RACE
AND
THE SUPREME COURT

DEFINING EQUALITY

Earl E. Pollock

the Peppertree Press
Sarasota, Florida

For information regarding permission,
call 941-922-2662 or contact us at our website:
www.peppertreepublishing.com or write to:
the Peppertree Press, LLC.
Attention: Publisher
1269 First Street, Suite 7
Sarasota, Florida 34236

ISBN: 978-1-61493-103-4

Library of Congress Number: 2012946309

Printed in the U.S.A.

Printed November 2012

For my wife Betty

TABLE OF CONTENTS

FOREWORD

THE VARIETIES OF EQUALITY

F rom Plato and Aristotle to the philosophers of our own day, equality has been a central moral and political ideal.[1] The original Constitution, however, did not contain any express requirement of equality. Nor did the Bill of Rights, adopted four years later.

It was not until the 1868 Fourteenth Amendment that the Constitution included such a requirement. The Equal Protection Clause provides that no State shall "deny any person within its jurisdiction the equal protection of the laws."

But what is "equal"?

Its meaning is certainly not self-evident. Nor is it a unitary concept. There are instead many different forms of equality, depending on the metric—the criterion to measure equality.

> "To say two persons or things are equal, does not mean that they are identical by every possible descriptive or prescriptive measure because no two persons or things can be identical by every possible measure. Nor does it mean that they are identical by any one possible descriptive or prescriptive measure because all persons and things are identical by some measures. It means, rather, that they are identical by the

---

[1] John Hoffman and Paul Graham, *Introduction to Political Theory* [Pearson 2d ed. 2009]: 58-77; Stefan Gosepath, "Equality," *Stanford Encyclopedia of Philosophy*, http://plato.stanford.edu/entries/equality.

relevant descriptive measure being the particular measure one stipulates as applicable."[2]

Frequently, therefore, "The question is not 'Whether equality?' but 'Which equality?'"[3]

Among, but by no means all, the various concepts of equality:

Moral equality. The Declaration of Independence proclaims "that all men are created equal"—i.e., that all are alike in some fundamental respects, particularly in terms of their moral worth and the commonality of their humanity. The United Nations' Universal Declaration of Human Rights (1948) states: "All human beings are born free and equal in dignity and rights." [4]

Equality of individuals. Equality is individual-centered when each individual is treated as the equal, with respect to the specified criterion, of all other individuals in the defined class. The wording of the Equal Protection Clause—"deny any *person*" equal protection—tends to support an individual-centered interpretation of the Clause. (Italics added.)[5]

Equality of groups. This standard measures equality between groups or subclasses (whose individual members may vary greatly in many respects) instead of equality among individuals. It was on a theory of group equality, for example, that the Supreme Court

---

2   Peter Westen, "The Concept of Equal Opportunity," *Ethics* (1985), reprinted in *Equality: Selected Readings* [Oxford 1997, Louis Pojman and Robert Westmoreland eds.]: 158, 162. See also Louis Pojman, "Equality: A Plethora of Theories," 24 *Journal of Philosophical Research* 193 (1999); Nicholas Capaldi, "The Meaning of Equality," *Liberty and Equality* [Hoover Press 2002]: 1-34.

3   Douglas Rae, *Equalities* [Harvard 1981]: 19 (italics in original).

4   See Felix Oppenheim, "Egalitarianism as a Descriptive Concept," 7 *American Philosophical Quarterly* 143 (1970): "Human beings can be said to be equal or unequal only with respect to certain characteristics which must be specified. It is elliptic, and hence meaningless to say that 'all men are equal.' With respect to any given characteristic, some men may be equal, but all are unequal. The only characteristic which they all share is a common 'human nature,' but that is a tautological statement."

5   Some framers, however, argued that the Amendment was more broadly intended to prohibit "caste" legislation that created or maintained a caste or otherwise subordinated a group through law. See, e.g., Steven Calabresi and Julia Rickert, "Originalism and Sex Discrimination," 90 *Texas Law Review* 1 (2011).

in Plessy v. Ferguson, 163 U.S. 537 (1896), upheld "separate but equal" facilities for the black and white races.[6]

Civil equality. Although the framers of the Thirteenth and Fourteenth Amendments expressed sharply different views of the scope of the Amendments, there was a broad consensus that at a minimum they granted ex-slaves what were them called, "civil rights," the fundamental elements of equality among citizens—such as rights with respect to contracts, property, lawsuits, and state protection from violence.[7]

Political equality. The framers did not give comparable support to granting the ex-slaves the political rights that are now commonly associated with citizenship, such as voting, jury service, and holding office. However, because of the Fifteenth Amendment's prohibition of voting discrimination and Supreme Court decisions (e.g., Strauder v. West Virginia, 100 U.S. 303 (1879)) prohibiting discrimination in other citizenship rights, the Court could claim in 1896 that "the Constitution of the United States, in its present form, forbids, *so far as civil and political rights are concerned*, discrimination by the General Government, or by the states against any citizen because of his race." [8](Italics added.)

Social equality. There was little or no framer support for what was called "social" equality—concerning matters that were generally regarded at that time as personal and private, such as marriage, schools, and public accommodations. Reflecting that view, the Court held in 1883 that the Reconstruction Amendments did not protect "social" rights as distinguished from "civil" rights;[9]

---

[6] A variant of "separate but equal" is the "equal disadvantage" theory that, until Loving v. Virginia, 388 U.S. 1 (1967), was invoked to defend miscegenation laws on the ground that the laws imposed the same penalty on both white and black partners. Pace v. Alabama, 106 U.S. 583 (1883).

[7] During and after Reconstruction, a tripartite typology of rights—civil, political, and social—was generally recognized. See, e.g., Richard Primus, *The American Language of Rights* [Cambridge 1999]: 128; Harold Hyman and William Wiecek, *Equal Justice under Law: Constitutional Development 1835-1875* [Harper & Row 1982]: 276-78; Jack Balkin, *Living Originalism* [Belknap 2011]: 221-25.

[8] Gibson v. Mississippi, 162 U.S. 565, 591 (1896). Note that "...a right called political in one place might easily be called civil in another." Primus, supra, at 128.

[9] Civil Rights Cases, 109 U.S. 3 (1883) (striking down the 1875 public accommodations law).

it emphasized in 1896 "[t]he distinction between laws interfering with the political equality of the negro and those requiring the separation of the two races in schools, theaters, and railway carriages....;"[10] and it declared in 1917 that the early civil rights laws "did not deal with the social rights of men, but with those fundamental rights in property which it was intended to secure upon the same terms to citizens of every race and color."[11]

Gender equality. Despite its broad wording ("any person"), the legislative history of the Equal Protection Clause indicates that the framers generally did not expect women to be included within its coverage.[12] It was not until 1971 that the Court invalidated a gender classification under the Fourteenth Amendment.[13]

Equality of result. This type of equality requires government preferences for some groups over others and allocation of benefits or positions on the basis of population or some other standard of proportionality. Policies designed to achieve equality of result may in turn generate claims of unequal treatment based on differences in ability, education, or other aspects of merit.[14]

Equality of access. Equal access requires that positions conferring advantages on their holders should be open to all in accordance with their qualifications ("to each according to his or her merit").

Equality of opportunity. Here the objective is to attempt to equalize outcomes to the extent that they are attributable to causes beyond a person's control, but to sanction differential outcomes insofar as they result from autonomous choice or ambition.

---

[10] Plessy v. Ferguson, 163 U.S. 537, 545 (1896). The dichotomy between civil/political rights and social rights was also accepted by the sole *Plessy* dissenter, Justice John Marshall Harlan, who (unlike the majority) regarded a citizen's travel on a common carrier as a civil—rather than social—right and therefore constitutionally protected. On the other hand, Harlan joined the opinion in Pace v. Alabama, 106 U.S. 583 (1883), sustaining miscegenation laws.

[11] Buchanan v. Warley, 245 U.S. 60, 79 (1917).

[12] The Court held in Bradwell v. Illinois, 83 U.S. 116 (1873), that a state could exclude women from the practice of law, and in Minor v. Happersett, 88 U.S. 121 (1875), that women did not have the constitutional right to vote.

[13] Reed v. Reed, 404 U.S. 71 (1971). It was not until the passage of the Nineteenth Amendment in 1920 that women were guaranteed the right to vote.

[14] These issues are addressed in Part V *Minority Preferences*.

Each of these concepts, as well as others, has influenced the Court's evolving treatment of race and definition of racial equality.

A threshold issue in tracing that evolution is "What is Race?." This is considered in Part I of the book with respect to both the scientific debate and the "race" categories employed by the federal government.

Part II, "The Legacy of the Peculiar Institution," recounts the founders' unsuccessful effort to reconcile the new nation's aspirations and the realities of slavery, the impact of the notorious *Dred Scott* decision, and the adoption of the Reconstruction Amendments that laid the foundation for the vindication of minority rights.

Against that background, the Court's response to equality issues is examined in each of the three categories of alleged discrimination on the basis of race: "Race Discrimination by Government" in Part III, "Race Discrimination by Private Actors" in Part IV, and "Minority Preferences" in Part V.

A Preliminary Note on Terminology

In earlier years, Supreme Court opinions and civil rights leaders commonly referred to "negroes" and "colored"—usages that today many regard as offensive (although organizations like the National Association for the Advancement of Colored People and the United Negro College Fund continue to use these terms in their titles). In 1968 more than two-thirds of black Americans described themselves as "Negro," but by 1974 "black" (popularized by the civil rights movement) had become the majority preference as an expression of racial pride.[15] Jesse Jackson is widely credited with popularizing "African-American" in 1988 before his second presidential campaign.[16] Later opinions of the Supreme Court refer to both "blacks" and "African-Americans."[17] The 2010 U.S. Census interchangeably employed the terms "black", "African-American," and "negro" as alternative designations.

According to a 2005 survey, there was then almost an even split among "Americans of African descent" on the question of whether they prefer the designation "black" or "African-American."[18] A 2007 Gallup survey found that a clear majority of "Americans of African descent" did not care which of the two designations is used.[19]

Given the apparent acceptability of both terms, "black" has generally been used In this book for several reasons: (1) the brevity of the term (in comparison with "African-American"); (2) its continued

[15] Brian Palmer, "When Did the Word Negro Become Taboo?," *Slate*, Jan. 11, 2010.

[16] Jesse Washington, "Some Blacks Insist: 'Don't Call Me African-American'," *Associated Press*, February 3, 2012.

[17] Apparently the last time the Supreme Court used the word "Negro" outside quotation marks or citations to other scholarship was in a 1985 opinion by Justice Thurgood Marshall, the first black Supreme Court Justice. Id.

[18] Lee Sigelman, Steven Tuch, and Jack Martin, "What's in a Name?: Preference for 'Black' versus 'African-American' among Americans of African Descent," 69 *Public Opinion Quarterly* 429 (2005). See also Marie Arana, "He's Not Black," *Washington Post*, November 30, 2008 (quotes poet Langston Hughes's statement that "I am not black.... I am brown").

[19] Frank Newport, "Black or African American?," *Gallup News Service*, September 28, 2007.

use by distinguished academics[20] as well as organizations such as the Congressional Black Caucus; (3) the opposition to the term "African-American" by blacks of Caribbean origin and the growing number of black immigrants born abroad;[21] and (4) the objection to the term "African-American" by blacks who consider "…the emphasis on their Africanness [to be] both physically inappropriate and culturally misleading."[22]

A caveat should also be noted about the terms "race" and "racial." In popular parlance those terms are often used to refer to Hispanics as well as blacks. However, although Hispanics share many cultural characteristics and a group history, and although some Hispanics prefer designation of their group as a race, Hispanics do not generally share biological or genetic traits and are therefore regarded by biologists as an ethnic group rather than a race.[23] Nevertheless, in order to avoid repeated references to "racial and ethnic" or "race and ethnic group," the book employs the common usage (with the foregoing caveat that it is not scientifically accurate) of including Hispanics in the terms "race" and "racial."

---

[20] See, e.g., William Julius Wilson, *More than Just Race: Being Black and Poor in the Inner City* [Norton 2009].

[21] See Washington, supra ("it's a misleading connection to a distant culture"); John McWhorter, "Why I'm Black, Not African American," *Los Angeles Times*, September 8, 2004. 27% of all blacks attending selective U.S. colleges and universities are first- or second-generation immigrants from other countries. James Taranto, "Off the Treadmill," *Wall Street Journal*, February 6, 2012; Douglas Massey et al, "Black Immigrants and Black Natives Attending Selective Colleges and Universities in the United States," *American Journal of Education* (February 2007). See also, e.g., Louis Chude-Sokei, "Redefining 'Black'," *Los Angeles Times*, Feb. 18, 2007 ("For black immigrants, African American culture can be as alien and as hostile as mainstream America"). Washington, supra, also notes that some whites of African descent object to "African-American" to refer only to blacks.

[22] Orlando Patterson, *The Ordeal of Integration: Progress and Resentment in America's "Racial" Crisis* [Civitas 1997]: xi. While rejecting emphasis on "Africanness," Professor Patterson nevertheless prefers the term "Afro-American."

[23] Various alternative terms have been suggested. For example, some writers prefer the term "ethno-racial groups." See, e.g., David Hollinger, *Postethnic America: Beyond Multiculturalism* [Basic Books 2005 ed.]: 9, 225-28.

PART I

WHAT IS "RACE"?

1. THE SCIENTIFIC DEBATE

Phrases like "racial equality" and "racial discrimination" presuppose the existence of a single accepted definition of the word "race." That word, however, has been used loosely in many different ways, sometimes suggesting biology ("the Caucasian race"), sometimes ethnicity ("the Hispanic race"), sometimes nationality ("the German race"), sometimes religion ("the Jewish race") and sometimes *everyone* ("the human race").[24] There continues to be considerable disagreement and confusion over the definition—and, indeed, whether there is even such a thing as "race."

In the eighteenth century, a different race was considered by many to be a different *type* of being—a different *species*.[25]

As one commentator pointed out:[26]

"The idea that 'race' is a crucial and immutable division of mankind is a product of the primitive social science of the nineteenth century. According to theorists of the day, all the peoples of the world were divided into four distinct races:

---

[24] Dinesh D'Souza, *The End of Racism: Principles for a Multiracial Society* [Free Press 1995]: 48.

[25] Ernst Mayr, "The Biology of Race and the Concept of Equality," *Daedalus* (Winter 2002).

[26] Stephan Thernstrom, "The Demography of Racial and Ethnic Groups," in *Beyond the Color Line: New Perspectives on Race and Ethnicity* [Hoover Press 2002]: 16.

white or 'Caucasian,' black or 'Negroid,' yellow or 'Oriental,' and red or Indian. White, black, yellow, and red people [it was believed] were profoundly different from each other, as different as robins from sparrows, trout from salmon, rabbits from squirrels.... If they were to mate across racial lines, their offspring would be biological monstrosities."

This notion that each race had its own blood type gave rise to the infamous "one-drop rule," which defined as black any person with as little as a single drop of "black blood." The antebellum South promoted the rule as a way of enlarging the slave population with the children of slave holders. [27]

Thirty states—in the North as well as the South—adopted statutory definitions of "Negro" or "black" or "colored" in order to implement discriminatory legislation using those terms, particularly anti-miscegenation laws forbidding marriage and sex between blacks and whites.[28] For example, as the Supreme Court pointed out in Plessy v. Ferguson, 163 U.S. 537, 552 (1896), some states provided "that any visible admixture of black blood stamps the person as belonging to the colored race (State v. Chavers, 5 Jones [N. C.] 1); others, that it depends upon the preponderance of blood (Gray v. State, 4 Ohio, 354; Monroe v. Collins, 17 Ohio St. 665); and still others, that the predominance of white blood must only be in the proportion of three-fourths (People v. Dean, 14 Mich. 406; Jones v. Com., 80 Va. 544)."

Several Southern states allowed persons of mixed black-white descent to define themselves as "white." For example, in Virginia during the 1800s, someone with less than one-fourth "Negro blood" could be classified as "white." In 1910, "white" was redefined as having less than one-sixteenth "Negro ancestry", and by 1924 persons defined as "white" in that way were prohibited from marrying anyone with "a single drop of Negro blood."

Ultimately, as a result of centuries of immigration and intermarriage, groups have become so intermixed that few people, if any, can claim to be of racially "pure" origins.[29] Indeed, it is estimated that

---

[27] Lawrence Wright, "One Drop of Blood," *The New Yorker*, July 24, 1994. As Wright points out, American Indians were not subject to the rule.

[28] As pointed out Chapter 12 *Extending the Scope of Brown*, 14 of the 30 repealed them in the 1950s or 1960s and 16 still had these laws on the books when the Supreme Court held them unconstitutional in Loving v. Virginia, 388 U.S. 1 (1967).

"at least seventy-five to more than ninety percent of the people who now check the Black [census] box could check Multiracial, because of their mixed genetic heritage."[30]

The great increase in mixed genetic heritage, coupled with revulsion for the earlier association between racism and primitive concepts of "race," led to a widely held theory—particularly among sociologists—that "race" is merely a "social construct"[31] or a "myth."[32] For example, the American Sociological Association's 2002 "Statement on the Importance of Collecting Data and Doing Social Scientific Research on Race" explains it as "a social invention that changes as political, economic, and historical contexts change." Similarly, in its 1998 Statement on "Race", the American Anthropological Association declared that "...physical variations in the human species have no meaning except the social ones that humans put on them." According to the social construct theory, any differences that exist among groups are merely cultural, not biological, and furthermore recognition of "race" only serves to foster prejudice.[33] That view was bolstered by findings that human beings share 99.9% of their DNA and that around 85% of human genetic variation occurs *within* the boundaries of what are commonly labeled as "race."

In his 1995 book *Postethnic America*, David Hollinger succinctly summarized the social construct theory: "Racism is real,but races are not."[34] And in June 2000, Craig Venter, the chief private scientist involved with the Human Genome Project, claimed that his analysis of the genomes of five people of different ethnicities had demonstrated that "race" was not a scientifically valid construct. Venter's claim, however, did not end the debate.[35]

---

[29] Thernstrom, supra, at 16.

[30] Wright, supra.

[31] See, e.g., Armand Marie Leroi, "A Family Tree in Every Gene," *New York Times,* March 14, 2005.

[32] E.g., Ashley Montagu, *Man's Most Dangerous Myth: The Fallacy of Race* [Columbia 1942]. See also Natalie Angier, "Do Races Differ? Not Really, Genes Show," *New York Times*, August 22, 2000 (stating that Dr. J. Craig Venter, head of the first successful human genome project, and researchers at the National Institutes of Health "had unanimously declared, there is only one race—the human race").

[33] Ann Morning, " 'Everyone Knows It's a Social Construct': Contemporary Science and the Nature of Race," *Sociological Focus* (Nov. 2007).

[34] David Hollinger, *Postethnic America: Beyond Multiculturalism* [Basic Books 1995 ed.]: 39.

Since that time the social-construct theory has come under strong attack. In a later edition of his widely praised book,[36] David Hollinger acknowledged that "...the geneticists make a strong case" and that his summary dismissal of the race concept was premature.[37]

Biologist Armand Marie Leroi observed: "Beneath the jargon, cautious phrases and academic courtesies, one thing was clear: the consensus about social constructs was unraveling. Some even argued that, looked at the right way, genetic data show that races clearly do exist."[38] Thus, "Like Lazarus, race quickly came back from the dead; the very science that was thought to lead to its demise has instead given it new life under the guise of modern genetics."[39]

In the view of many biologists, genes and race remain an important link, particularly in health matters. They contend that particular sets of genes are more common in particular racial and ethnic groups and that these genes alter the propensity of groups to be at risk from certain types of illness and raise questions as to whether medical treatment should vary on the basis of race or ethnicity.

As recently as 2001, an editorial in the prestigious journal *Nature Genetics* stated that "scientists have long been saying that at the genetic level there is more variation between two individuals in the same population than between populations, and that there is no biological basis for 'race.'" Only three years later, however, the same journal produced a special supplement containing the views of some two dozen geneticists on the medical uses of racial and ethnic classification.[40]

---

[35] E.g., Patricia McCann-Mortimer, Martha Augoustinoes, & Amanda LeCouteur, "'Race' and the Human Genome Project: Constructions of Scientific Legitimacy," 15 *Discourse & Society* 409 (2004).

[36] In a "Postscript" included in the 2005 edition of the book, reflecting post-1995 developments, Hollinger stated: "In the meantime, resounding voices in the biomedical sciences insist that the concept of race still has genuine utility after it is separated rigorously from the mistakes and prejudices of old-fashioned racial science" (pp. 226-27).

[37] These developments were strongly resisted by social scientists. See, e.g., Roger N. Lancaster, "Sex and Race in the Long Shadow of the Human Genome Project," Is Race "Real," a web forum organized by the Social Science Research Council, raceandgenomics.ssrc.org/Lancaster/ (June 7, 2006).

[38] Leroi, supra. See also, e.g., Gordon Allport, *The Nature of Prejudice* [Addison Wesley 1993]: 110: "To argue that the concept of race is badly abused and exaggerated does not, of course, alter the fact that some racial differences exist."

[39] Osagie K. Obasogie, "'Reports of My Death Have Been Greatly Exaggerated': Race and Genetics Ten Years After the Human Genome Project," *Huffington Post*, June 18, 2010.

Scientists at Howard University, including Dr. Charles Rotimi, acting director of the university's genome center, contended that there is no biological or genetic basis for race. But, in the same issue of the journal, several other geneticists such as Dr. Joanna Mountain and Dr. Neil Risch of Stanford University contended that new DNA data demonstrates a division of the human family into branches that coincide with the popular notion of race—principally Africans, East Asians, American Indians and Caucasians.

In 2005, the *New England Journal of Medicine* reported the news of a "race-based" drug (BiDil) targeted at blacks suffering from certain types of heart failure and the discovery of a gene that raises the risk of heart attack in blacks by more than 250 percent. More recently, researchers concluded that black patients' different response to beta blockers was genetic in nature. The September 2008 issue of *Clinical Pharmacology & Therapeutics* was devoted to "Pharmacoethnicity" and examined scientific, ethical, and regulatory considerations arising from new research showing that "Differences in response to medical products have been observed in racially and ethnically distinct subgroups of the US population."[41]

Expressing what appears to be an increasingly prevalent view, Harvard professor Ernst Mayr, one of the twentieth century's leading evolutionary biologists, stated:[42]

> "There is a widespread feeling that the word 'race' indicates something undesirable and that it should be left out of all discussions. This leads to such statements as 'there are no human races'. Those who subscribe to this opinion are obviously ignorant of modern biology. ...*Recognizing races is only recognizing a biological fact.*" (Italics added.)

The new scientific research, however, has raised concerns that it might be misapplied to support prejudice. Many geneticists,

---

[40] Nicholas Wade, "Articles Highlight Different Views on Genetic Basis of Race," *New York Times*, October 7, 2004.

[41] Gina Kolata, "Genes Explain Race Disparity in Response to a Heart Drug," *New York Times*, April 29, 2008; Nicholas Wade, "Genetic Find Stirs Debate on Race-Based Medicine," *New York Times*, November 11, 2005; Nicholas Wade, "Race Is Seen as Real Guide to Track Roots of Disease," *New York Times*, July 30, 2002.

[42] Mayr, supra. See also, e.g., Sally Satel, "I Am a Racially Profiling Doctor," *New York Times*, May 5, 2002.

sociologists and bioethicists argue that "black," "white," "Asian" and "Hispanic" are antiquated categories that may serve to justify discrimination.[43] Henry Louis Gates Jr., director of the W. E. B. Du Bois Institute for African and African American Research at Harvard University, cautioned: "We are living through an era of the ascendance of biology, and we have to be very careful. We will all be walking a fine line between using biology and allowing it to be abused."[44]

The issue may become even more explosive with the expected flood of studies analyzing the approximately 20,000-25,000 genes of the human genome.[45] As an *Economist* article predicted, "... [d]ozens of papers will report specific genes associated with almost every imaginable trait—intelligence, personality, religiosity, sexuality, longevity, economic risk-taking, consumer preferences, leisure interests and political attitudes," and these genome-wide association studies "...will reveal much less than hoped about how to cure disease, and much more than feared about human evolution and inequality, including genetic differences between classes, ethnicities and races."

---

[43] Rob Stein, "Race reemerges in debate over 'personalized medicine,'" *Washington Post*, July 31, 2011.

[44] Quoted in Amy Harmon, "In DNA Era, New Worries About Prejudice," *New York Times*, November 11, 2007.

[45] For example, in July 2011, two large genetic analyses published by the journals *Nature* and *Nature Genetics* found hundreds of genetic discrepancies between people of African American and European descent, and two papers published online by *Nature Genetics* found four unique genetic variations associated with asthma in people in Japan. Ibid.

[46] Geoffrey Miller, "The Looming Crisis in Human Genetics," *The Economist*, November 13, 2009. Scientists are now even examining the extent to which genes play a role in crimes. While there is broad agreement that there is no "crime gene," researchers are investigating the inherited traits that are linked to aggression and antisocial behaviors. Patricia Cohen, "Genetic Basis for Crime: A New Look," *New York Times*, June 19, 2011.

2. GOVERNMENT RACIAL CATEGORIES

Science has very little to do with the federal government's classification of racial and ethnic groups.

Instead, the categories used in compiling census data "are egregiously crude, are susceptible to strategic manipulation, and carry repellant historical associations."[47] As sociologist Nathan Glazer (author with Daniel Patrick Moynihan of *Beyond the Melting Pot*) stated: "The census questions, whatever we think of their incongruity and irrationality, are the direct result of powerful pressures from the ethnic groups concerned, from Congress, and from the Executive Office. And these are political not only in the sense that political actors are involved, but in the narrower and less respectable sense that they are often motivated by narrow and partisan considerations."[48]

The original census in 1790 recognized only three racial categories: white, black and Indian. These categories were required because of the three-fifths clause in Article I, Section 2, establishing the original formula for the apportionment of representatives and direct taxes among the states.[49] The number of classifications expanded in the late 1800s to account for the increased Chinese and Japanese populations.[50]

The final questionnaires for the 1970 census were already at the printers when, in response to demands of a member of the House Mexican-American Affairs Committee, President Nixon ordered the addition of a "Hispanic" ethnicity category,[51] resulting in "an officially

---

[47] Peter Schuck, *Diversity in America: Keeping Government at a Safe Distance* [Belknap Press 2003]: 25. In 2008 seven former Census Bureau directors—serving every President from Nixon to George W. Bush—signed a letter supporting a bill to make the Census Bureau an independent agency, concluding: "It is vitally important that the American public have confidence that the census results have been produced by an independent, non-partisan, apolitical, and scientific Census Bureau." John Fund, "Why Obama Wants Control of the Census," *The Wall Street Journal*, February 10, 2009.

[48] Nathan Glazer, "Do We Need the Census Race Questions?," *Public Interest* (Fall 2002), 21.

[49] See Chapter 3 *The Framers and Slavery*.

[50] See Peter Kirsanow, "2,000 Flavors and Counting," *National Review Online*, April 12, 2006.

[51] Glazer, supra.

sanctioned system of demographic classification that replicates precisely the crude, colloquial categories, black, yellow, white, red, and brown."[52]

This kind of political intervention has been bipartisan in nature. For example, in the late 1970s, when social scientists and the Census Bureau wanted to remove the "ancestry" census question because it was vague and uninformative (in comparison with the question on birthplace of respondents' parents which it replaced), the White House insisted that the ancestry question be retained regardless of the objections.[53]

In 1977 the Office of Management and Budget (OMB) issued Directive No. 15, "Race and Ethnic Standards for Federal Statistics and Administrative Reporting," governing race and ethnic standards for federal statistics and administrative reporting. The need for such standards arose because of the passage of several civil rights laws (Civil Rights Act of 1964, Voting Rights Act of 1965, Fair Housing Act of 1968, Equal Credit Opportunity Act of 1974, Home Mortgage Disclosure Act of 1975) requiring the federal government to monitor discrimination in a variety of areas. In order to assess discriminatory practices, the various affected agencies first had to specify the relevant protected groups, and this in turn led to the need for a uniform approach on a government-wide basis.[54]

The national impact of the resulting categories has far transcended government concerns. As Victoria Hattam has pointed out: "Although the directive was officially limited to federal statistics and administrative reporting, its categories quickly became the de facto standard for American society at large, setting the terms ever since for racial and ethnic classification in the United States."[55]

---

[52] David Hollinger, *Postethnic America: Beyond Multiculturalism* [Basic Books 2005 ed.]: 8.

[53] Glazer, supra, points out that even the phrasing of a census race question may be the subject of political interference. Before the 1990 census, both Houses of Congress passed legislation to require that "Taiwanese" be included as one of the "Asian and Pacific Islander" subgroups. The legislation never became law only because of President Reagan's pocket veto.

[54] Victoria Hattam, "Ethnicity and the Boundaries of Race: Rereading Directive 15," *Daedalus* (Winter 2005).

[55] Id.

The OMB's 1977 directive established four racial categories—American Indian or Alaskan Native, Asian or Pacific Islander, Black, and White—and two ethnicity categories—Hispanic origin and Not of Hispanic origin. Census respondents, whatever may be their mixed ancestry, were obliged to select one of the permitted boxes. The Directive stated that "These classifications should not be interpreted as being scientific or anthropological in nature...."

In 1997, the OMB amended Directive No. 15 to issue slightly revised standards for the 2000 census. Native Hawaiian or Other Pacific Islander was recognized as a fifth race, and Asian (previously linked together with Pacific Islander) now had its own category. There were also two ethnicity categories: Hispanic or Latino (defined as "A person of Cuban, Mexican, Puerto Rican, South or Central American, or other Spanish culture or origin, regardless of race") and Not Hispanic or Latino.[56] The amended Directive also revised the 1977 "not scientific" disclaimer to state: "The categories in this classification are social-political constructs and should not be interpreted as being scientific or anthropological in nature."

As Lawrence Wright pointed out, these changes were heavily influenced by the November 1993 hearings of the House Subcommittee on Census, Statistics, and Postal Personnel, where "...a variety of racial and ethnic groups were bidding to increase their portions of the federal pot. The National Coalition for an Accurate Count of Asian Pacific Americans lobbied to add Cambodians and Lao to the nine different nationalities already listed on the census forms under the heading of Asian or Pacific Islander. The National Council of La Raza proposed that Hispanics be considered a race, not just an ethnic group. The Arab American Institute asked that persons from the Middle East, now counted as white, be given a separate, protected category of their own. Senator Daniel K. Akaka, a Native Hawaiian, urged that his people be moved from the Asian or Pacific Islander box to the American Indian or Alaskan Native box."[57]

---

[56] Origin is defined as "the heritage, nationality group, lineage or country of the person or the person's parents or ancestors before their arrival in the United States."

[57] Lawrence Wright, "One Drop of Blood," *The New Yorker*, July 24, 1994.

17

Before the 1997 Directive was adopted, the addition of a "Multiracial" category was strongly urged in congressional hearings to reflect the mixed ancestry of large numbers of the population.[58] One in seven new marriages is now interracial or interethnic.[59] The effect of adding a "Multiracial" category would be far-reaching; "breaking up of the rigid distinction between black and white might has potential for the entire category scheme to lose its centrality as a marker."[60]

In response to the mixed-race proposal, minority groups mounted a successful political campaign to oppose any change in the demographic status quo.[61] In substance, their position was that they did not want "that kind of diversity" because it would undermine the sameness necessary for identity as a distinctive group.[62] In addition, "If a minority group were to lose members as a result of an exodus to the new mixed-race classification, the political clout of the group that loses its members would presumably diminish."[63] NAACP leader Julian Bond declared: "I very much oppose diluting the power and the strength of numbers as they affect legal decisions about race in this country."[64] Similarly, Jon Michael Spencer, a professor of Afro-American Studies at the University of North Carolina, argued that "To relinquish the notion of

---

[58] See Peter Wood, *Diversity: The Invention of a Concept* [Encounter 2003]: 25-26: "The idea was to recognize the Tiger Woods phenomenon. In 1997, when the golfer was asked by Oprah Winfrey how he classified himself, Mr. Woods replied that as a teenager he invented the word "Cablinasian"—CAucasian-BLack-INdian-ASIAN—in recognition of his father's mixed Caucasian, Black and Indian ancestry, and his mother's Thai heritage. Despite pressure from many African-Americans, who would prefer that Woods adhere exclusively to an "African-American" identity, he continues to refuse to pigeonhole himself in a single racial category." See also Stephan & Abigail Thernstrom, *America in Black and White: One Nation, Indivisible* [Simon & Schuster 1997]: 527.

[59] Susan Saulny, "Counting by Race Throws Off Some Numbers," *New York Times*, February 9, 2010.

[60] Randall Collins, "Ethnic Change in Macro-Historical Perspective," *Problem of the Century: Racial Stratification in the United States* [Russell Sage Foundation 2001, Elijah Anderson and Douglas Massey, editors]: 43.

[61] See, e.g., Thernstrom, supra, at 528.

[62] Hollinger, supra, at 102.

[63] Hollinger, supra, at 9. He further states: "While the demand to add mixed race to the federal census can be construed as merely an effort to turn the [ethno-racial] pentagon into a hexagon, the logic of mixed race actually threatens to destroy the whole structure." Id. at 45.

[64] Quoted by Ellis Cose, "One Drop of Bloody History," *Newsweek*, Feb. 13, 1995, page 72.

race—even though it's a cruel hoax—at this particular time is to relinquish our fortress against the powers and principalities that still try to undermine us."[65] As Orlando Patterson has acknowledged, "…the orthodox line among Afro-American leaders is now a firm commitment to the one-drop rule."[66]

Although rejecting a "Multiracial" category, the OMB did agree to allow census respondents to "check one or more" of the five categories and also, if they wish, select a sixth racial category "Some Other Race." The category was included to reduce the number of non-responses to questions about race, particularly by those Hispanics who do not identify with any of the five major race categories.

However, in March 2000, the Office of Management and Budget issued a directive (OMB Bulletin No. 00-02) providing that any response checking one minority race and the white race must be allocated to the minority race for purposes of "civil rights monitoring and enforcement" (i.e., to measure racial composition in education, employment, and public contracting).[67] OMB's directive effectively maximizes the size of minority groups; where previously mixed-race persons chose their own racial identities, the government's allocation rule now decides the matter for them.[68] Respondents who say they are white but also a member of a "minority race" will—regardless of how they might choose to identify themselves—be counted as belonging to the "minority race."

The 2010 census form asked a respondent to "mark one or more [of fifteen] boxes," including one box labeled "Some Other Race." The fifteen are: White; Black, African American, or Negro; American Indian or Alaska Native; Asian Indian; Chinese; Filipino; Japanese;

---

[65] Quoted by Wright, supra.

[66] Orlando Patterson, *The Ordeal of Integration: Progress and Resentment in America's "Racial" Crisis* [Civitas 1997]: 71.

[67] "Thus the federal government quietly reinserted into the tabulation of the census the principle of hypodescent that the opportunity to mark 'more than one' was publicly said to repudiate." Hollinger, supra, at 235.

[68] Schuck, supra, 144-145; Stephan Thernstrom, "One Drop—Still," *National Review,* April 17, 2000 ("If a significant proportion of African Americans reported themselves as partly white, they worried, it could mean fewer affirmative action slots at colleges and universities, fewer jobs for black applicants, a smaller share of public contracts set aside for black-owned businesses, fewer safe black seats on city councils, in state legislatures, and in Congress."). According to various estimates, because of their mixed ancestry, 75-90% of those who now check the "Black" box could properly check "Multiracial" if that option were available to them. Lawrence Wright, supra.

Korean; Vietnamese; Native Hawaiian; Guamanian or Chamarro; Samoan; Other Pacific Islander; Other Asian; and "Some Other Race."

Continuing efforts by some Hispanic organizations to obtain recognition of Hispanic as a separate "race" [69](rather than only as an "ethnic group") face considerable hurdles because of the extraordinary variety of the Hispanic category. It includes, for example, black Hispanics from the Dominican Republic, white Jews from Argentina, and Mexicans who would be counted as American Indians if they had been born north of the Rio Grande.[70] Hispanics as a group in this country, tend to identify themselves more by their shared set of cultural (rather than physical) traits like language and customs.[71]

In the 2010 census, OMB rejected the proposed "race" status for Hispanics. The 2010 forms stated that "For this census, Hispanic origins are not races," and the terms "Hispanic or Latino" were changed to "Hispanic, Latino or Spanish origin." 53 percent of Hispanics identified themselves as white and 37 percent (more than 18 million) identified themselves as "Some Other Race."[72]

Other agencies of the government employ other systems for compiling data on race and ethnicity. The resulting lack of uniformity makes comparison and analysis very difficult across fields and across time periods.[73]

In accord with OMB's 2000 directive, the Department of Education similarly requires that any student who acknowledges even partial Hispanic ethnicity must, regardless of any other racial ancestry, be reported to federal officials only as Hispanic. And students of non-Hispanic mixed parentage who choose more than one race are placed in a catchall "two or more races" category, so that a child of black and American Indian parents, for example, is

---

[69] See, e.g., Ian Haney Lopez, "Race in the 2010 Census: Hispanics and the Shrinking White Majority," *Daedalus*, Vol. 134 (2005).

[70] See Haya El Nasser, "Hispanic responses on race give more exact breakdown," *USA Today*, March 9, 2011

[71] Mireya Navarro, "For Many Latinos, Racial Identity Is More Cultural Than Color," *New York Times*, January 13, 2012

[72] Corkey Siemasko, "White population growing, census shows because Latinos checked white on forms," *New York Daily News*, Sept. 30, 2011.

[73] Susan Saulny, "Counting by Race Throws Off Some Numbers," *New York Times*, February 9, 2010.

counted in the same category as a child of white and Asian parents. The new standards will probably increase the nationwide student population of Hispanics, and could reduce the number of "black" students who will now be counted as Hispanic or as multiracial (in the "two or more races category").

The National Center for Health Statistics collects vital statistics from the states based on birth certificate information. However, a dozen states do not report race data in the newer manner that allows for the recording of more than one race. As a result, the Center cannot produce consistent national data documenting the health of the population.[74]

The Equal Employment Opportunity Commission mandates that most companies provide an annual count of their workers by race, ethnicity and gender. In 2007, the E.E.O.C. added a "two or more races" category.[75]

---

[74] Ibid.

[75] Ibid.

PART II

THE LEGACY OF THE "PECULIAR INSTITUTION"

3. THE FRAMERS AND SLAVERY

William Gladstone, the celebrated British statesman and prime minister, described the American Constitution as "the most wonderful work ever struck off at a given time by the brain and purpose of man."[1] It is now the oldest written constitution in the world and has survived the tribulations of practical politics, the holocaust of the Civil War, and the unrelenting tides of social and economic change.

But the Constitution, even after the addition of the Bill of Rights, was a deeply flawed document. This is scarcely surprising in view of the fundamental differences among the thirteen original States and the need to reconcile those differences through a series of often painful compromises.

The most famous of these was "the Great Compromise of 1787" (also called "the Connecticut Compromise"), the agreement reached between the larger States and the smaller ones concerning the composition of the two houses of Congress.[2]

---

[1] Article in the *North American Review* (September 1878). But see, e.g., Robert Dahl, *How Democratic Is the American Constitution?* [Yale 2001]; Sanford Levinson, *Our Undemocratic Constitution: Where the Constitution Goes Wrong (and How We the People Can Correct It)* [Oxford 2008]; Adam Liptak, " 'We The People' Loses Appeal With People Around the World," *New York Times*, February 6, 2012.

[2] Richard Beeman, *Plain, Honest Men: The Making of the American Constitution* [Random House 2009]: 150-51, 181-87, 223-25. The agreement to give each state equal representation in the Senate was regarded as so important that Article V of the Constitution prohibits any amendment that would change the Senate allocation.

The Framers' most infamous compromises, however, were made on the subject of slavery. The Declaration of Independence (called a "tour de force of disingenuousness" by one eminent historian[3]) had grandly proclaimed "that all men are created equal." Yet the Constitutional Convention agreed to several provisions accepting—although in oblique fashion—the then-existing reality of slavery.

On that basis, some critics—ranging from abolitionist Wendell Phillips (who called the Constitution a "covenant with death, an agreement with hell") to Justice Thurgood Marshall—have condemned the Framers as racist or worse.[4] But the inescapable fact is that if the Framers had not yielded, politics being the art of the possible, there would have been no Constitution and there would have been no United States of America.

As Abraham Lincoln (who has also been tarred as racist by revisionist writers) pointed out: "...when we established this government ... [w]e had slavery among us, we could not get our constitution unless we permitted them to remain in slavery, we could not secure the good we did secure if we grasped for more."[5] Would the slaves have been better off if no agreement had been reached? Would the cause of democracy have been enhanced if no agreement had been reached?

Remarkably, neither the word "slavery" nor "slave" appears in the Constitution. Instead, the Framers resorted to a kind of code as a substitute for the dreaded "s-word." As Lincoln said: "Thus, the thing is hid away, in the constitution, just as an afflicted man hides away a wen or a cancer, which he dares not cut out at once, lest he bleed to death; with the promise, nevertheless, that the cutting may begin at the end of a given time."[6]

The three principal provisions dealing with slavery were drafted in that artful fashion:

---

[3] Simon Schama, *Rough Crossings: Britain, The Slaves, and the American Revolution* [Ecco 2006]: 12.

[4] See Don Fehrenbacher, *The Slaveholding Republic: An Account of the United States Government's Relations to Slavery* [Oxford 2001]: 12, 39; Marshall Speech, 30 *Howard Law Journal* 915 (1987).

[5] Abraham Lincoln, *Selected Speeches and Writings* [Vintage 1992]: 147 (Speech at Chicago, July 10, 1858).

[6] Id. at 96-97.

Article IV §2, the fugitive slave provision, required that a slave escaping to a non-slave state "shall be delivered up on claim of the party to whom such service or labour may be due." To avoid any reference to the "s-word," the provision referred instead to "Person[s] held to Service or Labour in one State, under the Laws thereof." [7]

Article I §9 barred Congress from prohibiting the importation of slaves until 1808. The provision cryptically referred to slaves as "such Persons as any of the States now existing shall think proper to admit."[8]

Article I §2 provided that seats in the House (unlike the Senate) would be allocated on a population basis, but that a State's population would be calculated by adding together its "number of free persons" and "three fifths of all other persons"—a euphemistic reference to slaves, who of course had no vote but would nonetheless be fractionally counted increasing the number of House seats allocated to the slave states.[9]

Any notion that the South might have agreed to emancipation at the Convention is completely unrealistic. The Southern economy was largely based on its 650,000 slaves,[10] consisting of 40 percent of the total population of those states.[11] For example, as much as one-third of the wealth of Virginia was invested in slaves. If forced to choose between retention of their slaves or retention of the Articles of Confederation, the South would unhesitatingly have chosen to retain the Articles of Confederation.[12]

[7] "No Person held to Service or Labour in one State, under the Laws thereof, escaping into another, shall, in Consequence of any Law or Regulation therein, be discharged from such Service or Labour, but shall be delivered up on Claim of the Party to whom such Service or Labour may be due."

[8] "The Migration or Importation of such Persons as any of the States now existing shall think proper to admit, shall not be prohibited by the Congress prior to the Year one thousand eight hundred and eight, but a Tax or duty may be imposed on such Importation, not exceeding ten dollars for each Person."

[9] "Representatives and direct Taxes shall be apportioned among the several States which may be included within this Union, according to their respective Numbers, which shall be determined by adding to the whole Number of free Persons, including those bound to Service for a Term of Years, and excluding Indians not taxed, three fifths of all other Persons."

[10] Akhil Reed Amar, *America's Constitution: A Biography* [Random House 2005]: 94.

[11] Fehrenbacher, supra, at 15.

[12] Id. at 36, 39; Beeman, supra, at 320-35.

Nor did the Northern States seriously press the South on the issue. As Richard Beeman has observed, both "Southerners and Northerners, whatever their moral qualms about the institution, recognized slavery as a fact of life."[13]

The Northerners, of course, understood that the South's opposition to emancipation was non-negotiable. But their submission on the issue may have been influenced by other factors as well. Slavery at the time was by no means confined to the South; there remained large (although declining) numbers of slaves in the North (New York alone had 21,000). In addition, in the North as well as the South, there was then a widespread belief that blacks constituted a fundamentally inferior race.[14] This was a notion shared at the time not only by bigots and slave-owners but also later by many others deeply opposed to slavery, like Abraham Lincoln.[15] (Indeed, three of the leading philosophers of Western civilization—David Hume, Immanuel Kant, and Georg Hegel—accepted the theory of black inferiority.[16]) No matter how erroneous and offensive such views may seem today, they were pervasive among those then regarded as members of the ostensibly enlightened class.

THE FUGITIVE SLAVE CLAUSE

The fugitive slave clause did not merely countenance Southern slavery; it obliged Northern states that had abolished slavery to take an active role in keeping slaves in bondage.[17]

The provision was an outgrowth of the Convention's discussion of a clause dealing with the escape to another state of fugitives charged

---

[13] Id. at 310-11, 334.

[14] Id. at 314.

[15] Thus, in the First Lincoln-Douglas Debate in Ottawa, Illinois, August 21, 1858, although he argued that blacks are "entitled to all the natural rights enumerated in the Declaration of Independence, the right to life, liberty, and the pursuit of happiness," Lincoln said that he had "no purpose to introduce political and social equality between the white and black races" and that he was "in favor of the race to which I belong, having the superior position." Lincoln, supra, at149.

[16] D'Souza, supra, at 28-29.

[17] Fehrenbacher, supra, at 206-09. The language of the provision was substantially derived from §6 of the Northwest Ordinance of 1787, adopted almost concurrently by the Continental Congress. §6, while prohibiting slavery in the Northwest Territory, provided that a slave escaping into the territory from one of the original states "may be lawfully reclaimed and conveyed to the person claiming his or her labor or service...." Unlike the constitutional provision, the Northwest Ordinance applied only to a territory and did not intrude on the sovereignty of any existing state.

with crime. It was agreed that any such fugitive must be "delivered up" upon demand of the executive power of the state from which he fled. On the motion of southern delegates, an additional clause (with the usual reticence about the word "slave") was adopted requiring that a "Person held to Service or Labour in one State" who escapes into another shall be similarly "delivered up." The motion was unanimously approved without a single delegate raising his voice in protest.[18]

To implement the clause, Congress enacted the Fugitive Slave Act in 1793. There was, however, little enforcement of the Act until the Act was amended in 1850 to require federal marshals to assist in the capture and rendition of runaway slaves and to make the marshals financially liable for nonexecution of warrants and the escape of fugitives from their custody. The 1850 amendment was held constitutional by the Supreme Court (8-1) in Prigg v. Pennsylvania, 41 U.S. 539 (1842).

The intensified enforcement of the Fugitive Slave Act after its amendment was a key factor in generating antislavery sentiment in the North.[19]

THE SLAVE-TRADE CLAUSE

Article I §9 barred Congress from prohibiting the importation of slaves until 1808. James Madison defended the twenty-year exemption as a temporary evil that was necessary to prevent "dismemberment of the Union." Others hailed the clause as a major step toward abolition.[20]

In 1807, Congress adopted legislation to prohibit importation of slaves after 1808, as the clause permitted. However, in the preceding twenty-year period (1778-2008), the South imported 200,000 slaves—more than in any other twenty-year period, and only about 50,000 less than the total number of slaves imported to America in the preceding 170 years.[21] By 1810 importation and the high birth rate among slaves had increased the slave population to 1.4 million, more than double the number in 1787.

The 1807 statute provided for fines and imprisonment for violations but in the absence of special enforcement machinery the law

---

[18] Beeman, supra, at 330.
[19] Fehrenbacher, supra, at 44, 209-51.
[20] Id. at 37-38.
[21] Beeman, supra, at 333-34.

was largely ignored. Although legislation in 1819 and 1820 strengthened enforcement, "the illicit commerce reached such proportions as almost to constitute a 'reopening of the slave trade.'"[22]

THE THREE-FIFTHS CLAUSE

The notorious three-fifths clause—clearly the most important of the three slavery provisions—mandated that slaves be counted on a 3-to-5 basis in allocating seats in the House of Representatives.

The Clause has been justly condemned for its implication that a black is worth only three-fifths of a human being. But the Clause was adopted for a wholly different purpose. It was the South, in fact, that wanted slaves to be counted as whole persons. And the South's interest in doing so was, not because of any solicitude for its slaves, but instead to increase the number of House seats to be held by the South. The North, on the other hand, argued that slaves should not be counted at all because they were treated in the South as just a species of property.

The dispute was resolved by roughly "splitting the difference." The Convention adopted a three-fifths formula derived from the "federal ratio" proposed (but never implemented) to allocate the sharing of expenses under the Articles of Confederation.[23]

It is difficult to overstate the impact of the three-fifths clause on the nation's history. It took the Civil War and the Reconstruction Amendments to get rid of it. Until then, with only minor exceptions, the clause helped give the South virtual control of each of the three branches of the federal government.[24]

In Congress, including slaves in the count gave the slave states approximately one-third more seats in the House of Representatives than their free population warranted—47 seats instead of 33 in 1793, 76 instead of 59 in 1812, and 98 instead of 73 in 1833. In 1800, for

---

[22] Kenneth Stampp, *The Peculiar Institution: Slavery in the Ante-Bellum South* [Vintage 1956]: 271.

[23] See Fehrenbacher, supra, 21-25, 29-33, 41.

[24] Garry Wills, *"Negro President" Jefferson and the Slave Power* [Houghton Mifflin, 2003] 1-15, 50-61. Indeed, after the three-fifths clause was overturned by the Thirteenth Amendment abolishing slavery, the effect was to substantially increase the proportionate representation of the ex-slave states by fully counting the number of ex-slaves. See Fehrenbacher, supra, at 330. §2 of the Fourteenth Amendment provides for reduction of a state's representation if the right to vote is denied to qualified "male inhabitants," but the provision has never been enforced.

example, Massachusetts had a much larger free population than Virginia but Virginia had five more seats because of its nearly 300,000 non-voting slaves. From 1789 to 1861, 23 out of the 36 Speakers of the House were from the South.[25]

The three-fifths clause also greatly influenced the selection of the President. Since Article II §1 of the Constitution allocated to each state the same number of electoral votes as the "number of Senators and Representatives to which the State may be entitled in Congress," increasing the South's House seats by a third also increased the South's electoral votes by nearly a third.

For example, in the 1800 election—which except for the 1860 election was perhaps the most important in the Nation's history— Thomas Jefferson would never have been elected without the "extra" 12 to 16 electoral votes he received on the basis of the three-fifths clause. Instead, John Adams (who lost by only eight electoral votes, 73 to 65) would have been re-elected to a second term.[26] The Federalist Party never recovered from their defeat, and many in the Party bitterly scorned Jefferson as the "Negro President" because his election had depended on electoral votes attributable to counting slaves.[27]

From 1789 to the start of the Civil War in 1861, the President was a slaveholding Southerner for forty-nine years—or two-thirds of the time.[28] Twelve Presidents owned slaves, eight of them while in office. These included Washington, Jefferson, Madison, Monroe, and Jackson (the latter had also engaged in slave trading). In addition, some Northern Presidents in that period (like Van Buren, Pierce, and Buchanan) were notably sympathetic to the slave interest.

The three-fifths clause also had a profound impact on the third branch of the government—the Judiciary. By increasing the South's electoral votes by approximately a third in the election of the President (who of course appointed Justices), including slaves in the count led indirectly to Southern dominance of the Supreme Court. Before the Civil

---

[25] By contrast, for half a century after the Civil War, none of the Speakers of the House or presidents pro tem of the Senate came from the South. James McPherson, *Battle Cry of Freedom: The Civil War Era* [Oxford 1988]: 860.

[26] Amar, supra, at 345.

[27] Wills, supra, at 3-5, 62-72. See also John Ferling, *Adams vs. Jefferson: The Tumultuous Election of 1800* [Oxford 2004]: 47, 168.

[28] McPherson, supra, at 859-60. After the war a century passed before anyone from an ex-Confederate state was elected President. Id. at 860.

War, 20 of the 35 Supreme Court Justices were from the South, and 18 of the 20 had been slave-owners.[29]

The primary threat to Southern domination was the Nation's acquisition of huge new territories—the Louisiana Purchase, the annexation of Texas, the Oregon settlement with Britain, the Mexican cession, and the Gadsden Purchase. These acquisitions vastly increased the size of the United States, adding well over two million square miles and resulting by 1850 in the admission of 20 new states.

It was this expansion that increasingly polarized the South and the North over the political issue that ultimately ignited the Civil War—the issue of whether slavery would be permitted in the new states being carved out of the acquired territories.[30]

That issue, and *not* whether slavery could continue in the *existing* slave states, was the key bone of contention. Except for abolitionist groups, the North was generally resigned to accept slavery in the states where it already existed, but was strongly opposed to allowing its extension beyond those borders. Lincoln, for example, said that "Wrong as we think slavery is, we can yet afford to let it alone where it is, because that much is due to the necessity arising from its actual presence in the nation," but it cannot be allowed "to spread into the National Territories, and to overrun us here in these Free States."[31]

The South, on the other hand, claimed that slaves were merely another form of personal "property" and that the Constitution conferred a right to own and transport such "property" anywhere in the country. And congressional action to limit slavery in the new territories, the South greatly feared, might then lead to congressional action seeking to abolish slavery altogether. The South's highest priorities, therefore, were to establish a cordon of protective slave states surrounding the original slave states and to resist restrictions on the extension of slavery.

---

[29] In the half century after the war, only five of the 26 appointees to the Court were from the South. Ibid

[30] See Harold Hyman and William Wiecek, *Equal Justice under Law: Constitutional Development 1835-1875* [Harper & Row 1982]: 129-171.

[31] Lincoln, supra, at 251 (Cooper Institute Address, February 27, 1860). Lincoln contended that the Constitution did not allow congressional interference with slavery in the states where it already existed, and he even promised that he would not oppose a constitutional amendment permanently guaranteeing federal noninterference with slavery in those states. Fehrenbacher, supra, at 303, 314.

In 1820, Congress confronted this issue in the so-called Missouri Compromise. It was agreed to admit both Maine and Missouri as states—a free Maine and a slave Missouri. But even more significantly, as part of the Missouri Compromise, Congress established a formula to govern the subsequent admission of any other states in the massive Louisiana Purchase territory purchased from France in 1803. (The acquired territory included all of present-day Arkansas, Missouri, Iowa, Oklahoma, Kansas, Nebraska, parts of Minnesota south of the Mississippi River, most of North Dakota, nearly all of South Dakota, northeastern New Mexico, northern Texas, the portions of Montana, Wyoming, and Colorado east of the Continental Divide, and Louisiana west of the Mississippi River.) Under the formula, the territory north of the southern ("36-30") boundary of Missouri, excluding Missouri, would be free, and the territory below that line would be slave.

However, since the Missouri Compromise by its terms did not apply outside the Louisiana Purchase territory, it left open the question of whether slavery would be permitted in subsequently acquired territories. Acquisitions resulting from the Mexican War in 1846 thrust the issue to the forefront once again. In 1850, Congress provided for the admission of California as a free state and the eventual admission of the New Mexico and Utah territories as states "with or without slavery, as their constitution may prescribe" (that is, depending on how their settlers would vote) at the time of admission.

The 1850 New Mexico-Utah precedent led in 1854 to a demand for similar "squatter sovereignty" treatment of the huge Nebraska territory, which was part of the area that the Missouri Compromise had provided would be non-slave. Largely because of Southern opposition, four attempts to organize the Nebraska territory were defeated in Congress. To overcome the stalemate, the law finally adopted by Congress (known as the Kansas-Nebraska Act) divided the territory into two parts: Kansas, lying entirely west of Missouri and therefore convenient for settlement by slaveholding Missourians; and Nebraska, lying west of the free state of Iowa and the free territory of Minnesota. In disregard of the Missouri Compromise formula, the Act left the question of slavery in each of the two territories to the decision of the territorial settlers themselves. In addition, in response to Southern pressure, the Act was amended to include a provision that expressly repealed the Missouri Compromise.

The 1854 Act—which became law only with the benefit of 19 House seats directly attributable to the three-fifths clause—created a political upheaval in the North and led to the formation of the new Republican Party (later led by Abraham Lincoln).

It was against this background that the Supreme Court in 1857 considered the case of *Scott v. Sandford*.

4. THE *DRED SCOTT* DECISION

Scott v. Sandford, 60 U.S. 393 (1857)—characterized by a later Chief Justice, Charles Evans Hughes, as one of the Court's "self-inflicted wounds"—is widely regarded as the most egregious decision in the Court's history.[32]

Dred Scott was a slave born in Virginia. He moved with his master to St. Louis, Missouri, where he was sold to Dr. John Emerson, an army surgeon. In 1834, accompanied by Scott, Emerson was transferred to Fort Armstrong, Illinois (near what is now Rock Island) and in 1836 was transferred to Fort Snelling (near what is now St. Paul, Minnesota), located in the section of the Louisiana Purchase that had been designated as free territory by the 1820 Missouri Compromise.

After living in Fort Snelling for two years, Emerson and Scott returned to St. Louis, where Scott was sold to Sandford, a New York resident. In an attempt to obtain his freedom, Scott sued Sandford in the St. Louis federal court, claiming that he had become free when he lived in the free State of Illinois and a free territory in the Louisiana Purchase.[33] Scott contended that the federal court had jurisdiction of the suit on the basis of diversity of citizenship of the two parties.

In response, Sandford argued (1) that there was no diversity of citizenship (and hence no jurisdiction over the suit) because blacks were racially ineligible to be citizens, and (2) that, on the merits of the suit, Scott's status was controlled by Missouri law under which he was still deemed a slave despite his previously living in free areas. The trial judge agreed with Sandford on the merits and Scott appealed to

---

[32] See, e.g., Harold M. Hyman and William M. Wiecek, *Equal Justice under Law: Constitutional Development 1835-1875* [Harper & Row 1982]: 172-194.; Justice Stephen Breyer, "A Look Back at the Dred Scott Decision," 35 *Journal of Supreme Court History* 110, 117-18 (2010). The classic history of the litigation is Don E. Fehrenbacher, *The Dred Scott Case* [Oxford 1978]. See also, e.g., Carl Brent Swisher, *History of the Supreme Court of the United States: The Taney Period 1836-1864* [Macmillan 1974]: 592-652.

[33] Although Congress had repealed the Missouri Compromise in 1854 (three years before the *Dred Scott* decision), Scott relied on his residence in the Louisiana Purchase area during the interim pre-repeal period when the Missouri Compromise was in effect.

the Supreme Court, which held that Scott's case must be dismissed for lack of federal jurisdiction.

On the basis of its prior rulings, the Court could readily have decided the case on the sole ground that the determination of whether Scott was a Missouri citizen was controlled by Missouri law, and in the Court's deliberations it was initially agreed to dispose of the case on that ground.[34] Such a decision would have made it unnecessary to pass on the constitutionality of the Missouri Compromise and would likely have relegated *Dred Scott* to little more than a footnote in the Court's history. But instead of opting for the narrow ground, the majority attempted, with disastrous results, to put to rest the festering issue that divided the nation—the scope of congressional power to regulate slavery and, more specifically, whether Congress had the power to prohibit slavery in the territories.

The principal opinion was delivered by Chief Justice Taney. His opinion is captioned (presumably by Taney) as the "Opinion of the Court," but each of the other eight Justices also wrote an opinion expressing his individual views about the case. The nine opinions occupy 240 pages in the official report.

In holding that Scott's status had not been changed by living in territory that the Missouri Compromise had designated to be free, Taney and five other Justices held that Congress could not exercise any more authority over slaves than it could constitutionally exercise over property of any other kind.[35] Therefore, the majority reasoned, Congress did not have the constitutional power to ban slavery in the territories, the Missouri Compromise was unconstitutional, and the northern territory where Scott had lived had never been "free." It followed, in the majority's view, that Scott—still being a slave on this analysis—never achieved the status of a "citizen" entitled to bring suit in the federal courts.

Taney stated:

> "…the fifth amendment to the Constitution … provides that no person shall be deprived of life, liberty, and property, without due process of law. And an act of Congress which deprives a citizen of the United States of his liberty or property,

---

[34] Swisher, supra, at 618-19

[35] On that question, Curtis and McLean dissented, and Nelson (although rejecting Scott's claim on other grounds) expressed no view.

merely because he came himself or brought his property into a particular Territory of the United States, and who had committed no offence against the laws, could hardly be dignified with the name of due process of law.

"… Upon these considerations, it is the opinion of the court that the act of Congress [the Missouri Compromise] which prohibited a citizen from holding and owning property of this kind in the territory of the United States north of the line therein mentioned, is not warranted by the Constitution, and is therefore void; and that neither Dred Scott himself, nor any of his family, were made free by being carried into this territory; even if they had been carried there by the owner, with the intention of becoming a permanent resident."

As a second ground of his opinion, Taney wrote that blacks— whether slaves, former slaves, or freeborn—were racially ineligible to become "citizens" because, he contended, they had not been regarded as part of the political community created by the Constitution when it was adopted. On this issue, only two other Justices (Wayne and Daniel) expressed agreement with Taney; this part of Taney's opinion was not supported by a majority of the Court.

Taney declared:

"We think [blacks] are not, and that they are not included, and were not intended to be included, under the word 'citizens' in the Constitution, and can therefore claim none of the rights and privileges which that instrument provides for and secures to citizens of the United States. On the contrary, they were at that time considered as a subordinate and inferior class of beings, who had been subjugated by the dominant race, and, whether emancipated or not, yet remained subject to their authority, and had no rights or privileges but such as those who held the power and the Government might choose to grant them.

"…In the opinion of the court, the legislation and histories of the times, and the language used in the Declaration of Independence, show, that neither the class of persons who had been imported as slaves, nor their descendants, whether they had become free or not, were then acknowledged as a part of the people, nor intended to be included in the general words used in that memorable instrument.

"...They had for more than a century before been regarded as beings of an inferior order, and altogether unfit to associate with the white race, either in social or political relations; and so far inferior, that they had no rights which the white man was bound to respect; and that the negro might justly and lawfully be reduced to slavery for his benefit.

"...They show that a perpetual and impassable barrier was intended to be erected between the white race and the one which they had reduced to slavery, and governed as subjects with absolute and despotic power, and which they then looked upon as so far below them in the scale of created beings, that intermarriages between white persons and negroes or mulattoes were regarded as unnatural and immoral, and punished as crimes, not only in the parties, but in the person who joined them in marriage. And no distinction in this respect was made between the free negro or mulatto and the slave, but this stigma, of the deepest degradation, was fixed upon the whole race.

"...If any of its provisions are deemed unjust, there is a mode prescribed in the instrument itself by which it may be amended; but while it remains unaltered, it must be construed now as it was understood at the time of its adoption." (60 U.S. at 404-05, 407, 409, 426.)

As a third ground of his opinion, Taney held that Scott's status on his return to Missouri depended on Missouri law and that under Missouri law Scott remained a slave. According to Taney, the Missouri Supreme Court had held that a slave does not become entitled to his freedom if the slave's owner takes him to reside in a State where slavery is not permitted and afterwards brings him back to Missouri. This was the narrow ground on which the Court had initially agreed to decide the case before concluding that the validity of the Missouri Compromise should also be addressed.

Six other Justices joined Taney in rejecting (7-2) Scott's claim of entitlement to freedom, but they relied on a variety of grounds for doing so. Wayne completely accepted the Taney opinion. Daniel, contending that a slave was "strictly property," supported each of Taney's major points. Grier agreed with Taney on the unconstitutionality of the Missouri Compromise. Catron contended that the Missouri Compromise was invalid as a violation of the 1801 treaty acquiring the territory and that it also violated "that great fundamental condition of the Union—the equality of the States." Campbell, concurring only in the judgment, declared that the federal government could exercise "no power over the subject of slavery within the States, nor control the intermigration of slaves, other than fugitive slaves, among the States."

Nelson, without any discussion of the Missouri Compromise or Negro citizenship, agreed that Missouri law must be followed concerning the status of a former slave returning from free territory. Nelson filed as his separate opinion the draft he had earlier written as the proposed opinion of the Court before it was determined to deal with the power of Congress to regulate slavery in the territories.

Two Justices, Curtis and McLean, dissented. They rejected the majority's definition of "citizens" and supported Scott's entitlement to sue and invoke diversity of citizenship jurisdiction in the federal courts.[36]

In his powerful dissent of 67 pages, Justice Curtis contended that citizenship under the Constitution was "not dependent on the possession of any particular political or even of all civil rights" (p. 583); "citizens" in that context meant only "free inhabitants." With abundant documentation, he demonstrated that large numbers of free blacks had long been recognized as citizens in several states, were therefore citizens of the United States, and were accordingly entitled to sue and be sued in federal courts. Curtis found that Congress, which had outlawed the slave trade and restricted slavery in other ways as well, had the power to enact the Missouri Compromise restricting the scope of slavery in the territories, and he rejected Taney's suggestion that due process was violated by a limitation on the transportation of slaves.[37]

In his dissent, like Curtis, Justice McLean found the Missouri Compromise to be well within the constitutional powers of Congress. And he contended that the most appropriate definition of "citizen"

---

[36] See Carl Brent Swisher, *History of the Supreme Court of the United States: The Taney Period 1836-64* [Macmillan 1974]: 627-30.

[37] Breyer, supra, at 114-16.

was "a freeman" and that therefore an American-born slave automatically became a citizen upon becoming free.

As forcefully argued by the two dissents, neither of the two principal grounds of Taney's opinion is defensible. His opinion "…was built upon both a weak legal argument and a misrepresentation of history."[38] The decision essentially reflected an effort by a southern-dominated Court (five of the Justices in the majority had been slave-owners, and three of the Justices still owned slaves) to impose the South's view on the issue of Congress' power to regulate slavery. They may have hoped that the decision on the issue would reduce the danger of disunion. But the decision had the directly opposite effect; the result was to inflame the North and divide the country even more.

While the opinion was being drafted, the case became embroiled in one of the most notorious chapters in the Court's history. James Buchanan of Pennsylvania had just been elected President in 1856, primarily with southern support. In preparing his inaugural address, he wrote one of the Southern Justices, John Catron, to ask whether the Court's opinion in the case would decide the issue of the constitutionality of the Missouri Compromise. Catron informed Buchanan that the Court would decide the issue and intimated that the Court would hold the Missouri Compromise unconstitutional. Catron also suggested that Buchanan say in his inaugural address that the constitutional question was before the Supreme Court and that the whole matter should be left for its determination. Following Catron's advice, and of course knowing what the decision was going to be, Buchanan disingenuously proclaimed in his inaugural address that "it is a judicial question, which legitimately belongs to the Supreme Court of the United States," and that it was the President's duty, along with that of all good citizens, to "cheerfully submit" to the Court's decision, whatever it may be.[39]

He told the Buchanan what the ruling would be before it was made

---

[38] Fehrenbacher, supra, at 281

[39] See Don Fehrenbacher, *The Dred Scott Case* [Oxford 1978]: 307, 309, 312-313; Carl Brent Swisher, *American Constitutional Development* [Houghton Mifflin 1943]: 245-47

5. THE RECONSTRUCTION AMENDMENTS

Instead of settling the matter, the *Dred Scott* decision itself became a key political issue in the 1860 presidential election. As a result, the new Republican Party was vastly strengthened, while the Democratic Party was split along sectional lines, leading to Lincoln's election, the firing on Fort Sumpter, and the start of the Civil War.

This was followed by Congress' abolition of slavery in the District of Columbia and the territories, the 1861 Confiscation Act emancipating slaves supporting the Confederate military, the 1862 Confiscation Act emancipating slaves owned by Confederate officials, and Lincoln's Emancipation Proclamation on January 1, 1863.

The scope and effect of the Emancipation Proclamation are widely misunderstood. Although it altered the nature of the Civil War and the course of American history, it did not end slavery in America or even threaten to do so. The Proclamation, issued by Lincoln as a war measure, purported to free slaves only in Confederate-controlled areas and had no application to slaves in areas under Union control. All border states were exempted (including the new State of West Virginia consisting of the westernmost counties of Virginia). Moreover, as Lincoln acknowledged, the Proclamation might not survive the war; it might be repudiated by Congress (perhaps as part of a peace agreement with the Confederacy) or ruled unconstitutional by the Supreme Court.[40]

It was only with the approval of the Thirteenth Amendment in 1865 that slavery was abolished on a national basis.[41] §1 of the

---

[40] See, e.g., Lincoln, supra, at 446 (Response to Serenade, February 2, 1865): "A question might be raised whether the proclamation was legally valid. It might be added that it only aided those who came into our lines and that it was inoperative as to those who did not give themselves up, or that it would have no effect upon the children of the slaves born hereafter."

[41] See, e.g., Michael Vorenberg, *Final Freedom: The Civil War, the Abolition of Slavery, and the Thirteenth Amendment* [Cambridge 2001]: 1-35

Thirteenth Amendment provides that "Neither slavery nor involuntary servitude, except as a punishment for crime whereof the party shall have been duly convicted, shall exist within the United States, or any place subject to their jurisdiction." The Amendment, by abolishing slavery, also nullified the infamous three-fifths clause of Article I.

In drafting the Thirteenth Amendment, the Senate Judiciary Committee rejected a proposal by abolitionist Senator Charles Sumner to declare that all persons are "equal before the law"—a phrase derived from the French Declaration of Rights. Opting for a narrower approach, the Committee chose instead to borrow the principal terms used by Congress in the 1787 Northwest Ordinance, which prohibited "slavery and involuntary servitude" in the Northwest Territory, and which had been written in part by Thomas Jefferson.[42]

Although the Thirteenth Amendment abolished slavery, it said nothing expressly about granting ex-slaves either citizenship or the rights of citizens or protecting them from discrimination. Shortly after the adoption of the Thirteenth Amendment, Congress passed the Civil Rights Act of 1866.[43] The Act provided "[t]hat all persons born in the United States and not subject to any foreign power, excluding Indians not taxed, are hereby declared to be citizens of the United States." The Act further provided that all "such citizens, of every race and color, ... shall have the same right ... to make and enforce contracts, to sue, be parties, and give evidence, to inherit, purchase, lease, sell, hold, and convey real and personal property, and to full and equal benefit of all laws and proceedings for the security of person and property, as is enjoyed by white citizens...."

During consideration of the bill by the Senate and until shortly before its passage by the House, a draft of the bill provided far more broadly "[t]hat there shall be no discrimination in civil rights or immunities among the inhabitants of any State or Territory of the United States on account of race, color, or previous servitude...."

---

[42] See Vorenberg, supra, at 53-60. Vorenberg states that "The amendment could receive the necessary two-thirds support of Congress only if a sizeable minority of Democrats supported it" and the Republican majority "were sure to lose that support if they allowed either Sumner's name or his pet phrase, 'equal before the law', to become attached to the amendment" (p. 58).

[43] The substance of the 1866 Act is now codified in 42 U.S.C. §§ 1981-1982 and 18 U.S.C §242. The Supreme Court's interpretation of these provisions is reviewed in Chapter 21 *Federal Statutory Regulation of Private Discrimination*.

[handwritten: Emancipation proc didn't really free any slave border states were exempted]

Senator Lyman Trumbull and Representative James Wilson sought to give assurance that the bill would not affect state legislation on certain matters—voting, jury service, separate schools, and miscegenation. But, apparently in response to concern that such assurances might not be honored by the courts, the "no discrimination" clause was removed before House passage of the bill.[44]

Despite the removal of the "no discrimination" clause, the Act was vetoed by President Andrew Johnson, who contended that it exceeded Congress' authority under the Thirteenth Amendment. In his veto message Johnson contended that the bill "is another step, or rather stride, toward centralization and the concentration of all legislative powers in the national government." According to Johnson, "...if Congress can abrogate all State laws of discrimination between the two races in the matter of real estate, of suits, and of contracts generally," then Congress could "also repeal the State laws as to the contract of marriage between the two races" and "...repeal in the same way all State laws discriminating between the two races on the subjects of suffrage and office...."[45]

Although Congress overrode the veto, it was evident that a further constitutional amendment was essential to provide an adequate constitutional basis for the 1866 Act. The result was the Fourteenth Amendment, subsequently ratified in 1868.

The first sentence of §1 provides that:

> "All persons born or naturalized in the United States and subject to the jurisdiction thereof, are citizens of the United States and of the State wherein they reside."

This definition overturned Taney's holding in the *Dred Scott* case that blacks were ineligible for citizenship.

---

[44] Charles Fairman, *Reconstruction and Reunion 1864-88* [Macmillan 1971]: 1172-93; see also Harold Hyman and William Wiecek, *Equal Justice under Law: Constitutional Development 1835-1875* [Harper1982]: 394: "Republicans dropped suffrage because in the 1860s only 'radicals' merged civil and political rights. Suffrage was not the right of an American citizen, but a privilege a state should extend to its citizens.... Americans of the Civil War era did not entertain late-twentieth conceptions of 'civil rights'; the phrase came freighted with a different meaning for them than it does for us."

[45] Carl Brent Swisher, *American Constitutional Development* [Houghton Mifflin 1943]: 315-17; Hyman and Wiecek, supra, at 388-93; Fairman, supra, at 1194.

and south was in rebellion so would not abide north as hasn't in re...

The second sentence of §1 provides:

"No State shall make or enforce any law which shall abridge the privileges or immunities of citizens of the United States; nor shall any State deprive any person of life, liberty, or property, without due process of law; nor deny to any person within its jurisdiction the equal protection of the laws." [46]

This sentence is by any measure one of the most important in the entire Constitution and became the predicate for hundreds of Supreme Court decisions dealing with racial issues.[47]

§2 of the Fourteenth Amendment was designed to prevent the South's obtaining an advantage from the demise of the three-fifths clause that had been voided by the Thirteenth Amendment. With the end of slavery, ex-slaves would be counted as full persons for purposes of each state's representation in the House of Representatives, and thus, ironically, the South would benefit from its secession by substantially increasing its strength in Congress. To encourage states to provide black suffrage, §2 provided that, if a state excluded residents from voting in federal or state elections for any reason other than participation in the rebellion or conviction for crime, that state's congressional delegation would be reduced in proportion to the numbers of persons disfranchised. This provision, however, was never enforced and proved to remain a dead letter.

§3 of the Fourteenth Amendment barred from both federal and state office (unless Congress pardoned them) any persons who had held federal or state office and taken the oath to support the Constitution of the United States but then supported the rebellion.

§4 voided and rejected responsibility for "any debt or obligation incurred in aid of insurrection or rebellion against the United States, or any claim for the loss or emancipation of any slave."

---

[46] Two proposals for a broader prohibition were rejected by the drafters. Wendell Phillips, a leading abolitionist, had proposed that "No State shall make any distinctions ... on account of race, color, or descent;" and Thaddeus Stevens, a Republican Congressman, had proposed that "no discrimination shall be made on account of race and color." See Andrew Kull, *The Color-Blind Constitution* [Harvard 1992]: 57-69.

[47] It has been persuasively argued by historians that the epochal importance of the Thirteenth Amendment has been largely ignored—that Americans have "failed to remember that the amendment was once seen as the pinnacle of freedom instead of a mere precursor to the Fourteenth and Fifteenth Amendments." Vorenberg, supra, at 239. See also, e.g., Hyman and Wiecek, supra, at 386-89.

§5 of the Fourteenth Amendment (like §2 of the Thirteenth) provided that "The Congress shall have power to enforce, by appropriate legislation, the provisions of this article." As we shall see in succeeding chapters, the scope 0f this provision—the question what constitutes "appropriate legislation"—has been the subject of controversy in many Supreme Court decisions.

In 1870 the Fifteenth Amendment was adopted to prohibit discrimination in voting "on account of race, color, or previous condition of servitude" (§1). The need for a further amendment specifically dealing with voting became apparent because of the ineffectiveness of §2 of the Fourteenth Amendment that provided for the reduction of congressional representation if ex-slaves were barred from voting. The Fifteenth Amendment, like both of the other two Reconstruction Amendments, authorized Congress "to enforce this article by appropriate legislation" (§2).

The Reconstruction Amendments (set forth in full in the Appendix) fundamentally changed the nature and scope of the Constitution—from a document focused primarily on limiting federal power and protecting the independence of the States, to an evolving charter of individual rights enforceable against the States. And this "Second American Revolution" enormously expanded the role of the Supreme Court in the resolution of major public policy issues.

The remaining chapters deal with the Court's application of the Reconstruction Amendments—particularly the Equal Protection Clause of the Fourteenth Amendment—to three types of racial discrimination issues. Part III focuses on *governmental* discrimination *against* racial minorities; Part IV deals with racial discrimination by *private* actors *against* racial minorities; and Part V relates to claims of *governmental* discrimination *in favor of* racial minorities ("affirmative action").

PART III
RACE DISCRIMINATION BY GOVERNMENT

6. OVERVIEW OF THE EQUAL PROTECTION CLAUSE

Nearly 150 years after the 1868 adoption of the Fourteenth Amendment, there is still vigorous debate concerning the original intended scope of the Equal Protection Clause.[1]

Under one view, the Amendment was not intended by the framers to grant blacks political equality—the rights to vote, serve on juries, or hold political office. Under this view, the only equality to be given constitutional protection was *civil* equality, consisting primarily of the "civil rights" provided in the 1866 Civil Rights Act—the right to contract and own property; the right to testify, sue, and be sued in courts; freedoms of speech and religion; and the basic protections of the judicial process. Michael Klarman,[2] for example, states that this was "the

---

[1] See, e.g., Charles Fairman, *Reconstruction and Reunion: 1864-88 Part One* [Macmillan 1973]: 1260-1300.

[2] President Andrew Johnson's veto (subsequently overridden by Congress) of the 1866 Act led to the introduction of the proposed Fourteenth Amendment to "constitutionalize" the civil rights provided in the Act and to eliminate questions as to the adequacy of the Thirteenth Amendment to authorize the legislation. Harold Hyman and William Wiecek, *Equal Justice Under Law: Constitutional Development 1835-1875* [Harper & Row 1982]: 405-06. The 1866 Act granted blacks "the same right ... to make and enforce contracts, to sue, be parties, and give evidence, to inherit, purchase, lease, sell, hold, and convey real and personal property, and to full and equal benefit of all laws and proceedings for the security of person and property, as is enjoyed by white citizens."

original understanding of the postwar amendments" and that "...the framers of the [Fourteenth Amendment] refrained from prohibiting all racial classifications and repeatedly denied intending to protect political rights, such as voting and jury service."[3]

Other scholars, emphasizing the opposition of many framers to what was called "the civil rights formula," deny that the original understanding was so limited. Alexander Bickel theorized, for example, "that the Moderates and the Radicals reached a compromise permitting them to go to the country with language which they could, where necessary, defend against damaging alarms raised by the opposition, but which at the same time was sufficiently elastic to permit reasonable future advances."[4]

Richard Primus, referring to the Reconstruction "civil-political-social" typology, points out that "The most consistent feature of the scheme was that only 'civil rights' were guaranteed to all persons equally, and particular rights moved about among the categories in a kind of constitutional shell game depending on whether legislators or judges wanted to confer those rights on blacks."[5]

In Strauder v. West Virginia, 100 U.S. 303 (1879), the Supreme Court was confronted with a constitutional claim that by any definition combined both political and civil rights. At issue was the conviction of a black defendant tried by a jury from which all blacks had been excluded under a West Virginia statute barring them from jury service. The Court (7-2) reversed the conviction, concluding "that the statute of West Virginia, discriminating in the selection of jurors, as it does, against negroes because of their color, amounts to a denial of the equal protection of the laws to a colored man when he is put upon trial for an alleged offence against the State...." (p. 310).[6] In holding the statute

---

[3] Michael Klarman, *From Jim Crow to Civil Rights: The Supreme Court and the Struggle for Racial Equality* [Oxford 2004]: 40-43. See also Raoul Berger, *Government by Judiciary: The Transformation of the Fourteenth Amendment* [Liberty Fund 2d ed. 1997]: 8-9,198-220; Jack Balkin, *Living Originalism* [Belknap 2011]: 220-255.

[4] Alexander Bickel, "The Original Understanding and the Segregation Decision," 69 *Harvard Law Review* 1, 59-63 (1955); see also John Hart Ely, *Democracy and Distrust: A Theory of Judicial Review* [Harvard 1980]: 201.

[5] Richard Primus, *The American Language of Rights* [Cambridge 1999]: 128.

[6] According to the Court, "The colored race, as a race, was abject and ignorant, and in that condition was unfitted to command the respect of those who had superior intelligence. Their training had left them mere children, and, as such, they needed the protection which a wise government extend to those who are unable to protect themselves." (P. 306.) But, in a comment remarkably different from the view expressed 17 years later in *Plessy* on the effect of segregation, the Court also stated: "The very fact that colored people are singled out and expressly denied by a statute all right to

unconstitutional, the Court stated that the Fourteenth Amendment permitted a state to "confine the selection to males, to freeholders, to citizens, to persons within certain ages, or to persons having educational qualifications" but it could not do so on the basis of race.[7] The Court further held that the Fourteenth Amendment was not narrowly limited to only particular forms of discrimination singling out blacks (like the 1866 Civil Rights Act) and was instead broadly designed "to strike down all possible legal discriminations against" blacks (p. 310).

Strauder also recognized that blacks were not the only race protected by the Fourteenth Amendment—drafted broadly in terms of "any person." In a dictum (p. 308) the Court stated that the Amendment also barred racial discrimination against whites (or, for example, "all naturalized Celtic Irishmen").[8]

Yick Wo v. Hopkins, 118 U.S. 356, 369 (1886), applied the Equal Protection Clause to protect a group of 280 Chinese laundry owners (200 of them aliens) who, unlike their Caucasian competitors, had been denied city licenses to carry on their businesses. The Court declared that "the equal protection of the laws is a pledge of the protection of equal laws" and that the Fourteenth Amendment's provisions "are universal in their application, to all persons within the territorial jurisdiction, without regard to any differences of race, of color, or of nationality...."

---

participate in the administration of the law, as jurors, because of their color, though they are citizens, and may be in other respects fully qualified, is practically a brand upon them, affixed by the law, an assertion of their inferiority, and a stimulant to that race prejudice which is an impediment to securing to individuals of the race that equal justice which the law aims to secure to all others." (P. 308.)

[7] A year later, the Court ruled that, in the absence of a statute or other official state action excluding blacks from jury service on explicitly racial grounds, a defendant would have to prove deliberate discrimination in the defendant's case, and that it was insufficient to show "...that their race had never been allowed to serve as jurors in the [county] in any case in which a colored man was interested." Virginia v. Rives,100 U.S. 313, 322 (1880). Yet, in the following year, the Court in dicta implied that the complete absence of blacks from juries, despite Delaware's sizable black population, constituted prima facie evidence of discrimination. Neal v. Delaware,103 U.S. 370, 397 (1881).

[8] In the first case in which it was called upon to interpret the Equal Protection Clause, the Court expressed doubt whether "any action of a State not directed by way of discrimination against the negroes as a class, or on account of their race, will ever be held to come within the purview of this provision." Slaughterhouse Cases, 83 U.S. 36, 81 (1873) (suit by a New Orleans butchers association challenging a law granting another group a government-regulated monopoly to to operate a slaughterhouse in the city and surrounding area).

Under the broadly inclusive principle announced in *Yick Wo v. Hopkins*, the coverage of the Equal Protection Clause has ultimately been extended to a wide variety of groups, both racial and non-racial.[9] As the Court stated in upholding a discrimination claim by a group of Mexican-Americans, "...other differences [besides race] may define other groups which need the same protection. Whether such a group exists within a community is a question of fact. When the existence of a distinct class is demonstrated, and it is further shown that the laws, as written or as applied, single out that class for different treatment not based on some reasonable classification, the guarantees of the Constitution have been violated."[10]

Indeed, a group is apparently not essential. The Court has held that a valid equal protection claim may even be "brought by a 'class of one,' where the plaintiff alleges that she has been intentionally treated differently from others similarly situated and that there is no rational basis for the difference in treatment."[11]

To establish a claim under the Equal Protection Clause, a key requirement is proof of discriminatory intent or purpose. Such intent or purpose can be demonstrated in two ways. First, a law or policy is deemed discriminatory on its face if it expressly classifies persons on the basis of race or gender. Second, a law that is neutral on its face may be shown to have been applied in a discriminatory fashion.[12]

Statutory classifications are inevitable in the legislative process. Virtually all laws classify—and in that sense "discriminate"—by imposing special burdens or conferring special benefits on some people and not on others. In that context, the word "discriminate," stripped of the highly charged emotional connotation that it evokes, simply means to distinguish or to draw a line, and the fact that two groups receive different treatment under a statute is not, in itself, controlling.

---

[9] The applicability of the Equal Protection Clause to corporations was recognized in the *Granger Cases*, e.g., Chicago, B. & Q. R.R. v. Iowa, 94 U.S. 155 (1877).

[10] Hernandez v. Texas, 347 U.S. 475, 478 (1954) (holding that the Equal Protection Clause was violated by the systematic exclusion of persons of Mexican descent from service on juries).

[11] Village of Willowbrook v. Olech, 528 U.S. 562 (2000) (upholding a property owner's equal protection claim that a village had arbitrarily conditioned a water connection on her granting a 33-foot easement while requiring only a 15-foot easement from others).

[12] See Chapter 14 *The Discriminatory Purpose Requirement*.

Thus, in enacting a law, universal application of the law is not required; if every law had to apply to every person, in order to treat all persons identically, a legislature could not function.[13] A typical law, in fact, applies only to a specified subset of the population (e.g., real estate salesmen, bartenders, minors under 18, or one of an infinite variety of other groups), and such a law does not violate equal protection unless the criterion used for including some in the coverage and excluding others is found to be invalid. And in most instances—particularly in economic regulation matters—a legislature has broad discretion in creating such classifications.

As the Court has pointed out, "statutes create many classifications which do not deny equal protection; it is only 'invidious discrimination' which offends the Constitution."[14] But what is "invidious"? The term cannot be readily defined; it is instead a label used to refer to a classification that the Court concludes is too arbitrary or unreasonable to pass muster.

Until the Court's 1954 decision in *Brown v. Board of Education*, relatively few laws were held unconstitutional under the Equal Protection Clause. However, since *Brown*, the Clause has frequently been invoked to invalidate state action, frequently in cases that do not involve any racial issue.[15] As Archibald Cox noted, "Once loosed, the idea of equality is not easily cabined."[16]

---

[13] See, e.g., Ely, supra, at 135: "One thing we know the Constitution, the Equal Protection Clause in particular, cannot mean is that everyone is entitled to equal treatment by every law. In fact much of the point of most laws is to sort people out for differential treatment, often quite seriously differential treatment."

[14] Ferguson v. Skrupa, 372 U.S. 726, 732 (1963).

[15] The proliferation of such cases has led to considerable criticism. For example, Justice (future Chief Justice) William Rehnquist complained that "…"…this Court seems to regard the Equal Protection Clause as a cat-o'-nine-tails to be kept in the judicial closet as a threat to legislatures which may, in the view of the judiciary, get out of hand and pass 'arbitrary', 'illogical', or 'unreasonable' laws. Except in the area of the law in which the Framers obviously meant it to apply—classifications based on race or on national origin, the first cousin of race—the Court's decisions can fairly be described as an endless tinkering with legislative judgments, a series of conclusions unsupported by any central guiding principle." Trimble v. Gordon, 430 U.S. 762, 777 (1977) (dissenting opinion).

[16] Archibald Cox, "Constitutional Adjudication and the Promotion of Human Rights," 80 *Harvard Law Review* 91 (1966). The Court's increased reliance on the Equal Protection Clause may also be partly attributable to the almost concurrent decline of the substantive due process doctrine, which had fallen into growing disrepute, particularly in economic regulatory matters.

Another key factor responsible for increased reliance on the Equal Protection Clause is the Court's remarkably narrow interpretation of the Privileges or Immunities Clause ("No State shall make or enforce any law which shall abridge the privileges or immunities of citizens of the United States...."), which is also set forth in §1 of the Fourteenth Amendment. The framers' original design of the Fourteenth Amendment, in the view of most historians, was to establish the Privileges or Immunities Clause as the pivotal provision protecting citizens' fundamental rights from infringement by the states.[17] However, in the Slaughterhouse Cases, 83 U.S. 36 (1873), the Court largely nullified the Privileges or Immunities Clause by holding (5-4) that the rights of "citizens of the United States" did not include rights derived from state citizenship. Therefore, according to the decision, the Clause did not confer any new rights against state action and merely limited the Clause's protection to a very small group of national rights—for example, the rights to travel to the nation's capitol, to protection on the high seas and in foreign lands, and to access to the nation's ports and federal offices.[18] The four dissenting Justices, in an opinion by Justice Field, accused the majority of reducing the Clause to "a vain and idle enactment, which accomplished nothing, and most unnecessarily excited Congress and the people on its passage." (Pp. 96, 104.)[19]

The *Slaughterhouse* decision is still strongly criticized. But it has never been overruled, and in 2010 the Court "decline[d] to disturb" it."[21]

THE STRICT SCRUTINY STANDARD

In the last half century, in determining whether a claimed discrimination violates equal protection, the Court has adopted a hierarchy

---

[17] Raoul Berger, *Government by Judiciary: The Transformation of the Fourteenth Amendment* [Liberty Fund 2d ed.1997]: 57-69; Jack Balkin, *Living Originalism* [Belknap 2011]: 191-93; and see the second Justice Harlan's dissent in Oregon v. Mitchell, 400 U.S. 112, 163, 164 (1970).

[18] See Charles Fairman, *Reconstruction and Reunion: 1864-88 Part One* [Macmillan 1973]: 1301-1388.

[19] *Slaughterhouse* was reaffirmed in Bradwell v. Illinois, 83 U.S. 130 (1873) (the Privileges or Immunities Clause did not confer a right to practice law), Minor v. Happersett, 88 U.S. 162 (1875) (the Clause did not grant the right to vote), and Walker v. Sauvinet, 92 U.S. 90 (1876) (the Clause did not confer a right to trial by jury). And in United States v. Cruikshank, 92 U.S. 542 (1875), the Court relied on *Slaughterhouse* in emphasizing the limits on federal power to protect blacks from racial violence

[20] E.g., Akhil Reed Amar, "Substance and Method in the Year 2000," 28 *Pepperdine Law Review* 601, 631, 178n (2001) ("Virtually no serious modern scholar—left, right, and center—thinks that this [interpretation] is a plausible reading of the Amendment").

of standards of review that vary depending on the nature of the class allegedly discriminated against.[22]

Racial classifications are, at a minimum, subjected to a rigorous "strict scrutiny" standard. A discrimination subject to strict scrutiny is, as a practical matter, *presumed* to be invalid; the presumption can be overcome only by showing that the classification serves a "compelling" government interest and is narrowly tailored to serve that interest. Making such a showing, in order to meet the strict scrutiny standard, is almost invariably unsuccessful, so that the categorization of a claimed discrimination as subject to strict scrutiny will generally result in a finding of an equal protection violation.[23]

In addition to racial classifications, the strict scrutiny standard is applied to certain other "suspect" classifications, such as discrimination based on national origin and (with some exceptions) discrimination against aliens. The Court has also applied strict scrutiny to other equal protection claims based on rights found to be "fundamental," including procreation (Skinner v. Oklahoma, 316 U.S. 535, 541 (1942)), voting (Reynolds v. Sims, 377 U.S. 533, 562 (1964); Bush v. Gore, 531 U.S. 98 (2000)), access to the judicial process (Boddie v. Connecticut, 401 U.S. 371 (1971); Douglas v. California, 372 U.S. 353 (1963)), and interstate travel (Shapiro v. Thompson, 394 U.S. 618, 630 (1969)).[24]

GENDER DISCRIMINATION AND INTERMEDIATE REVIEW

An intermediate standard of review has been applied to classifications based on gender. Women have historically experienced discrimination, but many gender classifications are commonly accepted as legitimate—for example, separate bathrooms for men and women, separate men's and women's sports teams, and requiring men but not women to register for the draft. In addition, women are not a minority, and

---

[21] McDonald v. City of Chicago, 561 U.S. ___ (2010).

[22] Although the Court had declared in Korematsu v. United States, 323 U.S. 214, 216 (1944), that racial classifications are subject "to the most rigid scrutiny," the *Brown* opinion made no reference to reliance on a heightened standard of review.

[23] Only two Supreme Court decisions have found racial classifications to meet the strict scrutiny standard. *Korematsu*, supra (sustaining a wartime Japanese interment program), and Grutter v. Bollinger, 539 U.S. 306 (2003) (sustaining a law school's affirmative action program).

[24] See, e.g., Gerald Gunther, "In Search of Evolving Doctrine on a Changing Court: A Model for a Newer Equal Protection," 86 *Harvard Law Review* 1, 8-20 (1972).

insisting on identical treatment of the sexes could well disadvantage women by barring any legislation intended for their benefit.

Because of these competing considerations, in the evaluation of a law challenged for gender discrimination under the Equal Protection Clause, the Court generally applies a heightened standard of review but one that is less rigorous than strict scrutiny.[25] Under this intermediate standard, a challenged gender classification will not be upheld unless the governmental body demonstrates that the classification is substantially related to an "important" (even though not "compelling") government objective and is substantially related to achievement of that objective.

This standard has been applied with diverse results in numerous gender discrimination cases such as, for example, Craig v. Boren, 429 U.S. 190, 197 (1976), holding unconstitutional an Oklahoma law that allowed women to buy "near beer" at age 18 but forbidding men to do so until they were 21; United States v. Virginia, 518 U.S. 515 (1996), invalidating the exclusion of women from the Virginia Military Institute; Kirchberg v. Feenstra, 450 U.S. 455 (1981), holding unconstitutional a law that allowed men, but not women, to dispose of property without their spouse's consent); Kostker v. Goldberg, 453 U.S. 57 (1981), sustaining a federal law that required men, but not women, to register for the draft; and Geduldig v. Aiello, 417 U.S. 484 (1974), sustaining the validity of a state disability insurance system that excluded pregnancy-related disabilities.[26]

An intermediate standard of review was also applied in Plyler v. Doe, 457 U.S. 202 (1982), invalidating (5-4) under the Equal Protection Clause a Texas law that required payment of a full tuition fee to enable children of illegal immigrants to attend public schools. The Court acknowledged that undocumented aliens are not a suspect class and that education is not a fundamental right and therefore strict scrutiny review was not applicable. However, the majority

---

[25] Because their scope is far broader than the Equal Protection Clause, which applies only to "state action," federal and state laws have become the primary vehicle for regulation of gender and employment discrimination. See Chapter 21 *Federal Statutory Regulation of Private Discrimination.*

[26] The *Geduldig* decision was effectively overruled by Congress by enactment of the Pregnancy Discrimination Act, 42 U.S.C. §2000e(k), which defined sex discrimination to include pregnancy discrimination and prohibits discrimination on that basis.

concluded that a heightened standard was appropriate because of the importance of education to the affected children who (unlike their parents) were not responsible for their illegal status. On that basis, and rejecting Texas' contention that the policy furthered substantial governmental interests, the Court held the statute unconstitutional.[27]

RATIONAL BASIS REVIEW

All other classifications—all those not subjected to either strict scrutiny or the intermediate standard—are evaluated under the far more lenient "rational basis" test. This includes all social and economic legislation.[28]

Under the rational basis test, whoever challenges the alleged discrimination has the burden of showing that the legislature could have had no rational basis for adopting the classification—an extremely difficult standard to meet. The actual purpose of the law, moreover, is irrelevant and it must be upheld "if any state of facts reasonably may be conceived to justify" the classification. McGowan v. Maryland, 366 U.S. 420, 426 (1961). As the Court pointed out, "We many times have said, ... that rational basis review in equal protection analysis 'is not a license for courts to judge the wisdom, fairness, or logic of legislative choices.' ... Nor does it authorize 'the judiciary [to] sit as a superlegislature to judge the wisdom or desirability of legislative policy determinations made in areas that neither affect fundamental rights nor proceed along suspect lines.'" Heller v. Doe, 509 U.S. 312, 319-21 (1993).

Similarly: "[b]ecause we never require a legislature to articulate its reasons for enacting a statute, it is entirely irrelevant for constitutional purposes whether the conceived reason for the challenged distinction actually motivated the legislature.... [A] legislative choice

---

[27] In his dissent in *Plyler,* Chief Justice Burger argued that the Court's approach permitted patching "together bits and pieces of what might be termed quasi-suspect-class and quasi fundamental-right analysis" in order to spin "out a theory custom-tailored to the facts" of a case (p. 244).

[28] For example, in Williamson v. Lee Optical, 348 U.S. 483 (1955), the Court rejected a claim under the Equal Protection Clause that an Oklahoma law unconstitutionally discriminated against opticians by making it illegal for any one other than an optometrist or ophthalmologist to fit eyeglass lenses or to replace lenses except with a prescription from an optometrist or ophthalmologist. The Court upheld the law, despite its apparent purpose to protect optometrists and ophthalmologists from competition, on the ground that the Oklahoma legislature might rationally have concluded that eye examinations were critical not only for correcting vision but also for detection of ailments or diseases.

is not subject to courtroom factfinding and may be based on rational speculation unsupported by evidence or empirical data." Federal Communications Commission v. Beach Communications, Inc., 508 U.S. 307, 315 (1993).

Because of the heavy burden that a plaintiff must meet if an alleged discrimination is categorized as subject to the rational basis test, the result will almost always be a finding that the Equal Protection Clause was not violated. In the modern era, however, there have been a few rare cases in which the Court has deemed the classifications so arbitrary that they fail the rational basis test.[29]

Discrimination based on sexual orientation—against homosexual men or women—shares some characteristics applicable to other classifications that are reviewed under a heightened standard. But the Court has never held that such discrimination should be judged by any standard more exacting than the limited rational basis test. Ostensibly applying the rational basis test, the Court in Romer v. Evans, 517 U.S. 620 (1996), held (6-3) that the voters of Colorado violated the Equal Protection Clause when they adopted a state constitutional amendment barring antidiscrimination laws that give homosexuals special protection. In Lawrence v. Texas, 539 U.S. 558 (2003), again ostensibly applying the rational basis test, the Court held (6-3) that a Texas law prohibiting homosexual sodomy violated the Due Process Clause of the Fourteenth Amendment.

In a 1966 decision, the Court declared that "Lines drawn on the basis of wealth and property, like those of race, are traditionally disfavored." Harper v. Virginia Board of Elections, 383 U.S. 663, 668 (1966) (striking down a poll tax for state and local elections). But subsequent equal protection decisions have declined to apply heightened scrutiny to laws that, in their effects, allegedly discriminate against the poor. In Dandridge v. Williams, 397 U.S. 471, 485 (1970), upholding a state law that put a cap on welfare benefits to families regardless of their size, the Court characterized the state program as involving "state regulation in

---

[29] For example, applying the rational basis test in City of Cleburne, Texas v. Cleburne Living Center, Inc., 473 U.S. 432 (1985), the Court held unconstitutional a city ordinance requiring a special permit for the operation of a group facility for the mentally disabled. In Allegheny Pittsburgh Coal Co. v. County Commission, 488 U.S. 336 (1989), the Court unanimously held there was no rational basis for a county tax assessor's practice of valuing real property at 50% of its most recent sale price. But a subsequent decision, Nordlinger v. Hahn, 505 U.S. 1 (1992), sustained a state law embodying a practice essentially indistinguishable from the policy condemned in the Allegheny Pittsburgh case.

the social and economic field" and therefore not subject to the heightened scrutiny appropriate to civil liberty claims. In San Antonio School District v. Rodriguez, 411 U.S. 1 (1973), rejecting a challenge to Texas's system of relying heavily on local property taxes to pay for public education, the Court held (5-4) that poverty is not a suspect classification and that a disparity in school funding between affluent and poorer areas should only receive rational basis review. In his opinion for the Court, Justice Powell stated that "at least where wealth is involved, [the Equal Protection Clause] does not require absolute equality or precisely equal advantages" and that It was "not the province of this Court to create substantive constitutional rights in the name of guaranteeing equal protection of the laws." (Pp. 24, 33.)[30]

In determining what classifications should be deemed "suspect" and therefore entitled to a heightened standard of review, the Court has emphasized several factors. For example, immutable characteristics like race, national origin, gender, and illegitimate birth—characteristics that the person did not choose and cannot change—may warrant a more rigorous scrutiny than the minimal rational basis standard. Another factor given consideration is the ability of a group (such as aliens, who lack the right to vote) to protect itself through the political process.

---

[30] In Maher v. Roe, 432 U.S. 464, 471 (1977), upholding the government's refusal to fund abortions, the Court said that it "has never held that financial need alone identifies a suspect class for purposes of equal protection analysis." But in Plyler v. Doe, 457 U.S. 202 (1982), the 5-4 majority shifted to strike down Texas's refusal to provide any schooling at all to the children of illegal aliens.

[31] Samuel Eliot Morison and Henry Steele Commager, *Growth of the American Republic* [Oxford 1950]: 42-43.

7. JIM CROW AND THE "SEPARATE BUT EQUAL" DOCTRINE

In March 1867, as a result of the First Reconstruction Act (passed by Congress over President Johnson's veto), the civilian governments in the South were replaced by military rule, enforced by an army of occupation, some twenty thousand strong. Thousands of state and local officials were removed, civil courts were superseded by military tribunals, and anti-black laws were set aside or modified.[31]

In the 1876 presidential election, neither of the two presidential candidates, Republican Rutherford Hayes and Democrat Samuel Tilden, received the necessary electoral votes to be declared the winner. In the first few weeks of 1877, to avert a crippling national crisis, a compromise was reached in favor of Hayes. The price of southern agreement to the compromise included the Republicans' commitment to end Reconstruction, to withdraw the remaining troops from the South, and to stop enforcement of recently enacted federal civil rights laws.[32]

Former Confederate leaders, invoking white supremacy and demanding "Redemption" from the claimed injustices of Reconstruction, quickly returned to their old positions. The pre-Reconstruction slave codes regulating the conduct of blacks were reinstituted, although initially on a mostly extra-legal basis. According to C. Vann Woodward, "The new rulers did not, however, inaugurate any revolution in the customs and laws regarding racial relations. They retained such segregation practices as had grown up during Reconstruction, but showed no disposition to expand or universalize the system. ... More than a decade was to pass after Redemption before the first Jim Crow law was to appear upon the law books of a Southern state, and more than two decades before the older states of the seaboard were to enact such laws."[33] But by the early 1880s they became common, ultimately requiring segregation in schools, transportation (trains,

---

[32] See Chapter 20 *The Reconstruction Civil Rights Acts*.

[33] C. Vann Woodward, *The Strange Career of Jim Crow* [Oxford 3d rev. ed. 2002]: 31, 34.

buses, and steamboats), hotels, restaurants, theaters, education, housing, hospitals, libraries, cemeteries, employment, prisons, parks, and a multiplicity of other facilities and activities.

This development was by no means confined to the South. As Woodward points out, "One of the strangest things about the career of Jim Crow was that the system was born in the North and reached an advanced age before moving South in force."[34]

School segregation, since it had been enacted into law earlier and since it encountered less resistance among blacks, was particularly extensive. Moreover, constitutional challenges to school segregation had been rejected by more than a dozen decisions of state supreme courts and lower federal courts. The precedents were sufficiently uniform that contemporary legal commentators assumed that it was permitted by the Fourteenth Amendment.[35] And Congress continued to fund segregated schools in the District of Columbia.

THE PLESSY CASE

The first Supreme Court case challenging the constitutionality of state-enforced racial separation was Plessy v. Ferguson, 163 U.S. 537 (1896). At issue was an 1890 Louisiana statute requiring "equal but separate" railroad passenger cars "for the white and colored races." The statute, typical of many enacted in this period, provided "that all railway companies carrying passengers in their coaches in this state, shall provide equal but separate accommodations for the white, and colored races, by providing two or more passenger coaches for each passenger train, or by dividing the passenger coaches by a partition so as to secure separate accommodations...."

In large measure, these "car laws" reflected not only unwritten codes and customs governing black-white relations but also common-law doctrines concerning the rights and duties of railroads and other common carriers. The courts had long recognized that common carriers, although theoretically obliged to serve all passengers without discrimination, have broad discretion to develop and enforce rules for assigning passengers (notable examples being special cars for ladies

---

[34] Id. at 9, 17-21, 72-74

[35] Michael Klarman, *From Jim Crow to Civil Rights: The Supreme Court and the Struggle for Racial Equality* [Oxford 2004]: 24-26.

and smoking). And in many instances that principle was extended to include the assignment of whites and blacks to different cars.

A leading case on the issue was the 1867 decision by the Pennsylvania Supreme Court in West Chester and Philadelphia R. Co. v. Miles, 55 Pa. 209 (1867), two years after adoption of the Thirteenth Amendment. The court held that "it is not an unreasonable regulation to seat passengers so as to preserve order and decorum, and to prevent contacts and collisions arising from natural or well-known customary repugnancies which are likely to breed disturbances, where white and colored persons are huddled together without their consent."

Indeed, in an 1877 opinion nearly twenty years before it decided *Plessy*, the United States Supreme Court impliedly endorsed assignment of passengers on a racial basis. In Hall v. DeCuir, 95 U.S. 485 (1877), a steamboat owner challenged the constitutionality of an 1869 Louisiana law (enacted while the state was under federal control) that *prohibited* common carriers from racial discrimination in the transportation of passengers among the states. The Court unanimously held that the law interfered with interstate commerce and was therefore invalid under the Commerce Clause. In his opinion for the Court, Chief Justice Waite reasoned that the absence of specific congressional regulation of the subject constituted "the equivalent of a declaration that inter-state commerce shall remain free and untrammeled" and that "congressional inaction left Benson [the steamboat owner] at liberty to adopt such reasonable rules and regulations for the disposition of passengers upon his boat … as seemed to him most for the interest of all around," including the assignment of passengers on a racial basis.

The concurring opinion of Justice Clifford was even more explicit in supporting the validity of carrier-imposed regulations based on race. Although conceding that "substantial equality of right is the law of the State and of the United States," Clifford then added: "but *equality does not mean identity*, as in the nature of things identity in the accommodation afforded to passengers, whether colored or white, is impossible, unless our commercial marine shall undergo an entire change." (Italics added.)[36]

---

[36] See also Louisville, New Orleans and Texas Railway Company v. Mississippi, 133 U.S. 587 (1890), holding that a state statute requiring equal but separate railroad accommodations for whites and blacks did not violate the Commerce Clause in view of the state court's construction of the statute to apply only to intrastate commerce.

In Pace v. Alabama, 106 U.S. 583 (1883), involving the regulation of marriage and sexual relations, the Court unanimously sustained an Alabama statute imposing heavier penalties on interracial cohabitation. The Equal Protection Clause, the Court held, requires "not only accessibility by each one, whatever his race, on the same terms with others to the courts of the country for the security of his person and property, but that in the administration of criminal justice, he shall not be subjected for the same offense to any greater or different punishment." The Alabama statute was therefore upheld on the ground that, since both the black and white participants in the crime were subject to the same penalties, the races were being treated equally and there was not "any discrimination against either race." (The opinion was joined by Justice John Marshall Harlan, who in his *Plessy* dissent thirteen years later excoriated the Court for sustaining segregation in the seating of railroad passengers.)

Soon after the Interstate Commerce Commission was established in 1887, it received complaints from blacks who had been forced to ride in poorly maintained and less comfortable cars assigned to blacks. In response, the Commission interpreted the Interstate Commerce Act, which barred "undue or unreasonable prejudice or disadvantage," to permit segregation provided that facilities were equal. The Commission upheld railroad regulations requiring blacks to sit in separate cars, stating that "Public sentiment, whenever the colored population is large, sanctions and requires the separation of races," but ruled that cars of equal quality must be provided for both races on interstate trains. Following the Commission's ruling, every Southern state passed laws requiring "equal but separate" accommodations in public intrastate carriers.[37]

When the Louisiana car law was enacted in 1890, a group of several thousand New Orleans blacks (the "Citizens Committee to Test the Constitutionality of the Separate Car Law") undertook to challenge the validity of the statute, and Homer Plessy agreed to initiate the test.[38] When he refused to leave a "white-only" car despite having purchased a first-class ticket, he was charged with violating the statute and was briefly jailed until bond was posted. Before the case was tried, he petitioned the

---

[37] William H. Councill v. Western and Atlantic Railroad Co., 1 I.C.C. 346 (1887).

[38] Both the railroad (which opposed the law because of the additional expense it required) and the police cooperated in the test. Lawrence Goldstone, *Inherently Unequal: The Betrayal of Equal Rights by the Supreme Court, 1865-1903* [Walker 2010]: 152-54, 159.

court to dismiss the charge, alleging that he was "of mixed Caucasian and African blood, in the proportion of one-eighth African and seven-eighths Caucasian, the African admixture not being perceptible," and that he was entitled under the Thirteenth and Fourteenth Amendments to be seated in the car designated for whites. When his claims were rejected by the Louisiana courts,[39] Plessy appealed to the United States Supreme Court.

The Supreme Court's previous decisions under the Thirteenth and Fourteenth Amendments had applied the Amendments only to laws that discriminated against blacks by denying them the same rights granted to whites (as in, e.g., Strauder v. West Virginia, 100 U.S. 303 (1880), concerning exclusion of blacks from jury service). But the alleged discrimination imposed by the Louisiana car law was different in that it purported to treat both blacks and whites "equally"—each race was to have its own cars, and the law required that cars for blacks were to be comparable to those for whites. Was this also a forbidden discrimination? Or was it constitutional because of the requirement of equal facilities?

THE ISSUES PRESENTED TO THE COURT

Plessy was represented in the Supreme Court by three attorneys: Albion W. Tourgee, James C. Walker, and Samuel F. Phillips. Tourgee, a well-known lawyer and writer then living in New York State, had been retained as principal counsel by the Citizens Committee. Walker had been engaged by the Committee to serve as local New Orleans counsel. Tourgee arranged for Phillips, an old friend and like Tourgee an ardent supporter of the rights of blacks, to join him as co-counsel in the Supreme Court.

Phillips was a distinguished lawyer with a national reputation, having served as United States Solicitor General for over twelve years before reentering private practice in Washington, D.C. As Solicitor General, Phillips had extensive experience in Supreme Court practice, having argued many cases there on behalf of the Government, including such famous cases as United States v. Cruikshank, 92 U.S.

---

[39] The Louisiana Supreme Court held that Plessy's Privileges or Immunities claim was precluded by the decision in Slaughterhouse Cases, 83 U.S. 36 (1873). The court also relied heavily on sixteen cases that had upheld statutes or regulations mandating equal-but-separate facilities on common carriers and in public schools. As for the Equal Protection Clause, the court stated: "The statute applies to the two races with such perfect fairness and equality that the record brought up for our inspection does not disclose whether the person prosecuted is a white or a colored man." Ex parte Plessy, 45 La. Ann. 80 (1893).

542 (1875), and the Civil Rights Cases, 109 U.S. 3 (1883).

Three briefs (one by each of the attorneys) were filed for Plessy in the Supreme Court..[40] The briefs advanced a veritable potpourri of constitutional arguments and theories. Tourgee's brief set forth twenty-three "Points of Plaintiff's Contention" (each elaborated in a page or two).[41]

But, according to Tourgee, the "gist of our case" was that "... the State has no right to compel us to ride in a car 'set apart' for a particular race, whether it is as good as another as not." "The question," he contended, "is not as to the *equality* of the privileges enjoyed, but *the right of the State to label one citizen as white and another as colored* in the common enjoyment of a public highway, as this court has often decided a railway to be." (P. 29, italics in original.) Tourgee declared (p. 19) that "Justice is pictured blind and her daughter, the Law, ought at least to be color-blind" (thus introducing the "color-blind" expression into the case).

Phillips' brief also emphatically dismissed the relevance of equal facilities (p. 8, italics in original): "...*it is not of the smallest consequence that the car or compartment set apart for the Colored is* 'equal' *in those incidents which affect physical comfort to that set apart for the Whites. These might even be superior*, without such consequence!" The brief further declared that Plessy "...abhorred the equal accommodations of the car to which he was compulsorily assigned!"

Contrary to a common misconception of the case,[42] Plessy's counsel did not contend that racial segregation violated the Equal

---

[40] The briefs of Tourgee and Walker were bound together in the same document.

[41] Point I complained that the Louisiana statute denied equal protection by exempting the railroads and train officials for civil liability in enforcing the statute. (The Louisiana Supreme Court had held this exemption to be invalid.) Points II and III argued that Plessy's exclusion from the white car deprived him of property and liberty without due process of law. Point IV asserted that the statute interfered with "domestic rights" by potentially requiring the separation of husband and wife in different cars. Points V-XVI contended that the Louisiana law violated Plessy's rights of United States citizenship under the Privileges or Immunities Clause. Points XVII-XX contended, inter alia, that the construction urged by Plessy would not unduly impair the exclusive jurisdiction of the State. Points XXI and XXII claimed a violation of the Thirteenth Amendment. Point XXXIII invoked the Declaration of Independence.

[42] See, e.g., Andrew Kull, *The Color-Blind Constitution* [Harvard 1992]: 117-18: "The broader question for decision in Plessy was whether...the equal protection clause... imposed a different constitutional standard, more stringent than 'unreasonableness', for racial classifications generally." Kull similarly describes the Court as "[f]aced with the challenge to reconsider racial classifications with the guarantee of equal protection...." (p. 131).

Protection Clause. Instead, what Tourgee called "the gist of our case" against the Louisiana statute was based on the affirmative rights conferred by the Citizenship Clauses—the provisions of the Fourteenth Amendment declaring that all those born or naturalized here are "Citizens of the United States" and prohibiting "any state law which shall abridge the privileges or immunities of citizens of the United States." Those provisions, Plessy's counsel argued, guaranteed a citizen's right to travel on a public highway and therefore, since a railroad is deemed a public highway for that purpose, the Louisiana statute violated Plessy's citizenship rights by limiting his access on the basis of race.[43]

The "privileges or immunities" provision, as pointed out in Chapter 6, had been effectively nullified as a restraint on state action in The Slaughterhouse Cases, 83 U.S. 36 (1873), and United States v. Cruikshank, 92 U.S. 542 (1875). Plessy's briefs, instead of trying to deny the applicability of those decisions, argued that they were based on a "mistaken view, both of the character and effect of the XIVth Amendment" (Tourgee, pp. 19, 21). They further acknowledged "that Cruikshank's case is squarely against us" and that "Our contention is that the opinion in Cruikshank's Case cannot stand" (id. at 26).[44]

While pursuing a privileges or immunities theory that they conceded was inconsistent with two of the Court's decisions, Plessy's counsel chose to ignore the Equal Protection Clause on the constitutionality of racial segregation. The Equal Protection Clause was only incidentally invoked in Plessy's briefs for the limited purpose of challenging two collateral exemptions in the Louisiana statute—an exemption of railroads and train officials from civil liability for enforcing the statute, and an exemption for "nurses attending children of the other race." The civil liability exemption issue became moot after the Louisiana Supreme Court held that the exemption did not

---

[43] See, e.g., Olcott v. Supervisor, 83 U.S. 678 (1872); Crandall v. Nevada, 73 U.S. 35, 44 (1868); Williams v. Texas, 179 U.S. 270, 274 (1900).

[44] Citing Strauder v. West Virginia, 100 U.S. 30 (1880), Plessy's counsel asserted that the Court "had, in the interval, advanced from the position held in the Slaughter-House Case...." (p. 16). Strauder, however, did not purport to modify the Slaughterhouse decision concerning citizenship rights. Instead, it held that a statute barring blacks from jury service violated the Equal Protection Clause—which Plessy counsel wholly ignored except on two collateral issues.

apply in cases of wrongful assignment;[45] and the nurse exemption was likewise of no consequence since in any event the basic prohibition of the statute would be unaffected.

Particularly in terms of nineteenth century standards, Plessy's counsel were exemplary champions of the rights of blacks.[46] But it is quite incorrect to assume, as the standard narrative of the case would suggest, that they attacked the constitutionality of Jim Crow. In fact, in their argument to the Court, they *defended* the constitutionality of laws requiring school segregation and forbidding miscegenation. Those laws, Plessy's counsel explicitly reassured the Court, are justified under the State's police power and would still remain in force even if the Court struck down the Louisiana statute. The Phillips brief stated:

> "The institution of *Marriage*, including the *Family* and the rearing of the young, has, on the contrary, always been amenable to the laws of police. ... Whether therefore two races shall intermarry, and thus destroy both, is a question of police, and, being such, the *bona fide* details thereof must be left to the legislature. ... And if, instead of the old plan of allowing parents to educate children as they choose, government steps in and takes the matter into its own hands, no constitutional objection upon mere general grounds can be made to provisions by law which respect, so far as may be, a prevailing parental sentiment of the community upon this interesting and delicate subject. In educating the young, government steps 'in loco parentis', and may therefore in many things well conform to the will of natural parents. This is all a part of *Marriage* and *The Family*, and should be treated conformably therewith. *Separate races,* and *separate schools,* therefore, come under different orders of consideration." (Phillips, pp. 10-11, italics in original.)

This distinction was in substance the same that the Court had emphasized in the *Civil Rights Cases* (which Phillips had argued unsuccessfully for the Government)—the distinction between protected

---

[45] The Supreme Court's opinion (p. 549) further states that the Louisiana Attorney Gener al had conceded that the exemption was invalid.

[46] See, e.g., Owen Fiss, *History of the Supreme Court of the United States: Troubled Beginnings of the Modern State,1888-1910* [Cambridge 1993]: 354-60.

rights of citizenship and unprotected "social" rights.[47]

Plessy's support of school segregation and miscegenation laws also illuminates and qualifies the "color-blind" reference in Tourgee's brief. The "color-blindness" demanded by Plessy's counsel was limited to the affirmative rights conferred by the Citizenship Clauses and clearly did not extend to all government racial classifications.

As a result, the issue before the Court, as framed by the parties, was relatively narrow—and far more narrow than generally understood by later generations. Indeed, if the Court had granted Plessy *all* the relief he asked for, segregation on railroad passenger cars would have been prohibited *but school segregation and miscegenation laws would have remained fully intact.*

Given the existing environment in which the case arose, the result in the case was almost certainly inevitable regardless of how Plessy's counsel chose to argue the case. But several of their choices probably contributed to the result—including their acceptance of the constitutionality of school segregation and miscegenation laws, their disavowal of any claim that the passenger cars for blacks were inferior to those for whites, and foregoing any contention that segregation violates the Equal Protection Clause (which ultimately was of course the basis for striking down separate-but-equal in *Brown v. Board of Education*).

THE COURT'S DECISION

The Supreme Court has often noted—but not always followed—its general practice of declining to pass on constitutional issues that are unnecessary to dispose of the cases before them. If the Court had followed that practice in *Plessy v. Ferguson*, since Plessy's counsel had expressly acknowledged the validity of school segregation and miscegenation laws, the opinion would presumably have been confined to a ruling on railroad passenger cars under the Citizenship Clauses. But the Court chose instead to deal broadly with the constitutionality of the separate-but-equal doctrine.

---

[47] Their support of of school segregation and miscegenation laws might possibly explain why Plessy's counsel did not claim that segregation violated the Equal Protection Clause. Reliance on the Equal Protection Clause, because of its potentially broader scope, might have conflicted with their assurance to the Court that a decision in his favor on the Citizenship Clauses would not undermine school segregation and miscegenation laws. In addition, counsel were surely aware that Justice Harlan—their most likely supporter on the Court—had joined the unanimous opinion in Pace v. Alabama, 106 U.S. 583 (1883), upholding the constitutionality of miscegenation laws.

The Court (7-1) sweepingly upheld the doctrine under both the Thirteenth and Fourteenth Amendments. Ironically, the opinion was written by a northerner from Massachusetts, Justice Henry Billingsly Brown, and the dissent was written by a former slave-owner from Kentucky, Justice John Marshall Harlan.

Concerning the Thirteenth Amendment, the Court declared: "A statute which implies merely a legal distinction between the white and colored races—a distinction which is founded in the color of the two races, and which must always exist so long as white men are distinguished from the other race by color—has no tendency to destroy the legal equality of the two races, or re-establish a state of involuntary servitude." The Court thus denied that the racial classification in the Louisiana law constituted a forbidden discrimination. And, in response to the argument that acceptance of racial classifications would be abused, the Court stated: "The reply to all this is that every exercise of the police power must be reasonable, and extend only to such laws as are enacted in good faith for the promotion of the public good, and not for the annoyance or oppression of a particular class."

Similarly upholding the statute under the Fourteenth Amendment, the Court stated: "...we think the enforced separation of the races, as applied to the internal commerce of the state, neither abridges the privileges or immunities of the colored man, deprives him of his property without due process of law, nor denies him the equal protection of the laws, within the meaning of the fourteenth amendment...." (p. 548). According to the Court, even though "[t]he object of the amendment was undoubtedly to enforce the absolute equality of the two races before the law," "it could not have been intended to abolish distinctions based upon color, or *to enforce social, as distinguished from political, equality,* or a commingling of the two races upon terms unsatisfactory to either." (P. 544, italics added).[48]

On this predicate, the Court announced a constitutional standard

---

[48] In response to Plessy's argument that the Louisiana statute deprived him of the "property" of belonging to the dominant white race in violation of due process of law, the Court stated: "...we are unable to see how this statute deprives him of, or in any way affects his right to such property. If he be a white man, and assigned to a colored coach, he may have his action for damages against the company for being deprived of his so-called 'property.' Upon the other hand, if he be a colored man, and be so assigned, he has been deprived of no property, since he is not lawfully entitled to the reputation of being a white man." (P. 549.)

that was to govern black-white relations for over half a century (pp. 550-51):

> "...the case reduces itself to the question whether the statute of Louisiana is a reasonable regulation, and with respect to this there must necessarily be a large discretion on the part of the legislature. In determining the question of reasonableness, it is at liberty to act with reference to the established usages, customs, and traditions of the people, and with a view to the promotion of their comfort, and the preservation of the public peace and good order. Gauged by this standard, we cannot say that a law which authorizes or even requires the separation of the two races in public conveyances is unreasonable...."

Although gratuitously stating that enforced racial separation did not violate the Equal Protection Clause (and thereby implicitly rejecting an equal protection argument that Plessy's lawyers never made), the majority opinion gave little or no attention to defining "equal." Instead, according to the Court, the controlling constitutional test was "reasonableness," the same amorphous formulation used by the Court in its development of the substantive due process doctrine during the same period.[49] "Gauged by this standard," the Court stated, "we cannot say that a law which authorizes or even requires the separation of the two races in public conveyances is unreasonable, or more obnoxious to the fourteenth amendment than the acts of congress requiring separate schools for colored children in the District of Columbia, the constitutionality of which does not seem to have been questioned, or the corresponding acts of state legislatures." The Court (citing a Massachusetts state court decision[50]) also noted that separate schools for white and black children had been upheld "even by courts of states where the political rights of the colored race have been longest and most earnestly enforced."

The *Plessy* opinion rests on its premise that laws requiring racial separation "do not necessarily imply the inferiority of either race to the other...." In a key passage the Court piously observed: "We

---

[49] E.g., Allgeyer v. Louisiana, 165 U.S. 578 (1897), a landmark decision unanimously striking down a Louisiana statute on the ground that it violated an individual's "liberty to contract" based on the Due Process Clause of the Fourteenth Amendment.

[50] Roberts v. City of Boston, 59 Mass. 198 (1850).

consider the underlying fallacy of the plaintiff's argument to consist in the assumption that the enforced separation of the two races stamps the colored race with a badge of inferiority. If this be so, it is not by reason of anything found in the act, but solely because the colored race chooses to put that construction upon it."

Concluding, the Court denied that either the Constitution or legislation could provide a remedy for "social" (as distinguished from "civil and political") inequality:

> "When the government, therefore, has secured to each of its citizens equal rights before the law, and equal opportunities for improvement and progress, it has accomplished the end for which it was organized, and performed all of the functions respecting social advantages with which it is endowed. Legislation is powerless to eradicate racial instincts, or to abolish distinctions based upon physical differences, and the attempt to do so can only result in accentuating the difficulties of the present situation. If the civil and political rights of both races be equal, one cannot be inferior to the other civilly or politically. If one race be inferior to the other socially, the constitution of the United States cannot put them upon the same plane." (Pp. 551-52.)

The majority opinion, it should be noted, did not deny or even question the equality of "the civil and political rights of both races." The disagreement was instead over what is included in "civil and political rights" (and therefore constitutionally protected) and what conduct should be regarded as only "social" (and therefore unprotected).

THE HARLAN DISSENT

Of all the many dissenting opinions in the history of the Supreme Court, Justice Harlan's *Plessy* dissent is undoubtedly the most famous (and probably has been the most often cited). But it is also the most seriously misunderstood.

Like the majority, Harlan made no secret of his belief in the superiority of the white race. According to his dissent, "The white race deems itself to be the dominant race in this country. And so it is, in prestige, in achievements, in education, in wealth, and in power. So, I doubt not, it will continue to be for all time, if it remains true to its great heritage, and holds fast to the principles of constitutional liberty."[51]

But, he continued, white superiority is not determinative of the constitutional rights of black citizens. In his often-quoted words:

> "...in view of the constitution, in the eye of the law, there is in this country no superior, dominant, ruling class of citizens. There is no caste here. *Our constitution is color-blind,* and neither knows nor tolerates classes among citizens. In respect of civil rights, all citizens are equal before the law." (P. 559, italics added.)

That stirring declaration has been widely read—by, among others, eminent scholars—as a plea that all government racial classifications are *per se* unconstitutional, without the need of any further showing of unreasonableness or harm.[52]

For example, in his classic study of the *Plessy* decision, Charles Lofgren concluded that Harlan "...developed the position that legally mandated racial separation was by itself unconstitutional...."[53]

Similarly, in the most extensive analysis of the color-blindness doctrine, Andrew Kull states: "At the other extreme was the radical view, adopted in Harlan's dissenting opinion, that the equal protection clause prohibited racial classifications altogether;" "Justice Harlan's dissenting opinion [argued] that legal distinctions on the basis of race be altogether prohibited;" "Justice Harlan advanced a flat prohibition as the only alternative to a rule permitting reasonable racial classifications;" "...he was unwilling to rely on judges to distinguish a good racial classification

---

[51] Harlan's claim of superiority of the white race has been frequently criticized. E.g., Justice Ginsburg (joined by Justice Breyer) dissenting in Adarand Constructors, Inc. v. Pena, 515 U.S. 200, 272 (1995). In his dissent Harlan also stated, apparently approvingly, that "There is a race so different from our own that we do not permit those belonging to it to become citizens of the United States." (P. 537.) For an eloquent critique of that comment by an Asian-American law professor, see Gabriel Chin, "The Plessy Myth: Justice Harlan and the Chinese Cases," 82 *Iowa Law Review* 151 (1997).

[52] E.g., Charles Lofgren, *The Plessy Case: A Legal-Historical Interpretation* [Oxford 1987]; Andrew Kull, *The Color-Blind Constitution* [Harvard 1992; Owen Fiss, *History of the Supreme Court of the United States: Troubled Beginnings of the Modern State, 1888-1910* [Cambridge 1993]; Bernard Schwartz, *A History of the Supreme Court* [Oxford 1993]: 188.

[53] Lofgren, supra, at 195, 192, 205. His treatise meticulously notes all of Harlan's repeated qualifications limiting his argument to "civil rights," but Lofgren overlooks the central significance of the qualifications and apparently read Harlan's references to "civil rights" to include generally all personal constitutional rights as the term is now used..

from a bad one;" "The meaning of the Constitution must therefore be that classifications by race, regardless of its reasonableness in a particular instance, is beyond the legislative competence;" "The hostility toward the judicial evaluation of policy ... led Harlan to propose a per se prohibition of racial classifications...."[54]

Harlan's opinion, however, does not support such an expansive interpretation. His "eloquent mantra"[55] that "Our constitution is color-blind" did not relate to all racial classifications or to all Jim Crow laws. Further, like Plessy's counsel, Harlan did not contend that the Equal Protection Clause (which was scarcely mentioned in the dissent) prohibited segregation. And, although Harlan did not go as far as Plessy's counsel did in explicitly supporting the validity of school segregation and miscegenation laws, there is nothing in Harlan's opinion indicating that he regarded such laws as falling within his "color-blind" declaration.

Instead, Harlan's opinion was narrowly concerned with the fundamental rights of citizenship that he contended had been guaranteed by the Thirteenth Amendment (and then reinforced by the Fourteenth)—rights that were known in the nineteenth century as "civil rights." And, just as he had done thirteen years earlier in his *Civil Rights Cases* dissent, Harlan placed specific reliance in *Plessy* on a citizen's "civil right" to travel on a public highway. In the *Civil Rights Cases*, Harlan had contended "that the right of a colored person to use an improved public highway upon the terms accorded to freemen of other races is as fundamental, in the state of freedom established in this country, as are any of the rights which my brethren concede to be so far fundamental as to be deemed the essence of civil freedom." (109 U.S. at 39.) In *Plessy*, Harlan applied the identical argument to the Louisiana statute,

---

[54] Kull, supra, at 117, 118, 121, 123, 125. Owen Fiss, supra, at 363-64, reached the the same anticlassification conclusion but did so by reading the dissent as based on substantive due process and the limits of a state's police power. He contends that Harlan "...objected to the Louisiana statute on the ground that its purpose was to favor one-group (whites) over another (blacks)" and that such a law was "beyond the competence of any state." According to Fiss, Harlan applied in Plessy the same "liberty" doctrine that Harlan relied upon 12 years later in Adair v. United States, 208 U.S. 161 (1908) (striking down a federal prohibition against "yellow-dog" contracts as an interference with "freedom of contract"). Even apart from the absence of any reliance on substantive due process in the dissent, such an analysis would invalidate all Jim Crow legislation, contrary to both Harlan's focus on a limited class of fundamental citizenship rights and his acceptance of miscegenation laws and school segregation.

[55] Christopher Schmidt, "Brown and the Colorblind Constitution," 94 *Cornell Law Review* 203, 225 (2008).

concluding that it therefore violated Plessy's fundamental citizenship rights by "regulat[ing] the use of a public highway by citizens of the United States solely upon the basis of race." (167 U.S. at 553.)

After acknowledging that the Louisiana statute spoke of "persons," Harlan recast the issue more narrowly in terms of "citizens:" "While there may be in Louisiana persons of different races who are not citizens of the United States, the words in the act 'white and colored races' necessarily include all citizens of the United States of both races residing in that state." (P. 553.) Harlan then pointed out (just as he had argued in his *Civil Rights Cases* dissent) "That a railroad is a public highway ... is not, at this day, to be disputed" (p. 553).[56] On that foundation, Harlan argued that therefore the Louisiana statute encumbered and violated the "civil rights" of black citizens (p. 560).

In the nineteenth century, as Richard Primus pointed out in *The American Language of Rights*, the term "civil rights" was not—as it used today—a catchall phrase referring generally to a wide variety of (either recognized or claimed) constitutional rights.[57] Instead, it was then "... a limiting term referring to a subclass of rights ... that people must hold in order to act as private individuals in civil society, capable of personal independence and self-sufficiency."[58] And throughout his opinion Harlan inserted qualifying language to remove any doubt it was that subclass of rights on which he was focusing."[59]

---

[56] In support Harlan cited and quoted the same authorities on which he had relied in his *Civil Rights Cases* dissent, including Olcott v. Supervisors, 83 U.S. 678 (1872), which held "that railroads, though constructed by private corporations, and owned by them, are public highways, has been the doctrine of nearly all the courts ever since such conveniences for passages and transportation have had any existence."

[57] Richard Primus, *The American Language of Rights* [Cambridge 1999]: 128, 173-74.

[58] Richard Primus, "Canon, Anti-Canon, and Judicial Dissent," 48 *Duke Law Journal* 243, 289-90 (1998). See, e.g., Strauder v. West Virginia, 100 U.S. 303, 306, 309-10 (1879) (referring to jury service as a civil right and holding that excluding blacks violated the Fourteenth Amendment); Civil Rights Cases, 109 U.S. 3, 19, 24-26 (1883) (striking down the Civil Rights Act of 1875 on the ground that the public accommodation rights provided in the Act were not civil but social).

[59] T. Alexander Aleinikoff, "Re-Reading Justice Harlan's Dissent in Plessy v. Ferguson: Freedom, Antiracism, and Citizenship," 1992 *University of Illinois Law Review* 961, recognizes that the dissent only addressed fundamental citizenship rights, but then supports an interpretation of the dissent that is directly at odds with what Harlan said. Aleinikoff regards the "color-blind" reference as merely a forceful metaphor and

He used the term "civil rights" eleven times in his opinion (including three times in the paragraph containing the "color-blind" metaphor) and carefully limited his argument to "civil rights, common to all citizens" (pp. 554, 560), "when the civil rights of those citizens are involved" (p. 555), "so far as civil and political rights are concerned" (p. 556), and "[i]n respect of civil rights" (p. 559). He quoted from his own opinion issued thirty days earlier that "the Constitution of the United States, in its present form, forbids, *so far as civil and political rights are concerned*, discrimination by the General Government, or by the states against any citizen because of his race."[60] (Italics added.) And in his dissent in the *Civil Rights Cases* Harlan had similarly confined his argument to "civil rights necessarily growing out of freedom" and protecting the former slaves from "all discrimination against them, because of their race, *in respect of such civil rights as belong to freemen of other races*" (109 U.S. at 34, 36, italics added).

The limited parameters of Harlan's *Plessy* dissent are further demonstrated by his choice of examples of the consequences of the majority's decision. Each one relates to a right of citizenship—to travel on a highway or street; to observe courtroom proceedings; or to attend legislative sessions and political meetings. Harlan asked, if enforced passenger separation on railroads is permissible, does that mean that a state may "compel white citizens to keep on one side of a street, and black citizens to keep on the other?" May a state "punish whites and blacks who ride together in street cars or in open vehicles on a public road or street?" May a state "require sheriffs to assign whites to one side of a court room, and blacks to the other?" May a state "prohibit the commingling of the two races in the galleries of

---

reads the dissent as saying that "The Louisiana statute was unreasonable" because it was based on white supremacy. (Pp. 963-64969-70.) For several reasons, I do not believe such an interpretation is justified. All Jim Crow laws were based on white supremacy, but neither Harlan nor Plessy's counsel challenged the constitutionality of all Jim Crow laws. If the dissent only addressed fundamental citizenship rights and not all racial classifications, there would seem to be no obstacle to Harlan's regarding that limited subclass of rights as "color-blind." In addition, Harlan at length sharply criticized the courts' use of a "reasonableness" test to determine the validity of legislation. (167 U.S. at 558-59.)

[60] Gibson v. Mississippi, 162 U.S. 565, 591 (1896). Harlan also cited *Gibson* as one of five jury exclusion cases to illustrate "remov[al of] the race line from our governmental systems" (163 U.S. at 555-56).

legislative halls or in public assemblages convened for the consideration of the political questions of the day?" (Pp. 557-58.)

Conspicuously absent from Harlan's parade of horribles is any reference to the most widely prevalent Jim Crow laws requiring school segregation or prohibiting miscegenation. And his record both before and after *Plessy* contradicts any assumption that he included such racial classifications in his "color-blind" argument.

Thus, in *Pace v. Alabama*, Harlan joined the opinion sustaining a state miscegenation law on the ground that "The punishment of each offending person, whether white or black, is the same."

Three years after the *Plessy* decision, Harlan wrote the Court's opinion in Cumming v. Richmond County Board of Education, 175 U.S. 528 (1899), rejecting (9-0) a claim that a Georgia school board violated the Equal Protection Clause by closing its high school for blacks while continuing to maintain a high school for white girls. The board defended its action on the ground that its limited funds were more needed to support black primary schools for a much larger number of black children. The Court declined to pass on the constitutionality of the Georgia segregation statute on the ground that the issue had not been properly raised in the pleadings. But Harlan held that the board did not act unconstitutionally by refusing to withhold funds for the white high school in order to keep the black school open. Harlan stated: "...while all admit that the benefits and burdens of public taxation must be shared by citizens without discrimination against any class on account of their race, the education of the people in schools maintained by state taxation is a matter belonging to the respective states, and any interference on the part of federal authority with the management of such schools cannot be justified except in the case of a clear and unmistakable disregard of rights secured by the supreme law of the land. We have here no such case to be determined...." He added the caveat that "if it appeared that the board's refusal to maintain such a school was in fact an abuse of its discretion and in hostility to the colored population because of their race, different questions might have arisen in the state court." (P. 545.) In short, according to Harlan, the validity of the board's action would depend on the reasonableness of the board's action—a standard completely antithetical to a putative "color-blind" principle that all racial classifications are *per se* unconstitutional.[61]

It is evident that Harlan did not view either miscegenation or school segregation as involving "civil rights" that must be "color-blind" and exempt from a "reasonableness" standard. More broadly, Harlan did not disagree with the *Plessy* majority's premise that the Reconstruction Amendments did not protect what was then regarded as social equality. His disagreement with the majority was over the question whether the right sought by Plessy should be categorized as "civil" rather than "social."[62]

Even though the Harlan dissent was not cited in the Court's 1954 decision in *Brown v. Board of Education*,[63] some claim to find a close link between the two opinions. But "[t]he *Brown* decision actually reflected a conscious effort by the Justices to *not* accept the general principle of colorblind constitutionalism."[64] The holding in *Brown* was limited to public education and emphasized the harm to legally segregated black children. Other differences may also be noted: *Brown*, unlike the Harlan dissent, was based on the Equal Protection

---

[61] Justice Harlan also dissented in Berea College v. Kentucky, 211 U.S. 45 (1908), in which the college was convicted of violating a Kentucky statute that prohibited the teaching of both blacks and whites in the same place. The college appealed on substantive due process grounds, claiming that the application of the statute to a private college exceeded the state's police powers. The Court (7-2) declined to consider the college's constitutional claim by affirming the lower court decision solely upon the reserved authority of the Kentucky legislature to alter, amend, or repeal charters of its own corporations. In his dissent, Harlan disagreed with the majority's refusal to decide the constitutional issue and argued that the statute was "an arbitrary invasion of the rights of liberty and property guaranteed by the Fourteenth Amendment against hostile state action."

[62] See, e.g., Richard Primus, supra, at 243, 292; Jack Balkin, *Living Originalism* [Belknap 2011]: 225. Conversely, the majority did not deny that "civil rights," as then understood,, are "color-blind" but adhered to a far more restrictive view of what should be regarded as a "civil right."

[63] See Chapter 10 *The School Segregation Cases*.

[64] Schmidt, supra, at 208 (Italics in original); see also Kull, supra, at 151-51. Nor has any subsequent Supreme Court decision ever embraced the "color-blindness" doctrine. However, Harlan's dissent has frequently been cited by individual Justices on both sides of the ideological divide. For example, in Parents Involved in Community Schools v. Seattle School District No. 1, 551 U.S. 701 (2007), citations to the Harlan dissent appeared seven times in four separate opinions. In "The Color-Blind Court," 45 *American University Law Review* 791 (1996), Jeffrey Rosen correctly observes that four Justices "committed themselves to the principle that government can almost never classify citizens on the basis of race" (italics added), but significantly overstates by asserting that "The ideal of a color-blind Constitution is close to achieving five votes on the Supreme Court...." (p. 791). As subsequent decisions have confirmed, the "strict scrutiny" standard remains dominant.

Clause; Harlan relied instead on the "civil rights" conferred by the Thirteenth Amendment's grant of freedom. Thus *Brown* applied to all "persons" and Harlan's dissent was limited to those who were "citizens." *Brown* struck down school segregation; Harlan regarded such matters as "social" below the level of "civil rights' of citizens. And Harlan's assertion of the superiority and continued dominance of the white race is completely inconsistent with the premise and tenor of the *Brown* opinion.

THE CONTEMPORARY VIEW OF PLESSY

When the case was decided, neither the majority opinion nor Harlan's dissent received much public attention. The case was almost totally ignored in the press. In the *New York Times,* for example, the decision was noted in two brief paragraphs in a section concerning railroad news. The *Times* reported that the Louisiana law, "requiring the railroads of the State to provide separate cars for white and colored passengers," was upheld "by analogy to the laws of Congress and of many of the states, requiring the establishment of separate schools for children of the two races, and other similar laws." The *Chicago Tribune* [65] and the *Boston Globe* did not report the case at all. And the case remained in relative obscurity for several decades.[66]

More recently, the majority opinion in *Plessy v. Ferguson* has joined *Dred Scott* and the *Japanese Internment Cases* as one of the most reviled decisions in the history of the Supreme Court.[67]

As we now know, separate-but-equal proved to be an unmitigated disaster for the nation and particularly for its black citizens. To modern sensibilities, with the benefit of hindsight, *Plessy* and its racist premises are unconscionable. Contrary to the Court's apparent assumption, the inevitable effect of segregation was indeed to degrade the black race and stamp it "with a badge of inferiority." And it also became evident that the ostensible requirement that the facilities

---

[65] "Louisiana's Separate Car Law," *New York Times*, May 19, 1896.

[66] Lofgren, supra, at 196-97; Goldstone, supra, at 168. The decision was not even mentioned in Charles Warren's 1922 *The Supreme Court in United States History*, Henry Steele Commager's 1934 *Documents of American History*, or Carl Swisher's 1943 *American Constitutional Development*. Lofgren, supra, at 5.

[67] See Lofgren, supra, at 3-4, collecting examples of the invective concerning the decision.

be equal was almost invariably ignored. Judged by these standards, *Plessy* was in retrospect clearly wrong.

But the defects of separate-but-equal, although glaringly obvious today, were not as apparent in 1896. As Jack Greenberg, a key NAACP lawyer in the campaign to overturn separate-but-equal, observed: "The 1896 in which the *Plessy v. Ferguson* decision was handed down was a decidedly different milieu from the 1954 of the *School Segregation Cases,* and there is no doubt that the eras in which the cases were decided more than the formal logic involved in the controversies made the difference in result."[68] Similarly, historian Charles Lofgren has pointed out that "…simply condemning the decision promotes an understanding neither of it nor of America in the late nineteenth century."[69]

Plessy, moreover, did not originate the separate-but-equal doctrine. When the case was decided in 1896, the doctrine had already become deeply ingrained in the country's legal and social fabric. By applying the doctrine and giving it the imprimatur of the Supreme Court, *Plessy* undoubtedly facilitated the further growth of segregation. But, long before the decision, the rationale underlying *Plessy* and separate-but-equal was widely accepted as conventional wisdom. With all its many faults, the *Plessy* decision has been saddled with blame that in large measure is more justly attributable to a tragic failing of the nation.

[68] Jack Greenberg, *Race Relations and American Law* [Columbia 1959]: 8. See also Bernard Schwartz, *A History of the Supreme Court* [Oxford 1993]: 189.
[69] Lofgren, supra, at 4. See also Jack Balkin, *Constitutional Redemption: Political Faith in an Unjust World* [Harvard 2011]: 210.

8. THE *JAPANESE INTERNMENT CASES*

Justice Harlan called *Plessy v. Ferguson* "as pernicious as ... the *Dred Scott* case." Other candidates for that dubious distinction—and probably the Court's most harshly criticized decisions in the past century—are its decisions in the *Japanese Internment Cases*: Hirabayashi v. United States, 320 U.S. 81 (1943), and Korematsu v. United States, 323 U.S. 214 (1944).

These decisions upheld the imprisonment of approximately 120,000 Japanese-Americans—*two-thirds of them native-born American citizens*—solely on the basis of their racial ancestry and without evidence of disloyalty.[70] With few exceptions they were confined under appalling conditions in military-style "detention centers" for approximately three years.

After the Japanese attack on Pearl Harbor and the Declaration of War against Germany and Italy, President Franklin Roosevelt expressed his concern over reports that employees of Japanese, German, or Italian descent were being fired. He called that "as stupid as it is unjust" and reminded the nation that its fight was against nations convinced of their racial superiority. "We must not forget what we are defending: liberty, decency, justice," the President said. "I urge all private employers to adopt a sane policy regarding aliens and foreign-born citizens."[71]

Public clamor for the mass evacuation of Japanese was spurred by the January 24, 1942, report of the commission headed by Supreme Court Justice Owen Roberts to investigate the Pearl Harbor attack. One short passage of the report alleged—an allegation never documented but widely publicized—that Japanese spies in Hawaii had helped preparation for the attack. The report did not assert that any of the spies were Japanese-Americans (only that "some were Japanese

[70] The most detailed account is by Peter Irons, *Justice at War: The Story of the Japanese American Internment Cases* [California 1983].

[71] Jim Newton, *Justice for All: Earl Warren and the Nation He Made* [Riverhead 2006]: 123-24.

consular agents and others were persons having no ope[?]
the Japanese foreign service"). The evacuation deman[?]
include removal of citizens as well as aliens.[72]

On January 28 all Los Angeles city and county employees or
"Japanese parentage" were fired. On the same day the *Los Angeles
Times* called for the removal of Japanese-Americans "from the most
acute danger spots." And on January 29 the *Times* published a column by Henry McLemore calling "for immediate removal of every
Japanese on the West Coast to a point deep in the interior." The column added: "If making 1,000,000 innocent Japanese uncomfortable
would prevent one scheming Japanese from costing the life of one
American boy, then let 1,000,000 innocents suffer... Personally, I hate
the Japanese. And that goes for all of them."[73]

California Governor Culbert Olson announced in a radio speech
to the state that "It is known that there are Japanese residents of
California who have sought to aid the Japanese enemy by way of
communicating information, or have shown indications of preparation for fifth-column activities." Each of these reports, however,
proved to be false.[74]

The Commanding General of the Army Western Command,
General John L. DeWitt, told Defense officials in Washington that
"There's a tremendous volume of public opinion now developing
against the Japanese of all classes, that is aliens and non-aliens, to get
them off the land.... As a matter of fact, it's not being instigated or
developed by people who are not thinking but by the best people of
California. Since the publication of the Roberts Report they feel that
they are living in the midst of a lot of enemies. They don't trust the
Japanese, none of them." DeWitt told his superiors in Washington
that he now favored evacuating not only Japanese immigrants but
also Japanese-American citizens. [75]

Governor Olson, California Attorney General Earl Warren, and
most members of the West Coast congressional delegation now demanded that all persons of Japanese ancestry be removed from the

---

[72] Irons, supra, at 40-41; Newton, supra, at 125; Geoffrey Stone, *Perilous Times: Free
Speech in Wartime* [Norton 2004]: 291-92.

[73] Newton, supra, at 125-26.

[74] Id. at 138; Stone, supra, at 287.

[75] Newton, supra, at 128

West Coast.[76] Warren stated that he had "come to the conclusion that the Japanese situation as it exists today in this state may well be the Achilles heel of the entire civilian defense effort. Unless something is done it may bring about a repetition of Pearl Harbor." "It is difficult," he said, "to distinguish between a dangerous enemy alien, of which we are certain there are many here, and citizens who may be relied on to loyally support the United States war effort."[77]

An article titled "The Fifth Column on the Coast" written by the country's most prestigious columnist, Walter Lippman, was published on February 13. "Nobody's Constitutional rights include the right to reside and do business on a battlefield," he wrote. "And nobody ought to be on a battlefield who has no good reason for being there. There is plenty of room elsewhere for him to exercise his rights."[78] The fact that there had not been any evidence of subversion, according to Lippman, ws simply "a sign that the blow is well organized and held back until it can be struck with maximum effect."[79]

Another widely published journalist, Westbrook Pegler, wrote that "The Japanese in California should be under armed guard to the last man and woman right now—and to hell with habeas corpus until the danger is over."[80]

On February 14, General DeWitt proposed to the Secretary of War that all Japanese, aliens and citizens alike, be excluded from the West Coast. DeWitt wrote: "The Japanese race is an enemy race.... Along the Pacific Coast over 112,000 potential enemies, of Japanese extraction, are at large today. There are indications that these are organized and ready for concerted action at a favorable opportunity. The very fact that no sabotage has taken place to date is a disturbing and confirming indication that such action will be taken."[81]

In Washington, Attorney General Francis Biddle and Secretary of War Henry Stimson strongly disagreed about what should be

---

[76] Stone, supra, at 292

[77] Newton, supra, at 128-29.

[78] Id. at 132.

[79] Noah Feldman, *Scorpions: The Battles and Triumphs of FDR's Great Supreme Court Justices* [Twelve 2010]: 238-39.

[80] Irons, supra, at 60-61.

[81] Newton, supra, at 134; Hohri v. United States, 782 F.2d 227 (D.C. Cir. 1986).

done about the West Coast Japanese. Stimson argued for removal of some or all. Biddle, supported by FBI chief J. Edgar Hoover, opposed any such step.

On February 19, after a bitter battle within the Executive branch, President Roosevelt signed Executive Order 9066 authorizing United States military commanders to "prescribe military areas [from] which any or all persons may be excluded, and with respect to which, the right of any person to enter, remain in, or leave shall be subject to whatever restriction [the] Commander may impose in his discretion." The Executive Order declared that "the successful prosecution of the war requires every possible protection against espionage and against sabotage to national-defense material, national-defense premises, and national-defense utilities...."[82]

Attorney General Biddle protested that the order was "ill-advised, unnecessary, and unnecessarily cruel," to which the President responded, "[T]his must be a military decision."[83]

On March 21, 1942, again without any explicit reference to a particular race or nationality, Congress passed legislation making it a crime to violate an order of any military commander made pursuant to the Executive Order. Three days later, acting under this authority, General DeWitt designated California, western Oregon and Washington, and southern Arizona as "military areas" and issued a proclamation stating that "... the present situation within these Military Areas and Zones requires as a matter of military necessity the establishment of certain regulations pertaining to all enemy aliens and all persons of Japanese ancestry within said Military Areas and Zones ...." On this basis, General Dewitt then issued orders initially forbidding all persons of Japanese ancestry to leave their homes during "curfew" hours and then requiring the exclusion of all persons of Japanese ancestry from the West Coast until further orders shall permit. In addition, the exclusion order was paired with another order requiring all persons of Japanese ancestry to turn themselves in for transfer to the internment camps.

[82] A second Executive Order (No. 9102, March 18, 1942) established a War Relocation Authority that was authorized to formulate and effectuate a program for the removal, relocation, maintenance and supervision of persons designated under Executive Order No. 9066.

[83] Persico, supra, at 168.

Over the next eight months, approximately 120,000 individuals of Japanese descent (including infants in arms, children of high school age or younger, housewives, and the infirm and elderly) were forced to leave their homes in California, Washington, Oregon, and Arizona.[84] No differentiation was made between citizens and aliens, men and women, adults and children; no charges of disloyalty were brought against them; no hearings were conducted.[85] They were transported to desert and mountain camps that were hundreds, sometimes thousands, of miles from their homes. Most were incarcerated behind barbed wire for the balance of the war, resulting in many instances of the loss of their homes, cars, furniture, and a lifetime of savings.[86]

THE HIRABAYASHI CASE

Both Gordon Hirabayashi (a senior at the University of Washington) and Fred Korematsu (a welder in Oakland, California) were native-born citizens of Japanese descent. Although no question was raised as to either's loyalty, each was convicted of failing to report to a detention center. In addition, Hirabayashi was convicted on a second count of violating the curfew order. Hirabayashi challenged the constitutionality of both the curfew and internment charges.

In an opinion by Chief Justice Harlan Stone, the Supreme Court unanimously affirmed. However, in upholding Hirabayashi's sentence, the Court chose to consider only the curfew order on the ground that the sentences on the two counts were to run concurrently and thus the conviction on the second was sufficient to sustain the sentence. Holding that "The conviction under the second count [curfew] is without constitutional infirmity," the Court stated that therefore "we have no occasion to review the conviction on the first count...." based on the internment order and that "It is unnecessary to consider whether or to what extent such findings would support orders differing from the curfew order." (P. 105.)

Although ostensibly not dealing only with the internment order, the Court's rationale was far-reaching in its scope. Without any

---

[84] Ethnic Japanese in Hawaii were not interned even though Hawaii had by far the greatest concentration of individuals of Japanese descent and even though it had been the site of the Japanese attack. Id. at 295.

[85] Id. at 287.

[86] Newton, supra, at 136-37.

independent assessment of the evidence, the decision primarily rested on a constitutional assumption that in national security matters the Court must defer to the judgment of the military and of Congress as the "war-making branches." According to the opinion, "Whatever views we may entertain regarding the loyalty to this country of the citizens of Japanese ancestry, we cannot reject as unfounded the judgment of military authorities and of Congress that there were disloyal members of that population, whose number and strength could not be precisely and quickly ascertained." (P. 100.) Furthermore, "We cannot say that these facts and circumstances, considered in the particular war setting, could afford no ground for differentiating citizens of Japanese ancestry from other groups in the United States." Although "Distinctions between citizens solely because of their ancestry are by their very nature odious to a free people whose institutions are founded upon the doctrine of equality," the Court concluded that "The adoption by Government, in the crisis of war and of threatened invasion, of measures for the public safety, based upon the recognition of facts and circumstances which indicate that a group of one national extraction may menace that safety more than others, is not wholly beyond the limits of the Constitution and is not to be condemned merely because in other and in most circumstances racial distinctions are irrelevant." (P. 101.)[87]

Justices Murphy and Douglas joined the Stone opinion but also filed concurring opinions. Murphy warned of the great danger of having "one law for the majority of our citizens and another for those of a particular racial heritage" (p. 112). Douglas suggested, ambiguously, that Hirabayashi might possibly be able to obtain relief in some other forum. According to Douglas, "military measures of defense might be paralyzed if it were necessary to try [individual issues of loyalty]. But a denial of that opportunity in this case does not necessarily mean that petitioner could not have had a hearing on that issue in some appropriate

---

[87] The Court observed that "The Fifth Amendment contains no equal protection clause and it restrains only such discriminatory legislation by Congress as amounts to a denial of due process." (P. 100.) it is unclear how much weight the Court gave to this distinction. It seems unlikely that the Court would have sanctioned anti-Japanese legislation in a peacetime context. Eleven years later in Bolling v. Sharpe, 347 U.S. 497 (1954), in light of the *Brown* decision holding school segregation unconstitutional under the Fourteenth Amendment, the Court held that "it would be unthinkable that the same Constitution would impose a lesser duty on the Federal Government."

proceeding." Douglas, however, did not identify what that appropriate proceeding might be.[88]

THE KOREMATSU CASE

A year later, Fred Korematsu's case was appealed to the Supreme Court. Korematsu, unlike Gordon Hirabayashi, had been convicted on only a single count of failing to report to a detention center. In this case, therefore, the Court was obliged to face the issue of the constitutionality of the underlying internment program. In an opinion written by Justice Hugo Black, the Court (6-3) affirmed.

The opinion acknowledged—in a ringing declaration later often quoted in race discrimination cases—"that all legal restrictions which curtail the civil rights of a single racial group are immediately suspect" and "that courts must subject them to the most rigid scrutiny." (P. 216.) But, after enunciating that governing standard, the Court then proceeded to ignore it. Far from subjecting General DeWitt's order "to the most rigid scrutiny," the Court found it sufficient that the nation was at war, that Dewitt was authorized to issue such an order, and that DeWitt thought it was appropriate.

The majority held that its decision upholding the exclusion order was controlled by its decision in *Hirabayashi* sustaining General DeWitt's curfew order. According to Justice Black:

"Like curfew, exclusion of those of Japanese origin was deemed necessary because of the presence of an unascertained number of disloyal members of the group, most of whom we have no doubt were loyal to this country. It was because we could not reject the finding of the military authorities that it was impossible to bring about an immediate segregation of the disloyal from the loyal that we sustained the validity of the curfew order as applying to the whole group. In the instant case, temporary exclusion of the entire group was based by the military on the same ground." (Pp. 218-19.)

---

[88] Justice Black complained to Justice Frankfurter that Douglas was seeking to bring "a thousand habeas corpus suits in the district courts." Justice Jackson thought the idea of individual loyalty review so farfetched that he labeled it a "hoax." Douglas Kmiec, "The Supreme Court in Time of Hot and Cold War," 28 *Journal of Supreme Court History* 270, 273-74 (2003). See also Feldman, supra, at 241-42, 247-48.

Black denied that this was a "case of imprisonment of a citizen in a concentration camp solely because of his ancestry, without evidence or inquiry concerning his loyalty and good disposition towards the United States." Indeed, Black stated, the Court's "task would be simple, our duty clear, were this a case involving the imprisonment of a loyal citizen in a concentration camp because of racial prejudice." But, according to Black, even though there was "no doubt [most of those incarcerated] were loyal to this country," racial prejudice had nothing to do with requiring them to be "segregated":

> "To cast this case into outlines of racial prejudice, without reference to the real military dangers which were presented, merely confuses the issue. Korematsu was not excluded from the military area because of hostility to him or his race. He *was* excluded because we are at war with the Japanese Empire, because the properly constituted military authorities feared an invasion of our West Coast and felt constrained to take proper security measures, because they decided that the military urgency of the situation demanded that all citizens of Japanese ancestry be segregated from the West Coast temporarily, and, finally, because Congress, reposing its confidence in this time of war in our military leaders—as inevitably it must—determined that they should have the power to do just this." (P. 223.)[89]

Justice Frankfurter, concurring, found "nothing in the Constitution which denies to Congress the power to enforce such a valid military order by making its violation an offense triable in the civil courts. ... To find that the Constitution does not forbid the military measures now complained of does not carry with it approval of that which Congress and the Executive did. That is their business, not ours." (P. 225.)

---

[89] On the same day the Court decided the *Korematsu* case, it also issued its decision in Ex Parte Endo, 323 U.S. 283 (1944). Mitsuye Endo had challenged her detention in a habeas corpus proceeding and was conceded by the War Department to be loyal but yet had not been released. In an opinion by Justice Douglas, the Court (9-0) held that Japanese-American citizens who are found to be loyal must be freed. According to Douglas, since loyalty had been the claimed basis of the whole program, President Roosevelt could only have intended the continued detention of persons still suspected of disloyalty.

Three Justices who had joined the *Hirabayashi* decision the year before—Roberts, Murphy, and Jackson—dissented in *Korematsu*.

Rejecting Black's reliance on the curfew decision, Justice Roberts emphasized that "This is not a case of keeping people off the streets at night as in *Hirabayashi*...." but instead a "case of convicting a citizen as a punishment for not submitting to imprisonment in a concentration camp, based on his ancestry, and solely because of his ancestry, without evidence or inquiry concerning his loyalty and good disposition towards the United States." (P. 227.)

In a passionate dissent, calling the decision a "legalization of racism," Justice Murphy contended that "...it is essential that there be definite limits to military discretion, especially where martial law has not been declared." (Pp. 234, 242.) In his view, "no reasonable relation to an immediate, imminent, and impending public danger is evident to support this racial restriction, which is one of the most sweeping and complete deprivations of constitutional rights in the history of this nation in the absence of martial law." (P. 235.) Murphy found unsupportable each of General DeWitt's asserted reasons for ordering the exclusion and concluded: "The main reasons relied upon by those responsible for the forced evacuation ... appear, instead, to be largely an accumulation of much of the misinformation, half-truths and insinuations that for years have been directed against Japanese Americans by people with racial and economic prejudices." (P. 239.)

Justice Jackson's dissent pointed out that the Court's decision rested entirely on "General DeWitt's own unsworn, self-serving statement, untested by any cross-examination, that what he did was reasonable." Jackson asked: "How does the Court know that these orders have a reasonable basis in necessity? No evidence whatever on that subject has been taken by this or any other court." Furthermore, "...even if the orders of General DeWitt were permissible military procedures, I deny that it follows that they are constitutional. If, as the Court holds, it does follow, then we may as well say that any military order will be constitutional and have done with it." And Jackson warned: "...once a judicial opinion rationalizes such an order to show that it conforms to the Constitution, or rather rationalizes the Constitution to show that the Constitution sanctions such an order, the Court for all time has validated the principle of racial discrimination in criminal procedure and of transplanting American citizens."[90] (Pp. 245-46.)

AFTERMATH OF THE DECISIONS

Subsequent investigation demonstrated that, notwithstanding the rumors and suspicions leading to the curfew and internment programs, there was not a single documented act of espionage, sabotage, or treasonable activity committed by an American citizen of Japanese descent or by a Japanese national residing on the West Coast.

In 1976 President Gerald Ford issued a presidential proclamation acknowledging February 19 as "the anniversary of a sad day in American history," for it was "on that date in 1942 ... that Executive Order 9066 was issued" and "[w]we now know what we should have known then"—that the evacuation and internment of loyal Japanese-American citizens was "wrong."[91]

In 1980, Congress established an independent commission to review the exclusion and internment program. The commission heard the testimony of more than 720 witnesses, including key officials involved in the issuance and implementation of Executive Order 9066, and reviewed hundreds of documents that had not previously been available. After its study of the evidence, the commission unanimously concluded that the factors that shaped the internment decision "were race prejudice, war hysteria, and a failure of political leadership," rather than military necessity.

The criticism of the *Japanese Internment Cases* reached a new level of intensity with the discovery of archived documents demonstrating that the Government had deliberately misled the Supreme

---

[90] While urging that Korematsu's conviction be reversed, Jackson doubted that the Constitution allowed the Court to order the military to release the detainees: "In the very nature of things military decisions are not susceptible of intelligent judicial appraisal. They do not pretend to rest on evidence, but are made on information that often would not be admissible and on assumptions that could not be proved. Information in support of an order could not be disclosed to courts without danger that it would reach the enemy. Neither can courts act on communications made in confidence. Hence courts can never have any real alternative to accepting the mere declaration of the authority that issued the order that it was reasonably necessary from a military viewpoint." (P. 245.) See Feldman, supra, at 249-52.

[91] Newton, supra, at 305.

Court. In effect, the cases were decided on the basis of an intentionally doctored record.[92]

Among other things, the documents showed that there had been suppression of crucial evidence acknowledging that Japanese-Americans were not in fact a threat to national security. The FBI and the Office of Naval Intelligence had categorically denied that Japanese-Americans had committed any wrongdoing. The Director of the FBI, J. Edgar Hoover, ridiculed General DeWitt's proposal, saying "Every complaint in this regard has been investigated, but in no case has any information been obtained which would substantiate the allegation." Hoover further stated that "The necessity for mass evacuation is based primarily upon public and political pressure rather than on factual data" and that the FBI was fully capable of dealing with the small number of suspects then under surveillance.[93] Similarly, the Office of Naval Intelligence advised the Department of Justice that there was no basis for the allegation that Japanese-Americans had been engaged in shore-to-ship radio and light signaling to Japanese warships. This information contradicting DeWitt's report, however, was never disclosed to the Supreme Court.[94]

Even more strikingly, the documents showed that General DeWitt's "military necessity" claim—before it was revised to support the Government's position—was based on his characterization of the supposed racial traits of persons of Japanese ancestry. Dewitt's "Final Report" was dated June 5, 1943. But the original version of the report (printed and bound in final form) had been transmitted to the War Department nearly seven weeks earlier on April 15, 1943, and the original version dramatically differed from the "Final" version. Most significantly, the original report did not purport to rest on any military exigency, but instead declared that because of traits peculiar to persons of Japanese ancestry it would be impossible to separate the loyal from the disloyal. In addition, Dewitt stated flatly in the

---

[92] Hirabayashi v. United States, 828 F.2d 591 (9th Cir. 1987); Korematsu v. United States, 584 F.Supp. 1406 (N.D. Cal.). See also Irons, supra, at 186-219, 368-76; Stone, supra, at 305-07.

[93] Joseph Persico, *Roosevelt's Secret War* [Random House 2001]: 168; see also Stone, supra, at 289; Mark Weber, "World War II West Coast Camps for Japanese-Americans," http://www.ihr.org/jhr/v02/v02p-45_Weber.html.

[94] Hohri v. United States, 782 U.S. 227 (D.C. Cir. 1986).

foreword of the report his opposition to the return of any Japanese-Americans to the West Coast for the duration of the war.[95]

Other documents revealed that War Department officials (including Secretary John McCloy) were greatly alarmed after reading DeWitt's original report because it would likely undermine the Government's "military necessity" argument in the *Hirabayashi* case. They immediately tried to persuade DeWitt to revise it. Initially DeWitt refused. "My report to Chief of Staff," he radioed his deputy, "will not be changed in any respect whatsoever either in substance or form and I will not, repeat not, consent to any, repeat any, revision made over my signature." But DeWitt eventually capitulated. As a result, the report was rewritten after the War Department requested some fifty-five changes, particularly to eliminate racist characterizations and to emphasize—in line with the Government's litigation position in *Hirabayashi*—that military necessity was the controlling rationale. The expurgated document became the "Final" DeWitt report. The original report was never furnished or disclosed to the Department of Justice, then charged with the responsibility of defending the program in the Supreme Court.

War Department officials then ordered the destruction of all copies and evidence of the original report. One subordinate officer involved in carrying out the order reported that "War Department records have been adjusted accordingly." Another officer certified "...that this date I witnessed the destruction by burning of the galley proofs, galley pages, drafts and memorandums of the original report of the Japanese Evacuation."[97] The destruction order, however, did not prove entirely successful; one or more copies were subsequently found.

In 1983, when these facts were discovered, Fred Korematsu filed a petition in federal court to have his conviction set aside for "manifest injustice." In 1984, District Judge Marilyn Patel granted the petition, finding that the Government had knowingly and intentionally failed to disclose critical information that directly contradicted key statements in General DeWitt's report that the Government had relied upon to justify the mass evacuation.[97] Judge Patel concluded:

---

[95] See Irons, supra, at 206-212; Stone, supra, at 287; Richard Goldstein, "Gordon Hirabayashi, World War II Internment Opponent, Dies at 93," *New York Times*, January 3, 2012. (Fred Korematsu died in 2005.)

[97] Id. at 211.

[97] 584 F.Supp. at 1420.

"*Korematsu* remains on the pages of our legal and political history. As a legal precedent it is now recognized as having very limited application. As historical precedent it stands as a constant caution that in times of war or declared military necessity our institutions must be vigilant in protecting constitutional guarantees. It stands as a caution that in times of distress the shield of military necessity and national security must not be used to protect governmental actions from close scrutiny and accountability. It stands as a caution that in times of international hostility and antagonisms our institutions, legislative, executive and judicial, must be prepared to exercise their authority to protect all citizens from the petty fears and prejudices that are so easily aroused."

In 1987, on similar grounds, the Court of Appeals for the Ninth Circuit granted Gordon Hirabayashi's petition for a writ of *coram nobis* and vacated his conviction. The Ninth Circuit held that, given the importance that the Supreme Court attached to the Government's claims of military necessity in both *Hirabayashi* and *Korematsu*, "the reasoning of the Supreme Court would probably have been profoundly and materially affected" had it been advised "of the suppression of evidence" that would have "established the ... real reason for the exclusion order." The Ninth Circuit further stated: "The [Supreme] Court's divided opinions in *Korematsu* demonstrate beyond question the importance which the Justices in *Korematsu* and *Hirabayashi* placed upon the position of the government that there was a perceived military necessity, despite contrary arguments of the defendants in those cases. The majority in *Korematsu* reaffirmed the Court's deference in *Hirabayashi* to military judgments."[98]

The following year, Congress passed and President Reagan signed the Civil Liberties Act of 1988, which officially declared that the program had been a "grave injustice" that was "carried out without adequate security reasons" and without any documented acts of "espionage or sabotage." The Act declared that the program of exclusion and internment had been "motivated largely by racial

---

[98] 828 F.2d at 603-04.

prejudice, wartime hysteria, and a failure of political leadership." The Act included an official apology for the Government's actions and financial reparations.[99]

*****

As the history of the *Japanese Internment Cases* now makes clear, the primary vice of the decisions was not the Court's acceptance of a racial classification; segregation was not declared unlawful until ten years later in *Brown,* and even now other types of racial classifications (although presumptively invalid) may be shown to be justified in some limited circumstances.[100] Nor did the fault lie in the Court's taking wartime conditions into account; in determining whether a government action is constitutionally justified, context matters.[101]

Instead, particularly since the internment took place within the United States and not in a theater of war,[102] the primary vice of the decisions was the Court's failure to make the "rigid scrutiny" that *Korematsu* recognized was required. Had there been "rigid scrutiny"— or indeed any substantial consideration—of the Government's claim of necessity, the constitutional disaster would likely have been avoided.

---

[99] By 1998, the total payout ($20,000 to each surviving internee) was $1.6 billion, paid to 80,000 claimants. Stone, supra, at 307.

[100] See Chapter 13 *Evolution of the Equal Protection Standard..*

[101] For a limited defense of the internment order by a leading Court of Appeals judge, see Richard Posner, *Law, Pragmatism and Democracy* [Harvard 2003]: 293-95.

[102] Compare, e.g., Justice Black's opinion for the Court eight years later in the *Steel Seizure Case,* striking down President Truman's seizure of the steel mills and distinguishing "cases upholding broad powers in military commanders engaged in day-to-day fighting in a theater of war." Youngstown Sheet & Tube Co. v. Sawyer, 343 U.S. 579, 587 (1952).

9. CONFRONTING JIM CROW

In the nearly sixty years between *Plessy v. Ferguson* and *Brown v. Board of Education*, the separate-but-equal doctrine remained the controlling standard of the constitutionality of laws requiring racial segregation.

As recounted in Chapter 7, the first Supreme Court case involving school segregation was decided three years after *Plessy*. In Cumming v. Richmond County Board of Education, 175 U.S. 528 (1899), in an opinion by Justice Harlan (who had so forcefully dissented in *Plessy*), the Court (9-0) rejected the claim that a Georgia school board had violated the Equal Protection Clause by closing a black high school while continuing to support a high school for white girls. The board defended its action on the ground that its limited funds were needed more to support black primary schools for a much larger number of black children than the number who had attended the black high school.

The Court, after declining to consider the constitutionality of the Georgia school segregation statute because the issue had not been presented in the pleadings, held that the school board's decision did not present a "case of clear and unmistakable disregard of rights" since there was no showing that the school board had been motivated by a "hostility to the colored population because of their race." The board, Harlan stated, lacked the funds to support a black high school, and closing the white high school "would only ... take from white children educational privileges enjoyed by them, without giving to colored children additional opportunities." The Court acknowledged "that the benefits and burdens of public taxation must be shared by citizens without discrimination against any class on account of their race," but concluded that "the education of the people in schools maintained by state taxation is a matter belonging to the respective states, and any interference on the part of federal authority with the management of such schools cannot be justified except in the case of a clear and unmistakable disregard of rights secured by the supreme law of the land." (Pp. 544-45.)

In Chesepeake and Ohio R. Co. v. Kentucky, 179 U.S. 388 (1900), a Kentucky "equal but separate" railroad law was challenged as a violation of the Commerce Clause. Finding that the law applied only to intrastate commerce, the Court in an opinion by Justice Brown (who wrote the majority opinion in *Plessy*) concluded that "...so construing it there can be no doubt as to its constitutionality." In support of the decision, the Court relied in part on *Plessy* although noting that no Commerce Clause claim had been asserted in that case. Justice Harlan dissented without opinion.

In Berea College v. Kentucky, 211 U.S. 45 (1908), the college was convicted of violating a Kentucky statute that, although permitting education of both whites and blacks by the same corporation in different localities, prohibited the attendance of both races in the same place. The college appealed on substantive due process grounds, claiming that application of the statute to a private college violated the Fourteenth Amendment. The Court (7-2) declined to consider the Fourteenth Amendment claim by affirming the lower court decision solely upon the reserved authority of the Kentucky legislature to alter, amend, or repeal charters of its own corporations. Justice Harlan dissented, disagreeing with the Court's refusal to consider the constitutionality of the statute and arguing that the Kentucky statute was "an arbitrary invasion of the rights of liberty and property guaranteed by the Fourteenth Amendment against hostile state action."

In McCabe v. Atchison, Topeka, and Santa Fe, 235 U.S. 151 (1914), the Court emphasized that the separate-but-equal doctrine required that separate facilities must in fact be equal. But, even more significantly, the Court held that equality was to be measured on the basis of facilities provided to *individual* blacks. At issue in the case was an Oklahoma "equal but separate" law permitting railroads to provide sleeping, dining, and chair cars for whites without providing such cars for blacks if there was very little demand by blacks for those facilities. Although ultimately dismissing the case because the plaintiffs had not demonstrated personal injury, the Court (pp. 161-62) rejected the claim that limited black demand excused the failure to provide comparable facilities. According to the Court, in an opinion by Justice Charles Evans Hughes, the constitutional right of blacks to equal treatment did not "depend upon the number of persons who may be discriminated against" and "It is the individual who is entitled to the equal protection of the laws, and if he is denied…, a facility or convenience in the course of his journey which under substantially the same circumstances is furnished another traveler, he may properly claim that his constitutional privilege has been invaded." Chief Justice White and Justices Holmes, Lamar, and McReynolds concurred in the result.

Three years later in Buchanan v. Warley, 245 U.S. 60 (1917), the Court broke new ground—it struck down a segregation law and limited the scope of the *Plessy* separate-but-equal rationale. The unanimous decision invalidated a Louisville ordinance that prohibited blacks from moving into a block primarily occupied by whites and prohibited whites from moving into a block primarily occupied by blacks. The Court, however, based its decision on the Due Process Clause rather than the Equal Protection Clause. Relying on the then prevailing "liberty of contract" doctrine, the Court held that the ordinance was unconstitutional because it violated the rights of owners of property to acquire, use, and dispose of it (pp. 79-82):

> "The defendant in error insists that Plessy v. Ferguson, 163 U.S. 537, is controlling in principle in favor of the judgment of the court below. In that case, this court held that a provision of a statute of Louisiana requiring railway companies carrying passengers to provide in their coaches equal but separate accommodations for the white and colored races did not run counter to the provisions of the Fourteenth Amendment. It is to be observed that, in that case, there was no attempt to deprive persons of color of transportation in the coaches of the public carrier, and the express requirements were for equal, though separate, accommodations for the white and colored races. In Plessy v. Ferguson, classification of accommodation was permitted upon the basis of equality for both races.

> "…As we have seen, this court has held laws valid which separated the races on the basis of equal accommodations

in public conveyances, and courts of high authority have held enactments lawful which provide for separation in the public schools of white and colored pupils where equal privileges are given. But, in view of the rights secured by the Fourteenth Amendment to the Federal Constitution, such legislation must have its limitations, and cannot be sustained where the exercise of authority exceeds the restraints of the Constitution. We think these limitations are exceeded in laws and ordinances of the character now before us.

"It is the purpose of such enactments, and, it is frankly avowed, it will be their ultimate effect, to require by law, at least in residential districts, the compulsory separation of the races on account of color. Such action is said to be essential to the maintenance of the purity of the races, although it is to be noted in the ordinance under consideration that the employment of colored servants in white families is permitted, and nearby residences of colored persons not coming within the blocks, as defined in the ordinance, are not prohibited.

"The case presented does not deal with an attempt to prohibit the amalgamation of the races. The right which the ordinance annulled was the civil right of a white man to dispose of his property if he saw fit to do so to a person of color and of a colored person to make such disposition to a white person.

"It is urged that this proposed segregation will promote the public peace by preventing race conflicts. Desirable as this is, and important as is the preservation of the public peace, this aim cannot be accomplished by laws or ordinances which deny rights created or protected by the Federal Constitution.

"It is said that such acquisitions by colored persons depreciate property owned in the neighborhood by white persons. But property may be acquired by undesirable white neighbors or put to disagreeable though lawful uses with like results."

The *Buchanan* decision was of critical importance in limiting efforts to maintain all-white neighborhoods.[103] But, even more significantly, although the holding of the Court was cast in terms of protection of property rights and state police powers, the decision undermined key precepts underlying *Plessy*.

According to *Plessy*, the Louisiana segregation statute was constitutional because it was a "reasonable" exercise of police power. By contrast, *Buchanan* held that the Louisville segregation ordinance exceeded the "reasonable" bounds of police power because it violated individual rights, even though theoretically the ordinance imposed "equal" prohibitions on both blacks and whites. The Court also made clear that racial prejudice did not constitute a cognizable police-power justification for laws violating individual rights. Nor was it justified by expert opinion supporting the alleged value of racial separation or by the state's claim that integrated housing would lead to miscegenation, racial violence, and other social ills.[104]

Furthermore, although the decision was ostensibly based on liberty-of-contract grounds, the *Buchanan* opinion also relied on early Supreme Court anti-discrimination precedents such as Strauder v. West Virginia, 100 U.S. 303 (1880), and Ex parte Virginia, 100 U.S. 339 (1880), both involving the exclusion of blacks from jury service. The Court declared that the Amendments were designed "to protect all

---

[103] David Bernstein, *Rehabilitating Lochner: Defending Individual Rights against Progressive Reform* [Chicago 2011]: 83-84.

[104] The brief filed by Kentucky in support of the ordinance argued that segregation was divinely ordained and that housing segregation was necessary to prevent violence and lawlessness.. In response to the contention that the ordinance would restrict blacks to the poorest and least desirable sections of Louisville, the state argued that if "negroes carry a blight with them wherever they go ... on what theory do they assert the privilege of spreading that blight to the white sections of the city?" The state also submitted to the Court a voluminous appendix consisting of excerpts of books and articles justifying Southern treatment of blacks, claiming that an inherent racial instinct exists, stressing the purported negative effects of miscegenation; and asserting black inferiority. Bernstein, supra, at 80-81.

persons, white or black, against discriminatory legislation by the states" and that "This is now the settled law." The opinion also relied upon the 1866 and 1870 Civil Rights Acts, providing that blacks had the same right to make and enforce contracts and own and alienate property as did white persons. The Court stated that "These enactments did not deal with the social rights of men, but with those fundamental rights in property which it was intended to secure upon the same terms to citizens of every race and color. ... The Fourteenth Amendment and these statutes enacted in furtherance of its purpose operate to qualify and entitle a colored man to acquire property without state legislation discriminating against him solely because of color." (P. 79.)

Buchanan was thus the first Supreme Court decision recognizing that a law requiring segregation of the races—even with ostensibly equal facilities—may constitute an unconstitutional discrimination in at least some circumstances.

Despite the *Buchanan* ruling, separate-but-equal remained controlling. In Gong Lum v. Rice, 275 U.S. 78 (1927), the Court applied the doctrine in upholding the assignment of a Chinese child to a school for blacks under a Mississippi Constitution provision requiring that "Separate schools shall be maintained for children of the white and colored races." The Court pointed in particular to *Plessy*'s reliance on numerous precedents sanctioning the establishment of separate schools for whites and blacks, "even by courts of states where the political rights of the colored race have been longest and most earnestly enforced." The Court sustained the assignment to a black school, "assuming the cases above cited to be rightly decided, where the issue is as between white pupils and the pupils of the yellow races," and holding that "[t]he decision is within the discretion of the state in regulating its public schools, and does not conflict with the Fourteenth Amendment."

Starting in the 1930s, segregation in graduate schools was challenged in a series of Supreme Court cases. In each of the cases, the Court sustained the equal protection claim on the ground that the education offered to the black plaintiff was not equal. It was therefore unnecessary to pass on the validity of the separate-but-equal doctrine itself..

In Missouri ex rel. Gaines v. Canada, 305 U.S. 337 (1938), although no law school for blacks existed in the state, the all-white University of Missouri law school refused to admit a qualified

black Missouri resident. In an attempt to comply with the requirement of equal facilities, the state offered to pay the plaintiff's tuition at an out-of-state law school of equal reputation. The Court
(6-2) rejected the proposed alternative and ordered the applicant's
admission to the University of Missouri Law School. "The basic
consideration," the Court held, "is not as to what sort of opportunities other States provide, or whether they are as good as those
in Missouri, but as to what opportunities Missouri itself furnishes
to white students and denies to negroes solely upon the ground
of color" (p. 349). Relying on *McCabe*, the Court found that the
Equal Protection Clause was violated by a requirement that a
black student, but not a white student, would have to leave the
state to get a legal education.[105]

In Sipuel v. Oklahoma Board of Regents, 332 U.S. 631 (1948), the
Court applied its *Gaines* decision to invalidate Oklahoma's refusal
to provide legal education for blacks while maintaining a law school
restricted to whites. The state argued, unsuccessfully, that it was or-
ganizing a new law school for blacks. The Court held that the state
could not defer making such education available and must "provide
it as soon as it does for applicants of any other group."

On the same day in 1950, the Court decided two more graduate
school cases, Sweatt v. Painter, 339 U.S. 629 (1950), and McLaurin v.
Oklahoma, 339 U.S. 637 (1950). In each case, the Court unanimously
concluded that the facilities offered to the black student were inferior to
those provided to whites. Therefore, the Court stated, it was unnecessary
to "reach petitioner's contention that *Plessy v. Ferguson* should be re-ex-
amined in the light of contemporary knowledge respecting the purposes
of the Fourteenth Amendment and the effects of racial segregation."

In *Sweatt* the all-white University of Texas Law School had refused to admit a black applicant on the ground that the state had
created a new law school for blacks. The Court found that the two
schools were patently unequal. The University of Texas Law School
had sixteen full-time professors and substantial facilities, while the
black law school had only five professors and a small library. But, the

---

[105] The Court ordered the state to admit the plaintiff (Lloyd Gaines) but after the decision
he disappeared and no further proceedings in his case were possible. Subsequently,
however, the state established a law school for blacks. Jack Greenberg, *Race Relations
and American Law* [Columbia 1959]: 40.

Court added:

> "What is more important, the University of Texas Law School possesses to a far greater degree those qualities which are incapable of objective measurement but which make for greatness in a law school. Such qualities, to name but a few, include reputation of the faculty, experience of the administration, position and influence of the alumni, standing in the community, traditions and prestige."

The Court concluded that "we cannot find substantial equality in the educational opportunities offered white and Negro law students by the State...." (p. 633) and ordered the applicant's admission.

The *McLaurin* case involved a black Oklahoma resident seeking a doctorate in education. When his application to Oklahoma University was denied on racial grounds, a federal district court ordered the University to admit him but the University required him to sit in a separate row in class (separated by a railing with a "Reserved for Colored" sign) and to sit at separate tables in the library and cafeteria. The Supreme Court unanimously held that such segregation within the school hindered the black student's "ability to study, to engage in discussions, and exchange views with other students, and, in general, to learn his profession" (p. 641). And, referring to McLaurin's goal to become an educator: "Those who will come under his guidance and influence must be directly affected by the education he receives, Their own education and development will necessarily suffer to the extent that his training is unequal to that of his classmates. State-imposed restrictions which produce such inequalities cannot be sustained" under the Equal Protection Clause. McLaurin, the Court held, "must receive the same treatment ... as students of other races" (p. 642).[106]

---

[106]In a third racial discrimination opinion that day, Henderson v. United States, 339 U.S. 816 (1950), the Court applied the Interstate Commerce Act to invalidate the Southern Railway's discriminatory dining-car regulations. The Court held that special tables for black passengers were not permissible and that every ticket-holder entitled to use the diner must be equally free to do so: "The curtains, partitions and signs emphasize the artificiality of a difference in treatment which serves only to call attention to a racial classification of passengers holding identical tickets and using the same public dining facility." The Court had earlier invalidated state travel segregation laws under the Commerce Clause. Morgan v. Virginia, 328 U.S. 373 (1946).

These decisions effectively doomed reliance on the separate-but-equal doctrine at the graduate education level. The equality requirement, it was now clear, could not be met by sending black students out of state (*Gaines*), by opening a new but patently unequal law school (*Sweatt*), or by segregating black students within a school (*McLaurin*). The standards of equality adopted by the Court effectively precluded any possible justification for a white-only policy at a graduate school.

But this left unresolved a much more challenging issue—segregation in elementary and high schools in seventeen states. These schools, unlike the graduate schools, were equal or were being equalized. In addition, at the outset, desegregation at the graduate level opened the doors to only a relatively small number of black applicants to a few dozen graduate schools, and their admission did not require any large-scale changes in the structure or administration of the schools. By contrast, the desegregation of K-12 schools would require the uprooting and reorganization of thousands of separate white and black local school systems enrolling many millions of students. And exaggerated fears of the racial "mixing" of young boys and girls would undoubtedly arouse far more public resistance than the graduate schools' admission of black adults.

10. THE *SCHOOL SEGREGATION CASES*

After its victories in the *Sweatt* and *Mclaurin* cases in 1950, even though the black community was "deeply divided" about whether to attack segregation directly,[107] the NAACP reached the decision "to make desegregation, not equalization, the focus of all future cases."[108]

In 1952 the Court agreed to review five cases challenging the constitutionality of segregation in public schools in four states and the District of Columbia. In these cases, unlike the graduate school cases, it was not contended that separate schools for blacks were inferior to those provided for whites. Instead, the NAACP lawyers argued that government-imposed racial segregation is itself unconstitutional and that separate-but-equal should be overturned. The cases constituted a high-risk gamble, for if the gamble failed and if *Plessy* were reaffirmed, separate-but-equal would perhaps be entrenched forever as a principle of American constitutional law.

After hearing oral argument in December 1952 and reargument in December 1953, the Court on May 17, 1954 issued its decisions. Both opinions, written by Chief Justice Earl Warren, were unanimous. Brown v. Board of Education, 347 U.S. 483 (1954); Bolling v. Sharpe, 347 U.S. 497 (1954).

In its *Brown* opinion, dealing with the four state cases, the Court stated that an exhaustive review of the "consideration of the [Fourteenth] Amendment in Congress, ratification by the states, then existing practices in racial segregation, and the views of proponents

---

[107] Robert Carter, "The NAACP's Legal Strategy Against Segregated Education," 86 *Michigan Law Review* 1088-89 (1988); see also Jack Greenberg, *Crusaders in the Courts* [Basic Books 1995]: 86-87. Carter was general counsel of the NAACP, and Greenberg was a lawyer with the NAACP Legal Defense Fund (LDF) and later succeeded Thurgood Marshall as LDF director. Greenberg points out that one of the reasons for the black community's ambivalence was concern that school segregation would create problems for black teachers. Id. at 85.

[108] Greenberg, supra, at 118. There was disagreement among LDF lawyers whether the decision to attack segregation directly precluded also challenging the equality of the facilities. Marshall took the position that both arguments should be pressed. Id. At 86.

and opponents of the Amendment" had been insufficient "to resolve the problem with which we are faced" and "At best, they are inconclusive." The Court noted that the principal drafters of the Amendment had been sharply divided as to its scope and "What others in Congress and the state legislatures had in mind cannot be determined with any degree of certainty," particularly because of the fundamentally different status of public education at that time.

Having found the legislative history of the Fourteenth Amendment to be "inconclusive," the Court stated that it must consider "the effect of segregation itself on public education." Furthermore:

> "In approaching this problem, we cannot turn the clock back to 1868 when the Amendment was adopted, or even to 1896 when *Plessy v. Ferguson* was written. We must consider public education in the light of its full development and its present place in American life throughout the Nation. Only in this way can it be determined if segregation in public schools deprives these plaintiffs of the equal protection of the laws."

> "...In these days, it is doubtful that any child may reasonably be expected to succeed in life if he is denied the opportunity of an education. Such an opportunity, where the state has undertaken to provide it, is a right which must be made available to all on equal terms.

> "We come then to the question presented: Does segregation of children in public schools solely on the basis of race, even though the physical facilities and other "tangible" factors may be equal, deprive the children of the minority group of equal educational opportunities? We believe that it does.

> "In *Sweatt v. Painter*, supra, in finding that a segregated law school for Negroes could not provide them equal educational opportunities, this Court relied in large part on 'those qualities which are incapable of objective measurement but which make for greatness in a law school.' In *McLaurin v. Oklahoma State Regents*, supra, the Court, in requiring that a Negro admitted to a white graduate school be treated like all other students, again resorted to intangible considerations: '. . . his ability to

study, to engage in discussions and exchange views with other students, and, in general, to learn his profession.' Such considerations apply with added force to children in grade and high schools. To separate them from others of similar age and qualifications solely because of their race generates a feeling of inferiority as to their status in the community that may affect their hearts and minds in a way unlikely ever to be undone."

This view of the effect of segregation was diametrically opposed to the underlying premise of *Plessy v. Ferguson*, which in 1896 had denied that segregation subordinated blacks to an inferior status and had insisted that any such perception by blacks was "solely because the colored race chooses to put that construction upon it."

Fifty-eight years later in *Brown*, referring to a lower court finding that state-imposed segregation had a detrimental effect on the education of black children, the Court declared that "Whatever may have been the extent of psychological knowledge at the time of *Plessy v. Ferguson*, this finding is amply supported by modern authority" and that "Any language in *Plessy v. Ferguson* contrary to this finding is rejected."

The Court concluded:

"...in the field of public education the doctrine of 'separate but equal' has no place. Separate educational facilities are inherently unequal. Therefore, we hold that the plaintiffs and others similarly situated for whom the actions have been brought are, by reason of the segregation complained of, deprived of the equal protection of the laws guaranteed by the Fourteenth Amendment."

In the companion District of Columbia case, *Bolling v. Sharpe*, the Court held that the Due Process Clause of the Fifth Amendment prohibits public school segregation in a federal jurisdiction. The Court acknowledged that the Fifth Amendment (unlike the Fourteenth Amendment, which applies only to the states) does not contain an equal protection clause and rejected any implication "that the two are always interchangeable phrases." But the Court pointed out, as its prior decisions had recognized, that "the concepts of equal protection and due process, both stemming from our American ideal of fairness, are not mutually exclusive" and that "discrimination may be so unjustifiable as to be violative of due process."[109] On that basis, the Court concluded that, "In view of our decision [in *Brown*] that the Constitution prohibits the states from maintaining racially segregated schools, it would be unthinkable that the same Constitution would impose a lesser duty on the Federal Government." (347 U.S. at 499, 500.)[110]

*****

Viewed from the vantage point of over half a century later, the Court's rejection of separate-but-equal may now seem to have been inevitable. But in 1954 there was nothing inevitable about it.

Among the formidable obstacles: Each of the traditional standards of constitutional interpretation—text, precedent, custom, intent of the drafters, and original public understanding —tended to support adherence to *Plessy* rather than its reversal. Indeed, the same Congress that proposed the Fourteenth Amendment segregated the schools of the District of Columbia, and contemporaneously so did several northern states (including, as remarked in *Plessy*, "states where the political rights of the colored race have been longest and most earnestly enforced"). A strong argument could thus be made that the enactment of the Fourteenth Amendment was consistent

---

[109] As early as 1896, the Court unanimously declared that "the Constitution of the United States, in its present form, forbids, so far as civil and political rights are concerned, discrimination by *the General Government*, or by the states against any citizen because of his race." Gibson v. Mississippi, 162 U.S. 565, 591 (1896) (Italics added.). See also Buchanan v. Warley, 245 U.S. 60 (1917); Detroit Bank v. United States, 317 U.S. 329 (1943); Currin v. Wallace, 306 U.S. 1, 13-14 (1939); Steward Machine Co. v. Davis, 301 U.S. 548, 585 (1937).

[110] Despite the Court's rejection of such an implication, some have criticized *Bolling* for allegedly holding that the Due Process Clause of the Fifth Amendment incorporates the Equal Protection Clause of the Fourteenth Amendment. See, e.g., John Hart Ely, *Democracy and Distrust: A Theory of Judicial Review* [Harvard 1980]: 30; Richard Primus,"Bolling Alone," 104 *Columbia Law Review* 975 (2004); David Straus, *The Living Constitution* [University of Chicago Press 2011]: 130; Leonard Levy, *Original Intent and the Framers' Constitution* [Macmillan 1988]: 356-57. But, contrary to the premise of that criticism, the opinion did not treat due process and equal protection as fungible or otherwise purport to adopt a "reverse incorporation" doctrine. Instead, the Court only recognized that discrimination is one of the significant factors to be considered in applying the substantive aspect of due process. Jack Balkin, *Living Originalism* [Belknap 2011]: 249-55. Although due process was originally regarded as purely procedural rather than also substantive, that battle was lost many decades before *Bolling*. See cases cited in Washington v. Glucksberg, 521 U.S. 702, 720 (1997).

with the continuation of segregated schools. And under the doctrine of *stare decisis*, although it is not an ironclad rule, the Court has generally declined to set aside a precedent of long standing (in this instance nearly sixty years) if it has been extensively relied upon in the interim.

In addition to obstacles based on traditional standards of constitutional interpretation, there were justifiable fears of political turmoil and violence in the South. Justice Frankfurter told a close confidant: "Hugo Black [the only Justice from the Deep South] ... was scared to death—and he scared everybody else on the Court— of the political turmoil in the South that would follow from a decision ending racial segregation in public schools. ... Black was frightening the other Justices the most. He was saying to them, 'Now look, I have to vote to overrule *Plessy*, but this would mean the end of political liberalism in the South. ... The Klan is going to be riding again.'" [111]

In these circumstances, it would have been foolhardy to predict with any degree of confidence that *Plessy* would be overturned— let alone by a unanimous vote and without any separate individual opinions.

In the Court's conference after the first argument in December 1952, a multiplicity of views were expressed, as reflected in the Justices' conference notes.[112]

Chief Justice Fred Vinson indicated his opposition to overturning *Plessy*, emphasizing that there was a "Body of law back of us on separate but equal," "Congress pass no statute contrary," "For 90 years segregated schools in city [DC]," and "Hard to get away [from] long established acceptance in DC."

---

[111] Philip Elman, "The Solicitor General's Office, Justice Frankfurter, and Civil Rights Litigation, 1946-1960: An Oral History," 100 *Harvard Law Review* 817, 825, 828 (1987).

[112] See Kluger, supra, 10-11; Michael Klarman, *From Jim Crow to Civil Rights: The Supreme Court and the Struggle for Racial Equality* [Oxford 2004]: 293-300; Jim Newton, *Justice for All: Earl Warren and the Nation He Made* [Riverhead 2006]: 305-25; Bernard Schwartz, *Super Chief: Earl Warren and His Supreme Court* [NYU Press 1983]: 72-127; Bernard Schwartz, *The Unpublished Opinions of the Warren Court* [Oxford 1985]: 445-62; Mark Tushnet, with Katya Lezin, "What Really Happened in Brown v. Board of Education," 91 *Columbia Law Review* 1867 (1991). See also John Barrett (ed.), "Supreme Court Law Clerks' Recollection of Brown v. Board of Education," 78 *St. John's Law Review* 515 (2004).

Hugo Black "would vote ... to end discrimination."[113] He said "At first blush I would have said that it was up to Congress" but would reverse *Plessy* as contrary to the Fourteenth Amendment. However, he predicted "violence if [the] court holds segregation unlawful" and agreed with Vinson that South Carolina "might abolish [its] school system."

Stanley Reed would "Uphold segregation as constitutional" and believed "Negroes have not been thoroughly assimilated," "...a large opinion that separation of aces is for benefit of both," and "states should be left to work out the problem for themselves."

Felix Frankfurter was reluctant to admit that the Court had "long misread the Constitution" or to conclude that it was "unconstitutional to treat a Negro differently than a white" under the Fourteenth Amendment. He asked: "What justifies us in saying that what was equal in 1868 is not equal now[?]." But he had no similar doubts about the District of Columbia case; to permit school segregation in the nation's capital was "intolerable," and he was prepared "to vote today that [it] violates [the] due process clause" of the Fifth Amendment.

William Douglas thought that "Segregation is an easy problem ... "no classifications on the basis of race can be made. [The] Fourteenth Amendment prohibits racial classifications."

Robert Jackson, who like Frankfurter had sharply criticized the Court's abuses of judicial power in the New Deal era, said:[114] "[There is] nothing in the text that says this is unconstitutional. Nothing in the opinions of the courts that says it's unconstitutional. Nothing in the history of the Fourteenth Amendment. On [the] basis of precedent [I] would have to say segregation is ok."[115]

---

[113] Black (who generally—but not consistently—took an absolutist view of the Bill of Rights and the Reconstruction Amendments) was apparently the only Justice who contended that the Fourteenth Amendment was actually intended to abolish segregation. Noah Feldman, *Scorpions: The Battles and Triumphs of FDR's Great Supreme Court Justices* [Twelve 2010]: 375-81.

[114] Robert Jackson, *The Struggle for Judicial Supremacy* [Knopf 1949].

[115] In early 1954 Jackson prepared a draft concurrence reflecting his concerns. The draft acknowledged that the Court's decision "would be simple if our personal opinion that school segregation is morally, economically and politically indefensible made it legally so." But, he asked, "how is it that the Constitution this morning forbids what for three-quarters of a century it has tolerated or approved?"

Harold Burton was ready to reverse but said it "should be done in easy way as possible." He thought that "With [the] Fourteenth Amendment, states do not have the choice. Segregation violates equal protection. ... [It is] not reasonable to educate separately for a joint life."

Tom Clark was not yet ready to take a stand: "If we can delay action it will help. [The] opinion should give lower courts the right to withhold relief in light of troubles. [I] would go along with that. Otherwise [I] would say we had led the states on to think segregation is OK and we should let them work it out."

Sherman Minton: "[A] body of law has laid down [supporting the] separate but equal doctrine. That however has been whittled away in these cases [*Sweatt* and *McLaurin*]. Classification on the basis of race does not add up. It's invidious and can't be maintained."

According to Justice Douglas' recollection: [116]

"When the cases had been argued in December of 1952, only four of us—Minton, Burton, Black and myself—felt that segregation was unconstitutional. Vinson was Chief Justice and he seemed to be firm that *Plessy* v. *Ferguson* should stand, and that the states should be allowed to deal with segregation in their own way and should be given time to make the black schools equal to those of the whites. Justice Reed held that segregation was on its way out and over the years would disappear, and that meanwhile the states should be allowed to handle it in their own way.

"Frankfurter's view was that it was not unconstitutional to treat a Negro differently from a white but that the cases should be reargued. Jackson felt that nothing in the Fourteenth Amendment barred segregation and that it 'would be bad for the Negroes' to be put in white schools, while Justice Clark said that since we had led the states to believe segregation was lawful, we should let them work out the problem by themselves.

---

[116] William Douglas, *The Court Years 1939-1975* [Random House 1980]: 113.

"It was clear that if a decision had been reached in the 1952 Term, we would have had five saying that separate but equal schools were constitutional, that separate but unequal schools were not constitutional, and that the remedy was to give the states time to make the two systems of schools equal."

Douglas' count of probable votes and particularly his characterization of the position of Frankfurter (who was frequently at odds with Douglas) are open to serious question. Frankfurter, torn between his opposition to segregation and his devotion to judicial self-restraint, was unwilling at that point to reject *Plessy* but his overriding objective was to defer any decision until the Court could speak with a single voice.[117]

Richard Kluger, the preeminent historian of the *Brown* case, disputed Douglas' count:[118]

"Frankfurter thought the Court was divided five-to-four in favor of reversing *Plessy*, with himself in the majority. Burton thought the Court stood at six-to-three for reversing. Jackson counted anywhere from two to four dissenters if the Court voted to reverse, with himself in the majority camp, provided that an opinion palatable to him was drafted by Black or whoever might write for the Court."

Fortunately any decision in the 1952 Term was avoided by the Court's acceptance (Douglas dissenting) of Frankfurter's proposal to postpone a vote by ordering reargument of the cases.[119]

The stated purpose of the reargument was to obtain the views of counsel on five questions. The first two concerned the understanding of the framers of the Fourteenth Amendment about its effect on

---

[117] See, e.g., Philip Elman, "The Solicitor General's Office, Justice Frankfurter, and Civil Rights Litigation, 1946-1960: An Oral History," 100 *Harvard Law Review* 817, 825, 822-23 (1987): "[Frankfurter] did not want the segregation issue to be decided by a fractured Court, as it then was; he did not want a decision to go out with nine or six or four opinions. He wanted the Court to stand before the country on this issue united and speaking in a single voice. He felt that whatever it did had to go out to the country with an appearance of unity, so that the Court as an institution would best be able to withstand the attacks that inevitably were going to be made."

[118] Kluger, supra, at 614.

[119] See Feldman, supra, at 385-86. Frankfurter later stated that one reason he badly wanted to hold off a vote was his concern that Jackson might vote to affirm *Plessy*. Kluger, supra, at 610.

school segregation.[120] The third question addressed what proved to be the most difficult obstacle to reaching agreement among the Justices: "On the assumption that the answers to [the preceding questions] do not dispose of the issue, it it within the judicial power, in construing the Amendment, to abolish segregation in public schools?" The fourth and fifth questions asked, in the event that school segregation were found unconstitutional, how such a decision should be implemented—including whether the Court, "in the exercise of its equity powers, [may] permit an effective gradual adjustment."

A draft of the questions had been prepared by Frankfurter and distributed to the other Justices on May 27, 1953, with a memo stating: "These questions, I think, do not offend against the suggestion that we ought not to disclose our minds. Certainly as an entirety, they look in opposite directions. Some give comfort to one side and some to the other, and that is precisely the intention. Insofar as the questions dealing with remedies may indicate that a decision against segregation has been reached by the Court, I think it is not undesirable that an adjustment be made in the public mind to such a possibility. I know not how others feel, but for me the ultimate crucial factor in the problem presented by these cases is psychological—the adjustment of men's minds and actions to the unfamiliar and the unpleasant...."[121]

The reargument was originally scheduled for October 12, 1953. But on September 8, one month before the reargument was to be heard, Chief Justice Vinson died. If Vinson had lived, even if the Court were able to reach a decision rejecting *Plessy*, the decision would almost certainly have been deeply divided. A 5-4 or 6-3 vote overturning the separate-but-equal doctrine—accompanied by dissenting opinions and probably also concurring opinions, expressing a variety of individual views—would likely have been disastrous for both the cause of desegregation and the prestige of the Court.

---

[120] In late 1952 Justice Frankfurter instructed his clerk, Alexander Bickel, to review the Fourteenth Amendment debates in Congress and the states concerning segregation and particularly school segregation. Bickel (later a distinguished constitutional scholar) devoted a year to the project, concluding that the legislative history did not reveal a specific intent to prohibit segregation but was not so definitive that the Court was precluded from reaching that result. Frankfurter distributed the Bickel memorandum to the other Justices in August 1953. See Kluger, supra, at 653-55. The memorandum was later published. Alexander Bickel, "The Original Understanding and the Segregation Decision," 69 *Harvard Law Review* 1 (1955).

[121] See Kluger, supra, at 614-15.

Frankfurter, hopeful that the change in the Court's composition might break the logjam in the cases, told a close friend that "This is the first solid piece of evidence I've ever had that there really is a God."[122]

At the beginning of his administration, President Eisenhower had agreed with Earl Warren, then Governor of California, to appoint Warren to be Solicitor General in the Department of Justice, with the further understanding that Warren would be appointed to fill "the next vacancy" on the Supreme Court. Eisenhower, however, apparently assumed that "the next vacancy" would be an appointment as one of the eight Associate Justices, not as Chief Justice, and had not intended to appoint Warren as Chief Justice. Thus on Vinson's death Eisenhower offered the Chief Justice appointment to his Secretary of State, John Foster Dulles (who declined) and apparently also considered appointing Tom Dewey. When reminded of his discussion with Warren, Eisenhower tried to persuade Warren to wait for an Associate Justice vacancy. But Warren stood his ground, taking the position (according to Eisenhower's Attorney General, Herbert Brownell) that Warren "regarded the present vacancy as 'the next vacancy,'" and Eisenhower acceded.[123]

A that time the Senate was not in session. On September 30, in order to fill the vacancy before the beginning of the 1953 term in October, Eisenhower announced Warren's recess appointment as Chief Justice, and Warren immediately flew to Washington to assume his new position.[124]

---

[122] Norman Silber, *With All Deliberate Speed: The Life of Philip Elman* [University of Michigan Press 2004]: 219. Elman, a former Frankfurter clerk, was a long-serving Assistant to the Solicitor General.

[123] Jim Newton, *Justice for All: Earl Warren and the Nation He Made* [Riverhead 2006]: 7-9; Albert Lawrence, "Herbert Brownell, Jr.: The 'Hidden Hand' in the Selection of Earl Warren and the Government's Role in Brown v. Board of Education," 37 *Journal of Supreme Court History* 75, 76-81 (2012). This account is inconsistent with speculation that "...a politician is just what Eisenhower felt the Court needed; he intentionally chose Warren, according to this view, because he thought Warren was particularly suited to repair the damage wrought by Vinson." Tushnet, supra, at 1875; Kluger, supra, at 658.

[124] On October 5, Warren took the oath of office under his recess appointment. Article II of the Constitution provides that the "President shall have Power to fill up all Vacancies that may happen during the Recess of the Senate, by granting commissions which shall expire at the end of the next Session." There is a serious question whether the "vacancies" provision in Article II applies to judicial vacancies. Retired Justice John Paul Stevens, *Five Chiefs: A Supreme Court Memoir* [Little Brown 2011]: 84-86, has concluded that the provision is

To enable Warren to prepare for participation in the reargument (originally scheduled for October 12), the Court rescheduled it to December 7-9.

At the conference following the reargument, according to Douglas and Burton notes, Warren began the discussion by declaring that in his view the "separate but equal doctrine rests on [the] basic premise that the Negro race is inferior. That is [the] only way to sustain *Plessy*" and that he could not accept that premise. He contended that segregation was created by whites and imposed on blacks, and its purpose was to protect whites from blacks and to extend their power over blacks. But the "...Thirteenth, Fourteenth and Fifteenth Amendments were intended to make equal those who once were slaves." He could not see "how segregation can be justified in this day and age."

Black was absent because of the illness of a family member, but he sent word that his views had not changed and that the time had come to abandon school segregation.

Reed insisted that segregation was based "not on inferiority but on racial differences. It protects people against mixing races." If Congress wanted to change the law, it could, Reed argued. But he continued to believe that segregation was constitutional so long as the two races received substantially equal treatment.

According to Douglas, Frankfurter continued to worry about the application of the Fourteenth Amendment and said that the "history in Congress and in this Court indicates that *Plessy* is right."

Douglas reaffirmed his support for striking down segregation.

Jackson took the view that striking down segregation was the right thing to do but that it could only be done as an act of politics, not law. The Court "can't justify elimination of segregation as a judicial act."[125]

---

inapplicable to judicial vacancies and that Earl Warren did not become Chief Justice until March 20, 1954, when he was sworn in a second time after his Senate confirmation on March 1.

[125] In February 1954 Jackson prepared a memorandum clearly suggesting an intention to write a concurring opinion conceding the lack of a legal basis for overturning *Plessy*. The memorandum stated in part: "But we decide today that the unwritten law has long been contrary to a custom deeply anchored in our social system. Thus, despite my personal satisfaction with the Court's judgment, I simply cannot find, in surveying all the usual sources of law, anything which warrants me in saying that it is required by the original purpose and intent of the Fourteenth or Fifteenth Amendment." Kluger, supra, at 689.

Clark stressed the importance of a carefully considered remedy that would not antagonize Southern states or his native Texas.

Burton and Minton had previously made clear their view that school segregation should be abolished.

Together with the four who had already indicated their support for rejecting "separate but equal," Warren's position provided a majority for that view, but he proposed that any vote be deferred. Once votes are cast, they are harder to change, and Warren clearly wanted more than just a majority.[126]

Warren now focused on seeking to establish a consensus that would enable the Court to speak on the issue in one voice. For the next several months, through small lunches, private meetings in chambers, conversations at their homes, and walks around the block, Warren patiently warned his colleagues of the consequences of division.[127]

Douglas stated:

"On December 12, 1953, at the first Conference after the second argument, Warren suggested that the cases be discussed informally and no vote be taken. He didn't want the Conference to split up into two opposed groups. Warren's approach to the problem and his discussions in Conference were conciliatory; not those of an advocate trying to convince recalcitrant judges. Frankfurter maintained the position that history supported the conclusions in *Plessy* that segregation was constitutional. Reed thought segregation was constitutional, and Jackson thought the issue was 'political' and beyond judicial competence. Tom Clark was of the opinion that violence would follow if the Court ordered desegregation of the schools, but that while history sanctioned segregation, he would vote to abolish it if the matter was handled delicately."[128]

As Warren recounted: "We decided not to make up our minds on that first conference day, but to talk it over, from week to week,

---

[126]Kluger, supra, at 683. An additional possible consideration might have been that Warren, who was then still serving on the basis of a recess appointment, was not confirmed by the Senate until nearly three months later on March 1, 1953.

[127] Newton, supra, at 313-14.

[128] Douglas, supra, at 114.

dealing with different aspects of it—in groups, over lunches, in conference. It was too important to hurry it."[129]

Warren further explained:

"...we were all impressed with their [the decisions'] importance and the desirability of achieving unanimity if possible. Realizing that when a person once announces he has reached a conclusion it is more difficult for him to change his thinking, we decided that we would dispense with our usual custom of formally expressing our individual views at the first conference and would confine ourselves for a time to informal discussion of the briefs, the arguments made at the hearing, and our own independent research on each conference day, reserving our final opinions until the discussions were concluded.

"We followed this plan until the following February when it was agreed that we were ready to vote. On the first vote, we unanimously agreed that the 'separate but equal' doctrine had no place in public education. The question then arose as to how this view should be written—as a *per curiam* (by the Court) or as a signed, individualized opinion. We decided that it would carry more force if done through a signed opinion, and, at the suggestion of some of the Justices, it was thought that it should bear the signature of the Chief Justice."[130]

Warren's recollection of February as the time of the crucial vote appears to be mistaken. Justice Reed (who had prepared a draft of a dissenting opinion declining to overrule separate-but-equal) persisted in standing alone until April, when Warren put it to Reed directly: "Stan, you're all by yourself on this now. You've got to decide whether it's really the best thing for the country."[131] Despite serious reservations, Reed agreed to go along. It was only then that the drafting process began.

The writing of the *Brown* opinion was done under conditions of even greater secrecy than normally prevailed at the Court.[132] Warren

---

[129] Kluger, supra, at 683.

[130] Earl Warren, *The Memoirs of Chief Justice Earl Warren* [Doubleday 1977]: 285.

[131] Kluger, supra, at 698. See also Bernard Schwartz, *A History of the Supreme Court* [Oxford 1993]: 298-99.

[132] Bernard Schwartz, *The Unpublished Opinions of the Warren Court* [Oxford 1985]: 447.

later recalled that, at the conference at which unanimity was finally achieved, "the importance of secrecy was discussed. We agreed that only my law clerks should be involved, and that any writing between my office and those of the other Justices would be delivered to the Justices personally. This practice was followed throughout and this was the only time it was required in my years on the Court."[133]

After writing (in longhand) what he called a "Memorandum," Warren explained to his clerk what he wanted in the opinion: "... he wanted it to be short. He wanted it to be readable. He wanted it to be non-legalistic. He wanted it to be something that could be understood by the layman and, he said, 'Something that even could be published on the front page of a newspaper."[134] He also made clear that speed was of the essence; having finally obtained a consensus, he did not want to lose it.

Although subsequent drafts deleted substantial portions of Warren's Memorandum and also made substantial additions to the final version, the Memorandum established the basic framework of the *Brown* opinion and included two of its most well-known sentences—"...we cannot turn the clock of education back to 1868, when the Amendment was adopted, or even to [1896] when *Plessy v. Ferguson* was decided" and "To separate [black children]from others of their age in school solely because of their color puts the mark of inferiority not only upon their status in the community but also upon their little hearts and minds in a form that is unlikely ever to be erased."[135] (The wording of the latter sentence was somewhat modified in the revision process.)

Warren's Memorandum dealt with all five cases together. A May 3 draft separated them into two opinions—one opinion dealing with the four state cases governed by the Equal Protection

---

[133] Warren Memoirs, supra, at 285. Disclosure: The author served as law clerk to Chief Justice Warren in his first two terms (1953-55). See, e.g., John Barrett (ed.), "Supreme Court Law Clerks' Recollection of Brown v. Board of Education," 78 *St. John's Law Review* 515 (2004).

[134] See Newton, supra, at 319; John Barrett (ed.), "Supreme Court Law Clerks' Recollection of Brown v. Board of Education," 78 *St. John's Law Review* 515, 549 (2004).

[135] Many of the drafts and related documents are available in the Earl Warren Papers in the Library of Congress. Warren's Memorandum is also reproduced in Bernard Schwartz, *The Unpublished Opinions of the Warren Court* [Oxford 1985]: 452-55.

Clause of the Fourteenth Amendment, and the other opinion dealing with the District Columbia case (*Bolling v. Sharpe*) governed by the Due Process Clause of the Fifth Amendment.[136]

Among other changes, the May 3 draft deleted substantial portions dealing with the Fourteenth Amendment's background and early public education, as well as a statement attributing the *Plessy* decision to the Court's "attempt ... to serve two masters—(1) the master of equality under the laws, and (2) the master of racial concept as it existed at that time in the Southern States of the Union. It endeavored to retain both the philosophy of the *Dred Scott* case and the principle of the Fourteenth Amendment." Also deleted was the statement that segregation "has many other divisive results not necessary to enumerate here but which, in the aggregate, make the definition of 'separate but equal' inapplicable to education."

The May 3 draft added (after quoting a lower court finding concerning the effect of segregation on black school children) "In so far as there is language in *Plessy v. Ferguson* contrary to this finding with respect to public education, that case is overruled" and "We conclude that in the field of public education the doctrine of 'separate but equal' has no place. Separate educational facilities are inherently unequal." Also added was a summary of the six

---

[136] Id. at 551; Newton, supra, at 320. A cover memo to Warren with the May 3 revision stated:

Mr. Chief Justice:

Attached is a draft along the lines of your memo of last week. Like the memo, this draft covers all five cases in one consolidated opinion. I am inclined to think, however, that the District of Columbia case should be treated independently in a short, separate opinion accompanying the other one. This was the course adopted with respect to the restrictive covenant cases. See Shelley v. Kraemer, 334 U.S. 1 (states); Hurd v. Hodge, 334 U.S. 24 (District of Columbia). The material relating to the equal protection clause of the 14th Amendment has no direct relevance to the District of Columbia case, which, of course, is based primarily on the due process clause of the 5th Amendment. And the 5th Amendment has repeatedly been construed by this Court not to impose the same limits on federal discrimination as the 14th Amendment imposes on state discrimination. See Steward Machine Co. v. Davis, 301 U.S. 548, 584-585; Sunshine Coal Co. v. Adkins, 310 U.S. 381, 401; Helvering v. Lerner Stores, 314 U.S. 463, 468; Detroit Bank v. United States, 317 U.S. 328, 337.

In short, the legal problem in the states and the legal problem in the District are different and require somewhat different treatment. For the sake of clarity, a short, separate opinion in the District case is recommended. EP

[Memo from Earl Pollock to Chief Justice Warren, Papers of Earl Warren, Library of Congress, Box 571.]

post-*Plessy* education cases and a fuller explanation of the need to now confront the separate-but-equal issue.

On May 7, after further revisions, Warren decided that the drafts were ready for distribution to the other Justices. On the next day, a Saturday, Warren personally delivered copies to Justices who were in their chambers and to Jackson (then recovering from a heart attack) in the hospital. Warren's clerks brought Black's copies to him while he was playing tennis at his home in Alexandria and Minton's copies to him at his Washington apartment. In accordance with the effort to maintain secrecy, the drafts were then in typescript form, instead of being printed in the Court's printshop as usually done.

Warren's cover memo accompanying the drafts stated that "The attached drafts are offered as a basis for discussion and were prepared on the theory that they should be short, readable by the lay public, non-rhetorical, unemotional and, above all, non-accusatory."[137]

An earlier *undistributed* draft of Warren's cover memo, dated May 5, included additional "considerations which caused me to make this approach to the problem." Among other points, this draft stated that "On the question of segregation in education, this should be the end of the line....but we should not go beyond that. The applicability of the [separate-but-equal] doctrine in other contexts must await future decision."[138]

In the week of May 10, the other Justices responded to Warren with their comments, some in writing and some orally.

Douglas wrote: "I do not think I would change a single word... You have done a beautiful job." The other Justices also expressed agreement but proposed several editorial changes. Most were accepted by Warren, and some were not.

At Frankfurter's request, the words "generates a feeling of inferiority" were substituted for "puts the mark of inferiority" concerning the effect of segregation on black children. Also at Frankfurter's request the summary of the graduate school cases was revised to state that "lack of equality was found in that specific benefits were enjoyed by white students but were denied to Negro students of the same educational qualifications" and that "In none of these cases

---

[137] Papers of Earl Warren, Library of Congress, Box 571.
[138] Id.

was it necessary to reexamine the [separate-but-equal] doctrine to grant relief."

Frankfurter (and apparently Reed as well) questioned a sentence stating that "The record of congressional debates is not adequate for this purpose, and in many of the State Legislatures ratification was accomplished with little or no formal discussion," and the sentence was deleted.

At Black's request, instead of saying that the legislative history of the Fourteenth Amendment "casts little light" on the issue, the wording was changed to say that it casts "some" light "but not enough to resolve the problem."

In response to Burton, in the reference to states that prohibited the education of blacks before the Civil War, "most Southern States" was changed to "some states."

At Clark's request, the statement that "public education had already received wide acceptance in the North" was changed to "had already advanced further in the North."

In addition, in response to Clark's concern that a reader might assume he was the "Clark" cited in footnote 11 as the author of a social science study, the author's first two initials ("K.B.") were inserted before the name "Clark." (There does not appear to have been any other comment or objection by any of the Justices concerning Footnote 11, later a target of the decision's critics.)[139]

On May 12, revised drafts (again in typescript form) incorporating these changes were personally delivered by Warren to the other Justices.

The May 12 draft (like the May 7 draft) stated that *Plessy* was "overruled" in so far as it contained language contrary to the quoted district court finding. At Frankfurter's request, the sentence was changed to "Any language in *Plessy v. Ferguson* contrary to this finding is *rejected.*" (Italics added.)

On May 14 the revised drafts were sent to the Court's printshop for initial printing and copies were distributed to the other Justices.

Warren again delivered Jackson's copy to him in the hospital. In their discussion Warren was unwilling to make several of Jackson's suggestions dealing generally with segregation because Warren was insistent on confining the opinions to segregation in the

---

[139] See Schwartz, supra, at 458-60.

public schools.[140] But at Jackson's request a sentence was added that "Education of Negroes was almost non-existent, and practically all of the race were illiterate." A further change, probably also proposed by Jackson, was the addition of a sentence stating that "Today, in contrast, many Negroes have achieved outstanding success in the arts and sciences as well as in the business and professional world." According to Jackson's clerk, although Jackson did not believe that the history of the Fourteenth Amendment was "inconclusive" on the framers' view of school segregation, he was "so pleased that there was no blame" and thought Warren's opinion "was a master work."[141]

The drafts were reprinted to incorporate the further changes and were distributed to the other Justices on May 14. The next day, at its May 15 conference, the Justices gave final approval to the opinions and agreed they should be announced the following Monday, May 17.

At the beginning of the Court's noon session that day, the full Court was present, including Justice Jackson, who had come from the hospital to be there for the announcement. Justices Clark and Douglas and Chief Justice Warren read the opinions in several other pending cases. Then, at about 12:50 p.m., Warren startled the jammed courtroom by stating that "I have for announcement the judgment and opinion of the Court in No. 1-*Oliver Brown et al v. Board of Education of Topeka.*" He then read both the *Brown* and *Bolling* opinions word for word with one exception: In the sentence in *Brown* stating "We conclude that in the field of public education the doctrine of 'separate but equal' has no place," Warren inserted the word "unanimously" after "conclude," causing a noticeable stir in the courtroom.

Three days later, Frankfurter wrote Reed to praise him for resolving the "hard struggle . . . involved in the conscience of your mind" in a manner that was conducive to the nation's "great good."[142] In reply, Reed wrote Frankfurter that "there were many considerations that pointed to a dissent." But, he went on, "they did

---

[140] John Barrett (ed.), "Supreme Court Law Clerks' Recollection of Brown v. Board of Education," 78 *St. John's Law Review* 515, 554 (2004) (comment of Jackson's clerk E. Barrett Prettyman, Jr.).

[141] Id. At 554-55.

[142] Klarman, supra, at 302.

not add up to a balance against the Court's opinion . . . the factors looking toward a fair treatment for Negroes are more important than the weight of history." [143]

---

[143] Reed to Frankfurter, May 21, 1954, Frankfurter Papers, Harvard Law School, cited by Bernard Schwartz, *A History of the Supreme Court* [Oxford 1993]: 298.

11. THE IMPLEMENTATION OF *BROWN*

A further reargument was ordered for the following term to consider appropriate decrees to implement the Court's decision.

But it was already abundantly clear that desegregation would have to take place gradually.[144] Indeed, although questions remained as to the directions to be given the district courts, the Court could never have achieved unanimity in *Brown I* except on the assumption that it would be implemented on a gradual basis. For example, as a condition of joining the decision, Reed extracted from Warren a pledge that the Court's implementation decree would allow segregation to be dismantled gradually.[145] Similarly, Jackson had said that he "won't be a party to immediate unconstitutionality," and Clark said that he would "go along" if the opinion "g[a]ve lower courts the right to withhold relief in light of troubles."[146]

The gradualist approach had been proposed to the Court in an *amicus curiae* brief filed in December 1952 by the Department of Justice. Although supporting the plaintiffs on the unconstitutionality of school segregation, the Department contended that, if the Court held school segregation unconstitutional, "the Government would suggest that in shaping the relief the Court should take into account the need, not only for prompt vindication of the constitutional rights violated, but also for orderly and reasonable solution of the vexing problems which may arise in eliminating such segregation. ... It must be recognized that racial segregation in public

---

[144] The Court began to focus on gradual implementation in a conference held on January 16, 1954, several months before a vote was taken on the merits of the case. "For most of the Justices, though, overruling *Pessy* was bound up with devising a gradualist remedy ... The Court had achieved agreement on the merits in large measure because most of the Justices had a vague idea that they could avoid difficulty by allowing desegregation to occur gradually." MarkTushnet, with Katya Lezin, "What Really Happened in Brown v. Board, of Education," 91 *Columbia Law Review* 1867, 1914,1924, 1928 (1991).

[145] Kluger, supra, at 698.

[146] Klarman, supra, at 313

118

schools has been in effect in many states for a long time. Its roots go deep.... The practical difficulties which may be met in making progressive adjustment to a non-segregated system cannot be ignored or minimized."[147] The proposal—separating the constitutional principle from the remedy—offered the Court a middle ground "between reaffirming separate but equal, as urged by the states, and overruling *Plessy* and requiring immediate integration of public schools in all states, as urged by the NAACP."[148]

The gradualist approach was strongly opposed by the NAACP lawyers, who argued—with considerable merit as a legal matter—for a decree ordering desegregation "forthwith" of the plaintiff's constitutional rights that *Brown I* had affirmed. In the reargument on the remedy, NAACP chief counsel Thurgood Marshall stressed that black America could not accept any delay beyond a single year at most to implement the desegregation process.[149] The argument against delay was particularly powerful because delay would necessarily mean that the constitutional rights of many black students would never be vindicated.

Nevertheless, desegregation "forthwith" was never a realistic option. Even apart from the impossibility of obtaining unanimity on that basis, uprooting and reorganizing deeply entrenched educational systems in thousands of separate school districts in seventeen states could not be accomplished quickly. There was no state before the Court, but instead only a handful of local school districts, therefore necessarily requiring a multiplicity of lawsuits to enforce the decision against other districts that refused to comply voluntarily. As Justice Jackson commented during the 1953 argument,

---

[147] Brief for the United States as Amicus Curiae, *Oliver Brown, et al., v. Board of Education of Topeka*, December 1952, 27.

[148] Philip Elman, "The Solicitor General's Office, Justice Frankfurter, and Civil Rights Litigation, 1946-1960: An Oral History," 100 *Harvard Law Review* 817, 825, 828-29 (1987). The brief was primarily written by Elman, a lawyer in the Solicitor General's Office and a close confidant of Justice Frankfurter. In Elman's view, "If [the Court] had not had that alternative offered to them, one that came to them with the seal of approval of both the Democratic Truman and Republican Eisenhower administrations, who knows what would have happened. It would, in Frankfurter's judgment, have been an incredible godawful mess: possibly nine different opinions, nine different views on the Court. It would have set back the cause of desegregation; it would have hurt the public school systems everywhere; and it would have damaged the Court." (Pp. 828-29.)

[149] Kluger, supra, at 675.

even if state segregation statutes were held unconstitutional, "The only people we can reach with the judicial decree are the people who are before us in the case ... [s]o that if it is not acquiesced in and embraced, we have to proceed school district by school district...."[150] And different circumstances existed from one locality to another. From the inception of the cases, furthermore, there was a reasonable fear of violence, disorder, and school closures.

In October, a few months after the *Brown I* decision, Jackson died and John Marshall Harlan III—the grandson of the dissenting Justice in *Plessy*—was appointed to replace him. Because of delays in confirming Harlan, reargument on implementation was postponed until April 1955.

At the conference following the reargument, Warren said he thought that the Court should issue an opinion setting forth "factors for the courts below to take into account rather than a formal decree" and that "the opinion ought to give them some guidance" because it "would be rather cruel to shift it back to them and let them flounder." Among the key factors he emphasized: (1) these are class actions (as the Court had stated in its *Brown I* opinion), so enforcement would not be limited to just the named plaintiffs in each case; (2) the courts are entitled to take into consideration physical facts and financial problems ("but I wouldn't suggest psychological and sociological attitudes"); and (3) the courts must consider to what extent there has been movement toward desegregation.[151]

Black and Douglas disagreed. They contended that the Court should merely issue a simple order requiring admission of the few named plaintiffs to previously all-white schools. Black said that the "less we say the better" and that "Nothing is more important than that this Court should not issue what it cannot enforce."[152] They also objected to treating the cases as class actions, arguing that it should be left to future litigation to deal with other black students in segregated schools.[153] The position of Black and Douglas ultimately prevailed on the class action issue. But the majority refused to accept

---

[150] Leon Friedman (ed.), *Brown v. Board: The Landmark Oral Argument Before The Supreme Court* [The New Press 1969]: 253-54.

[151] Schwartz, *Super Chief*, supra, at 116-17.

[152] Id. at 118. According to Black, "The South would never be a willing party to Negroes and whites going to school together. There's no more chance to enforce this in the deep South than Prohibition in New York City."

[153] Tushnet, supra, at 1926-27; Kluger, supra, at 739-41.

their argument for a bare-bones decree and instead agreed with Warren that a statement of guidelines was necessary. [154]

On May 31, 1955, the Court issued its implementation decision, Brown v. Board of Education, 349 U.S. 294 (1955) (*Brown II*). In a unanimous opinion by Warren, the Court stated that its 1954 decision "declare[ed] the fundamental principle that racial discrimination in public education is unconstitutional" and that "All provisions of federal, state, or local law requiring or permitting such discrimination must yield to this principle."

The Court concluded that the cases should be remanded to the district courts:

"Full implementation of these constitutional principles may require solution of varied local school problems. School authorities have the primary responsibility for elucidating, assessing, and solving these problems; courts will have to consider whether the action of school authorities constitutes good faith implementation of the governing constitutional principles. Because of their proximity to local conditions and the possible need for further hearings, the courts which originally heard these cases can best perform this judicial appraisal."

At stake, the Court stated, was "the personal interest of the plaintiffs in admission to public schools as soon as practicable on a non-discriminatory basis:

"To effectuate this interest may call for elimination of a variety of obstacles. . . . Courts of equity may properly take into account the public interest in the elimination of such obstacles in a systematic and effective manner. But it should go without saying that the vitality of these constitutional principle cannot be allowed to yield simply because of disagreement with them."

---

[154] Warren's initial draft of the *Brown II* opinion stated that the district courts were to enter such orders and decrees as to ensure the nondiscriminatory admission to public schools of "the plaintiffs and those similarly situated in their respective school districts who may within such time as may be fixed by the District Courts become parties to these cases." This wording would have allowed not only the named parties, but also those similarly situated, to obtain the relief ordered on a class action basis. The draft was revised to order the district courts to enter such decrees as were necessary to admit to public schools "the parties to these cases." See Schwartz, supra, at 120.

The district courts were directed to "require that the defendants make a prompt and reasonable start toward full compliance with our May 17, 1954 ruling." Once such a start was made, additional time could be granted, but the burden would rest on the defendants to demonstrate that the extension was "in the public interest and is consistent with good faith compliance at the earliest practicable date."

But in determining an appropriate extension, the Court added that the district courts might consider administrative problems such as those "arising from the physical condition of the school plant, the school transportation system, personnel, revision of school districts and attendance areas into compact units to achieve a system of determining admission to the public schools on a nonracial basis, and revision of local laws and regulations which may be necessary in solving the foregoing problems."

Finally, without fixing a date on which the process must be concluded, the Court directed the courts

"...to take such proceedings and enter such orders and decrees consistent with this opinion as are necessary and proper to admit to public schools on a racially nondiscriminatory basis *with all deliberate speed* the parties to these cases."(Italics added.)

The phrase "with all deliberate speed" (which had not been in the Department of Justice's brief advocating a gradualist approach) was added to Warren's opinion at Frankfurter's request.[155]

Two days after *Brown II* was handed down, despite his disappointment with the decision's lack of timetables, NAACP chief counsel Thurgood Marshall expressed optimism: "Some people insist on having the whole hog ... I think it's a damn good decision! ... They've got to yield to the Constitution! And yield means yield! Yield means give up!"[156] But in the face of the South's massive resistance to implementation, any optimism soon faded and many—including those who had hailed *Brown I* as a path-breaking transformation—now

---

[155] Albert Lawrence, "Herbert Brownell, Jr.: The 'Hidden Hand' in the Selection of Earl Warren and the Government's Role in *Brown v. Board of Education*," 37 *Journal of Supreme Court History* 75, 87-88 (2012). The phrase had been used by Justice Oliver Wendell Holmes in Virginia v. West Virginia, 222 U.S. 17, 20 (1918), and had apparently originated in Francis Thompson's poem *Hound of Heaven* published in 1893.

condemned *Brown II* as too favorable to the states.

A wide variety of devices were employed to block desegregation, such as school closings, pupil placement laws, and residential zoning, as well as (in some instances) pressure, intimidation, and outright defiance.[157]

THE LITTLE ROCK CASE

The most dramatic confrontation involved the Little Rock, Arkansas school board and the Arkansas Governor, Orville Faubus.

Shortly after *Brown II,* a plan of gradual desegregation of the races in the Little Rock public schools was developed by the school board and approved by the lower courts. Under the plan, black students would be admitted to a previously all-white high school at the beginning of the 1957-58 school year. However, because of actions by the Arkansas Legislature and Governor Faubus and resulting threats of mob violence, black students were unable to attend the school until the Federal Government sent troops there. Finding that these events had resulted in chaos and turmoil disrupting the educational process, the District Court in Little Rock granted the school board's request that their plan of desegregation be suspended for two and one-half years, and that the black students be returned to segregated schools. The Court of Appeals reversed, and the school board applied to the Supreme Court for a stay.

In order to permit arrangements to be made for the beginning of the school year, the Court convened a special session on August 28, 1958, and scheduled oral argument for September 11. On September 12, the day after oral argument, the Court issued a *per curiam* order unanimously affirming the Court of Appeals decision and requiring immediate reinstatement of the earlier orders enforcing the school board's original desegregation plan. Cooper v. Aaron, 358 U.S. 1 (1958).[158]

---

[156] Peter Irons, *Jim Crow's Children: The Broken Promise of the Brown Decision* [Penguin 2004]: 170-71.

[157] This history is recounted by J. Harvie Wilkinson, *From Brown to Bakke: The Supreme Court and School Integration 1954-1978* [Oxford 1979]: 61-252; see also Klarman, supra, 321-43.

[158] Although the black students were admitted as a result of the Supreme Court's decision, that did not end Faubus' defiance. Subsequently he ordered both high schools closed during the 1958-1959 school year, and they were reopened only after a federal court declared the closing unconstitutional. Wilkinson, supra, at 94.

The *per curiam* order stated that the Court's opinion would be issued later.[159] On September 29, the Court issued a unanimous opinion signed by all nine Justices, stating (pp. 16-20):

"The constitutional rights of respondents are not to be sacrificed or yielded to the violence and disorder which have followed upon the actions of the Governor and Legislature. ... Thus law and order are not here to be preserved by depriving the Negro children of their constitutional rights. The record before us clearly establishes that the growth of the Board's difficulties to a magnitude beyond its unaided power to control is the product of state action. Those difficulties ... can also be brought under control by state action.

"The controlling legal principles are plain. ... Thus the prohibitions of the Fourteenth Amendment extend to all action of the State denying equal protection of the laws; whatever the agency of the State taking the action, ... or whatever the guise in which it is taken.... In short, the constitutional rights of children not to be discriminated against in school admission on grounds of race or color declared by this Court in the *Brown* case can neither be nullified openly and directly by state legislators or state executive or judicial officers, nor nullified indirectly by them through evasive schemes for segregation whether attempted 'ingeniously or ingenuously.'

"...[W]e should answer the premise of the actions of the Governor and Legislature that they are not bound by our holding in the Brown case. It is necessary only to recall some basic constitutional propositions which are settled doctrine.

"Article VI of the Constitution makes the Constitution the 'supreme Law of the Land.' In 1803, Chief Justice Marshall, speaking for a unanimous Court, referring to the

---

[159] The *Cooper* opinion was primarily written by Justice Brennan. Over the strong opposition of most other members of the Court, Justice Frankfurter—in addition to joining (and signing) the Court's opinion—insisted on filing a concurring opinion. His concurring opinion was not inconsistent with the main opinion but instead sought to appeal to moderate southern lawyers to support the Court's desegregation decisions. See Seth Stern & Stephen Wermiel, *Justice Brennan: Liberal Champion* [Houghton Mifflin 2010]: 150-52.

Constitution as 'the fundamental and paramount law of the nation,' declared in the notable case of Marbury v. Madison that 'It is emphatically the province and duty of the judicial department to say what the law is.' This decision declared the basic principle that the federal judiciary is supreme in the exposition of the law of the Constitution, and that principle has ever since been respected by this Court and the country as a permanent and indispensable feature of our constitutional system. It follows that the interpretation of the Fourteenth Amendment enunciated by this Court in the *Brown* case is the supreme law of the land, and Art. VI of the Constitution makes it of binding effect on the States 'any Thing in the Constitution or Laws of any State to the Contrary notwithstanding.' Every state legislator and executive and judicial officer is solemnly committed by oath taken pursuant to Art. VI, § 3, 'to support this Constitution. ...

"No state legislator or executive or judicial officer can war against the Constitution without violating his undertaking to support it."[160]

THE REJECTION OF "DELIBERATE SPEED"

Notwithstanding the Court's declaration in *Cooper*, Southern states continued to employ a variety of techniques to try to circumvent *Brown*. One of the most popular was a "pupil placement law" authorizing a state board to assign each student individually to a school on the basis of facially nondiscriminatory criteria, and requiring the exhaustion of state administrative remedies before each pupil seeking reassignment could bring individual litigation. Although eventually such devices were invalidated on the ground that they were

---

[160] Although applauding the result in the case, many legal scholars have sharply criticized the Court's characterization of its constitutional interpretations as "the law of the land" entitled to the same obedience as the Constitution itself. E.g., Sanford Levinson, revising Robert McCloskey, *The American Supreme Court* [Chicago 3d edition 2000]: 241; Philip Kurland, *Politics, the Constitution, and the Warren Court* [Chicago 1970]: 116, 186; Larry Kramer, *The People Themselves: Popular Constitutionalism and Judicial Review* [Oxford 2004]: 221; Alexander Bickel, *The Least Dangerous Branch: The Supreme Court at the Bar of Politics* [Bobbs-Merrill 1962]: 264; Akhil Reed Amar, "The Document and the Doctrine," 114 *Harvard Law Review*. 201 (2000); Frank Easterbrook, "Presidential Review," 40 *Case Western Law Review* L. Rev. 905, 926 (1990).

administered in a discriminatory manner, the desegregation process was excruciatingly slow. In response, the Supreme Court adopted a harder line with recalcitrant school districts and approved more aggressive remedies, including busing and judicial supervision of school operations, if such remedies were needed to eradicate racial practices found to violate the Fourteenth Amendment.

In 1964, when only one black child in a hundred had been enrolled in a racially mixed school in the South,[161] the Court declared that "[t]here has been entirely too much deliberation and not enough speed....." and "[t]he time for mere 'deliberate speed' has run out." Griffin v. County School Board, 377 U.S. 218, 229, 234 (1964).

In *Griffin*, the Court held (9-0) that Prince Edward County in Virginia had violated the Fourteenth Amendment by closing its public schools and providing tuition grants and tax credits to private schools attended only by white children. Declaring that "race and opposition to desegregation do not qualify as constitutional" grounds for abandoning public schools, the Court (Clark and Harlan disagreeing only as to the remedy) ordered the schools reopened and further authorized the district court if necessary to "require the [County] Supervisors to exercise the power that is theirs to levy taxes to raise funds adequate to reopen, operate, and maintain without racial discrimination a public school system in Prince Edward County like that operated in other counties in Virginia."

Green v. County School Board, 391 U.S. 430 (1968), inaugurated a fundamentally new phase in the implementation of *Brown*. The Court (9-0) held unconstitutional a "freedom of choice" plan that on its face was race-neutral but was commonly used as a device to avoid desegregation. The Court said that "[w]e do not hold that a 'freedom-of-choice' plan might of itself be held unconstitutional ... but [only] that in desegregating a dual system a plan utilizing 'freedom of choice' is not an end in itself" (pp. 439-440). The Court thus made clear that formal or nominal compliance was not sufficient in reviewing school districts' desegregation plans. Instead, the overriding requirement was "the disestablishment of a dual system," not only in theory but also in practice. (P. 442.)

The *Green* mandate was significantly expanded in Swann v. Charlotte-Mecklenburg Board of Education, 402 U.S. 1 (1970). After condemning continued "deliberate resistance" and "dilatory tactics,"

---

[161] Klarman, supra, at 362.

the Court (again by a 9-0 vote) announced new guidelines to deal with dual school systems that were still segregated fifteen years after *Brown II* (p. 13). The Court observed that the "constitutional command to desegregate schools does not mean that every school in every community must always reflect the racial composition of the school system as a whole" but only that "the very limited use of mathematical ratios was within the equitable remedial discretion of the District Court" to undo past unlawful action (pp. 24-25). Toward that end the Court sustained resort to revising attendance boundaries and busing students to desegregate dual school systems. The Court admonished, however, that the scope of the constitutional violation determined the scope of the remedy and that the district court's jurisdiction ended when "unitary" status was achieved.

Those limits were emphasized in Milliken v. Bradley, 418 U.S. 717 (1974), rejecting a plan to extend busing to adjacent school districts that had not engaged in segregation practices. For the purpose of desegregating the Detroit public schools, the district court ordered state officials to submit desegregation plans encompassing not only Detroit but also the three-county metropolitan area, despite the fact that the 53 outlying school districts in those three counties were not parties to the action and there was no claim that they had committed constitutional violations. In a bitterly divided 5-4 decision, the Supreme Court ruled that this was impermissible, stating that "[b]efore the boundaries of separate and autonomous school districts may be set aside by consolidating the separate units for remedial purposes or by imposing a cross-district remedy, it must first be shown that there has been a constitutional violation within one district that produces a significant segregative effect in another district." In short, according to the Court, "without an interdistrict violation and interdistrict effect there is no constitutional wrong calling for an interdistrict remedy" (p. 745).[162]

The same year that the Court in *Griffin* jettisoned "all deliberate speed," Congress finally took action. It enacted the Civil Rights Act of 1964, which in large measure was instrumental in eventually

---

[162] The majority distinguished its decision the previous year in Keyes v. Denver School District No. 1, 413 U.S. 189, 208 (1973), holding (6-2) that that a school district shown to have segregated one part of a large urban district created a rebuttable presumption that it had engaged in similar practices in other parts of the district as well.

ending the state-imposed segregation of public schools. The Act authorized the Department of Justice to bring lawsuits "for the orderly achievement of desegregation in public education." Even more significantly, the Act provided an additional form of leverage to pressure recalcitrant school districts; Title VI prohibited racial discrimination in federally funded programs, and the Department of Health, Education, and Welfare issued regulations threatening to withhold federal education funds from schools that continued to segregate.[163] "After the Civil Rights Act of 1964," as one commentator put it, "the South was squeezed in a tightening vise of new political and judicial determination."[164] These steps produced concrete results. The percentage of black children in desegregated schools increased to 6.1 percent in 1966, 16.9 percent in 1967, 32 percent in 1969, and an estimated 90 percent in 1973, with virtual completion of the process in succeeding years.[165]

In three cases in the 1990s, the Supreme Court approved the termination of federal court desegregation orders if the school district "had complied in good faith with the desegregation decree since it was entered, and ... the vestiges of past discrimination had been eliminated to the extent practicable." The Court directed that, "In considering whether the vestiges of *de jure* segregation had been eliminated as far as practicable, the District Court should look not only at student assignments, but [quoting *Green*] 'to every facet of school operations —faculty, staff, transportation, extra-curricular activities and facilities.'"[166] On that basis, more than 100 districts since 1990 have obtained release from desegregation orders.[167]

---

[163] See Andrew Kull, *The Color-Blind Constitution* [Harvard 1992]: 177-80.

[164] Wilkinson, supra, at 107.

[165] Klarman, supra, at 363. See also Stern & Wermiel, supra, at 355-65.

[166] Board of Education of Oklahoma City v. Dowell, 498 U.S. 237, 260 (1991); Freeman v. Pitts, 503 U.S. 467 (1992); Missouri v. Jenkins, 515 U.S. 70 (1995). In 2002 the Court also declined to review Belk v. Charlotte-Mecklenburg Board of Education, 269 F.3d 305 (4th Cir. 2001), in which the Court of Appeals for the Fourth Circuit found that the Charlotte-Mecklenburg school system had achieved desegregation status and that further busing was no longer necessary, thereby in effect terminating the *Swann* order.

[167] Greg Winter, "Long After Brown v. Board of Education, Sides Switch," *New York Times*, May 16, 2004.

SHOULD THE COURT HAVE DONE MORE?

The glacial pace of the desegregation process has been justifiably criticized. Frankfurter's addition of the phrase "with all deliberate speed," as Warren later acknowledged, proved to be a mistake.[168] The ambiguity of the phrase unfortunately enabled some to contend that *Brown II* authorized not only gradual enforcement but also procrastination in doing so. It is highly doubtful, though, that the Court could have done much more on its own before Congress intervened—ten years after *Brown I*—with enactment of the Civil Rights Act of 1964.

A leading critic of the gradualist approach, Michael Klarman, contends that "*Brown II* was a solid victory for white southerners" and that "In retrospect, the justices should have been firm and imposed deadlines and specific desegregation requirements." Yet Klarman then acknowledges: "Did their miscalculation matter much? Probably not. ... [C]ertain features of southern politics and the political dynamics of the segregation issue virtually ensured massive resistance.... Most white southerners would oppose desegregation until they were convinced that resistance was futile and costly. The Court was powerless to make that showing on its own."[169]

Quite a different criticism of the Court's role was made by Mark Tushnet—not on the ground that the Court failed to go far enough, but rather on the ground that it went too far.[170] Tushnet bases his criticism on what he considers the pernicious effect of *Brown II* in expanding the role of the judiciary, which thereafter "began to engage in structural reform, the major procedural innovation and source of expanded judicial power in the past generation." He contends that "Black and Douglas ... had a better understanding of the South" in opposing

---

[168] See Bernard Schwartz, *Super Chief: Earl Warren and His Supreme Court* [New York University Press 1983]: 123-24.

[169] Klarman, supra, at 318, 320. A harsher assessment of the Court's performance was made by J. Harvie Wilkinson (later a federal Court of Appeals judge), who charged that "...the Supreme Court fail[ed] to provide leadership and direction to the southern school controversy." According to Wilkinson, "the Court neglected to monitor deliberate speed, to insist on more than token progress, or to have done with naked stratagems for evasion and delay....By the time the Court awoke to its responsibilities, it already was too late....Much of the meaning of Brown had slowly trickled away." Wilkinson, supra, at 126-27.

[170] Mark Tushnet, with Katya Lezin, "What Really Happened in Brown v. Board of Education," 91 *Columbia Law Review* 1867, 1930 (1991).

any relief other than a simple order requiring admission of the few named plaintiffs to previously all-white schools. Black and Douglas, in Tushnet's view, "...believed, correctly, that all the Court could accomplish in the short run was a clear statement of fundamental principle regarding the unconstitutionality of segregation." If such a limited decree had been entered, Tushnet acknowledges, it would have provided only "token immediate relief," but he contends that "its effect on the framework of public law would have been much smaller."[171]

There is no reason, however, to think that a decree granting only "token immediate relief" would have ultimately advanced the desegregation process, and surely such a decision would have justifiably evoked national outrage except in the South. Nor is there any basis to believe that such a disposition would have been accepted by any of the other seven Justices.

---

[171] Ibid.

12. EXTENDING THE SCOPE OF *BROWN*

In deciding *Brown*, the Court of course fully understood that the separate-but- equal doctrine governed not only in public schools but also many other kinds of public facilities throughout the South.

The Court was also keenly aware that the application of separate-but-equal in public facilities was closely linked to miscegenation laws punishing black-white intercourse, cohabitation, and marriage. Even before *Plessy*, miscegenation laws had been upheld under the Equal Protection Clause in Pace v. Alabama, 106 U.S. 583, 585 (1883), on the ground that "The punishment of each offending person, whether white or black, is the same," and the *Plessy* opinion relied in part on the assumed legitimacy of miscegenation laws.

The miscegenation issue was raised, although in rather veiled terms, during the first argument in *Brown*. Justice Frankfurter asked one of the plaintiffs' counsel "whether it is your position that the Fourteenth Amendment or the Fifth ... automatically invalidates all legislation which draws a line determined because of race" and "... that marriage laws relating to race are ipso facto on the face of things, unconstitutional? ... Is it the all-embracing principle, that no legislation which is based on differentiation of race is valid?" Counsel replied that "I am invoking rather the principle which I think this Court involved in the Hirabayashi case when this Court said that legislation based upon race is immediately suspect: that is what I am invoking." Frankfurter then commented: "Well, that is a very candid and logical answer. That simply means that it can be valid. It is not an absolute prohibition, that good cause must be shown or great cause must be shown for the rule."[172]

But, irrespective of whether the purpose was to secure unanimity or for other reasons, the *Brown* decision was specifically limited to "the field of public education" and on its face the opinion did not

---

[172] Leon Friedman, ed., *Brown v. Board: The Landmark Oral Argument Before the Supreme Court* [The New Press 1969]: 111-17.

apply to either non-school facilities or miscegenation laws.[173] This limitation was emphasized in Warren's May 5, 1954 draft of a cover memo to send to the other Justices with his proposed opinions: "On the question of segregation in education, this should be the end of the line....but we should not go beyond that. The applicability of the doctrine in other contexts must await future decision."

That confrontation in other contexts was not long in coming. Shortly after the *Brown II* implementation decision, the Court summarily applied *Brown* to all public buildings, housing, transportation, and recreational and eating facilities. In 1955, in two very brief boilerplate orders issued without oral argument or opinion, the Court unanimously affirmed a Fourth Circuit decision that prohibited Baltimore's segregation of its public beaches, Mayor v. Dawson, 350 U.S. 877 (1955), and unanimously reversed a Fifth Circuit decision allowing a segregated municipal golf course in Atlanta. Holmes v. Atlanta, 350 U.S. 879 (1955). The following year, again without oral argument or opinion, the Supreme Court in Gayle v. Browder, 352 U.S. 903 (1956), affirmed a decision striking down the segregated bus system in Montgomery, Alabama. [174]

Unlike the *Brown* opinion, however, none of these orders contained any reference to harm suffered by blacks because of segregation. The result—although without saying so—was to convert the limited holding in *Brown* to the much broader principle that segregation of any public facility is conclusively presumed to be harmful to blacks and is therefore *per se* unconstitutional, without the need

---

[173] It was primarily on that ground that Judge Learned Hand criticized the *Brown* decision. Hand contended that the Court's focus on the single area of education—instead of dealing with segregation on an across-the-board basis—constituted impermissible second-guessing of legislative choices. Learned Hand, *The Bill of Rights* [Harvard 1958]: 54. In a letter to Hand after the *Brown* decision, Frankfurter insisted that it "did not rest on the absolute that the XIVth [Amendment] in effect said '[every] state law differentiating between colored and non-colored is forbidden.' ... I'm confident as comprehensive a proposition as yours in dealing with miscegenation would not have commanded unanimity. I know I would not have agreed to it—nor, I'm sure would several others." Gerald Gunther, *Learned Hand: The Man and the Judge* [Knopf 1994]: 669.

[174] The *Gayle* order, which like *Plessy* involved segregation in public transportation facilities, can arguably be said to have overruled *Plessy*—something that *Brown* (which had only "rejected language" in Plessy) had avoided doing. By 1963, the Court could declare categorically that "it is no longer open to question that a State may not constitutionally require segregation of public facilities." Johnson v. Virginia, 373 U.S. 61, 64 (1963).

to identify any specific harm to blacks (as *Brown* had done with respect to the educational disadvantage suffered by black children). Segregation's effect on black education, although the springboard for more broadly overturning separate-but-equal, could now be seen as but one example of a more pervasive vice—the pernicious effect of white subordination of blacks in all types of segregated public facilities.

But this left unresolved the incendiary and sexually charged question of the validity of miscegenation laws. Many in the South who were then resisting implementation of *Brown* claimed that de-segregation of schools would lead to "mongrelization of the white race," and Frankfurter in particular worried that a decision invali-dating miscegenation laws would increase southern resistance.[175] In 1954 the Court avoided the issue by exercising its discretion to deny certiorari in Jackson v. Alabama, 348 U.S. 888 (1954). But in 1955 and 1956 the issue was again presented to the Court in the case of Naim v. Naim, 350 U.S. 891 (1955), and 350 U.S. 985 (1956)—moreover, in a procedural posture in which review by the Court was ostensibly mandatory rather than discretionary. Nevertheless, the Court man-aged by a series of much-criticized stratagems to again defer deciding the constitutional issue.[176] Frankfurter wrote to Learned Hand that "We twice shunted it [the miscegenation issue] away and I pray we may be able to do it again, without being too brazenly evasive."[177]

Miscegenation again came before the Court in 1964, ten years after *Brown*. In McLaughlin v. Florida, 379 U.S. 184 (1964), the Court unanimously (Harlan, Douglas, and Stewart concurring) invalidat-ed a Florida criminal statute (§798.05) prohibiting cohabitation of an unmarried interracial couple. The Court held that the provision constituted an invidious racial classification in violation of the Equal Protection Clause "[b]ecause the section applies only to a white person and a Negro who commit the specified acts, and because no couple other than one made up of a white and a Negro is subject to conviction upon proof of the elements comprising the offense it pro-scribes…." (p. 184). In response to the state's claim that the provision

---

[175] Gunther, supra, at 666; Alexander Bickel, *The Least Dangerous Branch: The Supreme Court at the Bar of Politics* [Bobbs-Merrill 1962]: 174.

[176] Klarman, supra, at 322.

[177] Gunther, supra, at 667.

was designed to curb illicit extramarital and premarital promiscuity, the Court observed that "There is no suggestion that a white person and a Negro are any more likely habitually to occupy the same room together than the white or the Negro couple or to engage in illicit intercourse if they do" (p. 193).

Rejecting the state's reliance on the1883 *Pace* decision upholding miscegenation laws, the Court stated that "…*Pace* represents a limited view of the Equal Protection Clause which has not withstood analysis in the subsequent decisions of this Court" and that "Judicial inquiry under the Equal Protection Clause, therefore, does not end with a showing of equal application among the members of the class defined by the legislation" (p. 189). Although striking down the Florida cohabitation statute and repudiating the rationale on which *Pace* was based, the Court in *McLaughlin* deferred any ruling on the constitutionality of another Florida criminal statute (§741.11) prohibiting racial intermarriage. According to the Court, it did not have to pass on that issue "… even if we posit the constitutionality of the ban against the marriage of a Negro and a white," and "…without expressing any views about the State's prohibition of interracial marriage" (pp. 195-96).

Finally, three years after *McLaughlin* and 13 years after *Brown*, the Court in Loving v. Virginia, 388 U.S. 1 (1967), definitively held that all laws barring racial miscegenation were barred by the Equal Protection Clause. At the time of the decision, sixteen States still had such laws.[178]

The defendants in the *Loving* case were two Virginia residents, a black woman and a white man, who were married in the District of Columbia. When they returned to Virginia, they were indicted for violating Virginia's prohibition of interracial marriages.[179] They pleaded

---

[178] Alabama, Arkansas, Delaware, Florida, Georgia, Kentucky, Louisiana, Mississippi, Missouri, North Carolina, Oklahoma, South Carolina, Tennessee, Texas, Virginia and West Virginia. In the previous 15 years (1952-1967), such laws had been repealed by fourteen States: Arizona, California, Colorado, Idaho, Indiana, Maryland, Montana, Nebraska, Nevada, North Dakota, Oregon, South Dakota, Utah, and Wyoming.

[179] The Virginia statute provided that, "If any white person intermarry with a colored person, or any colored person intermarry with a white person, he shall be guilty of a felony and shall be punished by confinement in the penitentiary for not less than one nor more than five years." The statute further provided that "For the purpose of this chapter, the term 'white person' shall apply only to such person as has no trace whatever of any blood other than Caucasian; but persons who have one-sixteenth or less of the blood of the American Indian and have no other non-Caucasic blood shall be deemed to be white persons."

guilty and were sentenced to one year in jail, but the trial judge suspended the sentence on the condition that they leave the State and not return to Virginia together for 25 years. They subsequently filed a motion to vacate the judgment on the ground that the laws violated the Fourteenth Amendment. The motion was denied, and the Virginia Supreme Court affirmed.

In an opinion by Chief Justice Warren, the Supreme Court unanimously reversed. Quoting from the opinions in the *Japanese Internment Cases,* Hirabayashi v. United States, 320 U.S. 81, 100 (1943), and Korematsu v. United States, 323 U.S. 214, 216 (1944), the Court applied the principle that racial classifications are "odious to a free people whose institutions are founded upon the doctrine of equality" and must "be subjected to the 'most rigid scrutiny'... and, if they are ever to be upheld, they must be shown to be necessary to the accomplishment of some permissible state objective, independent of the racial discrimination which it was the object of the Fourteenth Amendment to eliminate."

Because of this "very heavy burden of justification," the miscegenation laws could not be sustained—as *Pace* had held—merely on the ground that the laws apply equally to both whites and blacks. Instead, "...the Equal Protection Clause requires the consideration of whether the classifications drawn by any statute constitute an arbitrary and invidious discrimination." Applying that test to the Virginia statute, the Court found "[t]here is patently no legitimate overriding purpose independent of invidious racial discrimination which justifies this classification." Such "...measures designed to maintain White Supremacy," the Court concluded, cannot be upheld. (Pp. 11-12.)

The Court's *Loving* decision is important for its definitive rejection of miscegenation laws. But in addition the case extended and explained the broader principle that all racial segregation laws (laws requiring physical separation of the races) are in substance *per se* unconstitutional.

Although the opinion reiterates the "rigid scrutiny" test, which presupposes that at least some racial classifications might be justifiable with appropriate proof, other passages in *Loving* make it clear that the possibility of such justification is precluded if the law requires racial separation—whether it be in public facilities or private bedrooms. By the very nature of such laws, because they are "designed to maintain White Supremacy," "[t]here is patently no legitimate overriding purpose independent of invidious racial discrimination" that might justify them. The result is to render them unconstitutional on their face and, in such a case, make irrelevant any need to show that the law imposes harm on the minority group. If the law requires racial separation, "rigid scrutiny" is redundant since it could have but one conclusion.[180]

---

[180] A temporary separation ordered by prison authorities, however, may be justified under the "strict scrutiny" standard if shown to be essential to prevent violence. Johnson v. California, 543 U.S. 499 (2005); Lee v. Washington, 390 U.S, 333 (1968). In *Johnson*, in rejecting an argument that a more deferential standard should be applied, the majority opinion stated that "all" racial classifications must be analyzed under strict scrutiny. In context the statement cannot be read as repudiating the *per se* invalidity of racial segregation of non-prison public facilities; instead the Court held in substance that all racial classifications must at a minimum be analyzed under strict scrutiny. If anything, the statement merely recognized that the need to prevent prison violence may in some unusual circumstances justify a limited factual inquiry. (In addition, if prisoners are temporarily separated on a racial basis to prevent violence, it does not denote white supremacy or the subordination of one race to another.)

13. EVOLUTION OF THE STANDARDS
OF EQUALITY

In its interpretation of the Equal Protection Clause, the Court has applied a series of evolving standards.

Invalidity of laws discriminating against black defendants charged with crimes—In Strauder v. West Virginia, 100 U.S. 303 (1880), the Court held unconstitutional the trial of a black criminal defendant by a jury from which blacks had been systematically excluded. It established the basic principle that rights enjoyed by whites cannot be denied to blacks on the basis of race.

Reasonableness—In Plessy v. Ferguson, 163 U.S. 537 (1896), the Court held (7-1) that a law requiring separate-but-equal facilities constituted a "reasonable" exercise of the state's police power. Under this amorphous standard, a law was "reasonable" if—in the Court's view—the law was not arbitrary and fell within the legitimate range of legislative discretion. The Court declined to regard a racial classification as unreasonable if the facilities provided to blacks were substantially equal to those provided to whites.

Color-blind test—The lone dissenting Justice in *Plessy*, John Marshall Harlan, stated in part (p. 559) that "Our Constitution is color-blind, and neither knows nor tolerates classes among citizens." Harlan's statement has been commonly (although not correctly, as pointed out in Chapter 7) understood as advocating that any racial classification is *per se* invalid. That test, of course, was not accepted in *Plessy* and has furthermore never been accepted by any other decision of the Supreme Court. [181]

---

[181] Individual opinions of some Justices, however, have expressed support for a color-blind rule. e.g., Justice Potter Stewart dissenting in Abington School District v. Schempp, 374 U.S. 203, 317 (1963); Justice Arthur Goldberg concurring in Bell v. Maryland, 378 U.S. 226, 287-88 (1964).

A stricter standard for review of racial classifications. In footnote 4 in
the Court's opinion in United States v. Carolene Products Co.,
304 U.S. 144, 152 (1938), in the course of dismissing a constitutional challenge to a state economic regulation, Justice Harlan
Stone observed that "There may be narrower scope for operation
of the presumption of constitutionality when legislation appears
on its face to be within a specific prohibition of the Constitution"
and in "the review of statutes directed at particular religious, or
national, or racial minorities." Greater protection for minorities,
Stone added, might be justified because they are characteristi-
cally subject to popular prejudices and may lack power to defend
themselves adequately in the political process. Although it received little attention at the time, the double standard suggested
in the footnote (which Justice Powell called "the most celebrated
footnote in constitutional law"[182]) ultimately achieved axiomatic
status and is now reflected in the established "strict scrutiny" test
for racial classifications.[183]

The underlying principle was recognized—although perhaps
not applied—in the *Japanese Internment Cases.* In Hirabayashi
v. United States, 320 U.S. 81 (1943) (also written by Stone), and
Korematsu v. United States, 323 U.S. 214 (1944), the Court declared that "Distinctions between citizens "solely because of their
ancestry are by their very nature odious to a free people" and "are
in most circumstances irrelevant and therefore prohibited" (320
U.S. at 100) and are "immediately suspect" and must be subjected
to the "most rigid scrutiny" (323 U.S. at 216). But in each case,
after a perfunctory review, the Court found that the test was satisfied by the Government's claimed justification for the internment program.

Rejection of separate-but-equal in public schools—In Brown v. Board
of Education, 347 U.S. 483 (1954), the Court rejected both (1)
the *Plessy* separate-but- equal doctrine as applied to public
schools and (2) the *Plessy* premise that enforced separation did

---

[182] Lewis Powell, "Carolene Products Revisited," 82 *Columbia Law Review* 1087 (1982).
[183] See, e.g., Bruce Ackerman, "Beyond Carolene Products," 98 *Harvard Law Review* 713 (1985).

not impose an inferior status on blacks. Although transformative in its effects,[184] the decision was in several respects quite narrow: The Court did not adopt a color-blind test that would invalidate all racial classifications (and that the NAACP had advocated in its briefs). Nor did the *Brown* opinion invoke the special scrutiny standard articulated in *Hirabayashi* and *Korematsu* (although the companion *Bolling v. Sharpe* opinion did so). Nor did the Court say that all government-mandated segregation is *per se* unconstitutional. Instead, emphasizing the impact on black children and their education, the *Brown* ruling was carefully limited to segregation in public schools.

Application of a per se rule to state-imposed segregation—As already pointed out, soon after the *Brown* decision, the Court in a series of summary orders outlawed state-imposed segregation in several other types of public facilities without any examination of their impact—thus applying a stricter standard than *Brown* did, and implicitly treating as irrelevant any claimed justification for laws requiring the physical separation of a racial group. The result is to make such a law, in substance, *per se* unconstitutional—without regard to the equality of facilities (as in *Plessy*) or a further demonstration of the effect on the subordinated group (as in *Brown*).

Racial classifications that neither segregate public facilities nor prefer one race over the other—In Loving v. Virginia, 388 U.S. 1 (1967), the Court further extended the anti-discrimination principle to miscegenation laws forbidding intermarriage. Relying on the anti-subordination rationale, the Court held that miscegenation laws were "measures designed to maintain White Supremacy," were not "necessary to the accomplishment of some permissible state objective," and were not excused because the prohibition applied to both races.

---

[184] See, e.g., Martin Luther King, Jr., *Stride Toward Freedom: The Montgomery Story* [Beacon Press 1958]: 191: *Brown* "marked a joyous end to the long night of enforced segregation" and "brought hope to millions of disinherited Negroes who had formerly dared only to dream of freedom;" David Garrow, "Hopelessly Hollow History: Revisionist Devaluing of Brown v. Board of Education," 80 *Virginia Law Review* 151 (1994).

Racial classifications that prefer minorities— As we shall see in Part V, the Court has also applied a "strict scrutiny" standard in determining the validity of minority preferences.

14. THE DISCRIMINATORY PURPOSE REQUIREMENT

In order to establish a violation of the Equal Protection Clause, a discriminatory *impact* is, without more, insufficient; it must also be found that the law has a discriminatory *purpose*. Thus, even if a law has a disproportionately adverse effect upon a racial minority, "...it is unconstitutional under the Equal Protection Clause only if that impact can be traced to a discriminatory purpose." Personnel Administrator of Massachusetts v. Feeney, 442 U.S. 256, 272 (1979). [185]

However, such proof is unnecessary if a law *expressly* assigns benefits or burdens on the basis of race. In those circumstances, a discriminatory purpose is indisputably implicit in the express classification.

But what if a law is race-neutral on its face? Such a law is not necessarily immunized from challenge. In some instances, a discriminatory purpose may be discerned from the facts even though the law is ostensibly neutral.

For example, in Yick Wo v. Hopkins, 118 U.S. 356 (1886), a San Francisco ordinance—containing no reference to race—required that laundries be located in brick or stone buildings unless a waiver was obtained from the board of supervisors. A Chinese alien who had operated a laundry for many years was refused a permit and was convicted and

---

[185] Such a discriminatory purpose should be distinguished from the subjective motives of the legislators who enacted the law. As Justice Black stated in Palmer v. Thompson, 403 U.S. 217, 225 (1971): "It is difficult or impossible for any court to determine the 'sole' or 'dominant' motivation behind the choices of a group of legislators." See also Justice Scalia dissenting in Edwards v. Aguillard, 482 U.S. 578, 636 (1987): "[W]hile it is possible to discern the objective 'purpose' of a statute (i.e., the public good at which its provisions appear to be directed), or even the formal motivation for a statute where that is explicitly set forth ..., discerning the subjective motivation of those enacting the statute is, to be honest, almost always an impossible task." But compare, e.g., Village of Arlington Heights v. Metropolitan Housing Development Corp., 429 U.S. 252, 264-65 (1977), holding that a facially neutral statute violates equal protection if it was motivated by discriminatory animus and its application results in a discriminatory effect.

imprisoned for illegally operating his laundry in violation of the ordinance. In a habeas corpus proceeding, the defendant successfully demonstrated that the ordinance was applied against Chinese nationals but not against other laundry shop operators. The authorities had denied the applications of over 200 Chinese subjects for permits to operate shops in wooden buildings, but granted the applications of 80 non-Chinese individuals to operate laundries in wooden buildings "under similar conditions." The Supreme Court unanimously reversed the conviction, stating (p. 373): "[T]he facts shown establish an administration directed so exclusively against a particular class of persons as to warrant and require the conclusion, that, whatever may have been the intent of the ordinances as adopted, they are applied by the public authorities charged with the administration, and thus representing the State itself, with a mind so unequal and oppressive as to amount to a practical denial by the State of equal protection of the laws..."[186]

Gomillion v. Lightfoot, 364 U.S. 339 (1960), involved a challenge to a law enacted by the Alabama legislature redrawing the boundaries of the city of Tuskegee. As a result of the change, the city was transformed from a square shape into "a strangely irregular twenty-eight-sided figure." Although the law contained no reference to race, its implementation would place virtually all of the 400 blacks in the city—but no whites—outside its boundaries. The plaintiff charged that the purpose of the law was to discriminatorily deprive blacks of the the right to vote in Tuskegee municipal elections. Given these allegations and in the absence of any other explanation, the Court held (p. 341), the plaintiffs were entitled to an opportunity to prove their claim: "These allegations, if proven, would abundantly establish that Act 140 was not an ordinary geographic redistricting measure, even within familiar abuses of gerrymandering. If these allegations, upon a trial, remained uncontradicted

---

[186] In United States v. Armstrong, 517 U.S. 456 (1996), in response to their indictment on "crack" cocaine and other federal charges, black defendants filed a motion for discovery or for dismissal, alleging that they had been selected for prosecution because they are black. The District Court and Court of Appeals upheld the discovery demand despite the lack of evidence that the Government had failed to prosecute nonblack defendants in similar circumstances. When the Government declined to comply with the discovery order, the indictment was dismissed. Distinguishing Yick Wo, the Supreme Court (8-1) reversed, holding that a defendant, in order to be entitled to discovery on a claim that he was singled out for prosecution on the basis of his race, must make a threshold showing that the Government had declined to prosecute similarly situated suspects of other races.

or unqualified, the conclusion would be irresistible, tantamount for all practical purposes to a mathematical demonstration, that the legislation is solely concerned with segregating white and colored voters by fencing Negro citizens out of town so as to deprive them of their pre-existing municipal vote."[187]

By contrast, for example, in Washington v. Davis, 426 U.S. 229 (1976), a discriminatory purpose could not be inferred from the results of a written personnel test that applicants for the police force in Washington, D.C., were required to take. The test was administered generally to prospective Government employees to determine whether applicants meet a uniform minimum standard of literacy—a requirement clearly relevant to the police function. Statistics showed that blacks failed the test much more frequently than whites, and it was contended on that basis that the test was racially discriminatory. The Court, however, held (7-2) that the evidence of disparity in results, without more, was insufficient to demonstrate a discriminatory purpose. The Court stated (pp. 246-47):

> "Respondents, as Negroes, could no more successfully claim that the test denied them equal protection than could white applicants who also failed. The conclusion would not be different in the face of proof that more Negroes than whites had been disqualified by Test 21. That other Negroes also failed to score well would, alone, not demonstrate that respondents individually were being denied equal protection of the laws by the application of an otherwise valid qualifying test being administered to prospective police recruits.

> "Nor on the facts of the case before us would the disproportionate impact of Test 21 warrant the conclusion that it is a purposeful device to discriminate against Negroes and hence an infringement of the constitutional rights of respondents as well as other black applicants. As we have

---

[187] The *Gomillion* majority resolved the case under the Fifteenth Amendment (pp. 342-348). In a concurring opinion, however, Justice Whittaker concluded that the "unlawful segregation of races of citizens" into different voting districts was cognizable under the Equal Protection Clause (p. 349). In Shaw v. Reno, 509 U.S. 630 (1993), the Court noted that "This Court's subsequent reliance on *Gomillion* in other Fourteenth Amendment cases suggests the correctness of Justice Whittaker's view."

said, the test is neutral on its face and rationally may be said to serve a purpose the Government is constitutionally empowered to pursue...."

The Court further cautioned that "A rule that a statute designed to serve neutral ends is nevertheless invalid, absent compelling justification, if in practice it benefits or burdens one race more than another, would be far reaching and would raise serious questions about, and perhaps invalidate, a whole range of tax, welfare, public service, regulatory, and licensing statutes that may be more burdensome to the poor and to the average black than to the more affluent white" (p. 247).

Statistical evidence was also found insufficient in McCleskey v. Kemp, 481 U.S. 279 (1987), holding (5-4) that evidence of discriminatory impact on a statewide basis in the past administration of the death penalty failed to show that the defendant had been convicted in violation of the Equal Protection Clause. A study of over 2000 Georgia murder cases found that the death penalty was imposed in 22 percent of the cases involving black defendants and white victims; in 8 percent of the cases involving white defendants and white victims; in 1 percent of the cases involving black defendants and black victims; and in 3 percent of the cases involving white defendants and black victims. The study further found that prosecutors sought the death penalty in 70 percent of the cases involving black defendants and white victims; 15 percent of the cases involving black defendants and black victims; and 19 percent of the cases involving white defendants and black victims. The study concluded that black defendants charged with killing white victims were 4.3 times as likely to receive a death sentence as defendants charged with killing blacks.

The Court, however, held that the study was not probative on the issue of the validity of the specific death penalty in the case under review. In an opinion by Justice Powell, the Court applied "the basic principle that a defendant who alleges an equal protection violation has the burden of proving 'the existence of purposeful discrimination'" and "that a criminal defendant must prove that the purposeful discrimination 'had a discriminatory effect' on him." Thus, "to prevail under the Equal Protection Clause, [a defendant] must prove that the decisionmakers in *his* case acted with discriminatory purpose." (Italics the Court's.) No such proof was presented by the defendant in the case before the Court: "He offers no evidence specific to his own case that would support an inference that racial considerations played a part in his sentence." (Pp. 292-93.) The Court further stated: "Each jury is unique in its composition, and the Constitution requires that its decision rest on consideration of innumerable factors that vary according to the characteristics of the individual defendant and the facts of the particular capital offense." (P. 294.)

Nor is the discriminatory purpose requirement satisfied by reliance on the foreseeable impact of the alleged discrimination. As the Court explained in Personnel Administrator of Massachusetts v. Feeney, 442 U.S. 256, 279 (1979), "'Discriminatory purpose,' ... implies more than intent as volition or intent as awareness of consequences. It implies that the decision-maker, in this case a state legislature, selected or reaffirmed a particular course of action at least in part 'because of,' not merely 'in spite of,' its adverse effects upon an identifiable group."[188]

In *Washington v. Davis*, while holding that the Equal Protection Clause requires a discriminatory purpose, the Supreme Court noted that legislatures could pass laws regulating disparate impacts that would be insufficient for a constitutional violation.[189] To relieve plaintiffs of the burden of proving discriminatory purpose, Congress in some civil rights statutes has provided a less stringent

---

[188] *Feeney* involved a challenge to a Massachusetts statute that gave veterans a preference in employment in the Massachusetts civil service. The effect of the preference was to exclude most women from the upper levels of the civil service, and the plaintiff argued that the Massachusetts legislature could readily have foreseen this effect since federal law in that period excluded most women from military service. The Court, however, held that the foreseeable impact of the statute was not sufficient to prove a discriminatory purpose under the Equal Protection Clause.

[189] 426 U.S. at 248: "...in our view, extension of the rule beyond those areas where it is already applicable by reason of statute, such as in the field of public employment, should await legislative prescription." Two states, North Carolina and Kentucky, have enacted "racial justice laws" that enable defendants sentenced to death to contest their sentences on the basis of evidence, including statistical patterns, indicating that race influenced their being sentenced to death. The North Carolina's law allows the use of statistics to prove that bias was a significant factor in death sentencing in the county where he was tried, or in the district, or even statewide. In April 2012 a North Carolina trial judge applied the law to order that a death sentence imposed 18 years ago be changed to life imprisonment without parole. The judge found that "race was a materially, practically and statistically significant factor" in the jury selection process not only in the defendant's trial but in trials across the county and state. The decision is being appealed. Campbell Robertson, "Bias Law Used to Move a Man Off Death Row," *New York Times*, April 20, 2012.

standard to establish claims under those statutes.[190] For example, as amended in 1982, the Voting Rights Act of 1965 provides that a violation of the statute may be established "based on the totality of circumstances" and that "[t]he extent to which members of a protected class have been elected to office [is] one circumstance which may be considered."

---

[190] See Chapter 17 *The Federal Voting Rights Act* and Chapter 25 *Title VII of the 1964 Civil Rights Act.*

15. CRIME AND "RACIAL PROFILING"

"Profiling" has become a pejorative term that many treat as synonymous with bigotry and harassment. And certainly profiling can be—and frequently has been—abused. But, in itself, profiling is morally neutral—neither good nor bad, neither just nor unjust.

As psychologist Gordon Allport recognized in his classic study *The Nature of Prejudice:* [191]

> "The human mind must think with the aid of categories (the term is equivalent to *generalizations*). Once formed, categories are the basis for normal prejudgment. We cannot possibly avoid the process. Orderly living depends upon it. ... A million events befall us every day. We cannot handle so many events. If we think of them at all, we type them. Open-mindedness is considered to be a virtue. But, strictly speaking, it cannot occur. A new experience *must* be redacted into old categories." (Italics in original.)

Walter Lippman made much the same point: "For the most part we do not first see, and then define, we define first and then see."[192] Thus, as Frederick Schauer concluded, "*profiling is inevitable*."[193]

Profiling furthermore "...remains a widespread and necessary weapon in the law enforcement arsenal. Tax inspectors use profiling to target certain taxpayers for intense audits, customs officials use profiling to determine which arriving passengers warrant close scrutiny, occupational safety and health officials use profiling to decide which businesses to inspect, and police detectives continue to

---

[191] Gordon Allport, *The Nature of Prejudice* [Addison Wesley 1979 ed.]: 20.

[192] Walter Lippman, *Public Opinion* [Harcourt, Brace 1922]: 81. See also, e.g., Douglas Massey, *Categorically Unequal: The American Stratification System* [Russell Sage Foundation 2007]: 9 ("...we are wired cognitively to construct general categories about the world in which we live and then to classify and evaluate the stimuli we encounter").

[193] Frederick Schauer, *Profiles, Probabilities, and Stereotypes* [Belknap 203]: 175 (italics added).

narrow the focus of their inquiries by constructing profiles of likely suspects."[194]

Such a profile may be formal—a prescribed written set of criteria to help identify probable violators.[195] Or more likely the profile will be quite informal—the criteria that the officer on the beat or the highway applies in identifying possible criminal activity on a case-by-case basis.

A typical profile, whether formal or informal, consists of several factors—primarily a combination of physical characteristics and behavioral patterns. However, if *race* is used as a profiling factor, particularly sensitive issues are presented. "[I]t is the use of race that has caused the hitherto largely unobjectionable practice of profiling to become so laden with political, moral, and emotional baggage."[196]

The "racial profiling" controversy is closely linked to the greatly disproportionate rate of black crime. Various causes for the disproportion have been suggested—unemployment, the learning achievement gap, broken homes, parental neglect, race discrimination, and others.[197] But whatever the causes, as prominent black scholars such as Randall Kennedy and Orlando Patterson acknowledge, the fact of the disproportion is beyond dispute.

Black men commit murders (93% of them are murders of other blacks) at a rate about eight times greater than that for white men—down from sixteen times in the late 1960s. In addition, the estimated rate at which black men commit burglary is three times higher than

[194] Id. at 159. In United States v. Sokolow, 490 U.S. 1, 10 (1989), sustaining (7-2) a DEA agent's reliance on a drug-courier profile, the Court held that "A court sitting to determine the existence of reasonable suspicion must require the agent to articulate the factors leading to that conclusion, but the fact that these factors may be set forth in a 'profile' does not somehow detract from their evidentiary significance as seen by a trained agent."

[195] The number of criteria in such a list may be large. For example, the Internal Revenue Service's "Discriminant Function" analysis includes 50 or more factors. Id. at 169.

[196] Schauer, supra, at 174.

[197] Khalil Gibran Muhammad. "Playing the Violence Card," *New York Times,* April 5, 2012, contends that "Black people were 'criminalized' through various institutions and practices, whether Southern chain gangs, prison farms, convict lease camps and lynching bees or Northern anti-black neighborhood violence and race riots ... stigmatizing black people as dangerous, legitimizing or excusing white-on-black violence, conflating crime and poverty with blackness, and perpetuating punitive notions of 'justice'—vigilante violence, stop-and-frisk racial profiling and mass incarceration—as the only legitimate responses."

it is for white men; for rape, it is five times higher.[198]

"People seeking solutions to America's massive racial problems," Randall Kennedy observes, "must resolutely eschew the temptation to prettify ugly realities:"

> "It does no good to pretend that blacks and whites are similarly situated with respect to either rates of perpetration or rates of victimization. They are not. A dramatic crime gap separates them. In relation to their percentage of the population, blacks on average both commit more crimes and are more often victimized by criminality. The familiar dismal statistics and the countless tragedies behind them are not figments of some Negrophobe's imagination. The country would be better off if that were so. Instead, the statistics confirm what most careful criminologists (regardless of ideological perspective) conclude: In fact (and not only in media portrayal or as a function of police bias) blacks, particularly young black men, commit a percentage of the nation's street crime that is strikingly disproportionate to their percentage in the nation's population."[199]

Sociologist Orlando Patterson similarly points out that "[Y]oung black men commit a disproportionate number of crimes, especially violent crimes, which cannot be attributed to judicial bias, racism or economic hardships." Further: "Afro-Americans constitute 25 percent of all arrestees in the United States, and 47 percent of all those arrested for violent crimes, nearly all against fellow Afro-Americans. ... On any given day almost one in three (32.2 percent) of Afro-American men between the ages of 20 and 29 is under some form of criminal justice supervision, in either prison or jail, or on probation or parole."[200] In addition, "Black

---

[198] James Q. Wilson, "Crime," *Beyond the Color Line* [Hoover Press 2002, Abigail & Stephan Thernstrom, eds.]: 116.

[199] Randall Kennedy, *Race, Crime, and the Law* [Vintage 1997]: 145. According to Bruce Western, *Punishment and Inequality in America* [Russell Sage Foundation 2006]: 18, "among the most socially marginal men—African Americans in their twenties and thirties who had dropped out of high school—incarceration rates were nearly fifty times the national average."

[200] Orlando Patterson, *The Ordeal of Integration: Progress and Resentment in America's "Racial" Crisis* [Civitas 1997]: 41. In 1992 blacks constituted 55.1 percent of those arrested for homicide, 42.8 percent of those arrested for rape, and 60.9 percent of those arrested for robbery. Kennedy, supra, at 22-23.

Americans, a mere 13 percent of the population, constitute half of this country's prisoners [one million]. .., [B]lacks are incarcerated at over eight times the white rate.... [O]ne in three male African-Americans in their 30s now has a prison record, as do nearly two-thirds of all black male high school dropouts...."[201]

Political scientist James Q. Wilson concluded that "The difference between blacks and whites with respect to crime, and especially violent crime, has, I think, done more to impede racial amity than any other factor."[202] "Of course," as he adds, "the average African American male is not likely to kill anybody. ... However low the absolute risk, the relative risk—relative, that is, to the chances of being killed by a white—is high, and this fact changes everything. When whites walk down the street, they are more nervous when they encounter a black man than when they encounter a white one."[203]

That nervous reaction, moreover, is not confined to whites. For example, Jesse Jackson has stated: "There is nothing more painful for me than to walk down the street and hear footsteps and start thinking about robbery. Then look around and see somebody white and feel relieved."[204] William Julius Wilson, a distinguished black University of Chicago professor, recently wrote: "...when I lived in a middle-class Chicago neighborhood that bordered a ghetto neighborhood, I, too, would tense up when I walked my dog at night and saw a black man or a group of black male teenagers approaching me on the street." Judge Theodore McKee, a black federal judge, stated: "If I'm walking down a street in Center City Philadelphia at two in the morning and I hear some footsteps behind me and I turn around and there

---

[201] Orlando Patterson, "Jena, O.J. and the Jailing of Black Americans," *New York Times*, September 30, 2007. As both Kennedy and Patterson point out, blacks are very disproportionately the victims of violent crime. Black teenagers are nine times more likely to be murdered than their white counterparts. Whereas black men were killed at the rate of 45 per 100,000 in 1960, by 1990 the rate was 140 per 100,000, compared with a figure of around 20 per 100,000 for white males. Douglas Massey, "Segregation and Violent Crime in Urban America," in *Problem of the Century: Racial Stratification in the United States* [Russell Sage Foundation 2001, Elijah Anderson and Douglas Massey, eds.]: 318.

[202] Wilson, supra, at 117.

[203] Id. at 116.

[204] Id.; Juan Williams, "The Trayvon Martin Tragedies," *Wall Street Journal*, March 27, 2012; Shelby Steele, "The Exploitation if Trayvon Martin," *Wall Street Journal*, April 4, 2012.

[205] William Julius Wilson, *More Than Just Race: Being Black and Poor in the Inner City* [Norton 2009]: 1-2.

are a couple a young white dudes behind me, I am probably not going to get very uptight. I'm probably not going to have the same reaction if I turn around and there is the proverbial Black urban youth behind me."[206] And in his celebrated 2008 civil rights speech President Barack Obama acknowledged that his white grandmother "loves me as much as she loves anything in this world, but ... once confessed her fear of black men who passed by her on the street...."[207]

Did Jesse Jackson, William Julius Wilson, Judge McKee, and Obama's grandmother react in that way because they are racists? Are they bigoted against black people? Of course not.

What triggered their response was not racism or bigotry but instead a crude but quite understandable form of "racial profiling"—an unconscious judgment that they were in increased danger based on the widely known facts concerning violent crime by black men (and particularly young black men). In nearly all such street encounters, this fear is probably unfounded. But their immediate reaction, in view of the many times greater rate of black crime, cannot be said to be irrational, at least not from the standpoint of those who suddenly find themselves alone in that highly charged situation.

Indeed, they almost certainly would have responded in the same way if their street encounter had been with a young white man who for some reason (for example, a threatening gang tattoo or a personal reputation for violence) triggered their fear of assault or robbery. What drives such a response, by black and white alike, is a basic human defense system that operates independently of consciousness and can be activated by an infinite variety of stimuli.[208]

Unquestionably, as one columnist observed, "Guilt isn't genetic. Color and culture don't dictate criminality. Innocence must be the default assumption. No one should be punished for another's sins."[209] But that undeniable truth does not change the reality of disproportionate black crime. Nor does it change, in many instances, the unfortunate perception based on that reality. Nor does it change the human reaction to such perception, regardless of whether the

---

[206] Kennedy, supra, at 15-16.

[207] Transcript, "Barack Obama Speech on Race," *New York Times*, March 18, 2008.

[208] See, e.g., Joseph LeDoux, *The Emotional Brain: The Mysterious Underpinnings of Emotional Life* [Simon & Schuster 1996]: 128-31.

[209] Charles Blow, "From O.J. to Trayvon," *New York Times*, April 6, 2012.

fear may prove to be (and in most instances is) unfounded. The alternative, as Randall Kennedy pointed out, is to seek "...self-protection only when the actual (as opposed to the feared) conduct of others warrant such a response. But the cost of waiting and individualizing one's judgment may be diminished security; sometimes it is too late to avoid a person when he finally gives you concrete reasons for doing so."[210]

And if this is true of those like Jesse Jackson, William Julius Wilson, Judge McKee, and Obama's grandmother, it is scarcely surprising that others less dedicated to racial equality might react the same way.

"STOPS" AND "STOPS-AND-FRISKS"

"Racial profiling" of a more serious type is involved in the controversy over the legitimacy of considering race in police "stops" and "stops-and-frisks."

A "stop" occurs when a police officer, by means of either physical force or show of authority, briefly (possibly for only a few moments) detains an individual in such a way that a reasonable person would have believed that he was not free to leave.[211] A stop typically does not result in an arrest, booking, or incarceration. Nevertheless, as the Supreme Court has recognized, "It is a serious intrusion upon the sanctity of the person, which may inflict great indignity and arouse strong resentment, and it is not to be undertaken lightly."[212]

A police stop is to be distinguished from an officer's approaching someone and asking a few questions. "[E]ven when officers have no basis for suspecting a particular individual, they may generally ask questions of that individual, ask to examine the individual's identification, and request to search his or her luggage—as long as the police do not convey a message that compliance with their requests is required."[213] But if the officer, by means of either physical force or show

---

[210] Kennedy, supra, at 15.

[211] Terry v. Ohio, 392 U.S. 1, 16-17 (1968): "...[W]henever a police officer accosts an individual and restrains his freedom to walk away, he has 'seized' that person within the meaning of the Fourth Amendment." Pertinent criteria include, e.g., the threatening presence of several officers, the display of a weapon by an officer, some physical touching of the person of the citizen, or the use of language or tone of voice indicating that compliance with the officer's request was being compelled.

[212] Id. at 16.

[213] Florida v. Bostick, 501 U.S. 429, 434-35 (1991); California v. Hodari D., 499 U.S. 621, 628 (1991).

of authority, restrains the person's liberty, the encounter constitutes a "seizure" subject to the Fourth Amendment.[214]

A stop, unlike an arrest, does not require the "probable cause" needed for an arrest. Probable cause requires "a fair probability that contraband or evidence of a crime will be found." By contrast, the Fourth Amendment permits a stop if the officer has a "reasonable suspicion" that the person has committed, is committing, or is about to commit a crime.[215] Reasonable suspicion requires something more than a "hunch" but less than the level of suspicion required for probable cause.[216]

If a stop is justified under the reasonable suspicion standard, and if in addition the officer reasonably believes that the person is armed and dangerous to the officer or others, he may also "frisk" the suspect—conduct a "patdown" of the suspect's outer clothing to search for concealed weapons or contraband. But reaching into a pocket or under a shirt is not allowed.[217]

The Supreme Court has held that the legality of a stop depends on "the totality of the circumstances—the whole picture:"[218]

> "The analysis proceeds with various objective observations, information from police reports, if such are available, and consideration of the modes or patterns of operation of certain kinds of lawbreakers. From these data, a trained officer draws inferences and makes deductions—inferences and deductions that might well elude an untrained person.

---

[214] The Fourth Amendment provides: "The right of the people to be secure in their persons, houses, papers, and effects, against unreasonable searches and seizures, shall not be violated, and no Warrants shall issue, but upon probable cause, supported by Oath or affirmation, and particularly describing the place to be searched, and the persons or things to be seized."

[215] Terry v. Ohio, 392 U.S. 1 (1968); United States v. Cortez, 449 U.S. 411, 417-18 (1981).

[216] Illinois v. Gates, 462 U.S. 213, 238 (1983).

[217] The Court has further held that, if there is probable cause for arrest, the subjective motivation of the arresting officer is immaterial, even if the police, under the guise of enforcing the traffic code, were seeking to identify violators of other laws (such as the narcotics laws). Whren v. United States, 517 U.S. 806, 813 (1996). And if there is an arrest, the officer may make a full search of the suspect and his automobile. In City of Indianapolis v. Edmond, 531 U.S. 32, 41-42 (2000), the Court (6-3) distinguished Whren from "checkpoint stops" and limited Terry to stops supported by individual suspicion: "Because the primary purpose of the Indianapolis narcotics checkpoint program is to uncover evidence of ordinary criminal wrongdoing, the program contravenes the Fourth Amendment."

[218] United States v. Cortez, 449 U.S. 411, 417-18 (1981).

"The process does not deal with hard certainties, but with probabilities. Long before the law of probabilities was articulated as such, practical people formulated certain common-sense conclusions about human behavior; jurors as factfinders are permitted to do the same—and so are law enforcement officers. Finally, the evidence thus collected must be seen and weighed not in terms of library analysis by scholars, but as understood by those versed in the field of law enforcement."

The calculations involved "are not technical; they are the factual and practical considerations of everyday life on which reasonable and prudent men, not legal technicians, act."[219] The Court has further emphasized that "the relevant inquiry is not whether particular conduct is 'innocent' or 'guilty,' but the degree of suspicion that attaches to particular types of noncriminal acts."[220]

Blacks and Hispanics charge that police engage in discriminatory "racial profiling" by stopping and searching on the basis of race. In support of that charge, in addition to numerous individual reports of police discourtesy or humiliation,[222] heavy reliance is placed on statistics showing that blacks and Hispanics are stopped and searched in numbers wholly out of proportion to their percent of the population.[222] For example, in 2011, the New York City police made 685,724 stops, and over 87% of those stopped were classified as black or Hispanic even though these groups make up only approximately 55% of the New York City population. Whites, by contrast, were involved in only 9% of all stops, although they constitute approximately 35% of the city's population. Furthermore, although young black and Hispanic men between the ages of 14 and 24 constitute only 4.7 percent of the city's population, they accounted for 41.6 percent

---

[219] Brinegar v. United States, 338 U.S. 160, 176 (1949).

[220] United States v. Sokolow, 490 U.S. 1, 10 (1989).

[221] See. e.g., Wendy Ruderman, "Rude or Polite, City's Officers Leave Raw Feelings in Stops," *New York Times*, June 26, 2012.

[222] See Peter Schuck, *Diversity in America: Keeping Government at a Safe Distance* [Belknap 2003]: 146: "State and city police departments must now collect data on the race, ethnicity, or national origin of all drivers or other individuals whom they stop. In order to do so, the officer must decide what the motorists' race, ethnicity, or national origin is and then record the data for the profiling monitor—without asking them, much less allowing them, to self-identify."

of the stops.[223] On the basis of such statistics, it is claimed that the police engage in racial discrimination by "profiling" minorities.[224]

In response, police and others contend that stops reduce crime and that racial statistics are misleading, particularly if considered in isolation from statistics of minority crime. While acknowledging that the number of minority stops is substantially disproportionate to population, they deny that such a comparison shows discrimination.[225] In their view, the disproportionate number of minority stops simply reflects urban reality and the necessity of assigning more police to high crime areas where both criminals (especially black male offenders aged 14 to 24) and most of their victims are located.[226]

More specifically, they contend that statistics comparing a city's entire population with the number of black and Hispanic stops would demonstrate discrimination only on the basis of two unsustainable assumptions: (1) that the rates of black and Hispanic crime are the same as those of other ethnic groups; and (2) that the incidence of crime is evenly distributed throughout the city.[227]

---

[223] Al Baker, "New York Police Release Data Showing Rise in Number of Stops on Streets," *New York Times*, May 12, 2012. In approximately half the 2011 stops the officer believed that the circumstances justified a frisk (i.e, a patdown to determine if the person is carrying a concealed weapon) but only 12% of the 2011 stops led to an arrest or summons. Ruderman, suupra.

[224] See, e.g., Editorial, "Injustices of Stop and Frisk," *New York Times*, May 13, 2012; Editorial, "Reform Stop-and-Frisk," New York Times, May 16, 2012.

[225] Peter Vallone, chairman of the New York City Council's Public Safety Committee, claimed that stop-and-frisks "usually increase as a result of the community's demands to do something to catch the culprits and eliminate illegal guns." Paul J. Browne, chief spokesman of the New York City Police Department, stated: "Minorities are disproportionately the victims of crime, and the police respond to where crime is reported." Al Baker, "Police Stops in City Rose Significantly Last Year," *New York Times*, February 11, 2009.

[226] Pointing to a significant reduction in the city's homicide rate, New York City Police Commissioner Raymond Kelly defended the department's practice: "I would submit that our strategies are saving lives. You look at the numbers in this city; you look at the lives that we're saving, and I would submit to you that the majority of those lives are minorities, and most of them are young men who are being killed for senseless reasons. We are saving those lives, and, quite frankly, we're saving them at a much greater degree and extent than other cities are." Al Baker, "New York Police Release Data Showing Rise in Number of Stops on Streets," *New York Times*, May 12, 2012.

[227] Heather Mac Donald, "Fighting Crime Where the Criminals Are," *New York Times*, June 25, 2010: "Based on reports filed by victims, blacks committed 66 percent of all violent crime in New York in 2009, including 80 percent of shootings and 71 percent of robberies. Blacks and Hispanics together accounted for 98 percent of reported gun assaults. And the vast majority of the victims of violent crime were also members of minority groups. ... The per capita rate of shootings in the 73rd Precinct—which covers Brooklyn's largely black Ocean Hill and Brownsville neighborhoods—is 81 times higher than in the 68th Precinct in largely white Bay Ridge. Not surprisingly, the per capita stop rate in the 73rd Precinct is 15 times higher than that in the 68th."

The disproportionate number of stops of blacks and Hispanics, it is contended, is a direct result of the much higher rates of crime by blacks and Hispanics, particularly in high crime areas primarily populated by blacks and Hispanics.[228] In short, statistics alone do not reveal whether police have complied with the reasonable suspicion standard.[229]

But statistics may support further inquiry whether there has been such compliance. For example, the steady increase in the number of stops in New York City from fewer than 100,000 in 2002 to nearly 700,000 in 2011 led to the claim (yet to be substantiated) that the increase is attributable to police disregard of the reasonable suspicion standard.[230] In a May 2012 pretrial order, a federal district court authorized class-action treatment of a suit charging that the New York Police Department had imposed on officers a "policy of establishing performance standards and demanding increased levels of stops and frisks."[231] While allowing the case to proceed as a class action, the court (pp. 16-17) added: "Hotly disputed, however, is whether the NYPD has set quotas governing the number of stops and summonses that NYPD officers must make on a monthly basis." That issue, unless a settlement is reached in the case, would have to be resolved at trial.

---

[228] See, e.g., Heather Mac Donald, "The Myth of Racial Profiling," *City Journal*, Spring 2001: "Trouble is, no one yet has devised an adequate benchmark against which to measure if police are pulling over, searching, or arresting 'too many' blacks and Hispanics. The question must always be: *too many compared with what?*" (Italics in original.)

[229] As the Supreme Court recognized in United States v. Armstrong, 517 U.S. 456, 465 (1996), discrimination against a minority group is not demonstrated by a higher rate of prosecutions than the group's percentage of the general public at large. Instead, the relevant comparison is with "*similarly situated* individuals of a different race [who] were not prosecuted." (Italics added.) See also Bush v. Vera, 517 U.S. 952, 968 (1996) (plurality opinion): "[R]acial disproportions in the level of prosecutions for a particular crime may be unobjectionable if they merely reflect racial disproportions in the commission of that crime."

[230] Police Commissioner Raymond Kelly and Mayor Michael Bloomberg responded that further steps are being taken to ensure that stops are conducted lawfully. Those measures, they said, would reduce the number of stops while increasing their quality. Ruderman, supra.

[231] Al Baker, "Judge Grants Class-Action Status to Stop-and-Frisk Suit," *New York Times*, May 16, 2012. A similar suit was filed in 2010 against the Philadelphia police department. The suit was settled by a consent decree that prohibits stops made solely on the basis of "furtive movement" or acting "suspiciously" or because the person was in a "high crime" or "high drug" area. See Editorial, "How to End Stop-and-Frisk Abuses," *New York Times*, May 23, 2012.

THREE TYPES OF "RACIAL PROFILING"

The term "racial profiling," among the many ways it is used, is broadly applied to *any* police stop based on *any* consideration of race or ethnicity.[232] Such use of the term fails to take account of the important differences among three quite different types of police stops:

(I) Stopping a black or Hispanic on the street or highway solely on the basis of race.

(II) Stopping a black or Hispanic in seeking to apprehend an alleged criminal in circumstances where the suspect's race was reported as one of the clues reported by the victim or a witness.

(III) Stopping a black or Hispanic in other circumstances where race is used as one factor among others in evaluating suspicious conduct.

The first type is patently illegal; the second is generally accepted; and the third remains a subject of controversy.

I.

Stopping someone solely on the basis of race—for, e.g., "driving while black" or "shopping while black"—is an indefensible perversion of profiling. (Indeed, a one-factor profile is not really a profile at all.)

A practice of this sort is universally and properly condemned.[233] For example, in United States v. Avery, 137 F.3d 343 (6th Cir. 1997),

---

[232] See, e.g., Richard Thompson Ford, *The Race Card: How Bluffing About Bias Makes Race Relations Worse* [Farrar, Straus and Giroux 2008]: 244: "...the consensus against racial profiling is a sham. It's easy for everyone from the ACLU and Amnesty International to Republican politicians and law enforcement agencies to condemn racial profiling, as long as no one insists on a precise definition of the term. Civil liberties groups play three-card monte by using the most narrow and extreme definition of profiling when describing it, but employing a more encompassing definition when seeking to prohibit it. Government and law enforcement play the same con game by heartily condemning racial profiling without defining it. Civil rights activists insist that racial profiling is always *irrational*, and police are happy to join them in rejecting 'irrational racial profiling'—leaving the door open to racial profiling that is rational. The activists attack the odious practice of targeting people 'because of race and race alone' and many states and police departments have seized on that rhetoric, prohibiting profiling based on race alone but tacitly exempting the type of profiling that police actually use, which is based on a combination of race and other factors." (Italics in original.)

[233] E.g., Gene Callahan and William Anderson, "The Roots of Racial Profiling," *Reason Magazine*, August/September 2001 issue.

the defendant claimed that he was stopped by law enforcement solely on the basis of his race. While the court affirmed his conviction, citing other factors utilized by the police in choosing to follow the defendant, the court stated that "[i]f law enforcement adopts a policy, employs a practice, or in a given situation takes steps to initiate an investigation of a citizen based solely upon that citizen's race, without more, then a violation of the Equal Protection Clause has occurred" (p. 355).[234]

II.

It does not follow, however, that all consideration of race in law enforcement is improper.

In particular, when police are trying to apprehend an alleged criminal whose race was described by the victim or a witness, consideration of race is recognized as legitimate. A key decision is Brown v. City of Oneonta, 221 F. 3d 329 (2d Cir. 1999), cert. denied, 534 U.S. 816 (2001).

In the *Oneonta* case, in a small college town, a man broke into a home shortly before 2:00 a.m and attacked a 77-year old woman who was sleeping. The woman struggled with the man before he ran away. The woman told the police who responded to the scene that she could not identify her assailant's face, but that he was wielding a knife; that he was a black man, based on her view of his hand and forearm; and that he was young, because of the speed with which he crossed her room. She also told the police that, as they struggled, the suspect had cut himself on the hand with the knife. A police canine unit tracked the assailant's scent from the scene of the crime toward the college campus, but lost the trail after several hundred yards. The police checked local hospitals and pharmacies to see if a young black man had requested treatment for a cut. The police also obtained a list of black male students at the college and attempted to locate all those on the list in order to examine their hands for cuts. When that effort yielded no suspects, the process was then extended to other young black men in the town. In all the police made approximately 200 of these stops. No one was arrested, and no one was ever charged with the crime.

---

[234] See also Chavez v. Illinois State Police, 251 F.3d 612, 635 (7th Cir. 2001) (any general policy of "utiliz[ing] impermissible racial classifications in determining whom to stop, detain, and search" would violate the Equal Protection Clause).

The black students whose names appeared on the list provided by the college (as well as others who were approached and questioned by the police) filed an action in the federal district court against the city, the college, and various police officials. In their complaint, the plaintiffs charged that the defendants had engaged in racial discrimination in violation of the Equal Protection Clause and federal civil rights laws. [235]

The Court of Appeals for the Second Circuit rejected the plaintiffs' discrimination claims. In its decision, the court recognized that initiating an investigation of a person based solely upon that person's race violates the Equal Protection Clause, but found that

> "...plaintiffs' factual premise is not supported by the pleadings; they were not questioned solely on the basis of their race. They were questioned on the altogether legitimate basis of a physical description given by the victim of a crime. Defendants' policy was race-neutral on its face; their policy was to investigate crimes by interviewing the victim, getting a description of the assailant, and seeking out persons who matched that description. This description contained not only race, but also gender and age, as well as the possibility of a cut on the hand. In acting on the description provided by the victim of the assault—a description that included race as one of several elements—defendants did not engage in a suspect racial classification that would draw strict scrutiny. The description, which originated not with the state but with the victim, was a legitimate classification within which potential suspects might be found." (P. 119.)

The court acknowledged that attempting to question every person fitting the general description of an alleged criminal may well have a disparate impact on a minority group, particularly in a small town such as Oneonta. But, citing *Washington v. Davis, supra,* the court held that such a disparate impact does not offend the Equal Protection Clause unless the challenged action was undertaken with discriminatory intent. Since the Oneonta investigation was initiated on reasonable non-racial grounds, the disparate impact of the investigation was found to be insufficient to sustain an equal protection

---

[235] The plaintiffs also charged violations of the Fourth Amendment. As to two of the plaintiffs, summary judgment for the defendants on their Fourth Amendment claims was reversed on the ground that their detention had been sufficiently long to constitute a "seizure"; as to the others, their Fourth Amendment claims were rejected for lack of any showing of a "seizure."

claim. The Supreme Court denied review.

Supreme Court review was also denied in United States v. Waldon, 206 F.3d 597, 604 (6th Cir. 2000), cert. denied, 531 U.S. 881 (2000), holding that "common sense dictates that, when determining whom to approach as a suspect of criminal wrongdoing, a police officer may legitimately consider race as a factor if descriptions of the perpetrator known to the officer include race."[236]

Randall Kennedy, although a strong critic of other types of racial profiling, has no objection to profiling "...in which police act against a person based on a detailed description that includes the suspect's race. In such a case, the person's skin color is being used no differently than information about the pants or jacket or shoes that the suspect was said to be wearing. [In that case] the person's race is not so much a category that embraces a large number of people as a distinguishing fact about the identity of a designated person."[237]

In short, as the *Oneonta* case illustrates, being black has a double significance: (1) it indicates membership in a racial group, but also (2) it is a "distinguishing fact" (or "clue") like gender or age or scars or clothing that may be highly relevant in identifying someone—regardless of his race—who is believed to have committed a crime.[238] To put the issue in equal protection terminology, if the police also customarily refer to other races (white, Asian, etc.) in describing particular suspects, the races are being treated alike without subordination of any race and hence there is no discrimination between persons "similarly situated."[239]

---

[236] See also, e.g., Buffkins v. City of Omaha, 922 F.2d 465, 468 (8th Cir. 1990).

[237] See also Sheri Lynn Johnson, "Race and the Decision to Detain a Suspect," 93 *Yale. Law Journal* 214, 242-43 (1983): "The use of race to identify a particular perpetrator ... does not disadvantage any racial group and thus does not require strict scrutiny. Although the suspect's race is noted and weighed in the decision to detain, no generalizations about the characteristics, behavior, or appropriate treatment of the racial group are employed. Rather, the suspect's race is used solely to help substantiate his identity as the individual involved in a particular offense. Because suspects in all racial groups will be identified in part by their race, reliance upon the witness's description of the perpetrator's race seems to impose equal burdens on all races."

[238] See, e.g., Schauer, supra, at 187: "[R]ace, gender, and age, ... have a visibility and a consequent salience that makes them stand out more than other factors."

[239] Critics of racial stereotyping recognize that even "[i]nvestigations of future conduct, such as plots to commit crimes, can also take account of race without being considered racial profiling if conducted in a targeted way." Michael Kirkpatrick and Margaret Kwoka, "Title VI Disparate Impact Claims Would Not Harm National Security—A Response to Paul Taylor," 46 *Harvard Journal on Legislation* 503, 523 (2009).

III.

But the consideration of race in other police stops—other than those aimed at apprehending a particular suspect—remains the subject of controversy even when race is only one of several factors relied upon to justify reasonable suspicion.

A. THE FOURTH AMENDMENT

In United States v. Brignoni-Ponce, 422 U.S. 873, 886-87 (1975), the Supreme Court held that "The likelihood that any given person of Mexican ancestry is an alien is high enough to make Mexican appearance a relevant factor, but standing alone it does not justify stopping all Mexican-Americans to ask if they are aliens."

In United States v. Martinez-Fuente, 428 U.S. 543, 563-64 (1976), in upholding the selection of motorists for questioning at a highway checkpoint, the Court sustained the reasonableness of Border Patrol stops based in part on ancestry. The Court stated that "...even if it be assumed that such referrals are made largely on the basis of apparent Mexican ancestry, we perceive no constitutional violation." In a footnote, the Court further stated that "...to the extent that the Border Patrol relies on apparent Mexican ancestry at the checkpoint, ... that reliance clearly is relevant to the law enforcement need to be served."[240]

Other courts that have confronted the issue have generally recognized the reasonableness of police consideration of race when it is but one of multiple factors relied upon.[241]

An example is the decision of the Court of Appeals of the Eighth Circuit in United States v. Weaver, 966 F.2d 391 (8th Cir. 1992). The defendant Weaver had been stopped and frisked at the Kansas City International Airport and found to be carrying a plastic bag filled with crack cocaine on his person and more than six pounds of crack

---

[240] In Davis v. Mississippi, 394 U.S. 721 (1969), the Supreme Court reversed the conviction of a young black boy for the rape of a white woman. The defendant had been arrested after an investigation in which the police interrogated and fingerprinted dozens of boys based simply on the victim's description of her assailant as a "Negro youth." The stated basis of the Court's reversal, however, was not the police's reliance on race but instead the inadmissibility of evidence obtained from the defendant while being illegally detained in violation of the Fourth Amendment.

[241] Kennedy, supra, at 141. Compare, e.g., United States v. Montero-Camargo, 208 F.3d 1122 (9th Cir. 2000).

cocaine in one of his bags. He was charged with possession of cocaine with intent to distribute. At trial DEA agent Hicks testified that several factors caused him to stop Weaver:

> "(1) that the agent had intelligence information and also past arrest history on two street gangs from Los Angeles called the Crips and the Bloods who are mostly young, roughly dressed male blacks and are notorious for transporting cocaine into the Kansas City area from Los Angeles for sale; (2) that Weaver got off a direct flight from Los Angeles, a source city for drugs; (3) that he was a roughly dressed young black male; (4) that he almost ran from the airplane toward a taxicab; (5) that he had two carry-on bags and no checked luggage; (6) that he had no identification on his person; (7) that he did not have a copy of his ticket; (8) that he appeared very nervous when he talked to the agent."

Weaver was convicted and he appealed, claiming that Hicks did not have reasonable suspicion to make the stop and therefore the seized evidence should have been suppressed. The Court of Appeals affirmed (2-1). The majority agreed "that a solely race-based suspicion of drug courier status would not pass constitutional muster" but held that in this case the agent "had knowledge, based upon his own experience and upon the intelligence reports he had received from the Los Angeles authorities, that young male members of black Los Angeles gangs were flooding the Kansas City area with cocaine." "To that extent," the majority concluded, race was a legitimate consideration "when coupled with the other factors Hicks relied upon...."[242]

B. THE EQUAL PROTECTION CLAUSE

Some critics contend that stops based on race—even in conjunction with other factors and even if the stops are valid under the Fourth Amendment—constitute racial discrimination under the Equal Protection Clause of the Fourteenth Amendment.

---

[242] In his dissent, Judge Arnold expressed concern about the use of race as a profiling factor but did not contend that it should be prohibited. In his view, the prosecution had failed to present enough evidence that being black actually correlated with a higher risk of drug trafficking. (P. 397.)

Law professor Randall Kennedy is the leading proponent of the theory, although he acknowledges that it is rational for the police to consider race in determining when to make a stop:[243]

"...there are circumstances in which, as a statistical matter, a police officer would be correct in estimating that a man's blackness identifies him as more likely than a similarly situated white person to be involved in criminal wrongdoing. Just as race can signal a heightened risk that a black person will die younger, earn less money, reside farther away from employment opportunities, experience more unpleasant encounters with police, and possess less education than a white person, so, too, can race signal a heightened risk that a black person will commit or has committed certain criminal offenses."[244]

He similarly acknowledges that "...in this context, race is not being used invidiously. It is not being used as a marker to identify people to harm through enslavement, or exclusion, or segregation. Rather, race is being used merely as a signal that facilitates efficient law enforcement" (p. 159).

Nevertheless, Randall Kennedy argues for outlawing race-dependent decisionmaking by police (except when seeking a specific alleged perpetrator) because it imposes a heavy "racial tax" on law-abiding blacks for the sins of others of their race.[245] As he concedes, adopting such a theory would almost certainly have a major detrimental effect on law enforcement.[246] And, ironically, the group most likely to be hurt would be blacks since the principal victims of black crime are other blacks[247] and "blacks far more than whites live in settings that make them particularly vulnerable to robbery, rape, murder, and the overall destruction of social life that occurs in areas in which street crime flourishes."[248] Nearly

---

[243] Kennedy, supra, at 147-64. See also, e.g., Johnson, supra, at 241-50.

[244] Kennedy, supra, at 145. Id. at 159.

[245] Id. at 159.

[246] Id. at 159-61 According to Kennedy, in order "to make up for any diminution in crime control caused by the reform I seek," the "racial tax" should be replaced by an increase in "taxes across the board" to pay for "spending more on other means of enforcement."

[247] See, e.g., Amy Wax, *Race, Wrongs, and Remedies: Group Justice in the 21st Century* [Rowman & Littlefield 2009]: 92

[248] Id. at 74-75.

50% of murder victims are black[249] and 93% of black murder victims are murdered by blacks.[250] In 2008 nearly as many blacks as whites were homicide victims, even though 80% of the population is white, and a black man is approximately six times as likely to be a homicide victim as a white man.[251]

Even critics of "profiling" accept the legitimacy of considering race and ethnicity to protect the public from terrorism, in view of the history of the disproportionate involvement of young Muslim men of Middle Eastern background in terrorist activities. "Nearly all of us," Orlando Patterson observes,[252] "have a civil liberties threshold: Imagine Pakistani madrassa graduates lining up at airport security; race matters in such cases, and need involve no animus."[253]

A similar double standard is approved in a policy statement issued by the Department of Justice.[254] The Department's "Guidance Regarding the Use of Race" asserts that racial profiling in "Traditional" law enforcement (such as traffic stops) "is not merely wrong, but also ineffective" and "is premised on the erroneous assumption that any particular individual of one race or ethnicity is more likely to engage in misconduct than any particular individual of another race or ethnicity." Accordingly, except in the case of a specific suspect description, "Federal law enforcement officers may not use race or ethnicity *to any degree*...." in "Traditional"

---

[249] Federal Bureau of Investigation, "2008 Crime in the United States," September 14, 2009.

[250] Juan Williams, "The Trayvon Martin Tragedies," *Wall Street Journal*, March 27, 2012; David Stout, "Violent Crime Fell Again in 2008, F.B.I. Says," *New York Times*, September 15, 2009.

[251] John R. Lott, Jr., "Reforms that Ignore the Black Victims of Crime," *Cato Unbound*, March 13, 2009. According to the Federal Bureau of Investigation, a young black man being shot to death by another black man is the most "typical" homicide in the United States; Stout, supra.

[252] See William Glaberson, "Racial Profiling May Get Wider Approval by Courts," *New York Times*, September 21, 2001. The article quotes Randall Kennedy: "The events of Sept. 11 are going to make it more difficult to get rid of racial profiling, both at the street level—what police actually do—and at the formal level of the courts."

[253] Orlando Patterson, "The Big Blind," *New York Times*, February 10, 2008. See also Richard Banks, "Racial Profiling and the War on Terror," 155 *University of Pennsylvania Law Review* 173, 175 (2007) ("Many people who condemned racial profiling in the War on Drugs were now convinced that it would be an effective tool in the War on Terror.").

[254] U.S. Department of Justice, Civil Rights Division, *Guidance Regarding the Use of Race by Federal Law Enforcement Agencies* (June 2003, updated July 2008), http://www.justice.gov/crt/split/documents/guidance_on_race.htm.

enforcement. (Italics added.)

But the policy statement then abruptly reverses course and declares that "The above standards do not affect current Federal policy" concerning "National Security and Border Integrity" matters such as terrorist investigations, screening air passengers, and border control. As to these matters, the Guidance endorses—"to the extent permitted by our laws and the Constitution"—the use of race and ethnicity in federal law enforcement. Although the Guidance refers to "the incalculably high stakes involved in such investigations," there is no explanation or suggestion why the use of race is "wrong but also ineffective" in one type of enforcement but yet is rational and effective in another type of enforcement.

According to Randall Kennedy, even though consideration of race in law enforcement is rational, it should nevertheless be forbidden because "[t]aking race into account in a small, marginal, even infinitesimal amount still constitutes racial discrimination."[255] But, contrary to Kennedy's premise, taking race into account clearly does *not* in itself constitute racial discrimination.[256] Indeed, consideration of race is widely accepted—and usually with the strong support of minority groups. For example:

- In the compilation of mountains of economic and social data concerning all aspects of American life.[257]

- In adopting policies to encourage a racially diverse student body, including strategic site selection of new schools, drawing attendance zones, allocating resources for special programs, recruiting students and faculty in a targeted fashion, and tracking enrollments.[258]

---

[255] Kennedy, supra, at 149. Proponents of the theory argue that such stops should be subject to the rigorous "strict scrutiny" standard of review. As the proponents recognize, such scrutiny is generally "fatal" in fact and would have the effect of making any police consideration of race virtually per se invalid. See Sheri Lynn Johnson, "Race and the Decision to Detain a Suspect," 93 *Yale Law Journal* 214, 241-46 (1983).

[256] As shown in Chapter 7, moreover, even the "color-blind" test unsuccessfully urged by the first Justice Harlan in *Plessy v. Ferguson* was narrowly limited to rights conferred by the Citizenship Clauses.

[257] See Chapter 2 *Government Racial Categories* concerning efforts to revise racial categories in the federal census.

[258] Parents Involved v. Seattle School District No. 1, 551 U.S. 701 (2007) (Justice Kennedy concurring). Because the other eight Justices were divided 4-to-4 in the case, Justice Kennedy's concurring opinion is the Court's controlling opinion.

- In the diagnosis and treatment of diseases (such as single-cell anemia and hypertension) particularly prevalent among blacks.
- In tracking comparative achievement levels in reading, math, and writing.[259]
- In designing entrance examinations in order to diminish the adverse impact on black applicants.[260]
- In redrawing voting districts.[261]

Taking race into consideration together with other factors does not demonstrate a discriminatory purpose, and such a purpose (together with a a discriminatory impact) is required for a violation of the Equal Protection Clause.[262] In an effort to satisfy the discriminatory purpose requirement, Randall Kennedy relies on the doctrine that proof of a discriminatory purpose is unnecessary if a law expressly classifies persons on the basis of race or gender.[263] But that doctrine would only apply—if at all—to the few formal profiles that still explicitly include a race factor, and even profiles of that sort would appear to be defensible as a rational response to disproportionate crime statistics. The doctrine concerning express racial classifications would have no bearing on the vast majority of stops that are made by officers on the basis of criteria they have developed on a case-by-case basis. If race is one of several factors relied on to justify such a stop, there is no basis (at least in the absence of extrinsic proof of a harassment purpose) for assuming that an officer's partial reliance on a concededly rational factor was motivated by racial animus.[264]

---

[259] See Chapter 29 *Affirmative Action and the Racial Achievement Gap* and Chapter 33 *Racial Preferences in Admissions.*

[260] See, e.g., Hayden v. County of Nassau, 180 F.3d 42, 48 (2d Cir. 1999): "This desire, in and of itself, however, does not constitute a 'racial classification.'"

[261] A legislature's deliberate consideration of race in redistricting is not an impermissible factor so long as it is just one among other factors; race must be demonstrated to have been the "predominant" purpose. See, e.g., Easley v. Cromartie, 532 U.S. 234, 257 (2001); Bush v. Vera, 517 U.S. 952 (1996) ("Strict scrutiny does not apply merely because redistricting is performed with consciousness of race ... For strict scrutiny to apply, the plaintiffs must prove that other, legitimate districting principles were 'subordinated' to race. ... By that, we mean that race must be 'the predominant factor motivating the legislature's [redistricting] decision.'").

[262] Washington v. Davis, 426 U.S. 229, 239-40 (1976).

[263] See, e.g., Adarand Constructors, Inc. v. Pena, 515 U.S. 200, 213, 227-29 (1995).

[264] See. e.g., United States v. Travis, 62 F.3d 170, 174-76 (6th Cir. 1995).

To summarize:

- Any stop based solely on race is a violation of both the Fourth Amendment and the Equal Protection Clause.
- The reasonableness of other stops under the Fourth Amendment depends on "the totality of the circumstances— the whole picture."
- The Constitution does not prohibit stops based on a particular race in seeking to apprehend a specific alleged criminal who has been identified as belonging to that race.
- Consideration of disproportionate black crime *as one of several factors* in assessing reasonable suspicion is not irrational, is not in itself racist or discriminatory, and does not violate the Equal Protection Clause.

Randall Kennedy is correct that stops impose an unfair "racial tax" on law-abiding blacks "even if the profiling is perfectly rational." That "tax," however, is only one aspect of the larger burden on blacks and whites alike resulting from disproportionate black crime —especially the burden on its victims, who are primarily black. In dealing with minorities, professional police conduct is a high priority. But an even more fundamental solution would be reduction of the crime rates on which the "racial tax" is based.[265]

---

[265] Wax, supra, at 92-93; Bob Herbert, "Too Long Ignored," *New York Times*, August 20, 2010 (...the heroic efforts needed to alleviate it will onot come from the government or the wider American society. This is a job that will require a campaign on the scale of the civil rights movement, and it will have to be initiated by the black community. ...Blacks in America have a long and proud history of overcoming hardship and injustice. It's time to do it again.")

16. RACIAL DISCRIMINATION IN VOTING

Voting, although left largely in the control of the States, is subject to restrictions imposed by several Amendments of the federal Constitution, as well as federal statutes enacted pursuant to those Amendments. In particular, the Fifteenth Amendment prohibits the denial of the right to vote "on account of race, color, or previous condition of servitude" and the Fourteenth Amendment prohibits discrimination in violation of the equal protection of the laws.[266]

These Amendments prohibit two types of voting discrimination: (1) discrimination that *prevents* certain citizens from voting and (2) discrimination *among voters* in the *exercise* of their right to vote.

VOTE PREVENTION

After the Civil War, to prevent blacks from voting, Southern States employed a variety of techniques, including literacy tests, grandfather clauses, property qualifications, "good character" tests, and the requirement that registrants "understand" or "interpret" certain matters. The Court initially declined to intervene. A remarkable example is an opinion by Justice Oliver Wendell Holmes in Giles v. Harris, 189 U.S. 475 (1903), called "the most legally disingenuous analysis in the pages of the U.S. Reports."[267] The Court held (6-3) that, if the Alabama voting system was a fraud on the Constitution as the plaintiffs alleged, then adding other voters to the fraudulent lists would make the Court a party to the unlawful scheme. But in later cases the Court held several of the exclusionary techniques unconstitutional. Thus, for example, grandfather clauses were invalidated in

---

[266]Other pertinent Amendments: the Nineteenth Amendment extending the right to vote to women; the Twenty-Fourth Amendment prohibiting poll taxes in federal elections; and the Twenty-Sixth Amendment fixing 18 as the voting age.

[267] Richard Pildes, "Democracy, Anti-Democracy, and the Canon," 17 *Constitutional Commentary* 295 (2000)). See also Michael Klarman, *From Jim Crow to Civil Rights: The Supreme Court and the Struggle for Racial Equality* [Oxford 2004]: 9, 135-42.

Guinn v. United States, 238 U.S. 347 (1915); the white primary was outlawed in Smith v. Allwright, 321 U.S. 649 (1944); and redrawing a city's boundaries to exclude blacks from voting was condemned in Gomillion v. Lightfoot, 364 U.S. 339 (1960).

Nevertheless, blacks in many states continued to be effectively disenfranchised. The Court narrowly interpreted the Fifteenth Amendment, refusing to invalidate laws that had been adopted to block black voting but were race-neutral on their face.[268] And, even when injunctions were obtained against discriminatory devices, some states merely switched to other devices that were not precisely covered by the decrees.

Frustration with the case-by-case approach and the South's continued defiance led to enactment of the Voting Rights Act of 1965, the landmark legislation summarized in the next chapter. Because its requirements for establishing a violation are considerably less rigorous than those of the Equal Protection Clause, the Voting Rights Act has largely replaced the Constitution as the governing standard for minority voting claims.

VOTE DILUTION

Even when citizens are not prevented from voting, there may still be voting discrimination in violation of the Equal Protection Clause if the votes of some are diluted by the government's election system.

One type of dilution—giving greater weight to voters in less populous districts in statewide elections—was recognized in Reynolds v. Sims, 377 U.S. 533 (1964), establishing under the Equal Protection Clause the "one person, one vote" rule.

In a case arising under the Voting Rights Act rather than the Equal Protection Clause, Allen v. State Board of Elections, 393 U.S. 544 (1969), the Court recognized a different type of voting dilution—the use of at-large voting and multi-member districts to dilute the power of black voters to elect the candidate of their choice.

---

[268] See, e.g., Williams v. Mississippi, 170 U.S. 213 (1898), holding that an amendment to the Mississippi constitution did not, on its face, discriminate on the basis of race by (1) making ability to read and understand any section of the United States Constitution a necessary qualification to a legal voter and (2) making the ability to read and write a necessary qualification for a grand or petit juror.

In holding that §5 applied even to a change from district voting to at-large voting for county supervisors, the Court declared (p. 569):

"The right to vote can be affected by a dilution of voting power as well as by an absolute prohibition on casting a ballot. See Reynolds v. Sims, 377 U.S. 533, 555 (1964). Voters who are members of a racial minority might well be in the majority in one district, but in a decided minority in the county as a whole. This type of change could therefore nullify their ability to elect the candidate of their choice just as would prohibiting some of them from voting."

In that brief paragraph, extending the concept of "dilution" of an individual's vote (in the context of its "one person, one vote" decisions) to the "dilution" of influence of a racial bloc, the Court approved a major expansion of the statute.[269]

At-large voting (rather than voting for a single representative in a limited area) and multi-member districts (districts in which two or more representatives are elected by all the voters in each district) tend to minimize the voting strength of minority groups by enabling the political majority in the district to elect *all* representatives. For example, if a city is sixty percent white and forty percent black, and if each of the two racial groups generally votes for candidates of its race, the result of an at-large election in which black and white candidates compete for each of five city council positions would be that the white candidate would likely prevail in every election, with about sixty percent of the vote.[270] By contrast, if a single representative is elected by the voters in a smaller subdistrict, a minority group that constitutes a majority in that more limited area is better able to elect a representative of their choosing.

So far as the Equal Protection Clause is concerned, however, the use of at-large voting and multi-member districts is not in itself forbidden. In Whitcomb v. Chavis, 403 U.S. 124 (1971), the Court admonished that vote dilution under the Constitution cannot become "a mere euphemism for political defeat at the polls."

---

[269] Andrew Kull, *The Color-Blind Constitution* [Harvard 1992]: 214-15.

[270] T. Alexander Aleinikoff and Samuel Issacharoff, "Race and Redistricting: Drawing Constitutional Lines after Shaw v. Reno," 92 *Michigan Law Review* 588, 589-90 (1993-94).

Rejecting a constitutional challenge in that case, the Court held (5-4) that "The mere fact that one interest group or another concerned with the outcome of Marion County [Indiana] elections has found itself outvoted and without legislative seats of its own provides no basis for invoking constitutional remedies where, as here, there is no indication that this segment of the population is being denied access to the political system."

But in White v. Regester, 412 U.S. 755 (1973), the Court affirmed a lower court decision finding that a multimember district violated equal protection because it "invidiously excluded Mexican-Americans from effective participation in political life, specifically in the election of representatives to the Texas House of Representatives." *White*, in light of the *Whitcomb* decision, left in doubt what standard was to be applied in determining the validity of at-large voting and multi-member districts.

That question was addressed more specifically in City of Mobile, Alabama v. Bolden, 446 U.S. 55 (1980), concerning an at-large system used by Mobile, Alabama to elect members of the city commission. The plurality opinion of Justice Stewart (joined by Burger, Powell, and Rehnquist) held that such election systems do not violate the Equal Protection Clause, even if there is proof of a discriminatory impact, unless there is proof of a discriminatory purpose—in short, the same standard applied to discrimination in employment, housing, and other contexts. "To prove such a purpose," the plurality stated, "it is not enough to show that the group allegedly discriminated against has not elected representatives in proportion to its numbers. ... A plaintiff must prove that the disputed plan was 'conceived or operated as [a] purposeful devic[e] to further racial ...discrimination'...." (p. 66). By a 6-3 vote, the Court (Stevens and Blackmun concurring) found no constitutional violation (White, Brennan, and Marshall dissented).

The *City of Mobile* decision created a firestorm in Congress, leading to enactment of the 1982 amendment of the Voting Rights Act. The amendment specifically prohibits election systems that dilute the voting power of a racial minority and eliminates the need for proof of discriminatory purpose in challenging an election system.

Voting strength of a minority group may also be diluted by *gerrymandering* district lines—by in effect placing voters in particular districts on the basis of how they are likely to vote. Racial gerrymandering may be employed either to limit or to increase minority representation.[271] Racial gerrymandering to limit minority representation is patently illegal under both the Voting Rights Act and the Equal Protection Clause. Racial gerrymandering to increase minority representation to facilitate the election of minority candidates—a form of affirmative action—is discussed in Chapter 37.

---

[271] Gerrymandering, in addition to use for racial objectives, is more commonly employed for political advantage. Political gerrymandering may involve, for example, drawing the lines of a district to provide a safe seat for an incumbent or drawing lines on a statewide basis to retain or increase control of a state legislature or congressional delegation. Efforts to impose judicial controls on political gerrymandering have so far been unsuccessful. See, e.g., Vieth v. Jubelirer, 541 U.S. 267 (2004).

17. THE FEDERAL VOTING RIGHTS ACT

The Voting Rights Act of 1965 (VRA) was upheld in South Carolina v. Katzenbach, 383 U.S. 301 (1966) (8-1), and Katzenbach v. Morgan, 384 U.S. 641 (1966) (7-2).

In the *South Carolina* case, the Supreme Court summarized the extensive legislative history of the Act (p. 309):

"First: Congress felt itself confronted by an insidious and pervasive evil which had been perpetuated in certain parts of our country through unremitting and ingenious defiance of the Constitution. Second: Congress concluded that the unsuccessful remedies which it had prescribed in the past would have to be replaced by sterner and more elaborate measures in order to satisfy the clear commands of the Fifteenth Amendment."

The Court concluded "that the portions of the Voting Rights Act properly before us are a valid means for carrying out the commands of the Fifteenth Amendment" (p. 337) and therefore constituted "appropriate legislation" under §2 of the Amendment.

When it was first enacted, the VRA was to expire in five years and was limited to prohibiting discrimination in voting rights. §2 provided that "No voting qualification or prerequisite to voting, or standard, practice, or procedure shall be imposed or applied by any State or political subdivision to deny or abridge the right of any citizen of the United States to vote on account of race or color."

The VRA was originally aimed at particular States (primarily in the South) that had a long history of racially discriminatory voting practices. §4 outlawed the use of any "test or device" restricting the opportunity to register and vote by any "covered jurisdiction."[272] The

---

[272] The VRA's definition of a "test or device" included such requirements as being able to pass a literacy test, establishing that he or she had good moral character, or having another registered voter vouch for his or her qualifications.

term "covered jurisdiction" was defined as any State or any political subdivision of a State in which (1) any such "test or device" was employed on November 1, 1964, and (2) less than 50 percent of the persons of voting age residing therein were registered on November 1, 1964, or less than 50 percent of such persons voted in the presidential election of November 1964. This resulted in the following States becoming, in their entirety, "covered jurisdictions" under the original Act: Alabama, Alaska, Georgia, Louisiana, Mississippi, South Carolina, and Virginia. In addition, certain political subdivisions (usually counties) in four other States (Arizona, Hawaii, Idaho, and North Carolina) were covered.

§5 provided that all "covered jurisdictions"—unless they first obtained preclearance from either the Attorney General or the District Court for the District of Columbia—were prohibited from implementing any change in "voting qualification or prerequisite to voting, or standard, practice, or procedure with respect to voting different from that in force or effect on November 1, 1964." The scope of §5, however, was greatly expanded by the Supreme Court's 1969 decision in Allen v. State Board of Elections, 393 U.S. 544 (1969), which held (7-2) "...that Congress intended to reach any state enactment which altered the election law of a covered State in even a minor way," and, even more significantly, that §5 encompassed any dilution of voting power affecting a minority's "ability to elect the candidate of their choice" (pp. 555, 569).[273] This made the preclearance requirement applicable, not only to practices that might prevent blacks from voting, but also to any change that "would lead to a retrogression in the position of racial minorities with respect to their effective exercise of the electoral franchise."[274] And the burden of proof is on a covered jurisdiction to demonstrate that

---

[273] On that basis, the Court held that §5 preclearance was required for each of the proposed actions in *Allen*: changing from district to at-large voting for county supervisors; making the office of county superintendent of education appointive rather than elective; barring any voter in a primary election from thereafter running as an independent candidate in the general election; and distributing a bulletin outlining new procedures for casting write-in votes.

[274] Beer v. United States, 425 U.S. 130 (1976).

the change does not have that effect.[275]

§5 thus "...placed political life in those jurisdictions under a form of administrative receivership...."[276] Changes subject to §5 range from just moving a polling place or keeping polls open an hour longer to redrawing district lines after a census. The preclearance requirement, moreover, applies to every political subdivision in a covered State, no matter how small.

In *South Carolina v. Katzenbach*, although voting to uphold the constitutionality of the rest of the VRA, Justice Black objected that "Section 5, by providing that some of the States cannot pass state laws or adopt state constitutional amendments without first being compelled to beg federal authorities to approve their policies, so distorts our constitutional structure of government as to render any distinction drawn in the Constitution between state and federal power almost meaningless." (383 U.S. at 358-59.) Other Justices have expressed similar misgivings about the constitutionality of §5.[277]

In 1970, Congress renewed the VRA for another five years, suspended the use of literacy tests on a nationwide basis, and added November 1968 as an alternative coverage date for determining the maintenance of a "test or device" and the levels of voter registration and electoral participation.

A 1975 amendment extended the VRA to 1982 and expanded its scope to include voting discrimination against members of "language minority groups," defined as "persons who are

---

[275] If a state or subdivision can demonstrate that no "test or device" has been used for a specified number of years for the purpose or effect of denying or abridging the right to vote on account of race or color, a covered jurisdiction may "bailout" of the preclearance requirement by obtaining a declaratory judgment in the District Court for the District of Columbia. The number of years is either seventeen (for jurisdictions covered by the original 1965 Act) or ten (for jurisdictions covered by the 1975 amendment of the Act).

[276] Samuel Issacharoff, "Is Section 5 of the Voting Rights Act a Victim of Its Own Success," 104 *Columbia Law Review* 1710 (2004). See also Richard Pildes, "The Future of Voting Rights Policy: From Anti-Discrimination to the Right to Vote," 49 *Howard Law Journal* 741 (2006) ("...the Act directly put (and continues to put) the election systems in certain parts of the country under what is, essentially, a form of federal receivership.")

[277] See, e.g., Justice Harlan in Allen v. State Board of Elections, 393 U.S. 544, 586, n.4 (1969); Justice Powell in Georgia v. Ashcroft, 539 U.S. 461, 545 (2003); Justices Powell, Rehnquist and Stewart in City of Rome v. United States, 446 U.S. 156, 200-06, 209-21 (1980); and Justice Thomas in Northwest Austin Municipal Utility District No. One v. Holder, 557 U.S. 193 (2009), discussed infra.

American Indian, Asian American, Alaskan Natives or of Spanish heritage." The 1975 amendment also made two changes in the coverage formula: (1) It added November 1972 as an alternative date for determining the maintenance of a test or device and the levels of voter registration and electoral participation. (2) The 1965 definition of "test or device" was expanded to include the practice of providing any election information, including ballots, only in English in states or political subdivisions where members of a single language minority constituted more than five percent of the citizens of voting age.

As a result of the changes made in the 1970 and 1975 amendments, the preclearance requirement was extended to political subdivisions in a number of additional states outside the Deep South, including Alaska, Arizona, and Texas in their entirety, and one or more counties or townships in California, Florida, Michigan, New Hampshire, New York, and South Dakota.

Today 16 states in whole or part remain subject to the VRA preclearance requirement.

Efforts began in Congress in early 1981 to renew the VRA once again. The focus of controversy became the issue of the appropriate standard of proof for identifying practices that "deny or abridge" the right to vote under §2. Supreme Court decisions had held that establishing a violation of the Equal Protection Clause required proof of discriminatory *purpose* in addition to discriminatory *effects*, and the *City of Mobile* decision held that the same standard is applicable to constitutional voting claims. Civil rights groups, claiming that the purpose test imposed an unduly burdensome litigation obstacle, argued that the VRA should be amended to adopt a more lenient "results" standard. Supporters of the purpose test countered that the "results" standard would lead to the establishment of racial quotas and proportional representation in elections.

Finally a compromise was reached that in effect endorsed "results" as the primary criterion, and the VRA was renewed in 1982 for 25 more years. As amended, §2 is violated when, based on "the totality of circumstances," the political process is "not equally open to participation" by members of a protected class and they "have less opportunities than other members of the electorate to participate in the electoral process and to elect representatives of their choice." §2(a) further provides that "The extent to which members of a protected class have been elected to office [is] one circumstance which may be considered" in evaluating "the totality of circumstances." This test, it should be noted, applies nationwide and to jurisdictions where minorities have never been disfranchised and have long held public office.

In 2006, it was again proposed to renew the VRA (then due to expire in 2007). Opponents contended that black voter registration and participation rates, along with the growth of minority officeholders, demonstrated that blacks were no longer disfranchised and that therefore the VRA's preclearance requirements were no longer necessary or appropriate to protect voting rights. Both the Senate and House committee reports accompanying the legislation acknowledged that "[I]n seven of the covered states, African-Americans are registered at a rate higher than the national average;" that "[I]n California, Georgia, Mississippi, North Carolina, and Texas, black registration and turnout in the 2004 election ... was higher than that for whites;" that "As of 2000, more than 9,000 African-Americans have been elected to office, an increase from the 1,469 officials who held office in 1970;" and that "[T]he number of African-American elected officials serving in the six original six States covered by the temporary provisions of the Voting Rights Act ... increased by approximately 1000 percent since 1965."[278]

Despite those fundamentally changed circumstances, Congress voted to renew the VRA for an additional 25 years, finding that "racially polarized voting" still continued. Reliance was also placed on the large number of preclearance applications to the Justice Department and anecdotal reports of alleged voting abuses in some of the covered jurisdictions.[279]

---

[278] Sen. Rep. No. 109-25, at 8; H.R. Rep No. 109-178, at 18.

[279] In renewing the Act in 2006, Congress also tightened the §5 "retrogression" test by providing that preclearance should be denied to any redistricting plan or voting law that "has the purpose of or will have the effect of diminishing the ability of any citizens of the United States on account of race or color [or language minority status] ... to elect their preferred candidates of choice...." Congress intended this revision to overturn the Supreme Court's decision in Georgia v. Ashcroft, 539 U.S. 461 (2003), which redefined the §5 "retrogression" standard to permit redistricting plans that opted for broader minority influence across a range of districts or in the legislature as a whole, as opposed to maintaining minorities' ability to elect their candidates of choice.

The constitutionality of the 2006 renewal was challenged in Northwest Austin Municipal Utility District No. One v. Holder, 557 U.S. 193 (2009), by a small Texas utility district with an elected board. The district, with no record of ever having engaged in any racial discrimination, filed suit under §4(a) seeking to "bailout" from the preclearance requirement or, in the alternative, contending that §5 is unconstitutional on the ground that the presumption of illegal voting practices could no longer be justified in view of the significant changed circumstances since the enactment of the VRA in 1965.[280] By devising what critics have called a "disingenuous" interpretation" of §5,[281] the Court (8-1) held that the statute authorized the plaintiff to seek "bailout" relief, thereby making it unnecessary for the Court to reach the plaintiff's claim that §5 is unconstitutional. Justice Thomas concurred in the judgment on the ground "that §5 exceeds Congress' power to enforce the Fifteenth Amendment."

Although avoiding a ruling on the constitutional issue, all of the other eight Justices (including those on both sides of the usual ideological divide), made clear their deep concern with the issue. They joined Chief Justice Roberts' opinion for the Court, stating that §5 "imposes current burdens and must be justified by current needs," and that "The statute's coverage formula is based on data that is now more than 35 years old, and there is considerable evidence that it fails to account for current political conditions." For example, the Court noted: When the VRA was first passed, registration of voting-age whites ran roughly 50 percentage points or more ahead of black registration in many covered States. Today, the registration gap between white and black voters is in single digits in the covered States; indeed, in some of those States, blacks now register and vote at higher rates than whites, and the racial gap in voter registration and turnout is lower in the States originally covered by §5 than it is nationwide. Many of the pre-VRA barriers to registration and turnout by minority voters have been eliminated. And minority candidates hold office at unprecedented levels.

---

[280] See, e.g., Sam Roberts, "2008 Surge in Black Voters Nearly Erased Racial Gap," *New York Times*, July 21, 2009 (younger blacks voted in greater proportions than whites for the first time and black women turned out at a higher rate than any other racial, ethnic and gender group).

[281] See, e.g., Richard Hasen, "Disenfranchised No More," *New York Times*, November 18, 2011.

The Court provocatively added that "The Act's preclearance require-ments and its coverage formula raise serious constitutional questions...." and concluded stating: "More than 40 years ago, this Court concluded that 'exceptional conditions' prevailing in certain parts of the country justified extraordinary legislation otherwise unfamiliar to our federal system. .... In part due to the success of that legislation, we are now a very different Nation. Whether conditions continue to justify such legis-lation is a difficult constitutional question we do not answer today."

Subsequently that question was directly addressed by the Court of Appeals for the District of Columbia Circuit in *Shelby County, Alabama v. Holder* (C.A.D.C. 2012). In a 2-to-1 decision, the court up-held the constitutionality of §5, rejecting the claim that the preclear-ance burdens imposed by VRA §5 are no longer justified in view of the significant changes pointed out by the Supreme Court. According to the *Shelby County* majority, "Congress drew reasonable conclu-sions from the extensive evidence it gathered" and "In this context, we owe much deference to the considered judgment of the people's elected representatives." The dissenting judge, Stephen Williams, concluded: "Whether the criteria are viewed in absolute terms (are they adequate in themselves to justify the extraordinary burdens of § 5?) or in relative ones (do they draw a rational line between covered and uncovered jurisdictions?), they seem to me defective."

It appears almost certain that the *Shelby County* case will be reviewed by the Supreme Court.[282]

---

[282] A similar issue is presented in an action filed in February 2012 by South Carolina challenging the Justice Department's blocking of the state's recently enacted voter identification law.

PART IV

RACE DISCRIMINATION BY PRIVATE ACTORS

18. THE STATE ACTION REQUIREMENT

The Fourteenth Amendment forbids "any *State* [to] deprive any person of life, liberty, or property, without due process of law [or] deny to any person within its jurisdiction the equal protection of the laws." The Fifteenth Amendment similarly forbids "any *State*" to deny citizens the right to vote "on account of race, color, or previous condition of servitude." (Italics added.).

In United States v. Cruikshank, 92 U.S. 542 (1876), involving the infamous Colfax Massacre in which a band of armed whites slaughtered fifty-nine blacks, the ringleaders of the attack were convicted under the 1870 Civil Rights Act for conspiring to prevent or hinder the free exercise of rights granted or secured by the Constitution or laws of the United States. The Supreme Court, in a much-criticized decision, unanimously dismissed all sixteen counts of the indictment.[1] Some of the counts were dismissed on the ground that they only alleged conduct by private individuals and therefore did not charge a violation of federal rights. The Fourteenth Amendment, the Court stated, "adds nothing to the rights of one citizen as against

---

[1] See Charles Lane, *The Day Freedom Died: The Colfax Massacre, the Supreme Court, and the Betrayal of Reconstruction* [Henry Holt 2008]: 244-47; Harold Hyman and William Wiecek, *Equal Justice under Law: Constitutional Development 1835-1875* [Harper 1982]: 489; Carl Swisher, *American Constitutional Development* [Houghton Mifflin 1943]: 342-55.

another. It simply furnishes an additional guaranty against any encroachment by the States upon the fundamental rights which belong
to every citizen as a member of society." According to the Court, although the Amendment prohibits a State from depriving any person
of life, liberty, or property without due process of law, "The only obligation resting upon the United States is to see that the States do not
deny the right. This the amendment guarantees, but no more. The
power of the national government is limited to the enforcement of
this guaranty." (Pp. 554-55.)

Seven years later, in its landmark decision in the Civil Rights Cases,
109 U.S. 3 (1883), the Court held that the Fourteenth Amendment
(and, by necessary implication, the Fifteenth Amendment as well) applies only to "state action" and does not apply to "private" conduct. The
case involved the constitutionality of the Civil Rights Act of 1875, prohibiting racial discrimination in public accommodations, including
common carriers, hotels, theatres, and other places of public amusement. The Court (8-1)) found the Act unconstitutional, holding that
it outlawed practices beyond the scope of both the Thirteenth and
Fourteenth Amendments.[2] Justice John Marshall Harlan dissented.[3]

The Court declared that the Fourteenth Amendment does not
apply to the "[i]ndividual invasion of individual rights" but instead
prohibits "state legislation, and state action of every kind" that violates the Amendment's commands and further authorizes Congress
to enforce the Amendment by appropriate legislation:

> "To enforce what? To enforce the prohibition. To adopt appro-
> priate legislation for correcting the effects of such prohibited
> state law and state acts, and thus to render them effectually
> null, void, and innocuous. This is the legislative power con-
> ferred upon congress, and this is the whole of it. It does not in-
> vest congress with power to legislate upon subjects which are

---

[2] The decisions in *Cruikshank* and the *Civil Rights Cases* are reviewed in greater detail
in Chapter 20 *The Reconstruction Civil Rights* Acts.

[3] While not denying that the Fourteenth Amendment required "state action," Justice
Harlan contended that the requirement was met by the states' regulation of the public accommodation companies: "In every material sense applicable to the practical
enforcement of the Fourteenth Amendment, railroad corporations, keepers of inns,
and managers of places of public amusement are agents or instrumentalities of the
State, because they are charged with duties to the public, and are amenable, in respect
of their dues and functions, to government regulation." (109 U.S. at 58.)

within the domain of state legislation; but to provide modes of relief against state legislation, or state action, of the kind referred to. It does not authorize congress to create a code of municipal law for the regulation of private rights...." (P. 11.)

As we shall see, however, the line between "state action " and "private" conduct is often far from clear. Conduct that might otherwise be regarded as "private" can be classified as "state action"—and therefore subject to the Constitution—if examination shows it to be in fact governmental in nature.

For example, Smith v. Allwright, 321 U.S. 649 (1944), one of the *White Primary Cases,*[4] involved efforts of the Texas Democratic Party to exclude blacks from participating in political primary elections. The Party claimed that it was a private association entitled to determine its own rules of eligibility. The Supreme Court (8-1) rejected that argument, holding that running an election for government office was "state action" within the meaning of the Fifteenth Amendment and must comply with the Constitution. According to the Court: "If the state requires a certain electoral procedure, prescribes a general election ballot made up of party nominees so chosen and limits the choice of the electorate in general elections for state offices, practically speaking, to those whose names appear on such a ballot, it endorses, adopts and enforces the discrimination against Negroes, practiced by a party entrusted by Texas law with the determination of the qualifications of participants in the primary" (p. 663).

A purportedly private organization may also be found to engage in state action if there is such a close relationship between the organization and the state that the private and public aspects are substantially intertwined. Thus, in Burton v. Wilmington Parking Authority, 365 U.S. 715 (1961), the Court held that a restaurant on leased premises in a parking building owned and operated by the city could not exclude blacks. It was emphasized that the restaurant was an integral part of the complex, that the restaurant and the parking facilities complemented each other, that the parking authority had regulatory power over the lessee, and that the financial success of the restaurant benefited the governmental agency.

---

[4] See also Nixon v. Herndon, 276 U.S. 536 (1927); Terry v. Adams, 345 U.S. 461 (1953).

However, the state action requirement is not met merely by showing that an otherwise private entity receives some governmental benefit or service. Nor is the state action requirement satisfied merely by showing that the otherwise private entity is to some extent state-regulated.

For example, Moose Lodge No. 107 v. Irvis, 407 U.S. 163 (1972), rejected a claim that a private club's state liquor license barred the club from engaging in racial discrimination. The license required the club to make such physical alterations in its premises as the state liquor board might require, file a list of the names and addresses of its members and employees, and keep extensive financial records. In addition, the board was authorized to inspect the premises at any time when patrons, guests, or members are present. The Court (6-3) concluded that "the operation of the regulatory scheme enforced by the [board] does not sufficiently implicate the State in the discriminatory guest policies of Moose Lodge to make the latter 'state action' within the ambit of the Equal Protection Clause of the Fourteenth Amendment." The Court stated that it:

> "...has never held, of course, that discrimination by an otherwise private entity would be violative of the Equal Protection Clause if the private entity receives any sort of benefit or service at all from the State, or if it is subject to state regulation in any degree whatever. Since state-furnished services include such necessities of life as electricity, water, and police and fire protection, such a holding would utterly emasculate the distinction between private as distinguished from state conduct.... Our holdings indicate that where the impetus for the discrimination is private, the State must have 'significantly involved itself with invidious discriminations,' ... in order for the discriminatory action to fall within the ambit of the constitutional prohibition." (P. 173.)[5]

---

[5] The *Moose Lodge* decision was recently applied by the Second Circuit Court of Appeals in dismissing a claim under 42 U.S.C. §1983 that several New York City nightclubs discriminated against men by charging them more than women for admission on "Ladies' Nights." The court relied on two grounds: (1) a liquor license is insufficient to establish state action; and (2) the state's liquor licensing laws did not cause the nightclubs to hold "Ladies' Nights" or charge lower prices to women. Roy Den Hollander v. Copacabana Nightclub, 624 F.3d 30 (2d Cir. 2010).

Nor is the state action requirement satisfied by just showing that the state provided financial assistance or tax benefits. For example, in Rendell-Baker v. Kohn, 457 U.S. 830 (1982), a private school for "problem" students referred by public institutions was heavily regulated by the State and received almost all of its operating budget from public funds. When the school fired a teacher for making political speeches, she claimed that her dismissal violated the First Amendment. The Supreme Court, however, held (7-2) that government funding, by itself, is not a basis for finding state action and that the Constitution did not apply without a showing that the State was involved in the dismissal, either through coercion or encouragement of the private entity to engage in the challenged conduct:. The Court concluded "... that the school's receipt of public funds does not make the discharge decisions acts of the State. The school ... is not fundamentally different from many private corporations whose business depends primarily on contracts to build roads, bridges, dams, ships, or submarines for the government. Acts of such private contractors do not become acts of the government by reason of their significant or even total engagement in performing public contracts." (Pp. 839-40.)

The "public function" theory of state action was introduced in Marsh v. Alabama, 326 U.S. 501 (1946), holding (5-3) that a company-owned town could not exclude Jehovah's Witnesses who wished to distribute literature there. The Court did "not agree that the corporation's property interests settle the question," for "[t]he more an owner, for his advantage, opens up his property for use by the public in general, the more do his rights become circumscribed by the statutory and constitutional rights of those who use it." The Court concluded that, "...balanc[ing] the Constitutional rights of owners of property against those of the people to enjoy freedom of press and religion, as we must here, we remain mindful of the fact that the latter occupy a preferred position." (Pp. 505-06.)

At issue in Evans v. Newton, 382 U.S. 296 (1966), was a testamentary trust that had created a park in Macon, Georgia, named the city as trustee, and required the park to be used by whites only. Although private trustees replaced the city as trustee, the Court held that the park could not be operated on a racially restrictive basis because the record showed that there had been no change in the city's maintenance of the park. But, as an alternative ground, the majority relied on the "public function" rationale: "A park ... is more like a fire department or police department that traditionally serves the community. Mass recreation through the use of parks is plainly in the public domain ...; and state courts that aid private parties to perform that public function on a segregated basis implicate the State in conduct proscribed by the Fourteenth Amendment. ... [T]he predominant character and purpose of this park are municipal." (Pp. 301-02.)

The dissent (by the second Justice John Marshall Harlan) attacked the majority's public function rationale as "vague," "amorphous," and "far-reaching." As the dissent pointed out, acceptance of the theory could be as readily applied to privately owned schools and colleges as well as "privately owned orphanages, libraries, garbage collection companies, detective agencies, and a host of other functions commonly regarded as nongovernmental though paralleling fields of governmental activity...." (p. 322).

Although *Marsh* has not been explicitly overruled, it is now of questionable status in light of the Court's later decisions.

Relying on *Marsh*, the Court in Amalgamated Food Employees Union Local 590 v. Logan Valley Plaza, 391 U.S. 308 (1968), held that a privately owned shopping center could not exclude striking laborers from picketing a store within the center. But the *Logan Valley* holding was sharply limited four years later in Lloyd Corp. v. Tanner, 407 U.S. 551 (1972), and was ultimately overruled in Hudgens v. National Labor Relations Board, 424 U.S. 507 (1976), concluding that the First Amendment does not provide a right to use a privately owned shopping center for speech.[6]

Jackson v. Metropolitan Edison Co., 419 U.S, 345 (1974), involved an action against a privately owned utility licensed and regulated by a state public utilities commission. It was claimed that the company's termination of the plaintiff's electric service constituted state action because the utility "provides an essential public service required to be supplied on a

---

[6] In PruneYard Shopping Center v. Robins, 447 U.S. 74 (1980), the Court distinguished *Hudgens* in holding that the Federal Constitution was not violated by a state constitutional provision providing a state right of access to shopping centers for speech purposes.

reasonably continuous basis by [state law] and hence performs a 'public function.'" Rejecting that claim, the Court (7-2) effectively limited the scope of *Marsh* to a private company's exercise "of some power delegated to it by the State which is traditionally associated with sovereignty." To hold otherwise, the Court held, "invites the expansion of this limited line of cases into a broad principle that all businesses 'affected with a public interest' are state actors in all their actions."[7]

---

[7] The Court reaffirmed the "carefully confined bounds" of the public function doctrine in Flagg Bros., Inc. v. Brooks, 436 U.S. 149 (1978).

19. APPLYING *SHELLEY V. KRAEMER*

The Supreme Court's decision in Shelley v. Kraemer, 334 U.S. 1 (1948), remains a kind of "wild card" in the law governing the state action requirement. Over sixty years later, the decision and its potential ramifications continue be a subject of argument and speculation.

In *Shelley*, black purchasers contracted with white sellers to buy homes in violation of racially restrictive covenants. The restrictive covenants, providing that the houses could only be occupied by Caucasians, were part of an agreement that had been executed by owners of properties in the neighborhood. The blacks were willing purchasers with adequate finances and the white owners were willing sellers. However, before the sales could be completed, owners of the neighboring properties (which also were subject to the covenants in the agreement) sued in the state courts to enjoin the sales. The state courts, treating the controversy as only a private dispute and therefore not subject to the Equal Protection Clause of the Fourteenth Amendment, enforced the restrictive covenants and enjoined the sales.

The Supreme Court reversed (6-0, Reed, Jackson, and Rutledge not participating) in an opinion by Chief Justice Vinson.[8] The Court recognized that, "So long as the purposes of those agreements are effectuated by voluntary adherence to their terms, it would appear clear that there has been no action by the State and the provisions of the Amendment have not been violated." But here, the Court emphasized, the purposes of the agreements were secured only by the state courts' enforcement of the restrictions:

> "We have no doubt that there has been state action in these cases in the full and complete sense of the phrase. The undisputed facts disclose that the petitioners were willing purchasers of

---

[8] In a companion case, the Court held that District of Columbia courts could not enforce racial covenants even though the Fourteenth Amendment is not applicable to the federal government. Hurd v. Hodge, 334 U.S. 24 (1948). The Court stated that such enforcement would violate the Civil Rights Act and would also be contrary to the public policy of the United States.

properties upon which they desired to establish homes. The owners of the properties were willing sellers; and contracts of sale were accordingly consummated. It is clear that, but for the active intervention of the state courts, supported by the full panoply of state power, the petitioners would have been free to occupy the properties in question without restraint."

The decision, if it were given its broadest interpretation, would—without more—establish a state action connection in a wide variety of matters now generally regarded as "private" and beyond constitutional protection. The role of government is so omnipresent in society—and, in particular, the reliance on government to enforce contracts and other property rights is so great—that arguably almost any private choice or transaction could be converted into an exercise of state action.

In Barrows v. Jackson, 346 U.S. 249 (1953), relying on *Shelley*, the Court held (6-1) that the Fourteenth Amendment also precluded an action for *damages* by a white homeowner against another white homeowner for selling to a black purchaser in violation of a racial covenant. The majority noted that permitting damage judgments would deter prospective sellers from selling to non-Caucasians. The only dissenter was the author of the *Shelley* opinion, Chief Justice Vinson, who contended that, unlike the innocent black purchaser in *Shelley*, the white homeowner who had agreed to the racial covenant lacked the requisite standing to claim the protection of the Fourteenth Amendment.

In Batson v. Kentucky, 476 U.S. 79 (1986), the Court applied the *Shelley* rationale to a prosecutor's use of "peremptory challenges" (requests to remove particular members of a proposed jury panel without the need to show cause for the removal). The Court held (7-2) that, if a prosecutor used peremptory challenges to exclude blacks from the jury in a criminal action against a black defendant, the prosecutor could be required to justify his peremptory challenges on "neutral" non-racial grounds. Later decisions expanded the *Batson* holding to apply to peremptory challenges of black jurors by *defense* attorneys in criminal cases and by attorneys for both plaintiffs and defendants in civil cases. *Batson* has also been extended to other ethnic minorities as well as women.

Evans v. Abney, 396 U.S. 435 (1970), was a sequel to the Court's decision in *Evans v. Newton* (discussed in Chapter 18). At issue was a state court ruling that approved reversion of the title to the donated park to the donor's heirs because the racial restriction in the donor's will had been blocked on constitutional grounds. This ruling, the Court held (6-2), did not constitute state discrimination under the Fourteenth Amendment. The Court found this case "easily distinguishable from [*Shelley*], where we held unconstitutional state judicial action which had affirmatively enforced a private scheme of discrimination against Negroes," because the prior decision "...eliminated all discrimination against Negroes in the park by eliminating the park itself, and the termination of the park was a loss shared equally by the white and Negro citizens of Macon."[9] Justices Douglas and Brennan dissented.

The scope of the *Shelley* doctrine was sharply contested in the "sit-in" cases of the 1960s. In many instances, when a "white-only" restaurant called the police to evict demonstrators protesting the restaurant's racial policy, the demonstrators were arrested and convicted of trespassing—presenting the question: Does the *Shelley* rationale bar enforcement of these trespass laws against persons excluded from private property when the exclusion by the restaurant owner is based on racial grounds?

That question remains undecided by the Supreme Court. In nearly all of the sit-in cases, the convictions were set aside without relying on *Shelley*. Garner v. Louisiana, 368 U.S. 157, 173-74 (1961), reversed the trespass convictions on the ground that there was no evidentiary support for the state's claim that the defendants were guilty of "disturbing the peace." In Peterson v. City of Greenville,

---

[9] Pennsylvania v. Board of Directors of Trusts, 353 U.S. 230 (1957), involved a will, probated in 1831, setting up a trust for a school solely for "poor white male orphans." The will named the City of Philadelphia as trustee; subsequently, a "Board of Directors of City Trusts," composed of city officials and persons named by local courts, was established to administer the trust and the college. When a group of black applicants were denied admission to the school on the basis of race, pursuant to the restriction in the will, the state court refused to order admission. Without any reference to *Shelley*, the Supreme Court reversed per curiam: "The Board which operates Girard College is an agency of the State. [Therefore,] even though the Board was acting as trustee, its refusal to admit [petitioners] was discrimination by the State." After that ruling, the state courts substituted private trustees to carry out Girard's will, and the Supreme Court denied certiorari.

373 U.S. 244 (1963), the Court based its decision on the city's participation in the restaurants' segregation policy: "When the State has commanded a particular result, it has saved to itself the power to determine that result and thereby 'to a significant extent' has 'become involved' in it, and, in fact, has removed that decision from the sphere of private choice." Similarly, in Lombard v. Louisiana, 373 U.S. 267, 273 (1963), the Court held that the discrimination was mandated by city officials and therefore "the city must be treated exactly as if it had an ordinance prohibiting such conduct."

Finally, in Bell v. Maryland, 378 U.S. 226 (1964), six Justices addressed the broader issue, but no consensus could be reached and the result was to decide to remand the case to the state courts for reconsideration in the light of intervening state legislation. Of the six Justices who reached the merits in their separate opinions, three (Douglas, Goldberg, and Warren) would have found a violation of equal protection, while three (Black, Harlan, and White) would have upheld the property right of the restaurant owner to choose his customers and exclude those he declined to serve.

In his concurring opinion, Justice Douglas (joined by Goldberg) contended that a business generally open to the public—like a restaurant—should not be able to invoke a state trespassing law in such circumstances (p. 259):

"Why should we refuse to let state courts enforce apartheid in residential areas of our cities but let state courts enforce apartheid in restaurants? If a court decree is state action in one case, it is in the other. Property rights, so heavily underscored, are equally involved in each case.

"The customer in a restaurant is transitory; he comes and may never return. The colored family who buys the house next door is there for keeps—night and day. If 'personal prejudices' are not to be the criterion in one case they should not be in the other. We should put these restaurant cases in line with Shelley v. Kraemer, holding that what the Fourteenth Amendment requires in restrictive covenant cases it also requires from restaurants."

Justice Goldberg also filed an opinion (joined by Warren) supporting reversal on that ground.

Justice Black (joined by Harlan and White) dissented, insisting that the Fourteenth Amendment "does not of itself, standing alone, in the absence of some cooperative state action or compulsion, forbid property holders, including restaurant owners, to ban people from entering or remaining upon their premises, *even if the owners act out of racial prejudice.*" (P. 326, italics added.) Black added:

> "[R]eliance [on *Shelley*] is misplaced. ... It seems pretty clear that the reason judicial enforcement of the restrictive covenants in Shelley was deemed state action was not merely the fact that a state court had acted, but rather that it had acted 'to deny to petitioners, on the grounds of race or color, the enjoyment of property rights in premises which petitioners are willing and financially able to acquire and which the grantors are willing to sell.' In other words, this Court held that state enforcement of the covenants had the effect of denying to the parties their federally guaranteed right to own, occupy, enjoy, and use their property without regard to race or color....

> "This means that the property owner may, in the absence of a valid statute forbidding it, sell his property to whom he pleases and admit to that property whom he will; so long as both parties are willing parties, then the principles stated in [Buchanan v. Warley, 245 U.S. 60 (1917)] and Shelley protect this right. But equally, when one party is unwilling, as when the property owner chooses not to sell to a particular person or not to admit that person, then ... he is entitled to rely on the guarantee of due process of law, that is, 'law of the land,' to protect his free use and enjoyment of property...." (Pp. 327-28, 330-31.)

The constitutional issue argued in the *Bell* case was to a large extent rendered moot by the enactment of the Civil Rights Act of 1964, which prohibits almost all restaurants from refusing to serve customers on a racially discriminatory basis.[10] In other contexts, however, determination of the scope of the *Shelley* doctrine remains unresolved.[11]

---

[10] See Chapter 22 *Public Accommodations and the 1964 Civil Rights Act* and Chapter 23 *Applying the Commerce Clause to Local Conduct.*

[11] The dilution of the state-action requirement led to some puzzling decisions such as Reitman v. Mulkey, 387 U.S. 369 (1967), holding unconstitutional a California voter initiative that repealed open housing laws (prohibiting private owners of residential property from discriminating in the rental of their property) and prevented the enactment of such future laws. Under the Fourteenth Amendment, discrimination by a private property owner does not constitute state action and therefore does not violate the Amendment. But in *Reitman* the Supreme Court (5-4) held that the California initiative adopting the same policy constituted state action that violated the Fourteenth Amendment. According to the majority, the initiative was unconstitutional because it "would encourage and significantly involve the State in private racial discrimination contrary to the Fourteenth Amendment." (P. 376.) But compare, e.g., the later decision in Crawford v. Board of Education, 458 U.S. 527 (1982), upholding a California initiative forbidding state courts to order the mandatory assignment or transportation of students unless a federal court would do so to remedy a violation of the Fourteenth Amendment.

20. THE RECONSTRUCTION CIVIL RIGHTS ACTS

Each of the Reconstruction Amendments—Thirteenth, Fourteenth, and Fifteenth—provides, in addition to its substantive terms, that "Congress shall have power to enforce this article by appropriate legislation." Relying on the grant of that constitutional authority, Congress soon enacted a series of civil rights statutes in 1866, 1870, 1871, and 1875 to implement the Amendments to protect the newly freed slaves.

Although the Thirteenth Amendment abolished slavery, it said nothing about granting ex-slaves either citizenship or the rights of citizens or protecting them from discrimination.[12] Nevertheless, shortly after the adoption of the Thirteenth Amendment, Congress passed the Civil Rights Act of 1866 providing "[t]hat all persons born in the United States and not subject to any foreign power, excluding Indians not taxed, are hereby declared to be citizens of the United States." The Act further provided that

> "such citizens, of every race and color, ... shall have the same right, in every State and Territory in the United States, to make and enforce contracts, to sue, be parties, and give evidence, to inherit, purchase, lease, sell, hold, and convey real and personal property, and to full and equal benefit of all laws and proceedings for the security of person and property, as is enjoyed by white citizens, and shall be subject to like punishment, penalties, and to none other, any law, statute, ordinance, regulation, or custom, to the contrary notwithstanding."[13]

---

[12] Michael Vorenberg, *Final Freedom: The Civil War, the Abolition of Slavery, and the Thirteenth Amendment* [Cambridge 2001], argues persuasively that the Thirteenth Amendment, although it did not expressly confer those rights, was intended to afford that protection to the ex-slaves. According to Vorenberg (p. 239), "the [Thirteenth] amendment was once seen as the pinnacle of freedom instead of a mere precursor to the Fourteenth and Fifteenth Amendments."

[13] The substance of the 1866 Act is now codified in 42 U.S.C. §§ 1981-1982 and 18 U.S.C §242. The Supreme Court's interpretation of these provisions is reviewed in Chapter 21 *Federal Statutory Regulation of Private Discrimination.*

The Act was vetoed by President Andrew Johnson but Congress overrode the veto and then undertook to supplement the Thirteenth Amendment by approving the Fourteenth Amendment ratified in 1868 and the Fifteenth Amendment ratified in 1870.

Congress then passed the 1870 Enforcement Act. The 1870 Act reenacted the 1866 Civil Rights Act, this time under the authority of the Fourteenth and Fifteenth Amendments, to shield the 1866 Act from claims that its scope exceeded the permissible limits of the Thirteenth Amendment. In addition, the 1870 Act prohibited conspiracies "to injure, oppress, threaten, or intimidate any citizen to prevent or hinder any citizen with intent to prevent or hinder his free exercise and enjoyment of any right or privilege granted or secured to him by the Constitution or laws of the United States...."[14]

§2 of the 1870 Act also imposed on state officers the duty to accept the votes of all citizens "without distinction of race, color, or previous condition of servitude." §3 imposed penalties on election inspectors who refused to accept a specified affidavit of compliance with state voting requirements; and §4 prohibited any person from engaging in force, bribery, threats, intimidation, or other unlawful means, to hinder, delay, prevent, or obstruct, any citizen from voting at any election.

§§ 3 and 4 of the 1870 Act were held unconstitutional in United States v. Reese, 92 U.S. 214 (1876). In *Reese* two inspectors of a municipal election in Kentucky were indicted under §§ 3 and 4 for refusing to receive and count the vote of a black citizen. The Court found that the language of the two statutory provisions did not in express terms limit the offense of an election inspector to a wrongful discrimination on account of "race, color, or previous condition of servitude" and therefore exceeded the scope of the Fifteenth Amendment. Stating that the Act reflects "a radical change in the practice, and the statute which creates it should be explicit in its terms" (p. 219), the Court held (7-2) that the

---

[14] The provisions of the 1870 Act are now in substance codified in 42 U.S.C. §1981 and 18 U.S.C. §241. The constitutionality of statutes prohibiting conspiracies to hinder the exercise of federal rights is well-established. See, e.g., Ex parte Yarbrough, 110 U.S. 651 (1884) (conspiracy to injure and intimidate a black citizen on account of his race, color, and previous condition of servitude to prevent and hinder his free exercise and enjoyment of the right to vote in a congressional election); Logan v. United States, 144 U.S. 263 (1892) (conspiracy to seize and injure several citizens of the United States while in the custody of a federal officer); In re Quarles, 158 U.S. 532 (1895) (conspiracy to murder an informant who had reported tax law violations to the government).

provisions were too broad to constitute "appropriate legislation" to enforce the Amendment.

In a case decided the same day, United States v. Cruikshank, 92 U.S. 542 (1876), arising out of the largest mass murder of blacks in American history, a conspiracy indictment under the 1870 Act was dismissed. The Court found that each count of the indictment was defective. The counts charging violation of the blacks' rights under the First Amendment (to peaceably assemble) and Second Amendment (to bear arms) were dismissed on the ground that those Amendments provided only protection from the national government. The counts charging deprivation of due process under the Fourteenth Amendment were dismissed on the ground that "The fourteenth amendment prohibits a State from depriving any person of life, liberty, or property, without due process of law; but this adds nothing to the rights of one citizen as against another" (p. 554). With respect to the counts alleging that the whites had conspired to deprive the blacks of their right generally to be treated equally with whites, the Court acknowledged that the 1866 Act established such a federal right, but held that these counts were also defective (even though other counts did allege a racial motive) "because ... it is nowhere alleged in these counts that the wrong contemplated against the rights of these citizens was on account of their race or color." Although the *Cruikshank* decision did not hold the 1870 Act unconstitutional, it imposed formidable obstacles to prosecutions under that Act as well as the 1866 Act.[15]

In response to racial violence in the South, Congress enacted the Civil Rights Act of 1871, also known as the Ku Klux Klan Act. §2 of the Act provided for punishment of private conspiracies to prevent the execution of any law of the United States or "to deny to any citizen of the United States the due and equal protection of the laws."[16]

In United States v. Harris, 106 U.S. 629 (1883), citing the *Reese* and *Cruikshank* decisions, the Court (9-0) held §2 of the 1871 Act unconstitutional. An armed mob of Tennessee whites had seized

---

[15] See Harold Hyman and William Wiecek, *Equal Justice under Law: Constitutional Development 1835-1875* [Harper 1982]: 489; Charles Lane, *The Day Freedom Died: The Colfax Massacre, the Supreme Court, and the Betrayal of Reconstruction* [Henry Holt 2008]: 251-52.

[16] The provisions of the 1871 Act are now in substance codified in 42 U.S.C. §§1983 and 1985. See Hyman and Wiecek, supra, at 495-98.

several blacks from the custody of a sheriff, killing one and beating the others. Although the indictment in the case charged violations of the federal rights of blacks, the Court held that the statute was constitutionally overbroad because the statutory language also covered instances of whites assaulting whites while the Thirteenth Amendment "simply prohibits slavery and involuntary servitude." The Fourteenth Amendment was held inapplicable because it only applied to actions by a state and was not violated by private discrimination.

The Civil Rights Act of 1875 outlawed private discrimination in public accommodations. §1 provided "That all persons within the jurisdiction of the United States shall be entitled to the full and equal enjoyment of the accommodations, advantages, facilities, and privileges of inns, public conveyances on land or water, theatres, and other places of public amusement, subject only to the conditions and limitations established by law and applicable alike to citizens of every race and color, regardless of any previous condition of servitude." §2 imposed criminal penalties for "denying to any citizen, except for reasons by law applicable to citizens of every race and color, and regardless of any previous condition of servitude, the full enjoyment of any of the accommodations, advantages, facilities, or privileges in said section enumerated, or by aiding or inciting such denial...."

However, both §§ 1 and 2 of the 1875 Act were declared unconstitutional in the Civil Rights Cases, 109 U.S. 3 (1883), on the ground that the provisions outlawed practices that were beyond the scope of both the Thirteenth and Fourteenth Amendments and therefore did not constitute "appropriate legislation" under the Amendments' enforcement clauses.[17] The Court (8-1) held that the Fourteenth Amendment only prohibits actions by the States and does not extend to the conduct of state-regulated organizations owned and operated by private entities, and that the Thirteenth Amendment (although not limited to actions by the States) applies only to slavery or involuntary servitude and does not extend to what the Court characterized as "social rights."

---

[17] The five cases involved charges that the defendants had violated the 1875 Act by denying hotel accommodations to a colored person, denying colored persons admission to the dress circle of Maguire's theatre in San Francisco, denying another person (color not stated) the full enjoyment of the accommodations of the Grand Opera House in New York, and refusing to allow a colored woman to ride in the ladies' car of a passenger train.

The Court's decision has had a profound effect in limiting—although not ultimately preventing—subsequent adoption of federal legislation prohibiting race discrimination by private parties.

In holding that the Fourteenth Amendment only prohibits actions by the states, not the individual invasion of individual rights, the Court stated that §5 of the Fourteenth Amendment

"...invests congress with power to enforce it by appropriate legislation. To enforce what? To enforce the prohibition. To adopt appropriate legislation for correcting the effects of such prohibited state laws and state acts.... This is the legislative power conferred upon congress, and this is the whole of it...

"If this legislation [the 1875 Act] is appropriate for enforcing the prohibitions of the [Fourteenth] amendment, it is difficult to see where it is to stop. Why may not congress, with equal show of authority, enact a code of laws for the enforcement and vindication of all rights of life, liberty, and property? ... The truth is that the implication of a power to legislate in this manner is based upon the assumption that if the states are forbidden to legislate or act in a particular way on a particular subject, and power is conferred upon congress to enforce the prohibition, this gives congress power to legislate generally upon that subject, and not merely power to provide modes of redress against such state legislation or action. The assumption is certainly unsound." (Pp. 11, 14-15.)

The Court recognized that the Thirteenth Amendment, unlike the Fourteenth Amendment, is not limited to actions by the States and vests in Congress the "power to pass all laws necessary and proper for abolishing all badges and incidents of slavery in the United States...." But the Court denied that "...the refusal to any persons of the accommodations of an inn, or a public conveyance, or a place of public amusement, by an individual, and without any sanction or support from any state law or regulation, ... inflict[s] upon such persons any manner of servitude, or form of slavery, as those terms are understood in this country." The Court stated:

"...we are forced to the conclusion that such an act of refusal [of access to public accommodations] has nothing to do with slavery or involuntary servitude.... It would be running the slavery argument into the ground to make it apply to every act of discrimination which a person may see fit to make as to the guests he will entertain, or as to the people he will take into his coach or cab or car, or admit to his concert or theater, or deal with in other matters of intercourse or business. Innkeepers and public carriers, by the laws of all the states, so far as we are aware, are bound, to the extent of their facilities, to furnish proper accommodation to all unobjectionable persons who in good faith apply for them. If the laws themselves make any unjust discrimination, amenable to the prohibitions of the fourteenth amendment, congress has full power to afford a remedy under that amendment and in accordance with it.

"When a man has emerged from slavery, and by the aid of beneficent legislation has shaken off the inseparable concomitants of that state, there must be some stage in the progress of his elevation when he takes the rank of a mere citizen, and ceases to be the special favorite of the laws, and when his rights as a citizen, or a man, are to be protected in the ordinary modes by which other men's rights are protected. There were thousands of free colored people in this country before the abolition of slavery, enjoying all the essential rights of life, liberty, and property the same as white citizens; yet no one, at that time, thought that it was any invasion of their personal status as freemen because they were not admitted to all the privileges enjoyed by white citizens, or because they were subjected to discriminations in the enjoyment of accommodations in inns, public conveyances, and places of amusement. Mere discriminations on account of race or color were not regarded as badges of slavery." (Pp. 24-25.)

The Court concluded "that no countenance of authority for the passage of the law in question can be found in either the Thirteenth or Fourteenth Amendments."[18]

Justice John Marshall Harlan dissented. According to Harlan, the

---

[18] See also Hodges v. United States, 203 U.S. 1 (1906), invalidating a federal law that made it a crime for private individuals to intimidate blacks to keep them from performing their contracts of employment. Explaining that the Thirteenth Amendment was intended only to prohibit slavery, the Court held that the Amendment did not authorize such special legislation for the freed slaves and that the Reconstruction Amendments had "declined to constitute them wards of the Nation ... doubtless believing that thereby, in the long run, their best interests would be subserved, they taking their chances with other citizens in the states where they should make their homes." (P.20.)

Thirteenth Amendment broadly conferred on the freemen "immunity from, and protection against, all discrimination against them, because of their race, in respect of such civil rights as belong to freemen of other races" and therefore Congress "...may enact laws to protect that people against the deprivation, on account of their race, of any civil rights enjoyed by other freemen in the same state; and such legislation may be of a direct and primary character, operating upon states, their officers and agents, and also upon, at least, such individuals and corporations as exercise public functions and wield power and authority under the state." (P. 36.) On the Fourteenth Amendment issue, Harlan contended: "In every material sense applicable to the practical enforcement of the Fourteenth Amendment, railroad corporations, keepers of inns, and managers of places of public amusement are agents or instrumentalities of the State, because they are charged with duties to the public, and are amenable, in respect of their dues and functions, to government regulation." (P. 58.)

In 1966 the Supreme Court came close to overruling the *Civil Rights Cases* interpretation of the Fourteenth Amendment. In United States v. Guest, 383 U.S. 745 (1966), upholding an indictment charging a conspiracy to deprive black citizens of federal rights, the majority opinion written by Justice Potter Stewart expressly declined to reach the question whether Congress could regulate private conduct under §5 of the Fourteenth Amendment. Because of other grounds supporting the decision, Stewart stated that the case "requires no determination of the threshold level that state action must attain in order to create rights under the Equal Protection Clause." In separate concurring and dissenting opinions, however, six Justices expressed support for the view that §5 gave Congress the constitutional authority to prohibit private discrimination. But in United States v. Morrison, 529 U.S. 598 (2000), the Court (5-4) specifically reaffirmed the *Civil Rights Cases* interpretation and disavowed the statements to the contrary in the *Guest* opinions as mere nonbinding dicta. [19]

---

[19] The *Morrison* case concerned the constitutionality of the Violence against Women Act, which provided a federal civil remedy for the victims of gender-motivated violence. The Court held that neither the Commerce Clause nor §5 of the Fourteenth Amendment provided a constitutional basis for the provision, stating (p. 626) that the Act "is not aimed at proscribing discrimination by individuals which the Fourteenth Amendment might not itself proscribe; it is directed not at any State or state actor, but at individuals who have committed criminal acts motivated by gender bias."

21. FEDERAL STATUTORY REGULATION OF PRIVATE DISCRIMINATION

In the *Civil Rights Cases*, the Court held that neither the Thirteenth nor Fourteenth Amendments authorized Congress to enact the 1875 Act prohibiting private discrimination by places of public accommodation. With respect to the Thirteenth Amendment, the Court held that the Act was beyond the scope of the Amendment because such discrimination did not impose a badge of slavery or involuntary servitude and instead concerned mere "social rights." The Court distinguished these unprotected "social rights" from "fundamental rights" such as those which Congress specifically protected on the basis of the Thirteenth Amendment in the 1866 Civil Rights Act (currently codified as 42 U.S.C. §1981)—"namely, the same right to make and enforce contracts, to sue, be parties, give evidence, and to inherit, purchase, lease, sell, and convey property, as is enjoyed by white citizens."[20] (109 U.S. at 22.). The Court held that "fundamental rights" of this character, "such as are guarantied by the constitution against state aggression, cannot be impaired by the wrongful acts of individuals, unsupported by state authority in the shape of laws, customs, or judicial or executive proceedings." (P. 17.)

This constrained reading of the Thirteenth Amendment—that it does not apply to private discrimination—continued in effect for nearly a century, sharply limiting the application of federal civil rights laws.

In Corrigan v. Buckley, 271 U.S. 323, 331 (1926), the Court rejected the claim that restrictive covenants prohibiting the sale of property to blacks or Jews violated what is now 42 U.S.C §1982 (derived from the 1866 Act) that "...citizens, of every race and color, ...

---

[20] Four years earlier, Virginia v. Rives, 100 U.S. 313, 317-18 (1879), had similarly interpreted the 1866 Act to be limited to "state action." The Court stated: "... the statutes partially enumerating what civil rights colored men shall enjoy equally with white persons ... are intended for protection against State infringement of those rights. Sect. 641 [derived from the 1866 Act] was also intended for their protection against State action, and against that alone."

shall have the same right, ... to inherit, purchase, lease, sell, hold, and convey real and personal property, ... as is enjoyed by white citizens...." The Court held that statutes implementing the Thirteenth Amendment, "...like the Constitutional Amendment under whose sanction they were enacted, do not in any manner prohibit or invalidate contracts entered into by private individuals in respect to the control and disposition of their own property" (pp. 330-31).

In Hurd v. Hodge, 334 U.S. 24, 31 (1948), the Court acknowledged that "...the statute does not invalidate private restrictive agreements [prohibiting sale of property to blacks] so long as the purposes of those agreements are achieved by the parties through voluntary adherence to the terms."[21]

But in 1968, on the basis of a sharply disputed reading of the legislative history,[22] the Court reversed its interpretation of both the 1866 Act and the Thirteenth Amendment.[23] In Jones v. Alfred H. Mayer Co., 392 U.S. 409 (1968), the Court held that the statute does indeed apply to private discrimination and that Congress has broad authority under the Thirteenth Amendment to determine how to enforce the prohibition against slavery and involuntary servitude.

The case involved a suit by a black couple against a private real estate developer for discriminatorily refusing to sell them a home in violation of the right provided in 42 U.S.C §1982 to "... inherit, purchase, lease, sell, hold, and convey real and personal property." The Court (7-2) concluded that the law prohibited private discriminatory refusals to deal, stating: "In light of the concerns that led Congress to adopt it and the contents of the debates that preceded its passage, it is clear that the [1866] Act was designed to do just what its terms suggest: to prohibit all racial discrimination, whether or not under color of law, with respect to the rights enumerated therein—including the right to purchase or lease property" (p. 436). According to the decision, Congress in 1866 had not only confirmed the capacity

---

[21] In the *Hurd* case and Shelley v. Kraemer, 334 U.S. 1 (1948), decided the same day, the Court held that judicial enforcement of such restrictive covenants violated the due process clauses of the Fifth and Fourteenth Amendments. See Chapter 19 *Applying Shelley v. Kraemer.*

[22] The Court's analysis of the legislative history is harshly criticized by, e.g., Fairman, supra, at 1207-59.

[23] See Michael Vorenberg, *Final Freedom: The Civil War, the Abolition of Slavery, and the Thirteenth Amendment* [Cambridge 2001]: 238-47.

of blacks to purchase property but also imposed a duty on all others to sell without regard to race.

Turning then to the constitutionality of the statute, Justice Stewart relied on the comments of the authors of the Thirteenth Amendment (pp. 340-43):

> "Surely Senator Trumbull was right. Surely Congress has the power under the Thirteenth Amendment rationally to determine what are the badges and the incidents of slavery, and the authority to translate that determination into effective legislation. Nor can we say that the determination Congress has made is an irrational one. For this Court recognized long ago that, whatever else they may have encompassed, the badges and incidents of slavery—its 'burdens and disabilities'—included restraints upon 'those fundamental rights which are the essence of civil freedom, namely, the same right ... to inherit, purchase, lease, sell and convey property, as is enjoyed by white citizens.' Civil Rights Cases, 109 U.S. 3, 22. Just as the Black Codes, enacted after the Civil War to restrict the free exercise of those rights, were substitutes for the slave system, so the exclusion of Negroes from white communities became a substitute for the Black Codes. And when racial discrimination herds men into ghettos and makes their ability to buy property turn on the color of their skin, then it too is a relic of slavery.

> "...At the very least, the freedom that Congress is empowered to secure under the Thirteenth Amendment includes the freedom to buy whatever a white man can buy, the right to live wherever a white man can live. If Congress cannot say that being a free man means at least this much, then the Thirteenth Amendment made a promise the Nation cannot keep."

A parallel reversal has taken place in the construction of civil conspiracy provisions. 18 U.S.C. §1985(c) provides a civil remedy for conspiracies to deny "the equal protection of the laws, or of equal privileges and immunities under the laws." In Collins v. Hardyman, 341 U.S. 651 (1951), the Court had narrowly interpreted the statute to reach only conspiracies under color of state law. But twenty years later, in Griffin v. Breckenridge, 403 U.S. 88 (1971), the Court unanimously rejected that interpretation and held §1985(c) applicable to private conspiracies to deprive blacks of their constitutional rights. The Court in *Griffin* sustained a damage suit by black victims of a racially motivated assault. The Court concluded that "It is thus evident that all indicators—text, companion provisions, and legislative history—point unwaveringly to 1985 (3)'s coverage of private conspiracies" that involve, "as an element of the cause of action, the kind of invidiously discriminatory motivation stressed by the sponsors of the limiting amendment" and that Congress had the constitutional authority to reach such a private conspiracy both under §2 of the Thirteenth Amendment and its power to protect the right of interstate travel (pp. 102-04, 104-06).[24]

In Runyon v. McCrary, 427 U.S. 160 (1976), the Court (7-2) applied the *Jones* rationale to hold that a private school's discriminatory refusal to admit qualified black children violated 42 U.S.C. §1981 (also derived from the 1866 Act) providing that all persons shall have "the same right ... to make and enforce contracts ... as is enjoyed by white citizens." The Court (p. 173) concluded "that §1981, like §1982, reaches private conduct" and therefore, "Just as in *Jones* a Negro's [statutory] right to purchase property on equal terms with whites was violated when a private person refused to sell to the prospective purchaser solely because he was a Negro, so also a Negro's [statutory] right to 'make and enforce contracts' is violated if a private offeror refuses to extend to a Negro, solely because he is a Negro, the same opportunity to enter into contracts as he extends to white offerees."[25]

Although §1981 (like §1982) refers only to the discriminatory denial of rights "enjoyed by white citizens," the Court in McDonald v. Santa Fe Trail Transportation Co., 427 U.S. 273 (1976), held (7-2)

---

[24] Justice Stewart added in a footnote that "We need not decide, given the facts of this case, whether a conspiracy motivated by invidiously discriminatory intent other than racial bias would be actionable under the portion of [the provision] before us." The scope of the *Griffin* decision was limited in United Brotherhood of Carpenters v. Scott, 463 U.S. 825, 830 (1983), holding (5-4) that a union's alleged conspiracy to violently interfere with nonunion workers' First Amendment rights did not violate §1985(3) without proof that "the State is involved in the conspiracy or that the aim of the conspiracy is to influence the activity of the State."

[25] The Court reaffirmed its *Runyon* holding in Patterson v. McLean Credit Union, 497 U.S. 164 (1989).

that §1981 also protects white persons from racial discrimination (in that case, an alleged discriminatory discharge from employment).[26]

The Civil Rights Act of 1964 vastly expanded the scope of federal regulation of private racial discrimination—in public accommodations (Title II), in federally funded programs (Title VI), and employment (Title VII). Each of these developments is reviewed in succeeding chapters.

---

[26] Quite apart from federal statutes, many state and local laws prohibit private discrimination not only on the basis of race but also on the basis of criteria that are not covered by federal legislation, such as sexual orientation, weight, appearance, or political affiliation (and even, in Minnesota, membership in a motorcycle gang).

22. PUBLIC ACCOMMODATIONS AND THE 1964 CIVIL RIGHTS ACT

For nearly 80 years after the 1875 Civil Rights Act was struck down, even as federal regulation of private discrimination continued to expand on the basis of the Thirteenth Amendment, the decision in the *Civil Rights Cases* stood as a formidable obstacle to any further attempt to prohibit private discrimination in places of public accommodations. Finally in 1964, in Title II of the epochal Civil Rights Act of 1964, Congress enacted sweeping legislation providing that "All persons shall be entitled to the full and equal enjoyment of the goods, services, facilities, privileges, advantages, and accommodations of any place of public accommodation, as defined in this section, without discrimination or segregation on the ground of race, color, religion, or national origin."

In considering the legislation, in light of the *Civil Rights Cases* precedent, Congress was keenly aware that the law would almost certainly be attacked as unconstitutional under the Fourteenth Amendment. In addition, while holding that the Fourteenth Amendment did not authorize Congress to regulate private discrimination, the *Civil Rights Cases* opinion noted that "...these remarks do not apply to those cases in which Congress is clothed with direct and plenary powers of legislation ..., as in the regulation of commerce among the several states." (109 U.S. at 18.) As a result, to bolster the case for the law's constitutionality, Congress explicitly based the 1964 Act on the Commerce Clause as well as the Fourteenth Amendment.

§201(b) of the Act provides that any of the following categories of business establishments (with minor exceptions) fall within the scope of the statute "if [the establishment's] operations *affect commerce*...." (italics added): any inn, hotel, or motel;[27] any restaurant

---

[27] An exception is provided for an establishment located within a building which contains not more than five rooms for rent or hire and which is actually occupied by the proprietor of such establishment as his residence.

or cafeteria; and any motion picture house. §201(c) then provides the criteria for determining whether the establishment's operations "affect commerce": any inn, hotel, or motel is deemed to affect commerce *per se*; restaurants and cafeterias affect commerce only if they serve or offer to serve interstate travelers or if a substantial portion of the food that they serve or products that they sell have "moved in commerce"; and motion picture houses affect commerce if they customarily present films, performances, etc., "move in commerce."

In actions brought to enjoin implementation of the Act, the constitutionality of Title II was unanimously upheld in Heart of Atlanta Motel, Inc. v. United States, 379 U.S. 241 (1964), and Katzenbach v. McClung, 379 U.S. 294 (1964), in two opinions written by Justice Tom Clark.

The Heart of Atlanta Motel, a 216-room motel in Atlanta, Georgia, restricted its clientele to white persons, three-fourths of whom are transient interstate travelers. The plaintiff in the *McClung* case operated "Ollie's Barbecue," a family-owned restaurant in Birmingham, Alabama, located on a state highway 11 blocks from an interstate highway and a somewhat greater distance from railroad and bus stations. The restaurant provides a take-out service for blacks and two-thirds of its employees are blacks, but the restaurant refused to serve blacks in its dining room since it opened in 1927. In the 12 months preceding the passage of the Act, the restaurant purchased locally approximately $150,000 worth of food, $69,683 (46%) of which was meat that it bought from a local supplier who had procured it from outside the State.

The *Heart of Atlanta* decision held that the Act, as applied to a motel that concededly serves interstate travelers, is within the power granted by the Commerce Clause, since Congress' power over interstate commerce extends to the regulation of local incidents thereof that might have a substantial and harmful effect upon that commerce. The decision in the *Civil Rights Cases* was deemed inapposite because, as the opinion in that case expressly acknowledged, the validity of the 1875 statute under the Commerce Clause had not been considered. It was therefore unnecessary, the *Heart of Atlanta* majority held, to address the question of whether the 1964 Act may also be supported under the Fourteenth Amendment.

In the *McClung* case, the Court acknowledged that the volume of food purchased by Ollie's Barbecue from out-of-state sources, viewed in isolation, was insignificant when compared with the total foodstuffs moving in commerce, but said, quoting Wickard v. Filburn, 317 U.S. 111 (1942), that "his contribution, taken together with that of many others similarly situated, is far from trivial." On the basis of the extensive congressional hearings on the matter, the Court concluded that it had a rational basis for finding that racial discrimination in restaurants had a direct and adverse effect on the free flow of interstate commerce.[28]

Justice Black, concurring, emphasized that the validity of the Act cannot be considered in terms of the effect on interstate commerce of only one isolated, individual, local event, without regard to the fact that a single local event when added to many others of a similar nature may impose a burden on interstate commerce by reducing its volume or distorting its flow. In light of the aggregate effect of a great number of such acts of discrimination, Black concluded that Congress has constitutional power to protect interstate commerce from the injuries bound to befall it from these discriminatory practices.

Justices Douglas and Goldberg concurred on the basis of both the Fourteenth Amendment and the Commerce Clause.[29]

---

[28] According to the Court, "Of course, the mere fact that Congress has said when particular activity shall be deemed to affect commerce does not preclude further examination by this Court. But where we find that the legislators, in light of the facts and testimony before them, have a rational basis for finding a chosen regulatory scheme necessary to the protection of commerce, oar investigation is at an end. The only remaining question—one answered in the affirmative by the court below—is whether the particular restaurant either serves or offers to serve interstate travelers or serves food a substantial portion of which has moved in interstate commerce." 379 U.S. at 303-04.

[29] Many states have also enacted public accommodation laws, and some of these laws have been broadly construed by state courts to prohibit private discrimination in a wide variety of organizations that are not traditionally considered "places of public accommodation." For example, the Little League Baseball organization was held to be a "place of public accommodation" under New Jersey law and was therefore required to admit girls. The New Jersey Supreme Court similarly held that the Boy Scouts of America constituted a "place of public accommodation." Boy Scouts of America v. Dale, 530 U.S. 640 (2000).

23. APPLYING THE COMMERCE CLAUSE TO LOCAL CONDUCT

As the *Heart of Atlanta* and *McClurg* cases demonstrate, so long as the *Civil Rights Cases* interpretation of the Fourteenth Amendment remains controlling, the primary source of Congress' power to regulate private discrimination is the Article I (§8) grant "To regulate Commerce ... among the several States." Since the New Deal revolution, the Court has construed the Clause to give Congress extraordinarily broad—although not unlimited—power.

In sustaining the 1964 Civil Rights Act on the basis of the Commerce Clause, the Court placed heavy reliance on Wickard v. Filburn, 317 U.S. 111 (1942), upholding the Agricultural Adjustment Act. One of the primary purposes of the AAA was to increase the market price of wheat and, to that end, limit the volume of wheat that could affect the market. Under the Act, each wheat farmer was assigned an allotment specifying how much wheat he would be allowed to grow.

Filburn owned a small dairy farm in Ohio. It was his practice to raise a small acreage of winter wheat, to sell a part of the crop to others, to feed part to poultry and livestock on the farm (some of which is sold), to use some on his farm to make flour for his own use, and to keep the rest for the following seeding. His allotment for 1941 was 222 bushels of wheat, but he grew 461 bushels and was fined $117 for the excess that he used for home consumption. He claimed that the federal law could not constitutionally be applied to the excess used for home consumption on the ground that it was not a part of interstate commerce. (P. 114.) Rejecting that contention, the Court (9-0) relied on the effect of all home-grown wheat on wheat prices in the national market. Even though the wheat grown by Filburn for home consumption only had a negligible impact on interstate commerce, the Court stated, his production was still held to be within the scope of federal regulation since "his contribution, taken together with that of many others similarly situated, is far from trivial" (p. 128). The Court concluded that "This record leaves us in no doubt that Congress may properly have considered that wheat consumed on the farm where grown if wholly outside the scheme of regulation would have a substantial effect in defeating and obstructing its purpose to stimulate trade therein at increased prices" (pp. 128-29).

The farmer in *Wickard v. Filburn*, it should be noted, did not claim that the wheat he sold to others was constitutionally exempt from regulation under the federal law. In addition, the decision was based on the particular record and statute in that case. However, *Wickard v. Filburn* and similar decisions established the principle that the Commerce Clause gives Congress the power to regulate, not only interstate commerce that actually crosses state lines, but also *intra-state* activities that on a cumulative basis have a "substantial effect" on interstate commerce.

For over 50 years after *Wickard v. Filburn*, not a single federal law was invalidated by the Court on the ground that the law exceeded the scope of Congress' power under the Commerce Clause.

But then in United States v. Lopez, 514 U.S. 549 (1995), the Court (5-4) struck down The Gun-Free School Zones Act of 1990, which made it a federal offense for an individual to knowingly possess a firearm in a school zone. Lopez, a 12th grade student, was convicted under the Act for possessing a concealed handgun and bullets at his San Antonio high school. The Court held that Lopez's conduct could not be said to substantially affect interstate commerce, stating: "Under the theories that the Government presents ..., it is difficult to perceive any limitation on federal power, even in areas such as criminal law enforcement or education where States historically have been sovereign. Thus, if we were to accept the Government's arguments, we are hard-pressed to posit any activity by an individual that Congress is without power to regulate.... To uphold the Government's contentions here, we would have to pile inference upon inference in a manner that would bid fair to convert congressional authority under the Commerce Clause to a general police power of the sort retained by the States."

Five years later, in United States v. Morrison, 529 U.S. 598 (2000), the Court applied the *Lopez* decision in striking down a provision in the Violence against Women Act that authorized a federal civil remedy for the victims of gender-motivated violence. The Court held (again 5-4) that such crimes did not constitute economic or commercial activity and were beyond the power of Congress to regulate under the Commerce Clause. The Court rejected "the argument that Congress may regulate noneconomic, violent criminal conduct based solely on that conduct's aggregate effect on interstate commerce."

In Gonzales v. Raich, 545 U.S. 1 (2005), the question presented was whether the Commerce Clause permitted application of the federal Controlled Substance Act to marijuana grown by two chronically ill patients for their own use for medicinal purposes as recommended by their doctors and pursuant to a California statute authorizing such use. Relying on *Lopez* and *Morrison*, the Ninth Circuit had held that the conduct at issue was completely noneconomic and therefore the aggregation principle of *Wickard v. Filburn* did not apply. The Supreme Court, however, reversed (6-3, Scalia concurring in the judgment).

The majority rejected the characterization of the conduct as noneconomic, stating that "In contrast [with *Lopez* and *Morrison*], the CSA regulates quintessentially economic activities: the production, distribution, and consumption of commodities for which there is an established, and lucrative, interstate market." The Court further stated: "In assessing the scope of Congress' authority under the Commerce Clause, ... [w]e need not determine whether respondents' activities, taken in the aggregate, substantially affect interstate commerce in fact, but only whether a 'rational basis' exists for so concluding. Given the enforcement difficulties that attend distinguishing between marijuana cultivated locally and marijuana grown elsewhere, ... and concerns about diversion into illicit channels, we have no difficulty concluding that Congress had a rational basis for believing that failure to regulate the intrastate manufacture and possession of marijuana would leave a gaping hole in the CSA. Thus, as in *Wickard v. Filburn*, when it enacted comprehensive legislation to regulate the interstate market in a fungible commodity, Congress was acting well within its authority to 'make all Laws which shall be necessary and proper' to 'regulate Commerce ... among the several States.'"

In his *Raich* concurrence, Justice Scalia relied on the Constitution's Necessary and Proper Clause in conjunction with the Commerce

Clause: "The regulation of an intrastate activity may be essential to a comprehensive regulation of interstate commerce even though the intrastate activity does not itself 'substantially affect' interstate commerce. ... That simple possession [of a controlled substance] is a noneconomic activity is immaterial to whether it can be prohibited as a necessary part of a larger regulation. Rather, Congress's authority to enact all of these prohibitions of intrastate controlled-substance activities depends only upon whether they are appropriate means of achieving the legitimate end of eradicating Schedule I substances from interstate commerce. ... I thus agree with the Court that ... Congress could reasonably conclude that its objective of prohibiting marijuana from the interstate market 'could be undercut' if those activities were excepted from its general scheme of regulation."

In United States v. Comstock, 560 U.S. ___ (2010), in a broad endorsement of federal power, the Court (7-2) ruled that Congress has constitutional power to authorize the continued civil commitment of sex offenders after they have completed their sentences for violation of federal laws. The challenged statute provides that prisoners (until they are no longer dangerous or a state assumes responsibility for them) may be detained if it is shown by "clear and convincing" evidence that they had engaged in sexually violent conduct, suffered from mental illness, and would have difficulty controlling themselves. In an opinion by Justice Breyer, relying on the Necessary and Proper Clause, the Court held that the challenged law "represents a modest addition" to Congress' undoubted powers to enact criminal laws in furtherance of its enumerated powers and to create a prison system to punish people who violate those laws. Justices Alito and Anthony voted to uphold the law but on more limited grounds.

In 2010, relying on the Commerce Clause, Congress enacted the Patient Protection and Affordable Care Act, providing in part that any individual not otherwise covered (by an employer or government insurance program) must purchase health insurance from a private insurer. Those who fail to do so must pay a penalty to the Internal Revenue Service with their taxes. Supporters of the constitutionality of this "individual mandate" requirement invoked Supreme Court precedents that had expansively construed the scope of the Commerce Clause, in particular the 1942 decision in *Wickard v.*

Filburn. Opponents claimed that the prior rulings were all distinguishable and that a decision validating the mandate would constitute in effect a sweeping rejection of any constitutional limit on Congress' power under the Commerce Clause.

In June 2012, in *National Federation of Independent Business v. Sebelius,* the Court held 5-to-4 that the individual mandate could not be sustained under the Commerce Clause. Five Justices (Roberts, Scalia, Kennedy, Alito, and Thomas) concluded that the exercise of the power to "regulate" commerce presupposes the prior existence of commercial activity subject to regulation. In their view, the individual mandate requirement does not regulate existing commercial activity but instead directs the creation of commerce by compelling individuals to purchase a product. On this issue, Justices Breyer, Ginsburg, Kagan, and Sotomayor dissented.

The constitutionality of the mandate, however, was sustained on another ground. A differently constituted majority (Chief Justice Roberts and the four dissenters on the Commerce Clause) upheld the mandate by the same 5-4 vote on the basis of Congress' "to lay and collect Taxes." On that issue, Justices Scalia, Kennedy, Alito, and Thomas dissented.

24. TITLE VI OF
THE 1964 CIVIL RIGHTS ACT

§601 of Title VI of the 1964 Act provides that "[n]o person in the United States shall, on the ground of race, color, or national origin, be excluded from participation in, be denied the benefits of, or be subjected to discrimination under any program or activity receiving Federal financial assistance."[30] Private individuals may sue to enforce §601 and obtain both damages and injunctive relief.

The scope of §601 was significantly limited—but only temporarily—by the Supreme Court's decision in Grove City v. Bell, 465 U.S. 555, 571-74 (1984), which adopted a strict interpretation of the phrase "program or activity." The Court ruled that the similarly worded prohibition of the Act's Title IX (dealing with gender discrimination) applies only to the specific part of the institution's operations that receives the federal funding. But, three years later, the *Grove City* interpretation was overturned by Congress' adoption of the Civil Rights Restoration Act of 1987, providing that federal funding of an entire institution is subject to termination if a violation is found in any part of the institution.

To establish a violation of §601, there must be proof of an intent to discriminate (disparate treatment, not just disparate impact). In Regents of University of California v. Bakke, 438 U.S. 265, 284-87 (1978), in what became the controlling opinion in the case, Justice Powell concluded that §601 is coextensive with the Equal Protection Clause, which prohibits only intentional discrimination.[31] As the Court stated in Alexander v. Choate, 469 U.S. 287, 293 (1985), rejecting the broader interpretation of the term "discrimination" in Title VII concerning employment, "Title VI itself directly reach[es] only

---

[30] 42 U.S.C. §2000d.
[31] The *Bakke* decision and the application of Title VI to affirmative action programs are reviewed in Chapter 30 *The Bakke Case* and Chapter 36 *Race-Based Scholarships*.

instances of intentional discrimination."32

Anomalously, however, a markedly different and substantially less rigorous standard is provided in administrative regulations issued by numerous federal agencies under §602, (which authorizes regulations "to effectuate the provisions of [§601].") These regulations—known as the "disparate-impact regulations"—prohibit not only intentional discrimination but also conduct that has a disparate impact, even without any discriminatory intent. The regulations forbid recipients of federal funds to "utilize criteria or methods of administration *which have the effect* of subjecting individuals to discrimination because of their race, color, or national origin" (italics added).[33] Since the disparate-impact regulations do not require proof of purposeful discrimination, they thus prohibit federally funded entities from engaging in conduct that is lawful not only under the Equal Protection Clause but also under §601 itself.

When confronted with this anomaly, the Supreme Court reaffirmed its position that §601 requires proof of discriminatory intent, yet at the same time declined to invalidate the regulations as an unauthorized expansion of §601. In Guardians Association v. Civil Service Commission of New York City, 463 U.S. 582, 610-11 (1983), none of the six opinions in the case was supported by a majority. The net result of the case, however, was that (1) seven Justices agreed that a Title VI violation requires proof of discriminatory purpose, (2) a majority of the Justices expressed the view in their individual opinions (at least as alternative grounds) that the disparate-impact regulations are valid, and (3) five Justices concluded that proof of disparate impact suffices to establish a violation of the regulations.

The question presented in Alexander v. Sandoval, 532 U.S. 275, 293 (2001), was whether the disparate-impact regulations (like §601 itself) can be enforced by a private action. In an opinion by Justice Scalia, the Court (5-4) acknowledged that, "Although Title VI has often come to this Court, it is fair to say (indeed, perhaps an understatement) that our opinions have not eliminated all uncertainty regarding its commands." The Court noted the "considerable tension" between

---

[32] As pointed out in Chapter 25 *Title VII of the 1964 Civil Rights Act,* the Court in Griggs v. Duke Power Co., 401 U.S. 424 (1971), held that "discrimination" in Title VII included a disparate-impact standard, subsequently codified by Congress.

[33] 34 C.F.R. §100.3(b) (2008).

the disparate-impact regulations and "the rule of *Bakke* and *Guardians* that §601 forbids only intentional discrimination." A footnote to the opinion added that "[w]e cannot help observing ... how strange it is to say that disparate-impact regulations" implement Title VI when the statute "permits the very behavior that the regulations forbid."

But, since the petitioner in the case had not challenged the validity of the regulations, the Court stated that it "must assume for purposes of deciding this case that regulations promulgated under §602 of Title VI may validly proscribe activities that have a disparate impact on racial groups, even though such activities are permissible under §601." (Pp. 281-82.) Although proceeding on the assumption that the disparate-impact regulations are valid, the Court ruled that there was neither Supreme Court precedent nor statutory authority for a private right of action to enforce the regulations. The Court held that a private right of action is not available for "a failure to comply with regulations promulgated under §602 that is not also a failure to comply with §601" (p. 286). [34]

To recapitulate the somewhat confusing state of the law in this area:

- A violation of either the Equal Protection Clause or Title VI requires a discriminatory intent (disparate treatment), but Title VII "discrimination" may be based on disparate impact as well as disparate treatment.

- A statutory violation of Title VI (disparate treatment) is subject to private actions as well as government administrative proceedings.

- A violation of disparate-impact regulations adopted under Title VI is subject to administrative enforcement, but not by private action.

---

[34] In his dissent, joined by three other Justices, Justice Stevens described the majority opinion as "unfounded in our precedent and hostile to decades of settled expectations." In his view, "The question the Court answers today was only an open question in the most technical sense." (Pp. 295, 317.) As an alternative remedy, Justice Stevens (p. 293) suggested that rejected private litigants could bring discrimination-impact cases under 42 U.S.C. 1983 (authorizing actions for deprivation of federal civil rights). Several federal courts of appeals have rejected this approach. See, e.g., Johnson v. City of Detroit, 446 F.3d 614, 629 (6th Cir. 2006); Camden Citizens v. New Jersey Department of Environmental Protection, 274 F. 3d 771, 774 (3d Cir. 2001); Harris v. James, 127 F.3d 993, 1010 (11th Cir. 1997).

25. TITLE VII OF
THE 1964 CIVIL RIGHTS ACT

Title VII forbids an employer "…to discriminate against any individual with respect to his compensation, terms, conditions, or privileges of employment, because of such individual's race, color, religion, sex, or national origin…." [35] Title VII applies to all private employers, state and local governments, and education institutions that employ 15 or more individuals.

Because of Title VII's much broader coverage (among other things, the Equal Protection Clause is limited to "state action"), Title VII has largely superseded the Equal Protection Clause in the regulation of employment discrimination.

Through administrative and judicial interpretation, subsequently codified in the Act, the term "discriminate" in Title VII has been transformed to include not only intentional discrimination ("disparate treatment") but also commonly accepted practices that have a disproportionately adverse effect on minorities ("disparate impact"), even in the absence of any intent to discriminate.

Intentional discrimination was the original target of Title VII.[36] It did not include any express prohibition of practices producing a disparate impact; and Congress went further by including a provision to bar liability based on statistical imbalance in an employer's workforce: "Nothing contained in this title shall be interpreted to require any employer … to grant preferential treatment to any individual or to any group because of the race … of such individual or group on account of an imbalance which may exist with respect to

---

[35] 42 U.S.C § 2000e.

[36] See, e.g., Richard Primus, "Equal Protection and Disparate Impact: Round Three," 117 *Harvard. Law Review* 493, 506 (2003): "…Title VII's language has never been the real source of disparate impact doctrine. Though formally a statutory matter, liability for disparate impact in employment practices was engineered by EEOC and the courts before it was ever clearly approved by Congress."

the total number or percentage of persons of any race ... employed by any employer ... in comparison with the total number or percentage of persons of such race ... in any community ... or in the available work force in any community...."[37] In addition, the floor managers of the bill, Senators Joseph Clark and Clifford Case, assured the Senate: "There is no requirement in title VII that an employer maintain a racial balance in his work force. On the contrary, any deliberate attempt to maintain a racial balance, whatever such a balance may be, would involve a violation of title VII because maintaining such a balance would require an employer to hire on the basis of race. It must be emphasized that discrimination is prohibited as to any individual." [38]

Nevertheless, in Griggs v. Duke Power Co., 401 U.S. 424, 430 (1971), the Supreme Court (8-0) approved application of the disparate-impact standard, holding that "good intent or absence of discriminatory intent does not redeem employment procedures or testing mechanisms that operate as 'built-in headwinds' for minority groups and are unrelated to measuring job capability" (pp. 432-33).[39]

On that basis, the Court held that the employer in Griggs had discriminated under Title VII by requiring applicants to pass a standardized test of general ability because disproportionate numbers of black applicants had failed the test. The Court found inapplicable the Title VII provision expressly approving employers' use of "any professionally developed ability test" that is not "designed, intended or used to discriminate because of race."[40]

According to the decision, it is immaterial whether the test has been constructed to be race-neutral and free of bias. Any test used for hiring purposes, the Court concluded (pp. 431, 436), is permissible only if the employer first demonstrates that it is essential to determine fitness for the specific job: "The touchstone is business necessity. If an employment practice which operates to exclude Negroes cannot be

---

[37] 42 U.S.C. §2000e-2(h).

[38] See also Albemarle Paper Co. v. Moody, 422 U.S. 405 (1975); Connecticut v. Teal, 457 U.S. 440 (1982).

[40] 42 U.S.C. §2000e-2(h). The floor managers of the bill assured the Senate that "There is no requirement in title VII that employers abandon bona fide qualification tests where, because of differences in background and education, members of some groups are able to perform better on these tests than members of other groups. An employer may set his qualifications as high as he likes, he may test to determine which applicants have these qualifications, and he may hire, assign, and promote on the basis of test performance." 110 Cong. Rec. 7213 (1964).

shown to be related to job performance, the practice is prohibited."[41]

Under the EEOC's "Uniform Guidelines on Employee Selection Procedures," an "adverse impact" may be presumed if the employer's rate of selection for any protected group is less than 80 percent of the rate for the most successful racial group.[42] Such a statistical presumption is necessarily based on the highly dubious premise that, absent racial discrimination, an employer's workforce would reflect proportional representation of the general population in terms of ability, training, intelligence, reliability, and other human differences.

In addition, according to the EEOC, "...any selection procedure which has an adverse impact on the hiring [or] promotion ... of members of any race, sex, or ethnic group will be considered to be discriminatory ... unless the procedure has been validated in accordance with" the Commission's requirements.[43] Thus, once an employer's practice is found to be "discriminatory in operation" even though otherwise race-neutral, the employer is required to meet "the burden of showing that any given requirement [has] ... a manifest relationship to the employment in question."[44]

The *Griggs* decision also held that requiring a high school education was properly presumed to be discriminatory because of the lower percentage of blacks who meet that requirement (p. 431). An infinite variety of other employment standards—ranging from being clean-shaven to non-addiction to drugs—have similarly been presumed to be discriminatory if a lower percentage of blacks would qualify under the standard.[45]

---

[41] See Kull, supra, at 202-07; Thernstrom, supra, at 427-34.

[42] 29 CFR 1607.4.D.

[43] 29 CFR 1607.3.A

[44] In *Griggs*, supra, 401 U.S. at 431-32. In order to demonstrate that denial of any particular felon's employment application is justified by business necessity, individualized consideration of each of these three elements is required by the EEOC: (1) the nature and gravity of the offense or offenses; (2) the time that has passed since the conviction and/or completion of the sentence; and (3) the nature of the job held or sought. EEOC Policy Statement on the Issue of Conviction Records under Title VII (2/4/87); EEOC Compliance Manual §15-V.B (page 22). The EEOC also prohibits employers from asking applicants about arrests which have not led to convictions, on the ground that such questions may discourage them from applying for a job. Apart from Title VII, however, many federal laws either flatly bar people with criminal records from holding a particular occupation or restrict their ability to do so.

[45] See, e.g., New York City Transit Authority v. Beazer, 440 U.S. 568 (1979) (rule against employing drug addicts); Dothard v. Rawlinson, 433 U.S. 321 (1977) (height and weight requirements).

Even consideration of an applicant's criminal conviction is presumed unlawful by the EEOC because the percentage of black and Hispanic men with such histories is so much higher than the comparable percentage of white men. In April 2012 the EEOC announced that it would intensify enforcement against employers whose consideration of applicants' criminal histories produce a disparate impact on the company's workforce. Furthermore, according to the EEOC, "evidence of a racially balanced work force will not be enough to disprove disparate impact."[47]

Because of the financial and other costs of demonstrating "business necessity" to the EEOC's satisfaction, overcoming the presumption arising from a statistical "disparate impact" is often an illusory alternative. And, even if "business necessity" is established, the employer will still be found guilty if "the person challenging the policy or practice can demonstrate that a less discriminatory alternative exists that meets the [employer's] business need...."[48]

The result, whether or not intended, is to give employers a strong incentive to avoid legal difficulties by taking the path of least resistance—adoption of a policy of racial balancing. As Justice O'Connor stated for the plurality in Watson v. Fort Worth Bank & Trust, 487 U.S. 977, 992-93 (1988), "...the inevitable focus on statistics in disparate impact cases could put undue pressure on employers to adopt inappropriate prophylactic measures" and it is "unrealistic to suppose that employers can eliminate, or discover and explain, the myriad of innocent causes that may lead to statistical imbalances in the composition of their work forces." Justice O'Connor added: "If quotas and preferential treatment become the only cost-effective means of avoiding expensive litigation and potentially catastrophic liability, such measures will be widely adopted. The prudent employer will be careful to ensure that its programs are discussed in euphemistic terms, but will be

---

[46] Steven Greenhouse, "Equal Opportunity Panel Updates Hiring Policy," *New York Times*, April 26, 2012 (quoting the EEOC: "National data supports a finding that criminal record exclusions have a disparate impact based on race and national origin.").

[47] Robb Mandelbaum, "U.S. Push on Illegal Bias Against Hiring Those With Criminal Records," *New York Times*, June 20, 2012.

[48] EEOC Compliance Manual, supra, at 21-22.

equally careful to ensure that the quotas are met."[49]

In 1989, the Court qualified the statistical analysis sanctioned in *Griggs*. The decision in Wards Cove Packing Company v. Atonio, 490 U.S. 642 (1989), reversed (5-4) a lower court decision that a prima facie case of "disparate impact" had been established solely on the basis of a statistical analysis of the racial composition of two different groups of employees (showing a high percentage of blacks in cannery jobs and a low percentage of blacks in other jobs). The Court stated (p. 652):

> "The Court of Appeals' theory, at the very least, would mean that any employer who had a segment of his work force that was—for some reason—racially imbalanced, could be halled into court and forced to engage in the expensive and time-consuming task of defending the 'business necessity' of the methods used to select the other members of his work force. The only practicable option for many employers would be to adopt racial quotas, insuring that no portion of their work forces deviated in racial composition from the other portions thereof; this is a result that Congress expressly rejected in drafting Title VII."

"[T]he dispositive issue," the Court held, "is whether a challenged practice serves, in a significant way, the legitimate goals of the employer" and on that issue "there is no requirement that the challenged practice be 'essential' or 'indispensable' to the employer's business for it to pass muster: this degree of scrutiny would be almost impossible for most employers to meet, and would result in a host of evils we have identified above." (P. 659.)

But two years later, rejecting the *Wards Cove* decision, Congress amended Tile VII and expressly approved the *Griggs* standard. The Civil Rights Act of 1991 provided that the employer must carry the burden of proving business necessity, that the challenged practice "must bear a significant relationship to successful performance of the job," and that the amendment was "meant to codify the meaning

---

[49] See also, e.g., Stephan and Abigail Thernstrom, *America in Black and White: One Nation Indivisible* [Simon & Schuster 1997]: 431: "If a firm's workforce was racially balanced—if the numbers were 'right'—the expense of hiring experts to justify particular employment criteria as matters of 'business necessity' could be spared. This was also the obvious way to keep litigators at bay. For those who wished to avoid an expensive, time-consuming, and image-damaging battle in the courts, the best defense was a good offense: anticipatory race-conscious hiring."

of 'business necessity' as used in Griggs v. Duke Power Co. ... and to overrule the treatment of business necessity as a defense in Wards Cove Packing Co., Inc. v. Atonio...."[50]

The 1991 Act, however, acknowledges that "The mere existence of a statistical imbalance in an employer's workforce on account of race, color, religion, sex, or national origin is not alone sufficient to establish a prima facie case of disparate impact violation." Disparate-impact liability may be imposed, the Act provides, "only if" the challenged employment practice cannot be shown by the employer to be "job related ... and consistent with business necessity" or the complaining party demonstrates the existence and availability of an equally valid alternative that results in less disparate impact and the government employer "refuses to adopt" that alternative.[51]

---

[50] 42 U.S.C. §2000e-2(k).

[51] An employer's refusal to adopt an equally valid alternative with less adverse impact provides some evidence "that the employer was using its tests merely as a 'pretext' for discrimination." Albemarle Paper Co. v. Moody, 422 U.S. 405, 425 (1975) (citing McDonnell Douglas v. Green, 411 U.S. 792, 804-05 (1973)).

26. "DISPARATE IMPACT" VERSUS "DISPARATE TREATMENT"

As noted in the previous chapter, a Title VII violation may be based on either disparate-impact or disparate-treatment standards. The result may place employers in the position of attempting to navigate between the Scylla of disparate impact liability (for discrimination against minority employees) and the Charybdis of disparate treatment liability (for discrimination against nonminority employees).

In Ricci *v*. DeStefano, 557 U.S. ___ (2009), the Court sought to reconcile these two commands of Title VII. The case also raises the question of whether there is an even more fundamental conflict—between Title VII's disparate-impact standard and the Equal Protection Clause of the Fourteenth Amendment.

The *Ricci* suit was brought by a group of nonminority firefighters employed by the City of New Haven, Connecticut. The plaintiffs charged that the City had violated Title VII by intentionally discriminating against them because of their race—disparate *treatment*—in the grant of promotions. But the City, by way of defense, claimed that its treatment of nonminority employees was legally justified in order to avoid a Title VII violation based on the disparate *impact* of its employment policies on its minority employees.

The New Haven city charter established a merit system requiring that civil-service vacancies be filled with the most qualified individuals as determined by job-related examinations. Supplementing that requirement, the City's contract with the New Haven firefighters' union specified that applicants for lieutenant and captain positions were to be screened using written and oral examinations, with the written exam accounting for 60 percent and the oral exam 40 percent of an applicant's total score.

In 2003, the City scheduled examinations to determine the eligibility of New Haven firefighters for promotion to the ranks of lieutenant and captain.

After reviewing bids from various consultants, the City hired a company (IOS) to develop and administer the examinations, at a cost to the City of $100,000. IOS specializes in designing examinations for fire and police departments. IOS engaged in extensive analyses to identify the tasks, knowledge, skills, and abilities that are essential for the lieutenant and captain positions in the New Haven fire department. At every stage of the analyses, IOS deliberately oversampled minority firefighters to ensure that the results would not unintentionally favor white candidates. With the job-analysis information in hand, IOS developed the written examinations to measure the candidates' job-related knowledge. Each test had 100 questions, as required by civil-service rules, and was written below a 10th-grade reading level. After IOS prepared the tests, the City gave candidates a three-month study period to review the source material for the questions, including the specific material from which the questions were taken. The oral examinations were scored by nine three-person panels—each consisting of one white, one black, and one Hispanic—selected from fire departments of similar size from outside Connecticut.

118 firefighters took the examinations. 77 candidates took the lieutenant examination—43 whites, 19 blacks, and 15 Hispanics. Of the 77, 34 passed—25 whites, 6 blacks, and 3 Hispanics; the top ten candidates to fill the eight vacant positions were white. 41 candidates took the captain examination—25 whites, 8 blacks, and 8 Hispanics. Of the 41, 22 passed—16 whites, 3 blacks, and 3 Hispanics; the top 9 candidates to fill the 7 vacant positions were 7 whites and 2 Hispanics.

When the test results showed that no black candidates had qualified for promotion to fill the vacant positions, the mayor and other local politicians strongly objected, and the City Civil Service Board refused to certify the test results. Soon after the denial of certification, the mayor "took credit for the scu[tt]ling of the examination results."

When certification was denied, 18 firefighters who would

otherwise have become eligible for promotion (17 whites and 1 Hispanic) filed suit. The plaintiffs alleged that, by discarding the test results, the City had discriminated against them because of their race, in violation of both Title VII of the Civil Rights Act of 1964 and the Equal Protection Clause of the Fourteenth Amendment.[52] In defense of the suit, the City and the other defendants argued that, if the results had been certified, the City might have faced liability under Title VII for adopting a practice that had a disparate impact on the black firefighters.

In granting summary judgment for the defendants, the District Court found that the City rejected the test results because of "a concern that too many whites and not enough minorities would be promoted were the lists to be certified." But the District Court concluded that "Defendants' motivation to avoid making promotions based on a test with a racially disparate impact ... does not, as a matter of law, constitute discriminatory intent...."; that the City did not deny the plaintiffs equal protection since "all applicants took the same test, and the result was the same for all because the test results were discarded and nobody was promoted"; and that, "while the evidence shows that race was taken into account in the decision not to certify the test results, the result was race-neutral: all the test results were discarded, no one was promoted, and firefighters of every race will have to participate in another selection process to be considered for promotion." (554 F.Supp.2d 142, 152, 160, 161, 162.)

The plaintiffs appealed to the Court of Appeals for the Second Circuit. The panel that heard the case affirmed (3-0) in a one-paragraph *per curiam* order adopting the opinion of the District Court. The full court (7-6) denied plaintiffs' petition for rehearing *en banc*.

In a 5-4 decision, the Supreme Court reversed, holding that the City's disparate treatment of the plaintiffs had violated Title VII. Because of its ruling on Title VII, the Court found it unnecessary

---

[52] The plaintiffs were able to assert both Title VII and Equal Protection claims because state and local public employers like New Haven are subject to Title VII and New Haven's conduct also constituted "state action" subject to the Fourteenth Amendment. Although New Haven is a public body, the Court's interpretation of Title VII is equally applicable, of course, to private employers subject to the Act.

to reach the question whether the City had also violated the Equal Protection Clause.

Justice Kennedy's majority opinion (joined by Roberts, Scalia, Alito, and Thomas) held that, before an employer can discriminate against nonminority employees for the asserted purpose of avoiding or remedying an unintentional disparate impact on minority employees, the employer must have a strong basis in evidence to believe it will be subject to disparate-impact liability if it does not take the discriminatory action. The City, the Court held, failed to meet that requirement and the plaintiffs were entitled to summary judgment:

> "The City's actions would violate the disparate-treatment prohibition of Title VII absent some valid defense. All the evidence demonstrates that the City chose not to certify the examination results because of the statistical disparity based on race—*i.e.*, how minority candidates had performed when compared to white candidates....

> "Allowing employers to violate the disparate-treatment prohibition based on a mere good-faith fear of disparate-impact liability would encourage race-based action at the slightest hint of disparate impact. ... That would amount to a *de facto* quota system, in which a 'focus on statistics ... could put undue pressure on employers to adopt inappropriate prophylactic measures'.... Even worse, an employer could discard test results (or other employment practices) with the intent of obtaining the employer's preferred racial balance....

> "Even if respondents were motivated as a subjective matter by a desire to avoid committing disparate-impact discrimination, the record makes clear there is no support for the conclusion that respondents had an objective, strong basis in evidence to find the tests inadequate, with some consequent disparate-impact liability in violation of Title VII....

> "The City, moreover, turned a blind eye to evidence that supported the exams' validity....

> "There is no genuine dispute that the examinations were job-related and consistent with business necessity. The City's assertions to the contrary are 'blatantly contradicted by the record'....

"On the record before us, there is no genuine dispute that the City lacked a strong basis in evidence to believe it would face disparate-impact liability if it certified the examination results. In other words, there is no evidence—let alone the required strong basis in evidence—that the tests were flawed because they were not job-related or because other, equally valid and less discriminatory tests were available to the City. Fear of litigation alone cannot justify an employer's reliance on race to the detriment of individuals who passed the examinations and qualified for promotions."

The Court accordingly ordered certification of the results of the promotion exams, as sought by the *Ricci* plaintiffs.[53]

In seeking to meet the formidable challenge of reconciling Title VII's two theories of liability, the Court clearly recognized that disparate treatment is the core prohibition of Title VII, with disparate impact occupying a secondary role when the two theories are in conflict. The primacy of disparate treatment is supported not only by its constitutional counterpart in the Equal Protection Clause but also by the statute's history. Disparate treatment was the thrust of Title VII as originally enacted; disparate impact was added only by the Civil Rights Act of 1991 and before then existed only as an administrative and judicial construct.

Justice Ginsburg (joined by Stevens, Breyer, and Souter) dissented, concluding that the plaintiffs "have not shown that New Haven's failure to certify the exam results violated Title VII's disparate-treatment provision."

---

[53] Subsequently another black New Haven firefighter (Michael Briscoe) sued the city under Title VII alleging that he had failed the same promotion exams because the results had a disparate impact on blacks. In Briscoe v. New Haven (No. 10-1975-cv Aug. 15, 2011), cert. denied (June 11, 2012), the Court of Appeals for the Second Circuit recognized that the Supreme Court in *Ricci* had apparently anticipated that its decision would protect the City from further disparate-impact liability relating to the exams. The Second Circuit, however, held that Briscoe was not precluded by the Supreme Court's decision (since he had not been a party to the *Ricci* case) and was therefore entitled to proceed with his claim (subject to what other defenses the City might assert). As one commentator noted, "Given the tense and complicated racial politics of New Haven, the city could be guilty of discrimination against both white and black firefighters." Richard Thompson Ford, "Now a Black Firefighter Is Suing New Haven," *Slate*, Oct. 23, 2009. See also, e.g., Charles Sullivan, "*Ricci v. DeStefano*: End of the Line or Just Another Turn on the Disparate Impact Road?," 104 *Northwestern University Law Review* 411, 423-26 (2010).

The dissent contended that the plaintiffs had "no vested right to promotion" and that the majority's "recitation of the facts leaves out important parts of the story," that "It took decades of persistent effort, advanced by Title VII litigation, to open firefighting posts to members of racial minorities," and that "By order of this Court, New Haven, a city in which African-Americans and Hispanics account for nearly 60 percent of the population, must today be served—as it was in the days of undisguised discrimination—by a fire department in which members of racial and ethnic minorities are rarely seen in command positions." In the dissenters' view, "New Haven had ample cause to believe its selection process was flawed and not justified by business necessity" because of "substantial evidence of multiple flaws in the tests New Haven used" and "the better tests used in other cities, which have yielded less racially skewed outcomes."

Justices Alito and Scalia, in addition to joining in the Kennedy majority opinion, filed concurring opinions. Justice Alito's opinion (joined by Scalia and Thomas) took issue with the dissent's characterization of the City's rejection of the test results. The record demonstrates, Alito contended, that "the City administration was lobbied by an influential community leader to scrap the test results, and the City administration decided on that course of action before making any real assessment of the possibility of a disparate-impact violation" and "that the City's real reason for scrapping the test results was not a concern about violating the disparate-impact provision of Title VII but a simple desire to please a politically important racial constituency."

Justice Scalia wrote separately

"...to observe that [the Court's] resolution of this dispute merely postpones the evil day on which the Court will have to confront the question: Whether, or to what extent, are the disparate-impact provisions of Title VII of the Civil Rights Act of 1964 consistent with the Constitution's guarantee of equal protection? The question is not an easy one. ...

"The difficulty is this: Whether or not Title VII's disparate-treatment provisions forbid 'remedial' race-based actions when a disparate-impact violation would *not* otherwise result—the question resolved by the Court today—it is clear that Title VII not only permits but affirmatively *requires* such actions when a disparate-impact violation *would* otherwise result. ... But if the Federal Government is prohibited from discriminating on the basis of race, Bolling *v.* Sharpe, 347 U.S. 497, 500 (1954), then surely it is also prohibited from enacting laws mandating that third parties—e.g., employers, whether private, State, or municipal—discriminate on the basis of race...

"The Court's resolution of these cases makes it unnecessary to resolve these matters today. But the war between disparate impact and equal protection will be waged sooner or later, and it behooves us to begin thinking about how—and on what terms—to make peace between them." (Italics Scalia's.)

In response to Scalia's opinion, Justice Ginsburg's dissent stated that "Until today... this Court has never questioned the constitutionality of the disparate-impact component of Title VII...." After *Ricci*, however, addressing this explosive issue may ultimately be unavoidable.

Justice Scalia's comment that "The question is not an easy one" is surely a massive understatement. The "evil day" when the question is directly confronted would force the Court to make a difficult choice.[54] A decision holding that the Equal Protection Clause invalidates Title VII's disparate-impact provisions would not only ignite a national firestorm but would also require the Court to repudiate its rulings in *Griggs* and other cases on which the disparate-impact doctrine was founded and developed.[55] A contrary decision, on the other hand, would presumably require a holding that the disparate-impact provisions meet the "strict scrutiny" standard.[56]

---

[54] The issue will presumably arise only in circumstances similar to those presented in the *Ricci* case—i.e., where those disadvantaged by the "disparate impact" are clearly identifiable. As Richard Primus pointed out: "...the race-conscious aspect of New Haven's decision to discard the results of the test became enormously and divisively salient, and its creation of visible victims was an important part of the reason why. Scrapping the test after it was administered and graded highlighted a specific set of innocent third parties at risk of being adversely affected." Richard Primus, "The Future of Disparate Impact," 108 *Michigan Law Review* 1341, 1373 (2110).

[55] Justice Ginsburg quotes and Justice Scalia cites an article by Richard Primus, "Equal Protection and Disparate Impact: Round Three," 117 *Harvard Law Review* 493, 585 (2003), commenting that "The very radicalism of holding disparate impact doctrine unconstitutional as a matter of equal protection suggests that only a very uncompromising court would issue such a decision." See also Linda Greenhouse, "The Next Time," *New York Times*, January 28, 2010.

[56] See, e.g., Richard Primus, "The Future of Disparate Impact," 108 *Michigan Law Review* 1341, 1375-82 (2110).

27. RACE AND FREE EXPRESSION

Race has also been deeply involved in many decisions interpreting the First Amendment's guarantee of free expression.

FREEDOM OF ASSOCIATION

In NAACP v. Alabama ex rel. Patterson, 357 U.S. 449, 460 (1958), Alabama sought to exclude the NAACP from doing business in the state on the ground that it had not complied with a state statute requiring qualification of foreign corporations.[57] When the NAACP took steps to comply, the state insisted the NAACP disclose its membership lists. The NAACP brought suit, claiming that the effect of compelled disclosure of the membership lists would be to abridge the rights of its rank-and-file members to engage in lawful association in support of their common beliefs. In support of their claim, the NAACP argued that revelation of the identity of its rank-and-file members had exposed these members to economic reprisal, loss of employment, threat of physical coercion, and other manifestations of public hostility.

The Court, in an opinion by Justice Harlan, found the law unconstitutional, stating (pp. 462-63): "... we think it apparent that compelled disclosure of petitioner's Alabama membership is likely to affect adversely the ability of [the Association] and its members to pursue their collective effort to foster beliefs which they admittedly have the right to advocate, in that it may induce members to withdraw from the Association and dissuade others from joining it because of fear of exposure of their beliefs shown through their associations and of the consequences of this exposure." In addition, "It is not sufficient to answer, as the State does here, that whatever repressive effect compulsory disclosure of names of petitioner's members may have upon participation by Alabama citizens in petitioner's activities follows not from state action but from private community pressures. The crucial factor is the interplay of governmental and private action, for it is only after the initial exertion of state power represented by the production order that private action takes hold."

THREATS AND CROSS-BURNINGS

Although the First Amendment is worded in absolute terms ("...shall make no law ... abridging the freedom of speech, or of the press"), it has long been recognized that not every communicative use of words is constitutionally protected. The Amendment has been construed to permit restrictions upon the content of speech in a few "well-defined and narrowly limited classes of speech, the prevention and punishment of which have never been thought to raise any Constitutional problem."[57] These unprotected activities include, for example, speech used in the commission of a crime such as perjury or bribery, so-called "fighting words" directed at another and likely to provoke a violent response, and the communication of a "true threat."

In Watts v. United States, 394 U.S. 705 (1969), a young black man was convicted of violating a federal law that prohibits threats against the president. During a protest in Washington D.C., he announced that he would refuse to respond to his draft notice and that "If they ever make me carry a rifle the first man I want to get in my sights is L.B.J. They are not going to make me kill my black brothers." The Supreme Court (5-4) reversed the conviction, holding that in context the statement would be understood by a reasonable person as political hyperbole rather than a true threat—"a kind of very crude offensive method of stating a political opposition to the President."

In NAACP v. Claiborne Hardware, 458 U.S. 886 (1982), the Court (8-0) reversed a Mississippi state court decision holding the NAACP and Charles Evers liable for damages for promoting a boycott of white-owned businesses. Names of boycott violators were read aloud at meetings at a black church and published in a local black newspaper. Evers, an NAACP official, had given impassioned speeches to blacks encouraging their compliance with the boycott and had declared: "If we catch any of you going in any of them racist stores, we're gonna break your damn neck."

Finding that Evers' statements did not constitute an incitement to imminent lawless action or a true threat, the Court stated: "Strong

---

[57] Chaplinsky v. New Hampshire, 315 U.S. 568, 571-72 (1942) ("fighting words" exception).

and effective extemporaneous rhetoric cannot be nicely channeled in purely dulcet phrases. An advocate must be free to stimulate his audience with spontaneous and emotional appeals for unity and action in a common cause. When such appeals do not incite lawless action, they must be regarded as protected speech" (p. 928). "Speech," the Court declared, "does not lose its protected character ... simply because it may embarrass others or coerce them into action" (p. 910).

Two "threat" cases involved challenges to convictions under legislation prohibiting the burning of crosses: R.A.V. v. St. Paul, 505 U.S. 377 (1992); and Virginia v. Black, 538 U.S. 343 (2003). In these cases, all the Justices except Justice Thomas rejected the claim that cross-burning should be regarded as outside the scope of the First Amendment and held instead that cross-burning is "speech" presumptively entitled to constitutional protection.

The Court, however, reached opposite conclusions on the constitutionality of the two challenged provisions on the basis of their different wording. In *R.A.V.* the St. Paul ordinance (prohibiting a cross-burning when it "arouses anger, alarm or resentment in others *on the basis of race, color, creed, religion, or gender*") was held to be content-based and therefore invalid because it singled out specific disfavored subjects for punishment. On the other hand, unlike the St. Paul ordinance, the Virginia statute in *Virginia v. Black* (prohibiting a cross-burning *"with the intent of intimidating any person or group of persons"*) was upheld on the ground that it is content-neutral because it contains no list of taboo subjects. (Italics added.)[58]

The vice of the St. Paul ordinance, the Court held, was that under the ordinance "Displays containing abusive invective, no matter how vicious or severe, are permissible unless they are addressed to one of the specified disfavored topics. Those who wish to use 'fighting words' in connection with other ideas—to express hostility, for example, on the basis of political affiliation, union membership, or homosexuality—are not covered. Displays containing some words—odious racial epithets, for example—would be prohibited to proponents of all views. But 'fighting words' that do not themselves invoke race, color, creed, religion, or gender—aspersions upon a person's

---

[58] While otherwise upholding the Virginia statute, the Court invalidated a section of the law providing that all cross-burnings were presumed to be intimidating.

mother, for example—would seemingly be usable ad libitum in the placards of those arguing in favor of racial, color, etc., tolerance and equality, but could not be used by those speakers' opponents." St. Paul, the Court concluded, "has no such authority to license one side of a debate to fight freestyle, while requiring the other to follow Marquis of Queensberry rules."

HATE CRIME LAWS

The term "hate crime law" is commonly applied to a law that provides *increased punishment* for those found guilty of certain crimes. A "hate crime law" does not criminalize conduct that is otherwise lawful. Instead, such laws enhance the penalty for violation of criminal statutes of general applicability (that prohibit, for example, homicide, assault, or other specified conduct regardless of the identity of the victim) if the victim of the crime was a member of a protected minority group and if it is also proved that the crime was motivated by bias against the group. Almost every state has some variety of hate crime laws.[59]

A statute of this type was unanimously upheld by the Supreme Court in Wisconsin v. Mitchell, 508 U.S. 476 (1993). The challenged Wisconsin statute provides that the maximum penalty for an offense shall be increased whenever the defendant "intentionally selects the person against whom the crime ... is committed ... because of the race, religion, color, disability, sexual orientation, national origin or ancestry of that person." The case arose from the severe beating of a white boy by a group of black men including the defendant. The defendant's prison sentence for aggravated battery (normally subject to a maximum sentence of two years) was increased to four years because of the jury's finding that the defendant had intentionally selected his victim because of his race.

Sustaining the validity of the statute, the Court stated: "Traditionally, sentencing judges have considered a wide variety of factors in addition to evidence bearing on guilt in determining what sentence to impose on a convicted defendant. The defendant's motive for committing the offense is one important factor. ... The Constitution does not erect a per se barrier to the admission of evidence concerning one's beliefs

---

[59] See Bill Keller, "Tyler and Trayvon," *New York Times*, April 1, 2012, for a persuasive critique of "hate crime" laws.

and associations at sentencing simply because those beliefs and associations are protected by the First Amendment." (P. 485.)

In addition to laws providing for enhanced punishment of crimes of general appliability, there are some criminal statutes—also sometimes called "hate crime laws"—that specifically prohibit conduct that injures members of certain protected groups because of their membership in such groups. Thus a federal statute, 18 U.S.C. §249(a)(1), provides for prosecution of anyone who "willfully causes bodily injury to any person or ... attempts to cause bodily injury to any person, because of the actual or perceived race, color, religion, or national origin of any person.." A violation of the statute involving a firearm or incendiary device is subject to a prison term of up to 10 years, while an offense involving murder, kidnapping, or sexual assault is subject to life imprisonment.

OFFENSIVE SPEECH

Offensive speech concerning race (or, for example, religion, gender, or sexual orientation) is often called "hate speech." But applying that label does not make it any it more subject to government regulation than other types of offensive speech. [60]

Unless it meets the requirements of an established exception to First Amendment protection (such as, e.g., "fighting words"), "hate speech" is constitutionally protected. Nor does it lose constitutional protection if (as is frequently the case) the effect of the "hate speech" is to inflict harm on a person or group. [61]

Sixty years ago, in Beauharnais v. Illinois, 343 U.S. 250 (1952), the Supreme Court upheld a state law that prohibited any publication that portrays "depravity, criminality, unchastity, or lack of virtue of a

---

[60] "Hate speech" if unaccompanied by conduct violating a criminal statute is to be distinguished from "hate crime laws" described above.

[61] As Michael McConnell observed in a recent book review: "Contrary to Waldron's apparent assumption, few people in the United States doubt that hate speech inflicts real harm on vulnerable minorities, any more than they doubt that lies about political candidates injure our democratic process; that vicious protests at the funerals of fallen soldiers inflict severe emotional injury on their families; that persistent use of extremely violent video games by adolescents aggravates antisocial behavior; that unlimited corporate and labor union contributions to candidates add to the appearance of political corruption; that public profanity degrades our culture; that raucous anti-abortion protests disturb patients seeking to end their pregnancies; or that the publication of state secrets undermines national security. This speech is all constitutionally protected — not because we doubt the speech inflicts harm, but because we fear the censorship more." Michael McConnell, "You Can't Say That," *New York Times*, June 22, 2012 (reviewing book by Jeremy Waldron).

class of citizens, of any race, color, creed, or religion [which exposes such citizens] to contempt, derision or obloquy or which is productive of breach of the peace or riots." The Court affirmed convictions under the law for urging the Mayor and City Council of Chicago to protect white neighborhoods from "encroachment, harassment, and invasion ... by the Negro" and called for "one million self respecting white people in Chicago to unite." According to the decision, just as a state could punish defamation, so may a state "punish the same utterance directed at a defined group."

Although *Beauharnais* has never has been expressly overruled, it has implicitly been repudiated by the Court's later decisions:

- The predicate of the *Beauharnais* ruling—that defamation liability is unlimited by the First Amendment—was expressly rejected by New York Times v. Sullivan, 376 U.S. 254 (1964).
- Brandenburg v. Ohio, 395 U.S. 444 (1969), expanded the scope of protected speech by holding (9-0) that the advocacy of the use of force or law violation is protected by the First Amendment "except where such advocacy is directed to inciting or producing imminent lawless action and is likely to incite or produce such action."
- *NAACP v. Claiborne Hardware Co.* similarly requires, in order to prohibit speech on the ground of incitement of violence, proof that there was a likelihood of imminent illegal conduct and that the speech was directed at causing imminent illegal conduct.
- Cohen v. California, 403 U.S. 15 (1971), held that a state does not have authority to prohibit "offensive speech" on the ground that others might find it objectionable.
- *R.A.V. v. St. Paul* reaffirmed that expression of racial hate is not outside First Amendment protection.

Notwithstanding these decisions, many state universities and colleges have adopted "speech codes" that prohibit and penalize certain types of offensive speech—speech that expresses bias or "hate" or "insensitivity" toward minorities or women. Whenever challenged on constitutional grounds, such codes have been rejected or withdrawn by state schools.

Typical is the University of Michigan regulation that subjected students to discipline for "[any] behavior, verbal or physical, that stigmatizes or victimizes an individual on the basis of race, ethnicity, religion, sex, sexual orientation, creed, national origin, ancestry, age, marital status, handicap or Viet Nam era veteran status" that "has the purpose or reasonably foreseeable effect of interfering with an individual's academic efforts, employment, participation in University sponsored extra-curricular activities or personal safety." The regulation was held unconstitutional under the First Amendment as overbroad and too vague.[62]

Efforts to justify such codes on the basis of the "fighting words" exception have proved unavailing. Moreover, the decision in *R.A.V. v. St. Paul* provides a formidable obstacle to the defense of any challenged speech code. If the code is limited to prohibiting certain forms of improper speech, it is likely invalid as impermissible content-based discrimination; but if the code is general in nature, it would likely fail on vagueness and overbreadth grounds.[63]

Nevertheless, these codes remain on the books at many universities and colleges and can have a chilling effect on students who do not want to risk the controversy or expense of challenging them.

A similar but less formal speech code—indeed, a code enforced by the federal government—continues in effect in the American workplace. Title VII of the 1964 Civil Rights Act has been interpreted to bar racial or sexual "harassment"—speech or conduct that creates a "hostile work environment." Many cases have found harassment on the basis (in whole or in substantial part) of offensive speech that the First Amendment protects outside the workplace—including content-based comments, jokes, magazines, and cartoons that insult or annoy minorities.[64]

---

[62] Doe v. University of Michigan, 721 F. Supp. 852 (E.D. Mich. 1989). Speech codes are also widely prevalent in private universities and colleges (which are not subject to court challenges under the First Amendment). Tufts University, for example, prohibits (among other things) "[h]arassment or discrimination against individuals on the basis of race, religion, gender identity/expression, ethnic or national origin, gender, sexual orientation, disability, age, or genetics," including "*attitudes or opinions that are expressed verbally or in writing*" (italics added).

[63] See Erwin Chemerinsky, *Constitutional Law: Principles and Policies* [Aspen 2d ed. 2002]: 979-80.

[64] See, e.g., Eugene Volokh, "What Speech Does 'Hostile Work Environment' Harassment Law Restrict?," 85 *Georgetown Law Review* 627 (1997); Kingsley Browne, "Title VII as Censorship: Hostile-Environment Harassment and the First Amendment," 52 *Ohio State Law Journal* 481 (1991).

PART V
MINORITY PREFERENCES

28. DEFINING "AFFIRMATIVE ACTION"

In his famous dissent in *Plessy v. Ferguson*, Justice John Marshall Harlan eloquently declared that "Our constitution is color-blind, and neither knows nor tolerates classes among citizens."[1] Harlan's dissent is widely (although incorrectly, as explained in Chapter 7) understood as arguing that all racial classifications are *per se* unconstitutional, without regard to the reasonableness or justification of such a classification.

This color-blind doctrine, although never adopted by any decision of the Supreme Court, was a key predicate of the campaign against segregation.[2] But in the mid-1960s the doctrine was repudiated by civil rights groups, contending that ending discrimination is insufficient to overcome the "under-representation" of minorities in important areas of American life.[3] Color-blindness

---

[1] 63 U.S. 537, 559 (1896).

[2] In *Brown v. Board of Education,* for example, the plaintiffs contended that "Classifications and distinctions based on race or color have no legal or moral validity in our society" and "That the Constitution is color blind is our dedicated belief." Brief for Appellants, 1953, Nos. 1, 2, and 4, p. 65.

[3] Andrew Kull, *The Color-Blind Constitution* [Harvard 1992]: 182-201; Terry Anderson, *The Pursuit of Fairness: A History of Affirmative Action* [Oxford 2004] 49-109; Dinesh D'Souza, *The End of Racism* [Free Press 1995]: 163-70, 205-06. Kull, supra, at 182, states: "The idea of the color-blind Constitution was largely eclipsed after 1968 because those who make national policy came to the view, contrary to the earlier beliefs of many of them, that race-specific measures were necessary means to imperative political ends."

(scorned by some critics as "reactionary" and even "racist"[4]) was rejected in favor of race-conscious "affirmative action."[5]

When granted by a private organization, minority preferences do not present a federal *constitutional* issue. As explained in Part IV, in the absence of the requisite "state action" involvement, the Fourteenth Amendment does not apply to private (non-governmental) conduct. But when racial preferences are granted by a government institution or by a private organization engaged in "state action," they are subject to challenge under the Equal Protection Clause. In addition, racial preferences by any federally funded organization, whether public or private, are subject to challenge on a statutory basis under Title VI of the 1964 Civil Rights Act.[6]

In a 1965 speech President Johnson declared his administration's support for minority preferences: "This is the next and the more profound stage of the battle for civil rights. We seek not just freedom but opportunity. We seek not just legal equity but human ability, not just equality as a right and a theory but equality as a fact and equality as a result."[7]

In 1969 President Nixon initiated the "Philadelphia Plan," the first significant federal minority preference program, to increase minority hiring in federal construction projects. The program ostensibly required only "goals and timetables" but in practical effect

---

[4]   See, e.g, Ian F. Haney Lopez, " 'A Nation of Minorities': Race, Ethnicity, and Reactionary Colorblindness," 59 *Stanford Law Review* 985, 989 (2007); Monica Williams, "Colorblind Ideology Is a Form of Racism," *Psychology Today* (December 27, 2011); Eduardo Bonilla-*Silva, Racism Without Racists: Color-Blind Racism. Inequality in the United States* [Rowman & Littlefield 2003]; Erin Winkler, "The Attack on Affirmative Action: The 'Race Neutral' Excuse," 33 *The Black Scholar* 37 (2007).

[5]   Thurgood Marshall, who in Brown had asked the Supreme Court to accept the color-blind doctrine, wrote in 1978: "During most of the past 200 years, the Constitution as interpreted by this Court did not prohibit the most ingenious and pervasive forms of discrimination against the Negro. Now, when a State acts to remedy the effects of that legacy of discrimination, I cannot believe that this same Constitution stands as a barrier." Regents of the University of California v. Bakke, 438 U.S. 265, 387 (1978) (concurring and dissenting).

[6]   See Chapter 24 *Title VI of the 1964 Civil Rights Act.*

[7]   Lyndon B. Johnson, "To Fulfill These Rights": Commencement Address at Howard University, June 4, 1965. As Kull points out, supra at 184-87, the genesis of the speech was a much-disputed report by Daniel Moynihan, then Assistant Secretary of Labor (later United States Senator), "The Negro Family: The Case for National Action," Office of Planning and Research, United States Department of Labor (March 1965).

imposed racial quotas.[8]

The shift in focus from discrimination to preferences led to strong opposition, including opposition by many ardent supporters of racial equality.[9] For example, in his critique of "the new racialism," Daniel Patrick Moynihan objected to "institutional strategies involving government-dictated outcomes directed against those institutions most vulnerable to government pressure" and warned that proportional representation policies would damage American universities.[10] And, in a much-quoted comment, Alexander Bickel protested: "The lesson of the great decisions of the Supreme Court and the lesson of contemporary history have been the same for at least a generation: discrimination on the basis of race is illegal, immoral, unconstitutional, inherently wrong, and destructive of democratic society. Now this is to be unlearned and we are told that this is not a matter of fundamental principle but only a matter of whose ox is gored. Those for whom racial equality was demanded are to be more equal than others. Having found support in the Constitution for equality, they now claim support for inequality under the same Constitution."[11]

Half a century later, the disagreement on the subject has, if anything, become more heated.

At the outset of any consideration of the controversy, the extraordinary ambiguity of the term "affirmative action" should be recognized. The term, somewhat confusingly, is often applied to government policies that are *not* restricted by the Equal Protection Clause. These include:

- *"Affirmative action" to eliminate racial discrimination against minorities.* For example, Executive Order 10925 issued by President Kennedy on March 6, 1961, required government contractors to "take affirmative action to ensure that applicants are employed, and that employees are treated during

---

8   Anderson, supra, at 118-26.

9   As a result of the shift, opponents of affirmative action and racial balancing have become the principal proponents of the color-blind doctrine. See, e.g., the repeated references to the Harlan dissent in the opinions of the Justices in Parents Involved in Community Schools v. Seattle School District No. 1, 551 U.S. 701 (2007).

10 Daniel Patrick Moynihan, "The New Racialism," *Atlantic Monthly* (August 1968), 35, 37.

11 Alexander Bickel, *The Morality of Consent* [Yale 1975]: 133.

employment, *without regard to their race, creed, color, or national origin.*"[12] (Italics added.)

- *"Affirmative action" through preferences to the economically
  disadvantaged on a race-neutral basis* (sometimes called
  "class-based affirmative action"). Such a program, by
  definition, does not involve minority preferences. Barack
  Obama, in his campaign for the presidency, indicated support for this kind of "affirmative action." In response to
  the question "Why should your daughters when they go to
  college get affirmative action?," Senator Obama stated: "I
  think that my daughters should probably be treated by any
  admissions officer as folks who are pretty advantaged, and
  I think that there's nothing wrong with us taking that into
  account as we consider admissions policies at universities.
  I think that we should take into account white kids who
  have been disadvantaged and have grown up in poverty
  and shown themselves to have what it takes to succeed."[13]

- *"Affirmative action" recruiting programs to expand the pool of
  eligible applicants on a race-neutral basis.* Again, if the program is race-neutral, no minority preferences are involved.[14]

By contrast, significant issues under the Equal Protection Clause
are presented by government preferences that are granted on a racial
basis to designated minorities by application of lower standards or
other means.

These policies have taken myriad forms. Examples include:

---

[12] The same language was used in President Lyndon Johnson's 1965 Executive Order
11246, but is markedly different from his statement of the policy in his 1965 Howard
commencement address, supra.

[13] May 13, 2007 television interview on *This Week with George Stephanapoulos* (ABC
network). In his best-selling book *The Audacity of Hope,* Obama criticized racial
preferences as a program that "dissect[s] Americans into 'us' and 'them'" and "can't
serve as the basis for the kinds of sustained, broad-based political coalitions needed
to transform America."

[14] See, e.g., Richmond v. J.A. Croson Co., 488 U.S. 469, 509-10 (1989): "Even in the absence of evidence of discrimination, the city has at its disposal a whole array of race-
neutral devices to increase the accessibility of city contracting opportunities to small
entrepreneurs of all races. Simplification of bidding procedures, relaxation of bonding
requirements, and training and financial aid for disadvantaged entrepreneurs of all
races would open the public contracting market to all those who have suffered the
effects of past societal discrimination or neglect."

- *Outright quotas*—devices (expressed in either numerical or percentage terms) widely used in earlier years to exclude or limit Jews, Catholics, and Asian-Americans,[15] but now used in some instances to prefer other minorities.

- *"Set-asides" or "reserved spots"*—the problem in the famous *Bakke* case (see Chapter 30).

- *"Bonus" arrangements*—Thus the law challenged in *Adarand Constructors, Inc. v. Pena* awarded a contractor a substantial bonus for selecting a minority subcontractor over a non-minority subcontractor.

- *"Critical mass" policies*—In the University of Michigan cases, it was contended that minority preferences were justified to establish a "critical mass" of students in each of three underrepresented racial groups.

- *"Race norming"*—a practice that was (until outlawed in 1991) widely used by federal and state government agencies to increase minority test scores to equalize the results for minorities and nonminorities.[16]

- *"Racial balancing"*—used in school boards' assignment of students to schools within a public school system on the basis of the students' race. This practice, a variant of "affirmative action," was rejected by the Court in Parents Involved in Community Schools v. Seattle School District No. 1, 551 U.S. 701 (2007).[17]

---

[15] See, e.g., Jerome Karabel, *The Chosen* [Mariner Books 2005]: passim.

[16] See, e.g., Peter Kilborn, " 'Race Norming' Tests Becomes a Fiery Issue," *New York Times*, May 19, 1991; Dinesh D'Souza, *The End of Racism: Principles for a Multiracial Society* [Free Press 1995]: 306-07.

[17] In addition to such voluntarily instituted programs, the term "affirmative action" has sometimes been loosely applied to court orders employed by courts as remedies to eradicate segregation previously found to violate the Fourteenth Amendment. E.g., Swann v. Charlotte-Mecklenburg Board of Education, 402 U.S. 1 (1971); Milliken v. Bradley, 418 U.S. 717 (1974); Sheet Metal Workers v. EEOC, 478 U.S. 421 (1986); United States v. Paradise, 480 U.S. 149 (1987). Thus, In *Swann* (402 U.S. at 25), the Court upheld the authority of a district court to order pupil assignments on a racial basis, emphasizing that such measures should be employed only on a temporary basis to eliminate purposeful segregation and as "a useful starting point in shaping a remedy to correct past constitutional violations." But, as the Court emphasized in Freeman v. Pitts, 503 U.S. 467, 495 (1992), "[w]here resegregation is a product not of state action but of private choices, it does not have constitutional implications" and "is beyond the authority and beyond practical ability of the federal courts to try to counteract these kinds of continuous and massive demographic shifts."

Despite the support of some Justices for a more lenient standard under the Equal Protection Clause, the Supreme Court has repeatedly held that government discrimination favoring minorities is subject to the same "strict scrutiny" standard of review applicable to government discrimination against minorities—i.e., whether the preference serves a compelling public interest and is narrowly tailored to serve that interest.[18]

---

[18] The Court has held that the creation of majority-black election districts—another form of affirmative action—is subject to a somewhat different standard. See Chapter 37 *Racial Preferences in Redistricting*.

29. AFFIRMATIVE ACTION AND THE RACIAL ACHIEVEMENT GAP

Although several different rationales have been invoked to justify affirmative action, their common (but often unstated) predicate is the tragic achievement gap—even among children from families of similar income—between black and Hispanic students, on the one hand, and whites and Asian-Americans on the other. If the gap did not exist, there would be no occasion to apply a double standard to eliminate or reduce the under-representation of blacks and Hispanics in several areas.

The causes of the achievement gap are intensely debated but its existence is beyond dispute.[19] As Christopher Jencks and Meredith Phillips concluded in their extensive study, "African Americans currently score lower than European Americans on vocabulary, reading, and math tests, as well as on tests that claim to measure scholastic aptitude and intelligence. This gap appears before children enter kindergarten ... and it persists into adulthood."[20] A recent study by Thomas Espenshade and Alexandria Radford similarly concludes that "A large body of evidence has demonstrated that the gap is real, it emerges early in children's lives, and it widens as children age and move through school."[21]

Moreover, except for some improvements in the 1970s and

---

[19] See, e.g., Christopher Jencks and Meredith Phillips, eds., *The Black-White Test Score Gap* [Brookings 1998]; William Bowen and Derek Bok, *The Shape of the River: Long-Term Consequences of Considering Race in College and University Admissions* [Princeton 1998]: 51; Michael Winerip, "Closing the Achievement Gap Without Widening a Racial One," *New York Times*, February 13, 2011 ("There is no more pressing topic in education today than closing the achievement gap....").

[20] Jencks and Phillips, supra, at 1. They also point out (p. 1 n.3) that, "Although this book concentrates on the black-white gap, similar issues arise when we compare either Hispanics or Native Americans to whites or Asians."

[21] Thomas Espenshade and Alexandria Radford, *No Longer Separate Not Yet Equal: Race and Class in Elite College Admission and Campus Life* [Princeton 2009]: 396.

1980s, the gap has been remarkably resistant to change.[22] And, as Jencks and Phillips point out, "...the gap shrinks only a little when black and white families have the same amount of schooling, the same income, and the same wealth."[23]

By the twelfth grade of high school, although obviously there are many outstanding black students (and many white students who do very poorly), black students *on average* are still two to three years behind whites and Asian-Americans, and Hispanics do not do much better.[24] On average, black and Hispanic students in high school are able to read and do math at only the average level of whites in junior high school.[25] Less than half of black students graduate from high school.[26]

The best evidence of long-term trends comes from the National Assessment of Educational Progress (NAEP), a federally sponsored series of national tests administered by the U.S. Department of Education and called "The Nation's Report Card." Beginning in the early 1970s, the NAEP has regularly tested representative samples of American elementary and secondary school pupils in various subjects, particularly reading and mathematics, at the ages of 9, 13, and 17. The NAEP examinations measure the skills that pupils have developed at key points in their school careers, and indicate how well prepared they are to move up to the next level of the educational system or to take

---

[22] See, e.g., John Yun and Chungmei Lee, "O'Connor's Claim—The Educational Pipeline and *Bakke*," in *Realizing Bakke's Legacy* [Stylus 2008]: 78: "In general, the research literature has come to a consensus that the Black-White test score gap has been difficult to narrow on nearly all longitudinal test-based measures of student achievement." Since the late 1980s, the gap has not significantly narrowed, Jaekyung Lee, "Racial and Ethnic Achievement Gap Trends: Reversing the Progress Toward Equity," *Educational Researcher*, Vol. 31, 3-12 (2002), notwithstanding the federal No Child Left Behind Act. Jaekyung Lee, *Tracking Achievement Gaps and Assessing the Impact of NCLB on the Gaps: An In-depth Look into National and State Reading and Math Outcome Trends* [Harvard Civil Rights Project 2006] (foreword by Gary Orfield); Sam Dillon, "'No Child' Law Is Not Closing A Racial Gap," *New York Times*, April 29, 2009.

[23] Jencks and Phillips, supra, at 2.

[24] Diana Jean Schemo, "It Takes More Than Schools to Close Achievement Gap," *New York Times*, August 9, 2006; Abigail and Stephan Thernstrom, *No Excuses—Closing the Racial Gap in Learning* [Simon & Schuster 2003]: 12.

[25] Sam Dillon, "Schools Slow in Closing Gaps Between Races," *New York Times*, November 20, 2006.

[26] Juan Williams, "The Trayvon Martin Tragedies," *Wall Street Journal*, March 27, 2012.

jobs in the workplace.[27]

In 1971 the average score in reading for black 17-year-olds was 239, compared to 291 for whites. By 1988 this gap of 52 had dramatically narrowed to 21 (295/274). Similarly, in the initial math scores (1973), the gap of 40 (310/270) for 17-year-olds had narrowed in 1990 to 21 (310/289).

There were similar changes in the scores of those aged 13 and 9. For 13-year-olds, the 1971 reading gap was 39 (261/222), reduced in 1988 to 18 (261/243); and the 1973 math gap was 40 (310/270), reduced in 1990 to 21 (309/289). For 9-year-olds, the 1971 reading gap was 44 (214/170), reduced in 1988 to 29 (218/189); and the 1973 math gap was 35 (225/190), reduced in 1990 to 27 (235/208).

But since 1990, despite those improvements in earlier years, the racial gap has not materially changed. Thus, by 2008, scores for minority students increased, but so did those of white students, leaving the achievement gap substantially the same.

In 2009 reading scores for twelfth grade students, the point gap was 27 (296/269).[28] In 2009 math tests, white fourth graders averaged 248 and blacks averaged 222, while white eighth graders averaged 293 and black eighth graders averaged 261. The gap of 32 points separating average black and white eighth graders represents about three years' worth of math learning.[29] A black student is about six times more likely than a white student to finish below the fifth percentile in a standardized math test but only about one-twentieth as likely as a white student to finish above the ninety-fifth percentile.[30]

---

[27] The NAEP achievement data strikingly parallel racial data concerning other significant criteria. E.g., college degree: Asian 49%, white 30%, black 17%; life expectancy: Asian 86, white 78, black 73; median earnings: Asian $31,518, white $30,485, black $23,025. *The American Human Development Report 2008-2009* (a project of the Social Science Research Council and based on 2005 census data). See also David Brooks, "The Limits of Policy," *New York Times*, May 4, 2010; Bob Herbert, "Too Long Ignored," *New York Times*, August 20, 2010.

[28] Sam Dillon, "12th-Grade Reading and Math Scores Rise Slightly After a Historic Low in 2005," *New York Times*, November 19, 2010. See also Sam Dillon, "'No Child' Law Is Not Closing A Racial Gap," *New York Times*, April 29, 2009.

[29] Sam Dillon, "Sluggish Results Seen in Math Scores," *New York Times*, October 15, 2009.

[30] Amy Wax, *Race, Wrongs, and Remedies: Group Justice in the 21st Century* [Rowman & Littlefield 2009]: 149.

Furthermore, according to a recent Department of Education study, the problem is not concentrated in just one section of the country. The nation's largest black-white gaps are no longer in Southern states like Alabama or Mississippi, but rather in Northern and Midwestern states like Connecticut, Illinois, Nebraska, and Wisconsin.[31] The gap on the national tests has remained constant in all major cities. In New York City, despite an intensive crash program, the difference between minority and white students in math proficiency is about the same in 2010 as it was in 2002.[32]

The problem is particularly acute for black males. According to a November 2010 report by the Council of the Great City Schools, an advocacy group for urban public schools, NAEP data concerning the gap between black and white males reveals a "national catastrophe." Among the findings: Only 12 percent of black fourth-grade boys are proficient in reading, compared with 38 percent of white boys, and only 12 percent of black eighth-grade boys are proficient in math, compared with 44 percent of white boys.[33]

Many theories have been advanced to explain the black-white gap.[34] There is widespread support for the view that it is wholly or largely attributable to cultural and environmental influences and is therefore subject to improvement.[35] Jencks and Phillips state: "The black-white test score gap does not appear to be an inevitable fact of nature ...[D]espite endless speculation, no one has found genetic evidence indicating that blacks have less innate

---

[31] Sam Dillon, "Racial Gap in Testing Sees Shift by Region," *New York Times*, July 15, 2009.

[32] Sharon Otterman and Robert Gebeloff, "A Triumph on the Racial Gap Withers in New York Schools," *New York Times,* August 16, 2010.

[33] Report of Council of the Great City Schools, A Call for Change (2010). See Trip Gabriel, "Proficiency of Black Students Is Found To Be Far Lower Than Expected," *New York Times*, November 9, 2010; Media Advisory, Council of the Great City Schools, November 4, 2010 (calling the data "jaw-dropping").

[34] See, e.g., Jenck and Phillips, supra, at 9-25; Felicia Lee, "Why Are Black Students Lagging?," *New York Times,* November 30, 2002; Dinesh D'Souza, *The End of Racism: Principles for a Multiracial Society* [Free Press 1995]: 431-76.

[35] See, e.g., William Julius Wilson, "Commentary," Christopher Jencks and Meredith Phillips, eds., T*he Black-White Test Score Gap* [Brookings 1998].

intellectual ability than whites."[36] In the view of Dr. Ronald Ferguson, director of the Achievement Gap Initiative at Harvard, "There's accumulating evidence that there are racial differences in what kids experience before the first day of kindergarten."[37] John McWhorter contends that "...the reason for the notorious achievement gap between even middle-class black students and white and Asian ones is not economics or racism, but a cultural factor: a facet of black peer culture that senses school as something separate from black culture."[38]

Poverty, although impacting achievement of all racial groups, accounts for only a part of the large disparity between the groups.[39] As Richard Rothstein has noted, "An aspect of the black-white gap that puzzles many observers is its persistence even for whites and blacks from families whose incomes are similar."[40] The 2010 report of the Council of the Great City Schools found that black middle-class boys do not do any better than poor white boys.[41] Indeed, the average SAT scores of black students from families in the *top*

---

[36] Jencks and Phillips, supra at 2. The publication of *The Bell Curve: Intelligence and Class Structure in American Life* [Free Press 1994] by Richard Herrnstein and Charles Murray created a national furor because of their conclusion that racial differences in IQ are genetically based (pages 269-368). The book led to an avalanche of harsh criticism. D'Souza, supra, at 431-37. Stephen Carter dismisses the theory of innate intelligence differences as "nonsense" but argues that it is wrong to bar discussion of such theories. Stephen Carter, *Reflections of an Affirmative Action Baby* [Basic Books 1991]: 181-86. See also, e.g., David L. Kirp, "After the Bell Curve," *New York Times,* July 23, 2006; Jim Holt, "Get Smart," *New York Times,* March 29, 2009

[37] Trip Gabriel, "Proficiency of Black Students Is Found To Be Far Lower Than Expected," *New York Times,* November 9, 2010. See also Michael Winerip, "Closing the Achievement Gap Without Widening a Racial One," *New York Times,* February 13, 2011.

[38] John McWhorter, *Winning the Race: Beyond the Crisis in Black America* [Gotham Books 2006]: 261. John Ogbu, an African-born anthropology professor, believes that the gap can be explained by the cultural behavior of blacks, like mocking hard-working classmates for "acting white." Felicia Lee, "Why Are Black Students Lagging?," *New York Times,* November 30, 2002.

[39] Wax, supra, at 49.

[40] Richard Rothstein, *Class and Schools: Using Social, Economic, and Educational Reform to Close the Black-White Achievement Gap* [Columbia 2004]: 47-50. See also, e.g., Thernstrom, *No Excuses,* supra, at 129 ("After taking full account of racial differences in poverty rates, parental education, and place of residence, roughly two-thirds of the troubling racial gap remains"); Amy Wax, supra, at 49.

[41] Report, supra, at 3. The report further found that the average black fourth-and-eighth grade male who is not disabled does no better in reading and math than white males who are disabled.

income bracket are *lower* than those of white students from families in the *bottom* income bracket.[42]

Nor is it explainable on the basis of differences in the schools attended. Improved schools benefit the education of both black and white students, but have only a modest effect in closing the gap between the two groups. In 1966 Congress ordered a study to determine whether black children's low achievement level was attributable to inferior schools. After conducting what was then the second largest social science research project in history—involving 600,000 children in 4,000 schools nationally—James S. Coleman and his colleagues issued their report *Equality of Educational Opportunity*. As Richard Rothstein has pointed out, Coleman "...concluded, to his own consternation, that variation in school resources had very little—almost nothing—to do with what we now term the test score gap between black and white children.... [S]cholarly efforts over four decades have consistently confirmed Coleman's core finding...."[43]

In the nearly 45 years since the Coleman study, the gap has not materially narrowed despite greater parity in the schools attended. Professor Amy Wax points out: "Along traditional dimensions of school quality (such as class size, student-teacher ratios, curriculum, and computer resources), the schools that blacks and whites attend became more similar during the 1980s and 1990s and now differ little on average."[44]

---

[42] Thernstrom, *Black and White*, supra, at 404-05; Shelby Steele, "The Age of White Guilt and the Disappearance of the Black Individual," *Harper's Magazine*, November 30, 1999

[43] Rothstein, supra, at 13-14. For example, a 1998 study of the well-financed schools in Shaker Heights, an affluent Cleveland suburb, left "the school administrators totally baffled. About half of the students in the Shaker Heights school system are black, but blacks are 7 percent of those in the top fifth of their class, and 90 percent of those in the bottom fifth." Abigail and Stephan Thernstrom, *Beyond the Color Line: New Perspectives on Race and Ethnicity* [Hoover Press 2002]: 264. Professor John Ogbu was invited by black parents to figure out why. "What amazed [him] is that these kids who come from homes of doctors and lawyers are not thinking like their parents.... They are looking at rappers in ghettos as their role models, they are looking at entertainers. The parents work two jobs, three jobs, to give their children everything, but they are not guiding their children." Felicia Lee, "Why are Black Students Lagging?," *New York Times*, November 30, 2002. See also Wax, supra, at 49-50;

[44] Wax, supra, at 48. She further states (p. 52): "In sum, the data reveal that the schools black children attend lag a bit on some measures of school quality, such as teacher experience, physical condition of the school, and number of advanced or enrichment courses, but are better on others, including student-teacher ratios and spending per student. The measured effects are not large in either direction."

Nor can the large gap be explained by the lack of education of the black students' parents. White students whose parents received only a high school education outscore black students whose parents attend or graduated from college. As Professor Wax states, "...[I]t is now well documented that differences in family income and education fail to explain most of the black-white achievement gap."[45]

---

[45] Id. at 49.

30. THE *BAKKE* CASE

Because of the achievement gap, if race-neutral standards are applied to selection processes in public education, employment, or contracting, a likely outcome will be substantial "under-representation" of one or more minorities. But if racial preferences are used to avoid that outcome by increasing minority representation, and if the resulting double standard operates to exclude better-qualified nonminority applicants, important constitutional questions are presented: Have the nonminority applicants been denied the equal protection of the laws? In making that determination, is discrimination against nonminorities subject to the same constitutional test as discrimination against minorities? To what extent, if any, may the government grant preferences on the basis of race?

The first Supreme Court decision on the validity of racial preferences was the landmark case of Regents of the University of California v. Bakke, 438 U.S. 265 (1978), concerning a system used by the medical school of the University of California at Davis to select applicants for admission.

The issue of the validity of racial preferences had been raised four years earlier in another graduate school case, DeFunis v. Odegaard, 416 U.S. 312 (1974), but the Supreme Court dismissed the case on procedural grounds without a decision on the merits. Marco DeFunis, a Phi Beta Kappa graduate of the University of Washington, brought suit in the Washington state courts, claiming that the University's law school had violated the Equal Protection Clause by rejecting his application for admission in favor of less qualified minority applicants. The trial court agreed and DeFunis, in accordance with the court's order, was admitted to the law school. After his admission, however, the trial court's decision was reversed by the Washington Supreme Court, upholding the law school's admission policies and thereby permitting the school to remove him from the school.

But execution of the Washington Supreme Court's judgment was stayed by Justice Douglas pending the U.S. Supreme Court's final disposition of the case, with the result that DeFunis was able to continue in the law school and had nearly completed his senior year by the time that the Court heard oral argument in 1974. In these circumstances, the Court (5-4 with Justices Burger, Blackmun, Rehnquist, Stewart, and Powell in the majority) dismissed the case as moot, holding that there was no issue before the Court requiring resolution since DeFunis would be graduating in any event.

The majority's refusal to rule on the constitutional issues elicited a sharp dissent from four Justices on the mootness issue. Written by Justice Brennan (joined by Douglas, White, and Marshall), the dissent accused the majority of "striving to rid itself of this dispute" and of doing so in a fashion that "clearly disserves the public interest." The dissent stated that "few constitutional questions in recent history have stirred as much debate" and correctly predicted that "they will not disappear" but "must inevitably return to the federal courts and ultimately again to this Court."

The only opinion on the merits of the constitutional issue was issued by Justice Douglas. In his dissent, in addition to disagreeing that the case was moot, Douglas contended that the law school's admissions policy was unconstitutional, stating in part: "There is no constitutional right for any race to be preferred.   There is no superior person by constitutional standards. A DeFunis who is white is entitled to no advantage by reason of that fact; nor is he subject to any disability, no matter what his race or color. Whatever his race, he had a constitutional right to have his application considered on its individual merits in a racially neutral manner." Justice Douglas also noted the problems associated with minority set-asides: "The reservation of a proportion of the law school class for members of selected minority groups is fraught with ... dangers, for one must immediately determine which groups are to receive such favored treatment and which are to be excluded, the proportions of the class that are to be allocated to each, and even the criteria by which to determine whether an individual is a member of a favored group." (416 U.S. at 336-37.)

Justice Douglas had retired from the Court when it next dealt with the affirmative action issue four years later in the Bakke case challenging the admission policy of the Medical School of the University of California at Davis.

Each applicant to the School was assigned a total "benchmark score," based on the applicant's interviews, grade point average, science grade point average, MCAT tests, recommendations, extracurricular activities, and other biographical data. The School, however, employed a special program for applicants who were members of minority groups ("Blacks," "Chicanos," "Asians," and "American Indians"). A minimum of 16 out of 100 places in the entering class were reserved for this group, and applicants in the special program were not required to meet a 2.5 grade point cutoff applied to others and were not ranked against those in the general admissions process.

Allan Bakke, a white male, applied to the School in 1973 and 1974. He was rejected both times, despite scores of 468 out of 500 in 1973 and 549 out of 600 in 1974. In both years applicants were admitted with significantly lower scores than Bakke's. After his second rejection, Bakke sued in state court alleging that he had been denied admission on the basis of his race, in violation of the Fourteenth Amendment, the California Constitution, and Title VI of the Civil Rights Act of 1964.[46] The California Supreme Court upheld Bakke's claim and ordered his admission, and the University appealed to the U.S. Supreme Court.

The central question in the case was what standard of judicial review should be applied in determining the validity of affirmative action programs under the Equal Protection Clause. Bakke's lawyers argued that preferences favoring minorities—and thereby discriminating against nonminorities—should be reviewed under the same strict scrutiny standard applied to discrimination against minorities. Under that standard, as explained in Chapter 6 *Overview of the Equal Protection Clause*, a racial classification disadvantaging minorities is unconstitutional unless the government carries the heavy burden of demonstrating a compelling public interest to justify the classification. Therefore, they contended, since the Equal Protection Clause guarantees equal protection to "any person," the color of the victim of the discrimination should not matter. The University's lawyers, on the

---

[46] §601 of the 1964 Act provides: "No person in the United States shall, on the ground of race, color, or national origin, be excluded from participation in, be denied the benefits of, or be subjected to discrimination under any program or activity receiving Federal financial assistance."

other hand, argued that strict scrutiny should be reserved for racial classifications that disadvantage minorities and that in other cases the state need only prove some rational basis for the policy.

After the oral argument, before the Court took a vote in the case, both positions received support in memos circulated among the Justices.[47] In a November 22, 1977, memo, Justice Powell endorsed applying strict scrutiny to the Davis program and found no compelling government interest that would justify setting aside a fixed number of slots for particular types of applicants. But Powell did not entirely rule out the consideration of race in admissions. As an example of what he believed could pass constitutional muster, he pointed to Harvard College's undergraduate admission program that "specifically eschews quotas" but "race or ethnic background might be deemed a 'plus' in a particular applicant's file."

In a memo to the other Justices the following day, Justice Brennan argued that "Short-term race consciousness is a necessary and constitutionally acceptable price to pay if we are to have a society indifferent to race." He contended that only racial classifications that insulted or stigmatized must be barred. "Government may not on account of race, insult or demean a human being by stereotyping his or her capacities, integrity or worth as an individual." But that was not the case here, according to Brennan, who believed the classification was benign. As for what kind of test to apply, instead of the strict scrutiny favored by Powell, Brennan suggested a "reasonableness" test.

The Supreme Court (5-4) affirmed. Justice Powell wrote the principal opinion, expressing his view that the School's policy violated the Equal Protection Clause, but none of the other eight Justices joined Powell's opinion. Four Justices in an opinion by Stevens, joined by Stewart, Burger, and Rehnquist, sustained Bakke's claim on the ground that the policy violated Title VI, without consideration of the applicability of the Equal Protection Clause. The other four Justices in a joint opinion by Brennan (who was the primary author[48]), White, Marshall, and Blackmun contended that the School's policy was valid under both the Equal

---

[47] This summary of the memos is derived from Seth Stern & Stephen Wermiel, *Justice Brennan: Liberal Champion* [Houghton Mifflin 2010]: 447-48.

[48] Id. at 453-55.

Protection Clause and Title VI. White, Marshall, and Blackmun also filed individual opinions.

In his opinion, Justice Powell held that government discrimination preferring minorities is subject to the same test as government discrimination against minorities: "Under the Equal Protection Clause, racial and ethnic classifications of any sort are inherently suspect and call for the most exacting judicial scrutiny" (p. 291). And Powell denied that any different test had been applied in post-*Brown* decisions temporarily allowing racial classifications to eradicate segregation that had been found to violate the Constitution. In those cases, "the racial classifications were designed as remedies for the vindication of clearly determined constitutional violations. Here, there has been no judicial determination of constitutional violation as a predicate for a remedial classification" (p. 300).

Powell stated that the University "...urges us to adopt for the first time a more restrictive view of the Equal Protection Clause and hold that discrimination against members of the white 'majority' cannot be suspect if its purpose can be characterized as 'benign.' ... The clock of our liberties, however, cannot be turned back to 1868. Brown v. Board of Education.... It is far too late to argue that the guarantee of equal protection to all persons permits the recognition of special wards entitled to a degree of protection greater than that accorded others." (Pp. 295-96.)

In addition, "the difficulties entailed in varying the level of judicial review according to a perceived 'preferred' status of a particular racial or ethnic minority are intractable. ... There is no principled basis for deciding which groups would merit 'heightened judicial solicitude' and which would not ... The kind of variable sociological and political analysis necessary to produce such rankings simply does not lie within the judicial competence—even if they otherwise were politically feasible and socially desirable." (Pp. 296-97.)

Furthermore, "It is settled beyond question that the 'rights created by the first section of the Fourteenth Amendment are, by its terms, guaranteed to the individual. The rights established are personal rights.' ... The guarantee of equal protection cannot mean one thing when applied to one individual and something else when applied to a person of another color. If both are not accorded the same protection, then it is not equal." And "Nothing in the Constitution supports the notion that individuals may be asked to suffer otherwise impermissible burdens in order to enhance the societal standing of other ethnic groups." (Pp. 289, 295, 298.)

The University advanced four justifications in support of the special program: (1) increasing the number of minorities in medical schools and the medical profession; (2) countering the effects of "societal discrimination"; (3) increasing the number of physicians who will practice in communities currently underserved; and (4) obtaining the educational benefits of an ethnically diverse student body. Applying a strict scrutiny standard of review, Justice Powell rejected each of the University's asserted justifications (pp. 307-15):

- "Preferring members of any one group for no reason other than race or ethnic origin is discrimination for its own sake. This the Constitution forbids."

- Helping certain groups "perceived as victims of 'societal discrimination' does not justify a classification that imposes disadvantages upon persons like Bakke, who bear no responsibility for whatever harm the beneficiaries of the special admissions program are thought to have suffered."[49]

- The University did not carry its burden of demonstrating that it must prefer members of particular ethnic groups in order to promote better health-care delivery to deprived citizens.[50]

- "The diversity that furthers a compelling state interest encompasses a far broader array of qualifications and characteristics; racial or ethnic origin is but a single though important

---

[49] Powell stated: "In the school cases, the States were required by court order to redress the wrongs worked by specific instances of racial discrimination. That goal was far more focused than the remedying of the effects of 'societal discrimination,' an amorphous concept of injury that may be ageless in its reach into the past. We have never approved a classification that aids persons perceived as members of relatively victimized groups at the expense of other innocent individuals in the absence of judicial, legislative, or administrative findings of constitutional or statutory violations. ... Without such findings of constitutional or statutory violations, it cannot be said that the government has any greater interest in helping one individual than in refraining from harming another. Thus, the government has no compelling justification for inflicting such harm." (Pp. 308-09.)

[50] Powell said that there was no proof that training more black doctors would mean that there would be more doctors actually practicing in minority communities. In addition, there might be other ways of achieving this goal more directly, such as by providing incentives for doctors to work in areas that are underserved.

element" and the School's special program was not necessary for that purpose and indeed "would hinder rather than further attainment of genuine diversity."

In rejecting "societal discrimination" as a permissible justification for minority preferences, Powell emphasized the individual-centered nature of equality protected by the Fourteenth Amendment:

"If it is the individual who is entitled to judicial protection against classifications based upon his racial or ethnic background because such distinctions impinge upon personal rights, rather than the individual only because of his membership in a particular group, then constitutional standards may be applied consistently. Political judgments regarding the necessity for the particular classification may be weighed in the constitutional balance, but the standard of justification will remain constant. This is as it should be, since those political judgments are the product of rough compromise struck by contending groups within the democratic process. When they touch upon an individual's race or ethnic background, he is entitled to a judicial determination that the burden he is asked to bear on that basis is precisely tailored to serve a compelling governmental interest. The Constitution guarantees that right to every person regardless of his background." (P. 299.)

In rejecting the Davis admissions program, Powell compared it with admissions programs of private universities that "expanded the concept of diversity to include students from disadvantaged economic, racial and ethnic groups" (pp. 315-19). Thus, at Harvard:

"When the Committee on Admissions reviews the large middle group of applicants who are 'admissible' and deemed capable of doing good work in their courses, the race of an applicant may tip the balance in his favor just as geographic origin or a life spent on a farm may tip the balance in other candidates' cases. ... In such an admissions program, race or ethnic background may be deemed a "plus" in a particular applicant's file, yet it does not insulate the individual from comparison with all other candidates for the available seats. The file of a particular black applicant may be examined for his potential contribution to diversity without the factor of race being decisive when compared, for example, with that of an applicant identified as an Italian-American if the latter is thought to exhibit qualities more likely to promote beneficial educational pluralism. Such qualities could include exceptional personal talents, unique work or service experience, leadership potential, maturity, demonstrated compassion, a history of overcoming disadvantage, ability to communicate with the poor, or other qualifications deemed important."

Such an admission program, Powell stated, treats each applicant as an individual since "The applicant who loses out on the last available seat to another candidate receiving a 'plus' on the basis of ethnic background will not have been foreclosed from all consideration for that seat simply because he was not the right color or had the wrong surname ... It would mean only that his combined qualifications, which may have included similar nonobjective factors, did not outweigh those of the other applicant. His qualifications would have been weighed fairly and competitively, and he would have no basis to complain of unequal treatment under the Fourteenth Amendment."

By contrast, Powell concluded, "...the fatal flaw in the Davis preferential program is its disregard of individual rights as guaranteed by the Fourteenth Amendment" (p. 319).[51]

Together with the four Justices who found a Title VI violation, Powell joined to affirm the California Supreme Court's judgment requiring Bakke's admission. However, because "the court below failed to recognize that the State has a substantial interest that legitimately may be served by a properly devised admissions program involving the competitive consideration of race and ethnic origin," Powell sided with the other four Justices to reverse "...so much of the judgment as enjoins Davis from any consideration of race of any applicant..." (p. 320).

The Brennan-Marshall-White-Blackmun joint opinion, in addition to arguing that Title VI was inapplicable, rejected Powell's analysis of the Equal Protection Clause and in particular Powell's reliance on the strict scrutiny standard. The opinion contended that Bakke's equal protection claim did not involve a "fundamental right." Furthermore: "Nor do whites as a class have any of the 'traditional indicia of

---

[51] A footnote to the Brennan-White-Marshall-Blackmun joint opinion (p. 326) states: "We also agree with Mr. Justice Powell that a plan like the 'Harvard' plan ... is constitutional under our approach, at least so long as the use of race to achieve an integrated student body is necessitated by the lingering effects of past discrimination."

suspectness: the class is not saddled with such disabilities, or subjected to such a history of purposeful unequal treatment, or relegated to such a position of political powerlessness as to command extraordinary protection from the majoritarian political process.' ... Nor has anyone suggested that the University's purposes contravene the cardinal principle that racial classifications that stigmatize—because they are drawn on the presumption that one race is inferior to another or because they put the weight of government behind racial hatred and separatism— are invalid without more." Instead of strict scrutiny, the joint opinion argued that the appropriate test for "remedial" racial classifications is the intermediate standard of review developed primarily in gender discrimination cases—whether they serve "important governmental objectives" and be "substantially related" to achieving those objectives. (Pp. 357-59.)

DECIPHERING THE BAKKE DECISION

Bakke established the fundamental framework in which affirmative action issues have since been contested. But just what did *Bakke* hold?

The bottom line, of course, is that Alan Bakke won his case. A majority of five Justices agreed that he should not have been denied admission. But a differently constituted majority agreed that flatly prohibiting any consideration of race in the admission process is wrong.

More broadly, the opinions in the case reflect a basic conflict (which still continues to this day) over what type of "equality" is protected by the Equal Protection Clause. The Powell and Stevens opinions espouse an *"individual-centered"* approach—focused on the impact of the government action on the individuals who are adversely affected. By contrast, the joint opinion of the other four Justices, as well as the individual opinions of White, Marshall, and Blackmun, are primarily *"group-centered"*—focused on the past treatment of a preferred minority as a class.[52]

Thus, in opposing application of strict scrutiny, the joint opinion argued that the Davis policy should be judged under a more relaxed standard because of past societal discrimination against minority

---

[52] See, e.g., Angelo Ancheta, "*Bakke,* Antidiscrimination Jurisprudence, and the Trajectory of Affirmative Action Law," in *Realizing Bakke's Legacy* [Stylus Publishing 2008, Patricia Marin & Catherine Horn eds.]: 15-40; Jack Balkin and Reva Siegel, "The American Civil Rights Tradition: Anticlassification or Antisubordination?," 58 *University of Miami Law Review* 9 (2003).

groups and because the policy did not stigmatize or overburden the white group. Whites, the joint opinion stated, had never been "...subjected to such a history of purposeful unequal treatment, or relegated to such a position of political powerlessness as to command extraordinary protection from the majoritarian political process" (p. 357). Furthermore, "Unlike discrimination against racial minorities, the use of racial preferences for remedial purposes does not inflict a pervasive injury upon individual whites in the sense that wherever they go or whatever they do there is a significant likelihood that they will be treated as second-class citizens because of their color" (p. 375).

Similarly, Justice Marshall in his individual opinion protested that "...today's judgment ignores the fact that for several hundred years Negroes have been discriminated against, not as individuals, but rather solely because of the color of their skins" (p. 400). And Justice Blackmun in his individual opinion, although acknowledging that "Bakke is not himself charged with discrimination and yet is the one who is disadvantaged," contended that "...in order to treat some persons equally, we must treat them differently" (p. 407).

By contrast, Justice Powell's opinion is premised on an individual-centered view of the Equal Protection Clause. Powell, however, recognized that the admission process need not be completely color-blind. He stated that "the courts below failed to recognize that the State has a substantial interest that legitimately may be served by a properly devised admissions program involving the competitive consideration of race and ethnic origin" (p. 320).

In short, according to Powell, although race-conscious selection might be permissible to some limited extent, the Davis program had gone far beyond an acceptable line. As to how far is too far, Powell suggested that, "without the factor of race being decisive," race might be considered as one of many factors considered in seeking student body diversity "to promote beneficial educational pluralism" (p. 317).

He emphasized that "The diversity that furthers a compelling state interest encompasses a far broader array of qualifications and characteristics of which racial or ethnic origin is but a single though important element." The kind of program Powell envisaged "treats each applicant as an individual in the admissions process" and "The applicant who loses out on the last available seat to another candidate receiving a 'plus' on the basis of ethnic background will not have been foreclosed from all consideration for that seat simply because he was not the right color or had the wrong surname." (P. 318.)

Although none of the other Justices joined in his opinion, Powell's views have generally been regarded as expressing the ultimate holding in *Bakke*. That, however, did not prevent substantial disagreement about how the decision should be applied in subsequent affirmative action cases.

*****

Following the decision, Allan "Bakke started class at Davis' medical school guarded by plainclothes police officers as one hundred noisy demonstrators protested outside. Four years later, Bakke quietly graduated not long before his forty-second birthday and went on to practice medicine at the Mayo Clinic in Rochester, Minnesota, where his patients later included Justice Powell."[53]

In November 1996, by a 55 percent to 45 percent margin, California voters approved a referendum ("Proposition 209") amending the California constitution to forbid government racial preferences. The amendment provides that "The state shall not discriminate against, or grant preferential treatment to, any individual or group on the basis of race, sex, color, ethnicity, or national origin in the operation of public employment, public education, or public contracting."

Several individuals and groups immediately brought suit alleging, inter alia, that the amendment violated the Equal Protection Clause. The district court granted a preliminary injunction barring the amendment's enforcement but the Ninth Circuit reversed in Coalition for Econonic Equity v. Wilson, 122 F.3d 692 (9th Cir. 1997). The court rejected the equal protection claim, holding that the amendment is constitutional because it "prohibits the State from classifying individuals by race or gender" and, therefore, "*a fortiori* does not classify individuals" impermissibly. The amendment prohibited preferential treatment, the court concluded, not "equal protection rights against political obstructions to equal treatment."

---

[53] Stern & Wermiel, supra, at 455.

The same group of plaintiffs subsequently brought a second suit, claiming that the Proposition 209 amendment had been applied by the University of California in violation of the Equal Protection Clause. They contended that the amendment allows admission officials to depart from the University's baseline admission criteria for any purpose—veteran status, income, geographical background, athleticism, or legacy—but not for "racial diversity" or to address "*de facto* racial segregation and inequality." This, the plaintiffs argued, treats black, Hispanic, and and Native American students unequally from their Asian-American and white counterparts. The plaintiffs further argued that the Supreme Court's intervening decision in Grutter v. Bollinger, 539 U.S. 306 (2003) (reviewed in Chapter 33), required invalidation of the Proposition 209 amendment. The Ninth Circuit rejected each of these contentions and again sustained the constitutionality of the amendment. Coalition for Economic Equity v. Brown, ___ F.3d ___ (9th Cir. 2012).

In the mid-1990s black students accounted for just over 4 percent of freshmen in the University of California multi-campus system. Although that level initially fell to 3 percent after Proposition 209 took effect, it subsequently returned to approximately the 1990s level, and graduation rates went up. Hispanic enrollment stood at 14-15 percent of the total before the amendment but by 2010 accounted for more than 22 percent of the system's freshmen.[54]

Referendums patterned after Proposition 209 were approved by voters in the States of Washington, Michigan, Nebraska, and Arizona. In addition, similar policies were adopted in Florida by a governor's executive order and in New Hampshire by a law enacted by the state legislature.

---

[54] Richard Perez-Pena, "To Enroll More Minority Students, Colleges Work Around The Courts." *New York Times*, April 1, 2012.

31. RACIAL PREFERENCES IN EMPLOYMENT

The meaning of "discrimination" in employment differs considerably depending on whether the case arises under the Equal Protection Clause or under statutes adopted by Congress. "Discrimination" in violation of the Equal Protection Clause requires both state action and an intent to discriminate. However, under a statute such as Title VII of the 1964 Civil Rights Act, neither of those elements is required to establish a violation, and a conclusion of "discrimination" means only that there has been a failure to comply with the requirements of the statute.

UNDER THE EQUAL PROTECTION CLAUSE

At issue in Wygant v. Jackson Board of Education, 476 U.S. 267 (1986), was a provision of a collective-bargaining agreement between a school board and a teachers' union. The provision stated that teachers with the most seniority would be retained if it became necessary to lay off teachers, except that at no time would there be a greater percentage of minority personnel laid off than the percentage of minority personnel employed at the time of the layoff. During certain school years, white teachers were laid off while black teachers with less seniority were retained. The white teachers brought suit, alleging violations of the Equal Protection Clause.

Applying a strict scrutiny standard of review, the Court (5-4) struck down the challenged provision. The Court held that the constitutional test does not change depending on which racial group is benefited or burdened by a racial preference and that such a preference can be justified only by showing that it serves a compelling governmental purpose and is narrowly tailored to effectuate that purpose. No such showing, the Court held, had been made by the school board.

Justice Powell's plurality opinion (joined by Burger and Rehnquist) stated that "a public employer ... must ensure that, before it embarks on an affirmative-action program [to remedy past discrimination], it has convincing evidence that remedial action is warranted. That is, it must have sufficient evidence to justify the conclusion that there has been prior discrimination." Moreover, even if prior discrimination was proved, the layoff plan would not have been constitutionally acceptable because, "as a means of accomplishing purposes that otherwise may be legitimate, the Board's layoff plan is not sufficiently narrowly tailored. Other, less intrusive means of accomplishing similar purposes, such as the adoption of hiring goals, are available." (Pp. 275-77.)

Justice Powell further emphasized (as he had done in his *Bakke* opinion) that "[s]ocietal discrimination, without more, is too amorphous a basis for imposing a racially classified remedy," and that "... as the basis for imposing discriminatory legal remedies that work against innocent people, societal discrimination is insufficient and over-expansive."

In addition, the plurality rejected the theory that the preferences for black teachers were justified to provide "role models" for black students. Such a theory, Justice Powell stated, "has no logical stopping point" and "allows the Board to engage in discriminatory hiring and layoff practices long past the point required by any legitimate remedial purposes. ... Moreover, because the role model theory does not necessarily bear a relationship to the harm caused by the past discriminatory hiring practices, it actually could be used to escape the obligation to remedy such practices by justifying the small percentage of black teachers by reference to the small number of black students."

Justices O'Connor and White concurred in the judgment. In her opinion, while agreeing with the plurality's rejection of the "societal discrimination" and "role model" justifications, Justice O'Connor emphasized that the board's plan to remedy past discrimination was erroneously based on the percentage of minority students in the school district, instead of the percentage of qualified minority teachers within the relevant labor pool. (Pp. 293-94.) Justice White concurred on the ground that "None of the interests asserted by the Board, singly or together, justify this racially discriminatory layoff policy and save it from the strictures of the Equal Protection Clause." (P. 295.)

Justice Marshall's dissent (joined by Brennan and Blackmun) argued that "…a public employer, with the full agreement of its employees, should be permitted to preserve the benefits of a legitimate and constitutional affirmative-action hiring plan even while reducing its workforce…." (P. 296.) In a separate dissent, Justice Stevens defended the "role model" justification for the plan: "In the context of public education, it is quite obvious that a school board may reasonably conclude that an integrated faculty will be able to provide benefits to the student body that could not be provided by an all white, or nearly all white, faculty." (P. 315.)

In an earlier public employment case, Washington v. Davis, 426 U.S. 229 (1976), the Court rejected a constitutional challenge to a written personnel test that applicants for the police force in Washington, D.C., were required to take. The Court held that evidence of the significantly lower scores of black applicants compared with those of white applicants did not, without more, demonstrate a denial of equal protection. As pointed out earlier (see Chapter 14 *The Discriminatory Purpose Requirement*), proof of a discriminatory impact is insufficient to establish a violation of the Equal Protection Clause; proof of a discriminatory purpose is also essential.

In *Washington v. Davis* the Court rejected the notion that the Fourteenth Amendment embodied a disparate impact standard, but in doing so it also suggested that Congress might create disparate impact standards at the statutory level.

UNDER TITLE VII OF THE 1964 CIVIL RIGHTS ACT

Title VII does not explicitly command that private employers give preferences to minorities. But the "disparate impact" rule of Title VII clearly has that effect. In hiring employees, employers—even in the absence of any discriminatory intent—are presumptively forbidden to consider commonly accepted criteria (such as a high school education or race-neutral test results) if consideration of the criterion would disproportionately exclude minorities. In order to rebut the presumption, an employer must demonstrate that meeting such a criterion is essential to fill the specific position. (See Chapter 25 *Title VII of the 1964 Civil Rights Act.*)

The redefinition of "discrimination" in Title VII to include "disparate impact" (in addition to "disparate treatment") markedly expanded the scope of government-required affirmative action. It was no longer limited to actions by government institutions and those seeking government contracts; now the statute requires minority preferences in hiring by all private employers meeting the jurisdictional criteria.

Because of its broad scope, Title VII has generally superseded the Equal Protection Clause in the regulation of employment discrimination.

Among the key differences:

- While Title VII applies to private employers (as well as state and local governments), the Equal Protection Clause requires "state action."

- As noted above, a discriminatory purpose is an indispensable element of a violation of the Equal Protection Clause; a discriminatory impact is insufficient (e.g., *Washington v. Davis, supra*). Title VII, however, prohibits not only intentional discrimination but also applies to "neutral" practices that do not involve any intent to discriminate. Thus a racial "imbalance" in an employer's workforce, or use of a test on which minority applicants fare poorly in comparison with nonminority applicants, creates—without more—a presumption of illegal discrimination. [55]

- The Court has held that Title VII, unlike the Equal Protection Clause (e.g., *Wygant v. Jackson Board of Education, supra*), does not protect nonminority employees from *intentional* discrimination by employers.

In a 1976 decision expanding the scope of Title VII, McDonald v. Santa Fe Trail Transp. Co., 427 U.S. 273, 283 (1976), the Court unanimously concluded that Title VII "prohibits all racial discrimination in employment, without exception for any group of particular employees," whether white or black. But three years later, in United Steelworkers of America v. Weber, 443 U.S. 193, 201 (1979), the Court ruled that the *McDonald* race-neutral principle did not apply to race discrimination incident to an affirmative action program.

---

[55] Griggs v. Duke Power Co., 401 U.S. 424 (1971). The Court stated (p. 431): "If an employment practice which operates to exclude Negroes cannot be shown to be related to job performance, the practice is prohibited." The *Griggs* decision also held that the requirement of high school education may be presumed to be discriminatory because of the lower percentage of blacks who meet that requirement.

In *Weber*, a white employee of Kaiser Steel brought a class action charging that Kaiser had violated Title VII by discriminating against them on the basis of race. Kaiser and a union had entered into an affirmative action agreement providing that blacks would be allocated 50% of openings in training programs. The Court (5-2) sustained the agreement, although acknowledging that the plaintiff's "reliance upon a literal construction of" Title VII "is not without force." According to the Court, "an interpretation of [Title VII] that forbade all race-conscious affirmative action would 'bring about an end completely at variance with the purpose of the statute and must be rejected'" and "The prohibition against racial discrimination ... must therefore be read against the background of the legislative history ... and the historical context from which the Act arose." The Court stated that "'[t]he crux of the problem [was] to open employment opportunities for Negroes in occupations which have been traditionally closed to them'" and the selection of the less senior black applicants over the white plaintiff was justified because taking race into account was consistent with Title VII's objective of "break[ing] down old patterns of racial segregation and hierarchy." (Pp. 201, 203, 208.)

Eight years later, the *Weber* decision was reaffirmed in Johnson v. Santa Clara County, 480 U.S. 616 (1987). The Court (6-3) rejected a claim that the defendant employer, pursuant to a voluntary affirmative action plan preferring women, had promoted a less qualified female employee instead of the plaintiff. The Court stated that "we do not regard as identical the constraints of Title VII and the Federal Constitution on voluntarily adopted affirmative action plans. ... Application of the 'prima facie' standard in Title VII cases would be inconsistent with Weber's focus on statistical imbalance, and could inappropriately create a significant disincentive for employers to adopt an affirmative action plan." (Pp. 632-33.)

It remains to be determined whether the authority of the *Weber* and *Johnson* decisions has been undermined by the Court's decision in Ricci v. DeStefano, 557 U.S. ___ (2009) (discussed in Chapter 26 *Disparate Impact versus Disparate Treatment*). The *Ricci* case involved what amounted to cross-claims under Title VII—the plaintiffs contended that their employer had violated Title VII by subjecting them to "disparate treatment" in favor of minority employees, while the employer also relied on Title VII to contend that the minority preferences were necessary to avoid a "disparate impact." The Court sought to reconcile the two Title VII claims by holding that the "disparate treatment" prohibition should be enforced unless there is a strong basis to fear "disparate impact" liability. At the risk of oversimplification, if Title VII's "disparate treatment" prohibition trumps the fear of legal liability for a "disparate impact" violation (as in *Ricci*), it would seem to follow that Title VII's "disparate treatment" prohibition should also trump a voluntary affirmative action program of the type involved in *Weber* and *Johnson*.[56]

§342 OF THE 2010 FINANCIAL REFORM ACT

Countless other federal and state statutes—even if not expressly incorporating a disparate impact standard like the amended Title VII—contain provisions that implicitly require private employers to meet the functional equivalent of a disparate impact standard.

The latest and perhaps most sweeping example is the 2010 financial reform legislation, entitled the "Dodd-Frank Wall Street Reform and Consumer Protection Act," adopted in July 2010. Before passage of the Act, although its provisions on banking regulation, derivative securities, bail-out contingencies, and consumer protection received extensive coverage in the media, §342 of the bill was largely ignored. [57] §342 further regulates the employment practices of any of the innumerable private financial institutions that do business with the government.

§342 establishes "Offices of Minority and Women Inclusion" in 20 agencies, including the Treasury, FDIC, SEC, Controller of the Currency, the Federal Reserve Board of Governors, and the 12 regional Federal Reserve banks. Each of these new 20 offices is to have its own director and staff to promote equal racial, ethnic, and gender diversity, not only of just the agency's workforce but also the

---

[56] See Charles Sullivan, "*Ricci v. DeStefano:* End of the Line or Just Another Turn on the Disparate Road?," 104 *Northwestern University Law Review* 411, 415 (2010): "This holding suggests a kind of hierarchy of discrimination theories— that is, that disparate treatment is the core prohibition of Title VII, with disparate impact playing a lesser role. In fact, the Court read the statute in this fashion, finding that disparate treatment was the thrust of Title VII as originally enacted, with disparate impact added only by the Civil Rights Act of 1991."

[57] Diana Furchgott-Roth, "Racial, Gender Quotas in the Financial Bill?," www.realclearmarkets.com (July 8, 2010). See also "Politicizing the Fed," *Wall Street Journal*, June 14, 2010.

workforces of each of its contractors and subcontractors.[58]

Each contractor is required to "ensure, to the maximum extent possible, *the fair inclusion of women and minorities* in the workforce of the contractor and, as applicable, subcontractors." (§342(c)(2), italics added.) The requirement broadly applies "...to all contracts of an agency for services of any kind, including the services of financial institutions, investment banking firms, mortgage banking firms, asset management firms, brokers, dealers, financial services entities, underwriters, accountants, investment consultants, and providers of legal services," and "...all contracts for all business and activities of an agency, at all levels, including contracts for the issuance or guarantee of any debt, equity, or security, the sale of assets, the management of the assets of the agency, the making of equity investments by the agency, and the implementation by the agency of programs to address economic recovery." (§342(d).)

To enforce the "fair inclusion" mandate, the Act provides that each of the 20 offices shall determine "...whether an agency contractor, and, as applicable, a subcontractor has failed to make a good faith effort to include minorities and women in their workforce" and if so shall "recommend... to the agency administrator that the contract be terminated." (§342(c)(3).) The Act further provides that each office shall annually report to Congress what percentage of funds was paid to minority and women contractors. (§342(e).)

In this context, the "fair inclusion" mandate can only be understood as meaning "fair" in one possible sense—not "fair" in terms of merit or competency or education or experience or productivity, but instead "fair" in numerical terms of increasing the percentage of minorities and women in the contractor's workforce. In the face of the incentives and disincentives provided in §342, that clear message—even without an express "set-aside" requirement—will scarcely be missed by any contractor trying to navigate within a safe harbor.[59]

---

[58] Each director's duties also include advising "the agency administrator on the impact of the policies and regulations of the agency on minority-owned and women-owned businesses." (§342(b)(3).)

[59] On learning of the provision in the Dodd-Franks bill, four members of the United States Civil Rights Commission urged the Senate to remove §342 before final enactment. They stated that "The likelihood that it will in fact promote discrimination is overwhelming." The requested change was not made.

32. RACIAL PREFERENCES IN CONTRACTING

The Court's decisions on contracting preferences pursued a zig-zag course in the 1980s and 1990s, before achieving substantial conformity with standards applied to other forms of affirmative action.

In Fullilove v. Klutznick, 448 U.S. 448 (1980), a federal minority "set-aside" program was challenged under the Fifth Amendment on equal protection grounds by nonminority contractors. A 1977 Act of Congress provided that, in the absence of an administrative waiver, 10% of federal funds granted for local public works projects must be allocated to businesses controlled by members of specified minority groups—Negroes, Spanish-speaking, Orientals, Eskimos and Aleuts. The law was upheld (6-3) but none of the three opinions was joined by a majority of the Justices; instead, the Court was divided into three groups advancing essentially inconsistent views.

Chief Justice Burger, joined by Justices White and Powell, emphasized the need of "appropriate deference to the Congress, a co-equal branch charged by the Constitution with the power to 'provide for the ... general Welfare of the United States' and 'to enforce by appropriate legislation,' the equal protection guarantees of the Fourteenth Amendment" (p. 472). In a concurring opinion, Powell contended that, unlike the medical school in *Bakke*, Congress was competent to make the past-discrimination findings necessary to sustain the program.

Justice Marshall, joined by Justices Brennan and Blackmun, concurred on the ground that an intermediate scrutiny standard should be used for racial classifications serving a remedial purpose: "The provision, therefore, passes muster under the equal protection standard I adopted in *Bakke*."

But the three dissenters argued that strict scrutiny was equally applicable to federal racial preferences and that the statute failed to meet that standard. Justice Stewart, joined by Justice Rehnquist, declared that "I think today's decision is wrong for the same reason that [*Plessy*] was wrong," that "The rule cannot be any different when the persons injured by a racially biased law are not members of a racial minority," and that "if a law is unconstitutional, it is no less unconstitutional just because it is a product of [Congress]." Justice Stevens based his dissent on the narrower ground that "this slapdash statute … cannot fairly be characterized as a 'narrowly tailored' racial classification because it simply raises too many serious questions that Congress failed to answer or even to address in a responsible way."

Nine years later, in Richmond v. J.A. Croson Co., 488 U.S. 469 (1989), the Court reached the opposite result in striking down an ordinance adopted by Richmond, Virginia. Richmond was then a majority-black city with a majority-black city council and a black mayor. The ordinance provided that any prime contractor awarded a city construction contract would be required to subcontract at least 30% of the dollar amount of each contract to one or more "Minority Business Enterprises." The term "Minority Business Enterprise" (MBE) was defined as any business owned and controlled (at least to the extent of 51%) by black, Spanish-speaking, Oriental, Indian, Eskimo, or Aleut citizens.

The Court (6-3) held that Richmond had failed to establish the type of past discrimination in the city's construction industry that would allow race-based relief under the strict scrutiny standard of review. *Fullilove* was distinguished on the ground "…that Congress, unlike any State or political subdivision, has a specific constitutional mandate to enforce the dictates of the Fourteenth Amendment" but "That Congress may identify and redress the effects of society-wide discrimination does not mean that, a fortiori, the States and their political subdivisions are free to decide that such remedies are appropriate." (P. 490.)

Speaking for the Court in *Croson*, Justice O'Connor declared that state and local racial classifications must be "strictly reserved for remedial settings" and justified by "proper findings" of "identified discrimination." The Court adopted and applied Justice Powell's rationale in *Wygant* (involving employment preferences) and *Bakke* (involving university admissions):

> "Like the 'role model' theory employed in *Wygant*, a generalized assertion that there has been past discrimination in an entire industry provides no guidance for a legislative body to determine

the precise scope of the injury it seeks to remedy.

"...Like the claim [in *Bakke*] that discrimination in primary and secondary schooling justifies a rigid racial preference in medical school admissions, an amorphous claim that there has been past discrimination in a particular industry cannot justify the use of an unyielding racial quota. It is sheer speculation how many minority firms there would be in Richmond absent past societal discrimination, just as it was sheer speculation how many minority medical students would have been admitted to the medical school at Davis absent past discrimination in educational opportunities." (Pp. 498-99.)

The Court found that none of the city's evidence demonstrated any identified discrimination in the Richmond construction industry: [60]

"...The 'evidence' relied upon by the dissent, the history of school desegregation in Richmond and numerous congressional reports, does little to define the scope of any injury to minority contractors in Richmond or the necessary remedy. The factors relied upon by the dissent could justify a preference of any size or duration.

"...We, therefore, hold that the city has failed to demonstrate a compelling interest in apportioning public contracting opportunities on the basis of race. To accept Richmond's claim that past societal discrimination alone can serve as the basis for rigid racial preferences would be to open the door to competing claims for "remedial relief" for every disadvantaged group. The dream of a Nation of equal citizens in a society where race is irrelevant to personal opportunity and achievement would be lost in a mosaic of shifting preferences based on inherently unmeasurable claims of past wrongs." (Pp. 498-99, 505-06.)

Further, "...the 30% quota cannot be said to be narrowly tailored to any goal, except perhaps outright racial balancing" (p. 507).[61]

---

[60] The *Croson* decision led to creation of a virtual industry devoted to the preparation of so-called "disparity studies" seeking to demonstrate that a sufficient evidentiary basis exists to initiate, maintain, or expand MBE programs. Very few of these "disparity studies" have been found to meet the *Croson* standard. See George R. La Noue, "Discrimination in Public Contracting," in *Beyond the Color Line*, supra, at 200, 203.

[61] The Court also found that "There is absolutely no evidence of past discrimination against Spanish-speaking, Oriental, Indian, Eskimo, or Aleut persons in any aspect of the Richmond construction industry" (p. 506).

Dissenting, and joined by Justices Brennan and Blackmun, Justice Marshall characterized the Court's decision as "a deliberate and giant step backward in this Court's affirmative-action jurisprudence" and "a grapeshot attack on race-conscious remedies in general." While agreeing that "[r]acial classifications drawn on the presumption that one race is inferior to another ... warrant the strictest judicial scrutiny....," Marshall contended that such a standard should not be applied to measures based on "the tragic and indelible fact that discrimination against blacks and other racial minorities in this Nation has pervaded our Nation's history and continues to scar our society." In his view, "Because the consideration of race is relevant to remedying the continuing effects of past racial discrimination, and because governmental programs employing racial classifications for remedial purposes can be crafted to avoid stigmatization, such programs should not be subjected to conventional strict scrutiny."

In a separate dissent Justice Blackmun acknowledged that "Today, for the first time, a majority of the Court has adopted strict scrutiny as its standard of Equal Protection Clause review of race-conscious remedial measures" (p. 551).

THE ADARAND CASE

The *Croson* decision distinguished—and left standing—the less rigorous standard applied to federal contracting by *Fullilove*. And, just a year after *Croson*, the Court applied *Fullilove* in Metro Broadcasting, Inc. v. FCC, 497 U.S. 547 (1990), sustaining (5-4) FCC policies that preferred minority-owned businesses in the grant of broadcast licenses. The specified groups to be given preference were persons of "black, Hispanic surnamed, American Eskimo, Aleut, American Indian, and Asiatic American extraction."

In an opinion by Justice Brennan, the *Metro Broadcasting* majority held that the FCC policies had been approved by Congress and that therefore the strict scrutiny standard of review applied in *Croson* is inapplicable. Instead, according to the majority, "...benign race-conscious measures mandated by Congress, even if those measures are not 'remedial' in the sense of being designed to compensate victims of past governmental or society discrimination, are constitutionally permissible to the extent that they serve important governmental objectives within the power of Congress and are substantially related to the achievement of those objectives." (Pp. 564-65.)

Justice O'Connor, the author of the *Croson* opinion, dissented in an opinion joined by Justices Rehnquist, Scalia, and Kennedy. Justice O'Connor contended that the strict scrutiny standard applicable to state racial classifications is equally applicable to racial classifications by the federal government. Furthermore: "'Benign' racial classification' is a contradiction in terms. Governmental distinctions among citizens based on race or ethnicity, even in the rare circumstances permitted by our cases, exact costs and carry with them substantial dangers. To the person denied an opportunity or right based on race, the classification is hardly benign." (Pp. 603-09.)

In a separate dissenting opinion joined by Scalia, Justice Kennedy likened "benign" racial classifications to South African apartheid, the internment of Japanese-Americans, and the *Plessy* "separate but equal" doctrine. Kennedy concluded: "I regret that after a century of judicial opinions we interpret the Constitution to do no more than move us from 'separate but equal' to 'unequal but benign.'" (Pp. 637-38.)

But the Court's approval of federal racial preferences was short-lived. Four of those in the *Metro Broadcasting* majority (Brennan, White, Marshall, and Blackmun) soon retired, and the *Metro Broadcasting* decision was expressly overruled (and *Fullilove* implicitly overruled) in Adarand Constructors, Inc. v. Pena, 515 U.S. 200 (1995). In *Adarand*, the Court held (5-4) that federal preferences were subject to the same strict scrutiny standard as state and local preferences: "Federal racial classifications, like those of a State, must serve a compelling governmental interest, and must be narrowly tailored to further that interest" (p. 235).

Adarand involved a highway construction contract awarded by the Department of Transportation (DOT). Like many federal statutes governing public contracts, a 1987 statute required that "not less than 10 percent" of DOT funds "shall be expended with small business concerns owned and controlled by socially and economically disadvantaged individuals." Federal statutes and regulations further provided that that a contract applicant should be presumed to be "socially and economically disadvantaged" if the applicant belonged to a racial or ethnic minority. Implementing these requirements, most federal

273

contracts contained a subcontractor compensation clause giving prime contractors financial incentive to hire minority subcontractors.

The contract at issue in *Adarand* was awarded by DOT to Mountain Gravel and Construction Company. The contract provided that Mountain would receive additional compensation if it hired subcontractors that were certified as small businesses controlled by "socially and economically disadvantaged individuals" and that "The contractor shall presume that socially and economically disadvantaged individuals include Black Americans, Hispanic Americans, Native Americans, Asian Pacific Americans, and other minorities...."

In response to its request for subcontractor bids, Mountain received bids for the guardrail portion of the project from Gonzalez Construction Company and Adarand Constructors. Gonzalez was certified as "socially and economically disadvantaged;" Adarand was not. Even though Adarand submitted the low bid, Gonzalez was awarded the subcontract instead of Adarand because of the additional payment Mountain would receive for choosing a minority contractor.

Adarand filed suit, claiming under the Fifth Amendment that the minority presumption unconstitutionally discriminated on the basis of race, and seeking declaratory and injunctive relief against any future use of subcontractor compensation clauses. From an adverse decision in the lower courts, Adarand appealed to the Supreme Court, which reversed (5-4).

In her opinion for the Court, Justice O'Connor summarized the guiding principles that the Court's decisions had now established with respect to governmental racial classifications: (1) Any preference based on racial or ethnic criteria must necessarily receive a most searching examination under strict scrutiny. (2) The standard of review under the Equal Protection Clause is not dependent on the race of those burdened or benefited by a particular classification. (3) Equal protection analysis under the Fifth Amendment is the same as that under the Fourteenth Amendment. These three propositions, O'Connor stated, lead to the conclusion that "any person, of whatever race, has the right to demand that any governmental actor subject to the Constitution justify any racial classification subjecting that person to unequal treatment under the strictest judicial scrutiny" and "We adhere to that view today, despite the surface appeal of holding 'benign' racial classifications to a lower standard...." (Pp. 224, 226.)

Justice O'Connor sought, however, "...to dispel the notion that strict scrutiny is 'strict in theory, but fatal in fact'." Government, she stated, is not disqualified from acting in response to the lingering effects of racial discrimination against minority groups in this country: "When race-based action is necessary to further a compelling interest, such action is within constitutional constraints if it satisfies the 'narrow tailoring' test this Court has set out in previous cases" (p. 237).

Justices Scalia and Thomas filed concurring opinions in *Adarand*. Scalia's opinion underscored his view that "government can never have a 'compelling interest' in discriminating on the basis of race in order to 'make up' for past racial discrimination in the opposite direction. ... [U]nder our Constitution there can be no such thing as either a creditor or a debtor race. That concept is alien to the Constitution's focus upon the individual ... and its rejection of dispositions based on race...."

In his opinion, Justice Thomas denied that there is any moral or constitutional difference "between laws designed to subjugate a race and those that distribute benefits on the basis of race in order to foster some current notion of equality." According to Thomas, "That these programs may have been motivated, in part, by good intentions cannot provide refuge from the principle that under our Constitution, the government may not make distinctions on the basis of race. ... In my mind, government-sponsored racial discrimination based on benign prejudice is just as noxious as discrimination inspired by malicious prejudice. In each instance, it is racial discrimination, plain and simple."

THE AFTERMATH OF THE ADARAND DECISION

While adopting the strict scrutiny standard for federal contracts, the Court left unanswered the ultimate question of whether the challenged requirements violated that standard. The Court instead sent the case back to the lower courts for reconsideration, noting that the Court of Appeals had not determined whether the interests served by the subcontractor compensation clause were compelling, or whether the clause was narrowly tailored and neither vague nor over- or under-inclusive. The Court also noted that the lower courts had not determined whether the agencies had considered race-neutral means to increase minority business participation.[62]

On remand, the Court of Appeals concluded that the Equal Protection Clause was violated by the preferences for "disadvantaged" small businesses that had been in force at the time of the Supreme Court's decision. But the Tenth Circuit held that the revised program, as amended in 1997, was narrowly tailored to serve a compelling governmental interest and passed constitutional muster.

However, by the time the case returned to the Supreme Court in 2001, the legal and factual framework of the case had been substantially altered by further changes in the challenged federal program. After hearing oral argument, the Supreme Court dismissed the case as "improvidently granted" because of several technical flaws making the case inappropriate for deciding the constitutional issues. Adarand Constructors, Inc. v. Mineta, 534 U.S. 103 (2001).[63]

The extent of federal agencies' compliance with the *Adarand* mandate is highly questionable. Most have resisted making more than modest changes in its preferential policies.[64] In September 2005,

---

[62] In her *Croson* opinion Justice O'Connor pointed out that the Equal Protection Clause does not prevent a government body from adopting race-neutral steps to assist minority contractors: "If MBE's disproportionately lack capital or cannot meet bonding requirements, a race-neutral program of city financing for small firms would ... lead to greater minority participation" (p. 507). In his concurring opinion in *Croson,* Justice Scalia similarly stated: "A State can, of course, act 'to undo the effects of past discrimination' in many permissible ways that do not involve classification by race. In the particular field of state contracting, for example, it may adopt a preference for small businesses, or even for new businesses—which would make it easier for those previously excluded by discrimination to enter the field. Such programs may well have racially disproportionate impact, but they are not based on race." (P. 526.)

[63] In 2004 the Court declined to revisit these issues when it denied review of the Eighth Circuit's ruling in Sherbrooke Turf, Inc. v. Minnesota Department of Transportation, 345 F.3d 964 (8th Cir. 2003), cert. denied, 541 U.S. 1041 (2004). Since the *Adarand* decision, while generally concluding that the federal government had a compelling interest for adopting such programs, the lower federal courts have disagreed on whether states or localities must independently justify the use of racial preferences to implement federal mandates within their individual jurisdictions. See, e.g., Western States Paving Co., Inc. v. Washington State Department of Transportation, 407 F.3d 983 (9th Cir. 2005); Rothe Development Corporation v. U.S. Department of Defense, 262 F.3d 1306 (Fed. Cir. 2001).

[64] See Thernstrom, supra, at 453-61.

the U.S. Commission on Civil Rights concluded that, ten years after the *Adarand* decision, federal agencies had still largely failed to comply with the strict scrutiny standard.[65] And under the revised Small Business Administration regulations, the extensive list of groups "presumed" to be "socially and economically disadvantaged" remains the same—in essence, anyone other than Caucasian:

> "Black Americans; Hispanic Americans; Native Americans (American Indians, Eskimos, Aleuts, or Native Hawaiians); Asian Pacific Americans (persons with origins from Burma, Thailand, Malaysia, Indonesia, Singapore, Brunei, Japan, China (including Hong Kong), Taiwan, Laos, Cambodia (Kampuchea), Vietnam, Korea, The Philippines, U.S. Trust Territory of the Pacific Islands (Republic of Palau), Republic of the Marshall Islands, Federated States of Micronesia, the Commonwealth of the Northern Mariana Islands, Guam, Samoa, Macao, Fiji, Tonga, Kiribati, Tuvalu, or Nauru); Subcontinent Asian Americans (persons with origins from India, Pakistan, Bangladesh, Sri Lanka, Bhutan, the Maldives Islands or Nepal); and members of other groups designated from time to time by SBA...."

Any individual who is not a member of one of the listed groups "must establish individual social advantage by a preponderance of the evidence" in order to qualify for certification. (13 CFR 124.103.)

---

[65] U.S. Commission on Civil Rights, *Federal Procurement after Adarand* (2005). In particular, the Commission charged that the agencies granted minority preferences without giving sufficient consideration to race-neutral alternatives to redress past discrimination.

33. RACIAL PREFERENCES IN ADMISSIONS

Starting with the *DeFunis* and *Bakke* cases, the constitutional battle over affirmative action has been primarily waged over admissions to state colleges and universities.[66]

As already pointed out (see Chapter 29 *Affirmative Action and the Racial Achievement Gap*), the black-white achievement gap has not substantially narrowed for many years, and black 17-year-olds by the twelfth grade of high school are still *on average* two to three years behind whites and Asian-Americans.

The racial gap among college-bound seniors is only slightly smaller. The average SAT scores of whites are nearly 24% higher than the average black scores. In 2010 the racial breakdown of SAT averages among all college-bound high school seniors was: Asian-Americans, 1636; whites, 1580; Hispanics, 1364; and blacks, 1277—i.e., 303 points lower than whites and 359 lower than Asian-Americans.[67] Comparable disparities exist with respect to applicants to selective colleges.[68]

---

[66] Admission programs of private colleges and universities generally do not involve "state action" subject to the Fourteenth Amendment. (See Chapter 18 *The "State Action" Requirement*.) However, Title VI of the 1964 Civil Rights Act prohibits discrimination on the basis of race, color, or national origin by all colleges and universities—including private ones—that receive federal financial assistance. (See Chapter 24 *Title VI of the 1964 Civil Rights Act*.) Enforcement of Title VI is the responsibility of the Department of Education's Office of Civil Rights, which only rarely has taken any action against minority preferences. See Jennifer Rubin, "The New Jews? Asian Admissions at the Ivies," *Weekly Standard*, September 1, 2008.

[67] Stephanie Banchero, "Students' SAT Scores Stay in Rut," *Wall Street Journal*, September 14, 2010 (the 2010 black and white averages were almost identical to those in 2009). See also Stephan & Abigail Thernstrom, *America in Black and White: One Nation, Indivisible* [Simon & Schuster 1997]: 398-99; Peter Schuck, *Diversity in America: Keeping Government at a Safe Distance* [Harvard 2003]: 148-49. Although criticized today because of the lower scores of minorities, the SAT test was introduced to democratize the selection process and break down the barriers to admission resulting from wealth and privilege. See, e.g., Andrew Ferguson, "The SAT and Its Enemies," *Weekly Standard*, May 4, 2009.

[68] Thomas Espenshade and Alexandria Radford, *No Longer Separate Not Yet Equal: Race and Class in Elite College Admission and Campus Life* [Princeton 2009]: 38 (referring to pre-2010 data).

Moreover, the SAT test—rather than being culturally biased against blacks—*over*-predicts their actual academic performance.[69] William Bowen and Derek Bok, leading proponents of affirmative action in college admissions, acknowledged that "The average rank in class for black students is appreciably lower than the average rank in class for white students *within each SAT interval* ... Black students with the same SAT scores as whites tend to earn lower grades" (italics in original).[70]

The gap is, if anything, even greater at the graduate school level. For example, admission to a top-ten law school generally requires a GPA of at least 3.5 and an LSAT score of at least 165. In 2002, 4,500 out of 91,000 law school applicants met that standard. Of the 4500, only 29 were black.[71]

Contrary to a widely held belief, poverty does not account for the SAT disparity. The average scores of black students from families in the *top* income bracket are *lower* than those of white students from families in the *bottom* income bracket.[72]

The achievement gap, however, does not preclude black or Hispanic high school graduates from going to college. There are approximately 4,200 degree-granting postsecondary institutions in the United States, including 2,300 four-year colleges and universities. Any high school graduate—even without the benefit of any racial preferences—has a choice of several accredited colleges to attend. In 2008 there were 2.5 million black college students, roughly double the number from 15 years earlier. Today blacks and Hispanics attend college at nearly the

[69] Schuck, supra, at 148. See also Stuart Taylor, "Sotomayor, Gates and Race," *National Journal*, Aug. 1, 2009 ("...the SAT is biased *in favor* of blacks and Hispanics; studies show that on average they do worse in college than whites with the same SAT scores") (emphasis in original).

[70] William Bowen and Derek Bok, *The Shape of the River: Long-Term Consequences of Considering Race in College and University Admissions* [Princeton 1998]: 77. According to the study, the average rank of black students was in the 23rd percentile of their schools, a full 30 percentile places lower than the average rank of whites. Furthermore, "...the black-white disparity in college grades is wider among students with high SAT scores." Jencks and Phillips, supra, at 39.

[71] John McWhorter, *Winning the Race: Beyond the Crisis in Black America* [Gotham Books 2006]: 264; Schuck, supra, at 148-49 ("The leading study of law school admissions in the early 1990s found that only a few dozen of the 420 blacks admitted to the eighteen most selective law schools would have been admitted to those schools absent affirmative action").

[72] Thernstrom, *Black and White*, supra, at 404-05; Shelby Steele, "The Age of White Guilt and the Disappearance of the Black Individual," *Harper's Magazine*, November 30, 1999.

same rate as whites (but only 17% graduate—about half the white rate).

The affirmative action issue therefore is not "college versus no college." Instead, from a constitutional standpoint, the issue arises only when minorities apply to so-called "highly selective" state schools—the relatively small number that receive far more applications than they can accept.

In choosing among applicants, these "highly selective" state schools (like their private counterparts) typically place heavy emphasis on objective criteria—grade point averages and tests like the SAT. As a result, if the same criteria are applied to all applicants, the percentage of black and Hispanic students who would be admitted would almost inevitably be far below the percentage of blacks and Hispanics in the population.[73] "The proportion of minority students at these [selective] colleges would be extremely low if admissions committees ignored the race or ethnicity of applicants."[74]

As a result, in order to increase the percentage of their minority enrollment, these schools (apart from, e.g., race-neutral outreach programs) are confronted with a difficult dilemma—they must lower their admission requirements either for all applicants or only for minority applicants.[75] But if a state school applies a double standard to admit some applicants *on a racial basis*, a significant constitutional issue is then presented under the Equal Protection Clause; for, in those circumstances, it necessarily follows that a government body is thereby excluding *on a racial basis* some nonminority applicants who are more qualified on the basis of the school's ostensible standard.

---

[73] See, e.g., McWhorter, supra, at 264 ("...simple and readily available data show that each year, there is but a sliver of black students with the grades and test scores considered sine qua non for serious consideration if students were white or Asian."); Schuck, supra, at 148-149 ("A recent study of forty-seven public institutions, moreover, found that the odds of a black student being admitted compared to a white student with the same SAT and GPA were 173 to 1 at Michigan and 177 to 1 at North Carolina State....").

[74] Thomas Espenshade and Alexandria Radford, *No Longer Separate Not Yet Equal: Race and Class in Elite College Admission and Campus Life* [Princeton 2009]: 347-48. If, for example, an elite college selected students solely on the basis of SAT scores, it would "produce... a college campus from which nearly all black students have disappeared." Id. at 365.

[75] McWhorter, supra, at 264 ("Pure logic requires that having a first-year class that is even 6 or 7 percent black requires each selective school to subject blacks to lower standards"). A black applicant to an elite school has (on average) an admission advantage of 230 to 400 SAT points. Espenshade, supra, at 93n.

Since the capacity of each "highly selective" school is limited, such a policy is necessarily a "zero-sum game" and therefore not "victimless." Race preferences do not just add minority applicants to the student body. Instead, for every winner based on race preferences, there is also a loser—an applicant denied admission who otherwise would have been admitted. For such an applicant denied admission, the process is not "benign."

The Equal Protection Clause, of course, does not require a school to adopt any particular standard for admission. The issue under the Equal Protection Clause is, instead, whether a public institution, in applying whatever standard it chooses to adopt (whether it be test scores, economic advantage, overcoming barriers, experience, character, or any other criteria), may grant preferences to some applicants over others on the basis of their race or ancestry.[76]

As already pointed out, the Supreme Court has repeatedly held that the Fourteenth Amendment imposes a very heavy burden to justify distinctions based on race,[77] that the validity of a racial classification "is not dependent on the race of those burdened or benefited by a particular classification,"[78] and that all racial classifications—whether characterized as "benign" or otherwise—are subject to the "most rigid scrutiny," rendering any racial classification invalid unless the government demonstrates, not only that the classification serves a "compelling" governmental interest, but also that the restriction is "narrowly tailored" to further that interest. The Court has also repeatedly held that racial preferences cannot be justified as a remedy for "societal discrimination."[79]

The effect of these decisions is to sharply limit the potential justifications that might be asserted to support minority preferences by

---

[76] The issue is further complicated by rules issued by the Department of Education in 2010 requiring universities and colleges to collect more information about race and ethnicity. The rules enable applicants with a multiracial ancestry to choose which parts of their background they wish to emphasize for admission purposes and disregard others. "...[T]ne rules offer students both a more accurate way to describe themselves—as well as, some counselors fear, yet another opportunity to perhaps game a competitive admissions system." Jacques Steinberg, "White? Black? Hispanic? Why Not All of the Above?," *New York Times*, June 13, 2011; Susan Saulny and Jacques Steinberg, "On College Forms, ation of Race, or Races, Can Perplex," *New York Times*, June 13, 2011.

[77] See, e.g., Loving v. Virginia, 388 U.S. 1, 9 (1967).

[78] See, e.g., McLaughlin v. Florida, 379 U.S. 184, 192 (1964).

[79] *Bakke*, supra; Wygant v. Jackson Board of Education, 476 U.S. 267 (1986); Shaw v. Hunt, 517 U.S. 899, 909-12 (1967).

colleges and universities. In particular, as Jerome Karabel pointed out in his study of elite college admission policies, the rejection of "societal discrimination" as an acceptable justification undercut "some of the main reasons that leading colleges and universities adopted affirmative action in the first place: to right the wrongs of the past and to integrate the elite of the future," and the decisions thus "eroded the moral foundations on which affirmative action was built."[80]

Because of the rejection of other possible justifications for minority preferences, the only remaining alternative was reliance on the diversity rationale suggested by Justice Powell's individual comments in *Bakke*. As Jerome Karabel observed: " 'Diversity', a flexible ideology that in the past had been used to limit the number of Jews ... was now being deployed to increase the numbers of historically underrepresented minorities...."[81]

The initial prospects of succeeding with a diversity defense were not impressive. Powell's comments in *Bakke* on diversity assumed that an acceptable admission program would be based on a highly individualized analysis of multiple factors—a process that very few public universities could claim to utilize. In addition, elite schools employing minority preferences have shown little or no desire to promote *non*-racial diversity: "Most elite universities seem to have little interest in diversifying their student bodies when it comes to the numbers of born-again Christians from the Bible belt, students from Appalachia and other rural and small-town areas, people who

---

[80] Jerome Karabel, *The Chosen* [Mariner Books 2006]: 498-99. A "societal discrimination" rationale, furthermore, would be inapplicable to many black applicants. A large percentage of blacks attending elite schools are not "African-American" descendants of slaves. According to a study published in the *American Journal of Education*, more than a quarter of black students at selective universities are immigrants from Africa, the West Indies, and Latin America, and "the more elite the school, the more black immigrants are enrolled." Darryl Fears, "In Diversity Push, Top Universities Enrolling More Black Immigrants," *Washington Post*, March 6, 2007. In 2004 Harvard professors Lani Guinier and Henry Louis Gates Jr. estimated that as many as two-thirds of Harvard's undergraduates were West Indian and African immigrants or their children, or to a lesser extent, children of biracial couples. Sara Kimer and Karen Aronson, "Top Colleges Take More Blacks, but Which Ones?," *New York Times*, June 24, 2004.

[81] Karabel, supra, at 499. See also Peter Schuck, *Reflections on Grutter*, Yale Law School, Public Law Working Paper No. 61, available at SSRN: http://ssrn.com/abstract=430606 or doi:10.2139/ssrn.430606: "Every sophisticated observer who can see through the rhetorical fog thrown up by the now-obligatory diversity-talk (including all members of the Court, one supposes) understands that this remedy, not diversity, is the law school's true motive."

have served in the U.S. military, those who have grown up on farms or ranches, Mormons, Pentecostals, Jehovah's Witnesses, lower-middle-class Catholics, working class 'white ethnics,' social and political conservatives, wheelchair users, married students, married students with children, or older students first starting out in college after raising children or spending several years in the workforce."[82] Although such groups do not have even close to a "critical mass" at most American universities, they would likely add at least as much to campus diversity as racial minorities.

Particularly lacking is any diversity in terms of economic advantage. The student bodies of the elite schools are still drawn overwhelmingly from the upper middle class. At the 146 most competitive four-year colleges and universities, 74% of students come from the top quarter of the socioeconomic distribution (based on family income and parental education and occupation) and *only 3% of all students (and only 2% of white students)* come from families in the bottom quarter.[83] Minority students at selective colleges are also overwhelmingly middle class; an extensive study supporting affirmative action found that 86 percent of black students at selective colleges were from middle or high socioeconomic backgrounds.[84]

For these and other reasons, a diversity justification for racial preferences was viewed skeptically "as a rhetorical Hail Mary pass, an argument made in desperation now that all other arguments for preferences have failed."[85]

---

[82] Russell K. Nieli, "How Diversity Punishes Asians, Poor Whites and Lots of Others," *Minding the Campus: Reforming Our Universities,* http://www.mindingthecampus.com/originals, July 12, 2010. See also Ross Douthat, "The Roots of White Anxiety," *New York Times,* July 18, 2010 ("The most underrepresented groups on elite campuses often aren't racial minorities; they're working-class whites (and white Christians in particular) from conservative states and regions.").

[83] Espenshade, supra, at 348. See also Karabel, supra, at 554; Bowen and Bok, supra, at 48. Only 15 % of the class of 2010 at the country's 193 most selective colleges came from the bottom half of the income distribution, while 67 % came from the highest-earning fourth of the distribution. David Leonhardt, "Top Colleges, Largely for the Elite," *New York Times,* May 24, 2011.

[84] McWhorter, supra, at 264; Bowen and Bok, supra, at 49.

[85] Peter Schuck, *Diversity in America: Keeping Government at a Safe Distance* [Belknap 2003]: 161. See also Peter Wood, *Diversity: The Invention of a Concept* [Encounter Books 2003]: 103 ("The idea of defending racial quotas by citing the advantages of diversity had indeed been kicking around for several years, but it was just one of several hypothetical sales pitches for countering the increasingly sharp attacks on the unfairness of affirmative action"); Karabel, supra, at 499.

It was against this background that the Supreme Court in 2003 decided two important cases involving the admission policies of the University of Michigan.

One of the two cases involved undergraduate admissions; the other involved admissions to the law school. The plaintiffs in both cases alleged that they had been denied admission because of the University's affirmative action policies in violation of the Equal Protection Clause of the Fourteenth Amendment and Title VI of the Civil Rights Act of 1964.

The University admitted the use of race preferences but, relying on Justice Powell's comments on diversity in the *Bakke* case, sought to justify the preferences on the ground that increased enrollment of three statistically "under-represented groups"—blacks, Hispanics, and Native Americans—would enhance diversity in the student body.

THE GRATZ CASE

In the undergraduate case, Gratz v. Bollinger, 539 U.S. 244 (2003), applicants for admission were evaluated on the basis of a "point system" assigning to each applicant a certain number of points for SAT scores, high school grade averages, and other academic credentials. In addition, an automatic "bonus" of 20 points was given to any applicant from one of the three favored groups. The result of the "bonus" was to admit almost every applicant from the three groups that met minimal standards; by contrast, a Caucasian or Asian-American of equal qualifications would have only about a 1-in-3 chance of admission.

The Supreme Court in *Gratz* held (6-3) that the "bonus" for minorities violated the equal protection of the laws. In an opinion by Chief Justice Rehnquist, the Court rejected the University's effort to justify its undergraduate policy on the basis of the diversity rationale suggested by Justice Powell in *Bakke*:

> "Justice Powell's opinion in *Bakke* emphasized the importance of considering each particular applicant as an individual, assessing all of the qualities that individual possesses, and in turn, evaluating that individual's ability to contribute to the unique setting of higher education. The admissions program Justice Powell described, however, did not contemplate that any single characteristic automatically ensured a

specific and identifiable contribution to a university's diversity.... Instead, under the approach Justice Powell described, each characteristic of a particular applicant was to be considered in assessing the applicant's entire application. The [University's undergraduate] policy does not provide such individualized consideration.... The only consideration that accompanies this distribution of points is a factual review of an application to determine whether an individual is a member of one of these minority groups." (Pp. 271-72.)

Three Justices dissented, including Justice Ginsburg, whose opinion predicted that colleges and universities—despite the majority decision—would still seek to maintain minority enrollment "through winks, nods, and disguises" (p. 305).

THE GRUTTER CASE

On the same day, in Grutter v. Bollinger, 539 U.S. 306 (2003), a differently constituted majority (in an opinion by Justice O'Connor, who had joined the *Gratz* majority to strike down the undergraduate policy) voted 5-to-4 to uphold the law school's admission program.

Of the 3,500 applications received each year for the law school's freshman class, only approximately 350 are accepted—about one in ten. Admissions officials place substantial reliance on each applicant's undergraduate grade point average (GPA) and Law School Admissions Test (LSAT) score. In 1992 the School initiated a policy of trying to increase the enrollment of students from members of three "underrepresented minorities"—blacks, Hispanic, and Native American. By 2000 the result was to increase the law school's minority admissions by 400%.

When Barbara Grutter, a white Michigan resident with a 3.8 GPA and a 161 LSAT score, was denied admission, she filed suit, alleging that her academic qualifications were substantially superior to many of the applicants admitted from the three minority groups and that the School had unconstitutionally discriminated against her on the basis of race.

The Law School defended its admission policy on diversity grounds. The School contended it gave special consideration to blacks, Hispanics, and Native Americans in order to achieve a "critical mass" of students in each of the three minorities because "a critical mass of underrepresented minority students could not be enrolled if admissions decisions were based primarily on undergraduate GPAs and LSAT scores" (p. 318). The law school's expert testified that in 2000 35% of applicants in the three groups—approximately one out of every three—were admitted and that if race were not considered only 10% of those applicants would have been admitted and the three groups would have comprised only 4% of the entering class instead of the actual figure of 14.5%. (Pp. 318-20.)

In upholding the law school program, Justice O'Connor reiterated each of the limitations established in prior decisions (including her own opinions in *Croson* and *Adarand*) restricting minority preferences. She acknowledged that "the Fourteenth Amendment 'protect[s] *persons*, not *groups*,'" that admitting "some specified percentage of a particular group merely because of its race or ethnic origin' ... would amount to outright racial balancing, which is patently unconstitutional," that all racial classifications imposed by government "must be analyzed by a reviewing court under strict scrutiny" and "are constitutional only if they are narrowly tailored to further compelling governmental interests," and that is done to "'smoke out' illegitimate uses of race by assuring that [government] is pursuing a goal important enough to warrant use of a highly suspect tool." (Pp. 326-27, italics in original.)

But, in the application of these standards, the majority's scrutiny of the law school's program was far from strict. While purporting to apply Justice Powell's *Bakke* opinion as "the touchstone for constitutional analysis of race-conscious admissions policies" (p. 323), the *Grutter* decision brushed aside Powell's precondition for accepting a diversity justification. The diversity program that Powell endorsed was one in which "the race of an applicant may tip the balance in his favor just as geographic origin or a life spent on a farm may tip the balance in other candidates' cases," and in which "race or ethnic background may be deemed a 'plus' in a particular applicant's file, yet it does not insulate the individual from comparison with all other candidates for the available seats." (438 U.S. at 316-18.)

In *Grutter*, in contrast with the type of program required by Powell in *Bakke*, the law school did not employ diversity "to tip the balance" resulting from a holistic evaluation of all candidates according to their varied backgrounds and talents. On the contrary, the school did precisely what Powell condemned—that is, "insulate the individual from comparison with all other candidates for the available seats" in order to admit a predetermined percentage of minority applicants. The law school's own admission statistics seemingly permit no other conclusion.

In every year of the relevant 1995-2000 period, as the dissenting opinions pointed out, the percentage of admitted applicants of each of the three minority groups was almost identical to the percentage of applications received from members of that minority. In 1995, for example: 9.7% of the applicants were black, and 9.4% of those admitted were black; 5.1% of the applicants were Hispanic, and 5.0% of those admitted were Hispanic; 1.1% of the applicants were Native American, and 1.1% of the applicants admitted were Native American. As to each of the minority groups in each year in the period, the inference is unavoidable that the school consistently applied a formula (rather than any holistic analysis) to determine how many members of each group would be admitted.

Denying the school's application of a quota, the *Grutter* majority responded that "...the number of underrepresented minority students *who ultimately enroll* in the Law School differs substantially from their representation in the applicant pool and varies considerably for each group from year to year" and that this variance shows "a range inconsistent with a quota." (P. 336, italics added.) But the number of students "who ultimately enroll"—unlike the number of applicants that the school had previously offered to admit—will of course vary depending on whether those given offers elect to enroll at Michigan or go elsewhere. Any variance in the ultimate enrollment figures is immaterial to determine the basis on which the school chose to admit applicants. And, whether or not the law school's program is called a quota, it surely constitutes racial balancing, which the majority opinion acknowledges is "patently unconstitutional."

Furthermore, even if educational diversity may in some circumstances be accepted as a compelling objective, the law school's program was scarcely designed to achieve it. As one commentator put it, if the program were really about enrolling students of diverse backgrounds, why would the program ignore "those other demographic factors (religion or partisanship, say) that directly represent the different world views with which educational diversity is supposedly concerned? Would a fundamentalist Christian or a conservative Republican or an anarchist, for that matter, create less diversity-value for Michigan's students than an applicant whose only special claim to diversity value is his surname or the color of his skin?"[86]

Achievement of true educational diversity, moreover, would require far greater attention to the notorious under-representation of students from low-income families. As already noted, 74 percent of the enrollments of elite colleges and universities come from the top quarter of the socioeconomic distribution, and only 3 percent come from the bottom quarter.[87] Recently published scholarship shows, moreover, that the achievement gap between rich and poor children has dramatically widened.[88] One study found that the gap in standardized test scores between affluent and low-income students had grown by about 40 percent since the 1960s, and is now double the testing gap between blacks and whites. A second study found that the imbalance between rich and poor children in college completion— the single most important predictor of success in the work force— has grown by about 50 percent since the late 1980s.

*****

The University of Michigan's victory in the law school case proved to be short-lived. In November 2006, by a 58 to 42 margin, Michigan voters approved a state constitutional amendment called the Michigan Civil Rights Initiative that in effect barred application of the *Grutter* decision in Michigan. The amendment (in language similar to referendums adopted in California,

---

[86] Peter Schuck, *Reflections on Grutter*, Yale Law School, Public Law Working Paper No. 61, available at SSRN: http://ssrn.com/abstract=430606 or doi:10.2139/ssrn.430606. Schuck observes: "The only convincing explanation for the school's program has little to do with the goal of educational diversity and everything to do with a goal the Court has insisted is constitutionally insufficient to justify preferences: the laudable wish to remedy the historic injustices suffered in America by (at least two of) those groups."

[87] Espenshade, supra, at 348.

[88] Sabrina Tavernise, "Education Gap Grows between Rich and Poor, Studies Say," *New York Times*, February 12, 2012. The studies were published in 2011 by the Russell Sage Foundation in *Whither Opportunity? Rising Inequality, Schools, and Children's Life Chances* (Greg Duncan and Richard Murnane, eds.).

Washington, Arizona, and Nebraska, a governor's executive order in Florida, and a law enacted by the New Hampshire legislature) provides that the University of Michigan "...and any other public college or university, community college, or school district shall not discriminate against, or grant preferential treatment to, any individual or group on the basis of race, sex, color, ethnicity, or national origin in the operation of public employment, public education, or public contracting."

A group of organizations and individuals brought an action to enjoin the amendment on the ground that it violated the Equal Protection Clause. The Sixth Circuit Court of Appeals rejected the claim. Coalition to Defend Affirmative Action v. Granholm, 473 F.3d 237, 249 (6th Cir.2006).

34. RACIAL BALANCING IN PUBLIC SCHOOLS

The *Gratz* and *Grutter* decisions have by no means ended the debate over the validity and scope of affirmative action in education. Even if these decisions continue to be controlling, questions may be raised whether other affirmative action plans are sufficiently "individualized" (and therefore valid under *Grutter*) or too much like a "quota" (and therefore invalid under *Gratz*).

Controversy also continued on a closely related issue—the validity of so-called "voluntary integration" to mitigate "imbalances" between white and minority students. The vast majority of school districts do not take race into account when assigning students.[89] However, even in the absence of any government-imposed segregation and without the compulsion of a remedial desegregation order, some school districts elected on their own to make assignments to schools on a racial basis, in order to increase the low percentage of whites attending schools in which minorities constitute most of the enrollment.[90]

These programs are "voluntary" in the sense that they were not ordered by a court, but they are not "voluntary" on the part of students who are assigned to schools on a racial basis. Although the programs were defended as efforts to deal with "segregation," the targeted imbalances did not result from "segregation" in any legal sense. As the Supreme Court pointed out, "[T]he differentiating factor between *de jure* segregation and so-called *de facto* segregation . . . is *purpose* or *intent* to segregate."[91]

The imbalances instead arise primarily from demographic residential patterns (where the students' homes are located) and the

---

[89] James Ryan, "The Supreme Court and Voluntary Integration," 121 *Harvard Law Review* 131, 144 (2007).

[90] The background of this movement is traced in Andrew Kull, *The Color-Blind Constitution* [Harvard 1992]: 172-199.

[91] Keyes v. School Dist. No. 1, 413 U.S. 189 (1973) (italics in original).

preference of many parents (minority parents as well as white ones) to have their children attend neighborhood schools rather than bused to distantly located schools. But a more fundamental cause of the imbalances is the relatively small percent of white students attending public schools in major cities. In 2000-01 white enrollment in 25 of the 26 largest school districts averaged a mere 17 percent. Whites made up only 10% of the public school students in Los Angeles, 17% in Philadelphia, 15% in New York City, 11% in Miami, 10% in Chicago and in Houston, 8% in Dallas, and 4% in New Orleans and Detroit.[92] Of the ten largest school districts; only two had more than 30% white enrollment; the rest had a white enrollment of between 3 and 14%.[93]

There is, in short, a marked shortage of white students in these districts to "balance" against the much larger number of minority students.[94] Although the nation's cities are now more racially integrated than at any time since 1910,[95] the relative paucity of white students in these districts is likely to continue (and perhaps increase) as a result of a higher minority birth rates, the movement of immigrants (both legal and illegal) to the cities, and "white flight" from the cities to the suburbs.[96]

In Parents Involved in Community Schools v. Seattle School District No. 1, 551 U.S. 701 (2007), the Court considered the constitutionality of plans adopted by school districts in Seattle, Washington, and Jefferson County, Kentucky. Both plans provided, under specified conditions, for mandatory assignment on a racial basis—the assignment of white

---

[92] Abigail & Stephan Thernstrom, "Have We Overcome?," *Commentary* (Nov. 2004).

[93] Ryan, supra, at 145.

[94] Nationally, in 2000, 72 % of black children attended a school where minority children constituted more than half of the students, and 37% attended a school with more than a 90% minority. Of the nearly 16,000 school districts in the country, more than half have a student enrollment that is greater than 90% white or 90% minority. Ryan, supra, at 145.

[95] Edward Glaeser and Jacob Vigdor, *The End of the Segregated Century: Racial Separation in America's Neighborhoods, 1890-2010* [Manhattan Institute 2012]. See Sam Roberts, "Segregation Curtailed in U.S. Cities, Study Finds," *New York Times*, January 30, 2012.

[96] Racial balancing plans may have the unintended result of accelerating the decline of white enrollment by increasing "white flight" to the suburbs and transfers to private schools, particularly in the largest school districts. James Coleman, Sara Kelly, and John Moore, *Trends in School Integration* [Urban Institute 1975]. See David Armor and Christine Rossell, "Desegregation and Resegregation in the Public Schools," *Beyond the Color Line: New Perspectives on Race and Ethnicity* [Hoover 2002]: 221.

students to predominantly minority-attended schools and the assignment of minority students to predominantly white-attended schools.

To implement the plans, Seattle students were classified as either "white" or "nonwhite" (including not only blacks, but also Asian-Americans, Latinos, and Native Americans), while Jefferson County students were classified as either black or "other" (all races, including Asian-American). The classifications were generally made according to the race specified in the student's registration materials. In Seattle, however, if a parent declined to specify a race, the district classified the student through a visual inspection of the parent or the student.

Both plans were challenged under the Equal Protection Clause in suits brought by the parents of students who were denied assignment to particular schools solely because of their race. In the Seattle case, for example, Andy Meeks' mother sought to enroll him in a special program because he suffered from attention deficit hyperactivity disorder and dyslexia. He was found qualified for the program but was denied admission because of his race. The children of Jill Kurfurst and Winnie Bachwitz, because of their race, were denied admission to a school near their home and instead were assigned to a school on the other side of Seattle. To attend that school, the two students faced a daily multi-bus round-trip commute of over four hours; the parents instead enrolled the children in private schools. Similarly, when Joshua McDonald's family moved into the Jefferson County district, he was assigned to a kindergarten class in a school located ten miles from his home. When his mother sought a transfer to a school only a mile from his new home, the transfer was denied on the ground that it would adversely affect racial balances.

The Seattle plan was upheld by the Court of Appeals for the Ninth Circuit *en banc* and the Jefferson County plan was upheld by the Court of Appeals for the Sixth Circuit. The Supreme Court held (5-4) that both plans violated the Equal Protection Clause.

There were three main opinions—Roberts' plurality opinion (joined by Scalia, Alito, and Thomas), the concurring opinion of Kennedy (who also joined part of the Roberts opinion), and Breyer's dissent (joined by Stevens, Souter, and Ginsburg). In addition, Thomas wrote a separate concurrence and Stevens wrote a separate dissent. The rhetoric of the opinions was unusually heated; for example, Roberts and Breyer called each other's opinion "lawless" and Thomas equated Breyer's dissent with arguments made by segregationists.

The Seattle and Louisville plans, according to the Roberts plurality opinion, improperly based assignment decisions solely on the race of the student; and because race was the determinative factor and race-neutral alternatives had not been sufficiently considered, the districts' plans were not narrowly tailored. Roberts concluded that, even if obtaining a diverse student body were a compelling state interest justifying the use of race, the Seattle and Louisville plans were not aimed at achieving diversity. Instead, they were attempting to remedy *de facto* segregation by balancing the black and white enrollments so that they mirrored the demographics of surrounding districts. "Racial balancing," he wrote, "is not transformed from 'patently unconstitutional' to a compelling state interest simply by relabeling it 'racial diversity'" and "The way to stop discrimination on the basis of race is to stop discriminating on the basis of race."

Unlike Thomas in his concurrence, Roberts did not support a color-blind test that would bar any consideration of race.[97] Roberts' opinion rejected the two plans primarily on the ground that under the plans "race is not considered as part of a broader effort to achieve 'exposure to widely diverse people, cultures, ideas, and viewpoints.'" (Pp. 723-25.)[98]

Roberts declined to opine on the validity of other race-conscious policies that do not involve the racial assignment of students: "These other means—for example, where to construct new schools, how to allocate resources among schools, and which academic offerings to provide to attract students to certain schools—implicate different considerations than the explicit racial classifications at issue in these cases, and we express no opinion on their validity."

Kennedy, concurring, stated that he was unwilling to join the Roberts opinion in its entirety because it "is at least open to the interpretation that the Constitution requires school districts to ignore the problem of *de facto* resegregation in schooling," According to

---

[97] In denying that the *Brown* decision supported racial balancing in the public schools, both Roberts and Thomas quoted from NAACP briefs in the *Brown* case that espoused a color-blind test. Surviving members of NAACP legal team in *Brown* responded with outrage. Christopher Schmidt, "*Brown* and the Colorblind Constitution," 94 *Cornell Law Review* 203, 204, 225-29 (2008).

[98] Quoting Grutter v. Bollinger, 539 U.S. 306, 329-30 (2003).

Kennedy, "To the extent the [Roberts] plurality opinion suggests the Constitution mandates that state and local school authorities must accept the status quo of racial isolation in schools, it is, in my view, profoundly mistaken." At the same time Kennedy assailed the dissenters' apparent willingness to allow school boards virtually untrammeled authority to use racial balancing techniques, even to the extent of deciding whether individual students should be admitted on the basis of skin color. He further contended that the dissent's proposed standard of review (which Kennedy said "bears more than a passing resemblance to rational-basis review") would "invite widespread governmental deployment of racial classifications." (P. 791.)

In view of the split of views among the other eight Justices, Kennedy's concurrence constitutes in effect the Court's controlling opinion in the case. In his view, "individual racial classifications employed in this manner may be considered legitimate only if they are a last resort to achieve a compelling interest." (P. 790.) Kennedy did not completely rule out consideration of race in student assignments as part of a "holistic" multi-factor plan of the sort suggested by Powell in *Bakke*. In addition, Kennedy would allow some race-conscious steps to reduce racial isolation in K-12 schools, provided that they "address the problem in a general way and without treating each student in different fashion solely on the basis of a systematic, individual typing by race." Such steps, Kennedy said, include "strategic site selection of new schools; drawing attendance zones with general recognition of the demographics of neighborhoods; allocating resources for special programs; recruiting students and faculty in a targeted fashion; and tracking enrollments, performance, and other statistics by race" and "it is unlikely any of them would demand strict scrutiny to be found permissible." However, "[a]ssigning to each student a personal designation according to a crude system of individual racial classifications is quite a different matter; and the legal analysis changes accordingly." (Pp. 788-89.)[99]

---

[99] Similarly, in Richmond v. J.A. Croson, 488 U.S. 469 (1989), Justices O'Connor and Scalia both expressed approval of cities' use of race-neutral methods to assist minorities in obtaining public contracts—for example, "city financing for small firms" to meet bonding requirements (p. 507) or giving "a preference for small businesses, or even for new businesses" in awarding contracts (p. 526).

THE IMPACT OF THE PARENTS INVOLVED DECISION

In *Grutter*, the Court sustained the University's search for a "critical mass" of minority students and permitted "some attention to numbers" of minority students. In *Parents Involved*, the Court found that the school districts' focus on numbers, without evidence that those numbers were tied to "any pedagogic concept of the level of diversity needed to obtain the asserted educational benefits," was unconstitutional. Although *Parents Involved* did not purport to overrule *Grutter*, the majority's scepticism about numerical goals and racial assignments is hard to reconcile with *Grutter*'s approval of a "critical mass" standard.

However, despite Justice Breyer's dire predictions (pp. 858-63), the *Parents Involved* decision is not likely to have a significant impact on American education. When asked what effect the decision would have on his district, Seattle's School Superintendent said: "In reality, none."[100] As a leading critic of the Court's decision recognizes, "The truth is that racial integration is not on the agenda of most school districts and has not been for over twenty years" and "[r]ace-neutral alternatives remain available for consideration and have already been used in places like Seattle with some success."[101] One increasingly popular race-neutral alternative is to switch emphasis from racial diversity to class-based diversity.[102]

A principal reason for the growing disenchantment with racial balancing is the backlash in a significant part of the black community, particularly in cities where balancing involves busing black children to schools distant from their own neighborhoods. In some of these cities (including Louisville and Nashville), black parents have instituted lawsuits to resist balancing plans and to terminate desegregation orders.[103]

---

[100] Ryan, supra, at 146-47 ("Looking across various accounts of race-based student assignment plans, I count fewer than thirty districts that have plans similar to those in effect in Seattle and Louisville, where students are given a broad choice among regular public schools and where that choice is constrained by racial guidelines. The number may be as low as ten. …[M]ost racial segregation exists between rather than within districts. In many metropolitan areas, therefore, racial integration would only be a plausible goal if students could attend school outside of their home districts. But opportunities to do so are rare.").

[101] Id. at 148.

[102] See Emily Bazelon, "The Next Kind of Integration," *New York Times Magazine*, July 20, 2008, concerning steps taken by school boards after Parents Involved to achieve diversity by a primarily class-based method.

[103] See, e.g., Greg Winter, "Long After Brown v. Board of Education, Sides Switch," *New York Times*, May 16, 2004.

As the *New York Times* reported in 2004, black "[c]ritics of mandatory integration contend that there is nothing wrong with having predominantly black schools; in fact, they say, it is racist to suggest otherwise. What is more, the fatigue of busing their children for hours each day, only to see them do poorly at predominantly white schools, has led some black parents to almost yearn for the type of tight-knit network of black educators that integration disbanded."[104]

These critics also contend that any benefits to blacks of balancing "do not outweigh the immeasurable cultural and psychological losses," including "the black school as a community center and resource, the leadership training of black students in their own teams, clubs, and activities, and the close involvement of black parents in their children's education."[105] Lani Guinier, a prominent black law professor at Harvard, observed: "I find enormous nostalgia for the world pre-*Brown*. This is very disconcerting but not surprising. People feel like what was lost was a sense of community."[106]

In addition, demographic assumptions underlying the rationale for racial balancing (including assumptions relied upon by Justice Breyer in his *Parents Involved* dissent) are probably no longer valid. As demonstrated by a comprehensive study *The End of the Segregated Century* published in January 2012, the degree of racial separation in America has in recent years fundamentally changed.[107] The study, based on census results from thousands of neighborhoods and supported by a broad spectrum of other experts, found that the nation's cities are now more racially integrated than at any time since 1910, that all-white enclaves "are effectively extinct," and that black urban ghettos are shriveling. According to the study, only 0.5% of America's 70,000 neighbourhoods are now all-white and the proportion of

---

[104] Ibid. See also, e.g., Juan Williams, "Don't Mourn Brown v. Board of Education," *New York Times*, June 29, 2007 ("In a series of cases in Atlanta, Oklahoma City and Kansas City, Mo., frustrated parents, black and white, appealed to federal judges to stop shifting children from school to school like pieces on a game board. The parents wanted better neighborhood schools and a better education for their children, no matter the racial make-up of the school.").

[105] Peter Irons, *Jim Crow's Children: The Broken Promise of the Brown Decision* [Penguin 2004]: 343.

[106] Winter, supra.

[107] Edward Glaeser and Jacob Vigdor, *The End of the Segregated Century: Racial Separation in America's Neighborhoods, 1890-2010* [Manhattan Institute 2012]. See Sam Roberts, "Segregation Curtailed in U.S. Cities, Study Finds," *New York Times*, January 30, 2012; "The dream is getting closer," *The Economist*, February 11, 2012.

blacks living in ghetto neighbourhoods (more than 80% black) has dropped from nearly half to about 20%. An influx of immigrants and the gentrification of black neighborhoods contributed to the changes, the study said, but suburbanization by blacks was even more instrumental. Indeed, contrary to earlier patterns, "…suburbs are often among the most integrated parts of America."

Racial Balancing and "the Promise of Brown"

Brown v. Board of Education "was the catalyst that shook up Congress and culminated in the two major Civil Rights acts of the century….," and "…there was in *Brown* the spirit that altered daily dealings of the races so profoundly, that displaced the indignities of caste with new respect."[108] In large measure *Brown* marked the real beginning of the "Second Reconstruction."[109] Nevertheless the scope of the Court's holding should not be overstated.

In *Parents Involved*, in supporting a group-centered rather than individual-centered approach, the dissenters acknowledged that "This is not to deny that there is a cost in applying 'a state-mandated racial label'" (p. 867). This "cost" of course would have to be paid by students such as Andy Meeks, Joshua McDonald, and the other children who are assigned to distant schools on a racial basis against their will.

Although not explicitly claiming that such a result was required by *Brown*,[110] the dissenters nevertheless invoked the popular mantra of "the promise of *Brown*." According to Justice Breyer, the majority's decision "undermines *Brown*'s promise of integrated primary and secondary education" and "To invalidate the plans under review

---

[108] J. Harvie Wilkinson, *From Brown to Bakke—The Supreme Court and School Integration: 1954-1978* [Oxford 1979]: 49.

[109] See C. Vann Woodward, *The Strange Career of Jim Crow* [Oxford 3d rev. ed. 2002]: 8-10

[110] Among those similarly decrying a breach of the "promise of *Brown*," Peter Irons, supra, at 338, acknowledges that the only integration sought by the NAACP lawyers in *Brown* was the integration of schools that had been segregated by law. But he nevertheless contends that the *Brown* decision promised to use busing and other means to integrate any school that was all-black or predominantly black—regardless of whether the school's racial composition was due to government discrimination or was wholly attributable to demographic concentrations, "white flight," and the strong preference (of both races) for neighborhood schools. See esp. pages xi-xiii, 289-94, 338-47.

is to threaten the promise of *Brown*." (P. 868.) [111]

Brown, however, did not and could not promise "integrated primary and secondary education" consisting of school classes of a certain racial composition. And there is not the slightest basis for believing that *any* Justice in 1954 would have voted to make such a promise. Nor did the Court find or suggest that black children were harmed by the lack of a sufficient number of white classmates. Instead, what *Brown* promised was desegregation of schools to end governmentally imposed racial subordination.

And that is precisely the relief that the plaintiffs in *Brown* sought. In the first oral argument in the *Brown* case, Thurgood Marshall, the NAACP's principal lawyer in the case, expressly disclaimed any support for racial balancing. What the plaintiffs wanted, Marshall declared, was an order prohibiting the admission of students "on the basis of race or color." He further stated that, "If the lines are drawn on a natural basis, without regard to race or color, then I think that nobody would have any complaint. For example, the colored child that is over here in this school would not be able to go to that school."[112] Five years after the *Brown* decision, the same view was stated by Jack Greenberg, who succeeded Marshall as director of the NAACP Legal Defense Fund and also represented the plaintiffs in *Brown*: "If ... there were complete freedom of choice, or geographical zoning, or any other nonracial standard, and all Negroes still ended up in certain schools, there would seem to be no constitutional objection."[113]

---

[111] Even more broadly, Justice Breyer claimed that "*Brown* held out a promise. It was a promise embodied in three Amendments designed to make citizens of slaves. It was the promise of true racial equality—not as a matter of fine words on paper, but as a matter of everyday life in the Nation's cities and schools. It was about the nature of a democracy that must work for all Americans. It sought one law, one Nation, one people, not simply as a matter of legal principle but in terms of how we actually live." (P. 868.)

[112] Leon Friedman (ed.), *Brown v. Board: The Landmark Oral Argument before the Supreme Court* [New Press 2004]: 48. Justice Frankfurter then asked, if drawing lines "on a natural basis" would lead to some schools "only Negro children would [attend], and there would be no white children mixed with them, or vice versa—why would it not involve Negro children saying, 'I want to go to this school instead of that school'?" Marshall replied that "They could move over into that district, if necessary. Even if you get stuck in one district, there is always an out, as long as this [segregation] statute is gone." Id.

[113] Jack Greenberg, *Race Relations and American Law* [Columbia 1959]: 240.

That was in substance the same position advanced by Chief Justice Roberts in his *Parents Involved* opinion: "What do the racial classifications do in these cases, if not determine admission to a public school on a racial basis? Before *Brown*, schoolchildren were told where they could and could not go to school based on the color of their skin. The school districts in these cases have not carried the heavy burden of demonstrating that we should allow this once again—even for very different reasons." (P. 747.)

35. THE *FISHER* CASE

On February 21, 2012, the Supreme Court granted certiorari to review *Fisher v. University of Texas*, an important affirmative action case decided by the Court of Appeals for the Fifth Circuit. Oral argument in the case will likely be heard in October or November, 2012, shortly after the beginning of the Court's 2012-13 term.

Fisher differs from previous affirmative action cases in several respects:

- Even before instituting the challenged racial preference program, the University (UT) had a highly diversified racial enrollment—almost 50% of its entering freshman are Hispanic, black, or Asian-American.[114]
- Because of the large numbers of Hispanics and blacks admitted to UT, there already existed a "critical mass" of each group at the University.
- Because of the existing racial diversity on a UT campus-wide basis, the UT preference plan goes considerably further; the plan seeks to achieve a "critical mass" of Hispanics and blacks on a departmental and classroom basis.
- Because of the large number of students admitted to UT each year under the Texas "Top Ten Percent Law" (automatically admitting the top 10% of graduates of all Texas high schools), there is room to admit only a relatively small number of applicants on the basis of racial preferences.
- *Fisher* is the first major affirmative action case to reach the Supreme Court where the primary beneficiaries are Hispanics rather than blacks.

---

[114] In 2007, the incoming freshman class was 19.7 percent Hispanic, 19.7 percent Asian American and 5.8 percent black. UT announced that "[t]hese [we]re record highs for each group." According to the 2010 census, 37.6% of the state's population are Hispanic, 11.8% are black, and 3.8% are Asian. On that basis, whites (45.3%) constitute a slightly smaller group than the total of the three groups frequently characterized as minorities. Asians, clearly a statistical minority, are treated under the UT program together as whites as part of the overrepresented group. Asian-American organizations appear to be divided over the UT affirmative action program. Scott Jaschik, "Asian-American group urges Supreme Court to bar race-conscious admissions", *Chronicle of Higher Education*, May 30, 2012.

Although the case is unusual in these respects, the Court's decision in *Fisher* is nevertheless likely to have a profound effect on the validity of racial preferences in its various contexts.

In 1996, the Fifth Circuit decided Hopwood v. Texas, 78 F.3d 932 (5th Cir. 1996), holding that educational diversity did not constitute a compelling governmental interest and that therefore the racial preferences then granted by UT's law school violated the Equal Protection Clause. The decision was not appealed to the Supreme Court. The Attorney General of Texas opined that the *Hopwood* ruling flatly prohibited the use of race as a factor in admissions by any undergraduate or graduate program at public universities in Texas. In 1997 the Texas legislature enacted the "Top Ten Percent Law" requiring UT to accept the application of all Texas high school seniors ranking in the top ten percent of their classes. The initial result was automatic admission under the Top Ten policy of approximately 80 percent of UT's entering freshman classes. In 2009 the law was amended to reduce the percentage of automatic admissions under Top Ten to 75 percent.[115]

After the Supreme Court's 2003 decision in *Grutter* (which in effect overruled the Fifth Circuit's *Hopwood* decision), UT re-instituted a program of racial preferences of Hispanics and blacks while continuing in effect the Top Ten policy. Declaring that there were "significant differences between the racial and ethnic makeup of the University's undergraduate population and the state's population" and a lack of diversity in its "classrooms," UT announced that it "would modify its admissions procedures to ... combine the benefits of the Top 10 Percent Law with affirmative action programs that can produce even greater diversity."[116] For the non-Top Ten spots, under a system known as "holistic review," applicants are rated on factors including test scores, essays, activities, socioeconomic status, and cultural background as well as race and ethnicity.[117]

---

[115] James McKinley Jr., "Texas Vote Curbs a College Admission Guarantee Meant to Bolster Diversity," *New York Times*, May 31, 2009. University records show that about two-thirds of the white freshmen were admitted automatically, compared with 80 percent of the black students and 85 percent of the Hispanic students. Tamar Lewin, "At the University of Texas, Admissions as a Mystery," *New York Times*, April 1, 2012.

[116] The 2011-2012 freshman class of 7,000 students is 46 percent white, 23 percent Hispanic, 20 percent Asian and 6 percent black. Lewin, supra.

[117] Lewin, supra.

In 2008 Abigail Fisher applied for undergraduate admission to UT. Since her grade average was below the top tenth of her high school class, she did not qualify for automatic admission under the Top Ten law. Her application was therefore considered in competition against other non-Top Ten applicants, including Hispanics and blacks who were allegedly admitted despite having lesser qualifications than white applicants in the group. After being denied admission, she and a group of other unsuccessful non-Top Ten applicants sued UT, charging violations of the Equal Protection Clause and federal civil rights laws on the ground that they were denied admission because they were white and that minority applicants with lower grade averages had been accepted under the plan. The claim was rejected by the District Court and the Fifth Circuit.

The Fifth Circuit held that the challenged program met the requirements of *Grutter*. Judge Higginbotham, writing for himself and another judge on the panel, concluded that "*Grutter's* 'serious, good faith consideration' standard" had been satisfied and that under *Grutter* "a university admissions program is narrowly tailored" so long as it avoids express quotas or specified preference points and "allows for individualized consideration of applicants of all races." The panel endorsed UT's "good faith" determination that the use of race would further UT's interests in having its already diverse student population mirror the racial demographics of Texas and in attaining "classroom diversity."

Judge Emilio Garza "specially concurred." He characterized the panel opinion as "a faithful, if unfortunate, application of" what he considered *Grutter's* erroneous "digression in the course of constitutional law." Judge Garza viewed *Grutter* as "abandon[ing] [strict scrutiny] and substitut[ing] in its place an amorphous, untestable, and above all, hopelessly deferential standard that ensures that race-based preferences in university admissions will avoid meaningful judicial review for the next several decades." In particular, he protested the panel's approval of "the University's reliance on race at the departmental and classroom levels, [which] will, in practice, allow for race-based preferences in seeming perpetuity." He further contended that "[UT]'s use of race has had an infinitesimal impact" on minority enrollment and thus race has been "completely ineffectual in accomplishing its claimed compelling interest."[118]

Rehearing en banc was denied by a vote of 9 to 7. Writing for five of the dissenting judges, Chief Judge Jones contended that UT's admissions program was not justified by *Grutter*. In her view, the panel decision "essentially abdicates judicial review of a race-conscious admissions program for undergraduate students that favors two groups, blacks and Hispanics, in one of the most ethnically diverse states in the United States." She charged that the panel had improperly extended *Grutter* by "watering down" strict scrutiny to authorize the use of race in college admissions when "a race-neutral state law (the Top Ten Percent Law) had already fostered increased campus racial diversity," and by validating UT's "unachievable and unrealistic goal of racial diversity at the classroom level to support the University's race-conscious [admissions] policy."

Since its 2003 decision in *Grutter*, the composition of the Supreme Court has changed: Samuel Alito succeeded Sandra Day O'Connor (who was the author of the *Grutter* opinion), Sonia Sotomayor succeeded David Souter; and Elena Kagan succeeded John Paul Stevens. Because Justice Kagan has disqualified herself in *Fisher*, apparently because she had some involvement in the case when she was Solicitor General, the decision will presumably be made by an eight-Justice Court.

Justices Roberts, Kennedy, Scalia, Alito, and Thomas constituted the majority in the *Parents Involved* case, invalidating racial balancing in public schools. And Justice Kennedy, widely regarded as the Court's swing Justice (since O'Connor was replaced by Alito), has never voted to uphold an affirmative action program. In his dissent in *Grutter*, he charged that the O'Connor opinion was based on excessive deference to the judgment of university administrators and that the majority's review of the evidence was "nothing short of perfunctory."

---

[118] He noted that in 2008, of the 363 black freshmen from Texas admitted and enrolled, 305 were the product of the Top Ten plan, and just 58 were admitted through merit or a combination of merit and race. For in-state Hispanics, 1,322 were admitted through the Top Ten plan and just 158 through merit or a combination or merit and ethnicity. He estimated that the number of "underrepresented" minority students admitted on the basis of race was less than 1% of the 2008 freshman class and concluded that UT's use of race "has had an infinitesimal impact on critical mass in the student body as a whole." In the *Parents Involved* case the Supreme Court suggested that a plan's minimal impact of race indicated the use of race was not really necessary.

In light of their previous votes and opinions, if the Court reaches the constitutional issue,[119] it appears likely that five of the eight Justices participating in the *Fisher* case would vote to reverse the Fifth Circuit. Depending on the Court's rationale, however, the decision need not necessarily overrule *Grutter* or repudiate diversity as a permissible "compelling state interest." For example, while ostensibly adhering to *Grutter*, a less sweeping disposition might hold that the UT plan nevertheless fails to meet "strict scrutiny," either because UT had already achieved racial diversity or because UT's extension of racial preferences to the departmental and classroom levels is unwarranted. But regardless of the particular grounds relied upon, a reversal of the Fifth Circuit decision would at the very least severely weaken the argument for the constitutionality of racial preferences.

---

[119] In opposing the grant of certiorari, UT contended that the case is moot because after Ms. Fisher had been denied admission to UT she enrolled at another university (Louisiana State University) and had received a college degree. Fisher countered that she is still seeking damages for the harm she claimed she suffered in being denied admission. In addition, an exception to the mootness doctrine allows adjudication of a recurring issue that otherwise would escape review because of the lengthy time required by the justice system to address the issue. See, e.g., Roe v. Wade, 410 U.S. 113 (1973). Compare DeFunis v. Odegaard, 416 U.S. 312 (1974), dismissing (5-4) a racial preference claim as moot where the claimant had been admitted to the school that had initially refused to admit him.

36. RACE-BASED SCHOLARSHIPS

The validity of race-based scholarships—as distinguished from race-based college admissions—has not been directly addressed by the Supreme Court. The issue, however, received considerable attention from the Department of Education (DOE).

On December 4, 1990, the DOE Assistant Secretary for Civil Rights declared that Title VI of the 1964 Civil Rights Act prohibits race-based scholarship programs of any federally funded university or college.[120] But only a few months later on March 20, 1991, after intense opposition by civil rights leaders, the policy was rescinded by a newly appointed Secretary of Education, Lamar Alexander, who stated that DOE "would continue to interpret Title VI as permitting federally funded institutions to provide minority scholarships."

On February 18, 1994, after receiving comments from the public and relying heavily on Justice Powell's comments in the *Bakke* case, DOE issued guidelines supporting the use of race-based financial aid to promote diversity.[121] According to the guidelines, universities and colleges "may consider race or national origin with other factors" in awarding financial aid "if this use is narrowly tailored, or, in other words, if it is necessary to further its interest in diversity and does not unduly restrict access to financial aid for students who do not meet the race-based eligibility criteria to promote diversity."

The guidelines listed the following "considerations that affect a determination of whether awarding race-targeted financial aid is narrowly tailored to the goal of diversity": (1) whether race-neutral means of achieving that goal have been or would be ineffective; (2)

---

[120] Title VI provides that "[n]o person in the United States shall, on the ground of race, color, or national origin, be excluded from participation in, be denied the benefits of, or be subjected to discrimination under any program or activity receiving Federal financial assistance." See Chapter 24 *Title VI of the 1964 Civil Rights Act.* The Department of Education is charged with responsibility to enforce Title VI with respect to universities and colleges.

[121] 59 Federal Register 8756-58.

whether a less extensive or intrusive use of race or national origin in awarding financial aid as a means of achieving that goal has been or would be ineffective; (3) whether the use of race or national origin is of limited extent and duration and is applied in a flexible manner; (4) whether the institution regularly reexamines its use of race or national origin in awarding financial aid to determine whether it is still necessary to achieve its goal; and (5) whether the effect of the use of race or national origin on students who are not beneficiaries of that use is sufficiently small and diffuse so as not to create an undue burden on their opportunity to receive financial aid.

The guidelines further provided that scholarships could be awarded on the basis of race to help "remedy past discrimination" even in the absence of any court or administrative finding that the school had engaged in illegal discrimination.[122]

"The Secretary," the guidelines state, "anticipates that most existing programs will be able to satisfy the principles set out in this final guidance."

Shortly after the issuance of the guidelines (but without any reference to Title VI or the guidelines), the Court of Appeals for the Fourth Circuit held that a race-based scholarship program at the University of Maryland at College Park violated the Equal Protection Clause. In Podberesky v. Kirwan, 38 F.3d 147 (4th Cir. 1994), cert. denied, 514 U.S. 1128 (1995), a Hispanic student challenged a scholarship program reserved solely for black students. The Fourth Circuit, applying strict scrutiny, held that race-conscious remedial measures are constitutional only if the proponent of the measure provides strong evidence for their necessity and if the measure is narrowly tailored to meet the remedial goal. The court, relying on the *Croson* decision, found (p. 161) that "the University has not shown that its programs and quota goals are narrowly tailored...." and reversed the district court's denial of the plaintiff's summary judgment motion.[123]

---

[122] Catherine Manegold, "U.S. Officially Backs Race-Based Scholarships," *New York Times*, February 18, 1994.

[123] See also Flanagan v. President and Directors of Georgetown College, 417 F. Supp. 377 (D.D.C. 1976). In *Flanagan* a federal district court ruled that a financial aid program at the Georgetown law school violated both the Equal Protection Clause and Title VI because the program allocated more aid to minority students than white students even though some white students had a greater need of financial assistance.

More specifically, the court ruled that the university had failed to provide sufficient evidence of the linkages between the university's past discriminatory practices and its contemporary problems—the university's poor reputation among blacks, a racially hostile campus environment, and the under-representation of blacks in the student body—in order to justify using the challenged scholarship program as a remedy. The court also concluded that the scholarship program that the university employed as a recruitment tool for high-achieving black students from both Maryland and outside the state was not narrowly tailored to addressing any past discrimination committed by the university.

After the Supreme Court denied certiorari in the *Podberesky* case, the Clinton administration reaffirmed its position on the legality of race-based scholarship programs. In a September 7, 1995 letter to counsel for colleges and universities, the DOE general counsel "confirm[ed] that the Department of Education's policy guidance on race-targeted student financial aid has not changed.... While we disagree with the result in *Podberesky*, the decision does not require the Department to modify its policy guidance on remedial race-targeted scholarships. ... The Department will continue to implement its financial aid policy under Title VI of the Civil Rights Act and to support race-targeted aid programs that are consistent with our policy."

However, after the *Gratz* and *Grutter* decisions of 2003, DOE (even though it has never revoked its 1994 guidelines) changed its position and now opposes race-based financial aid. As a result, facing threats of litigation and pressure from Washington, as many as half of the four-year universities and colleges in the United States have modified such programs to eliminate racial exclusivity as a condition of eligibility—a trend likely to continue.[124]

---

[124] See, e.g., Jonathan Glater, "Colleges Open Minority Aid to All Comers," *New York Times*, March 14, 2006. In 2003, following a campaign by two anti-affirmative action groups who threatened to file Title VI complaints against them with the DOE, at least ten universities (including Princeton and M.I.T.) terminated minority-only scholarships and summer programs. In his second book, then-Senator Barack Obama supported a "modest" scholarship program for minorities. Barack Obama, *The Audacity of Hope: Thoughts on Reclaiming the American Dream* [Crown/Three Rivers]: 244: "Given the dearth of black and Latino Ph.D. candidates in mathematics and the physical sciences, for example, a modest scholarship program for minorities interested in getting advanced degrees in these fields (a recent target of a Justice Department inquiry) won't keep white students out of such programs, but can broaden the pool of talent that America will need for all of us to prosper in a technology-based economy...."

37. RACIAL PREFERENCES IN REDISTRICTING

Although initially designed to prohibit voting discrimination against blacks, the Voting Rights Act of 1965[125] (VRA) was soon expanded by judicial interpretation to include a potent instrument of affirmative action to increase the power of black voters.

In Allen v. State Board of Elections, 393 U.S. 544 (1969), the Court held that the preclearance requirement of §5 was not limited to discriminatory tests or devices covered in §4 but also applied to changes that "diluted" black voting power. The Court declared (p. 569):

> "The right to vote can be affected by a dilution of voting power as well as by an absolute prohibition on casting a ballot. See Reynolds v. Sims, 377 U.S. 533, 555 (1964). Voters who are members of a racial minority might well be in the majority in one district, but in a decided minority in the county as a whole. This type of change could therefore nullify their ability to elect the candidate of their choice just as would prohibiting some of them from voting."

Whether intentionally or not, that short paragraph in the *Allen* opinion reconstructed the VRA in much in the same way that Griggs v. Duke Power Co., 401 U.S. 424 (1971), had reconstructed Title VII of the 1964 Civil Rights Act.[126] As Andrew Kull has pointed out, the ruling was necessarily based on the unstated assumption that—without regard to discriminatory intent—black voters are effectively disenfranchised unless they elect a black candidate by a black majority.[127]

---

[125] See Chapter 17 *The Federal Voting Rights Act.*

[126] As noted by Kull, supra, at 215: "The radical transformation of the meaning of 'discrimination' is the same one that has been observed in the case of school assignments and employment practices." See Chapter 25 *Title VII of the 1964 Civil Rights Act.*

[127] Kull, supra, at 210-24. See also Abigail Thernstrom, *Voting Rights—and Wrongs: The Elusive Quest for Racially Fair Elections* [AEI 2009]: 32-34, 49-53.

The Court, moreover, did not examine the constitutional implications of its interpretation of §5. If black-white voting is completely polarized, as *Allen* assumes, there would appear to be only two ways to ensure that a black candidate will be elected in any district: either (1) give more weight to the vote of each black voter in comparison with the weight given the vote of a white voter, or (2) gerrymander district lines on a racial basis to create a black-majority district. The first alternative would be directly contrary to the "one person, one vote" mandate of *Reynolds v. Sims*, the very decision on which *Allen* relies. Implicitly, therefore, the *Allen* ruling could only be implemented by the gerrymander alternative.

Relying on the *Allen* concept of dilution, the Justice Department adopted a policy of denying preclearance under §5 to any proposed redistricting proposal that did not include, in the Department's view, a sufficient number of black-majority districts. In blunter terms, the Department demanded the racial gerrymander of districts to *predetermine* the election of black representatives. To accomplish that objective, a district has to be drawn to include not only enough black voters to constitute a majority but also a minority of nonblack "filler people" who can vote but have no real prospect of electing their preferred candidate.[128] These "filler people"—assigned on a racial basis to *lose* the election—"should not be expected to compete in any genuine sense for representation in the district to which they have been assigned, lest they undo the redistricting assignment of that district to the specified minority group."[129]

This policy was challenged under the Equal Protection Clause in United Jewish Organizations of Williamsburgh, Inc. v. Carey, 430 U.S. 144 (1977) (*UJO*). At issue was a New York State reapportionment plan that the Justice Department insisted must include a district composed of at least 65% blacks. Under the VRA, because three counties (including Kings County) had not provided Spanish-election materials in the 1960s, preclearance by the Department was required. In order to comply with the 65% requirement, the State's plan bisected a Brooklyn

---

[128] See T. Alexander Aleinikoff and Samuel Issacharoff, "Race and Redistricting: Drawing Constitutional Lines after Shaw v. Reno," 92 *Michigan Law Review* 588, 601, 649 (1993).

[129] Samuel Issacharoff, Pamela Karlan, and Richard Pildes, *The Law of Democracy: Legal structure of the Political Process* [Foundation Press 1998]: 567.

Hasidic community (which previously had all been located in the same district) into two of the proposed districts. The Hasidic community brought suit under the Fourteenth and Fifteenth Amendments, alleging that the plan's purpose was to achieve a racial quota, that they were assigned to districts solely on the basis of race, and that this racial gerrymander diluted their own voting power.

The Supreme Court (7-1) upheld the constitutionality of the plan, finding the discrimination to be "benign." Justice White's plurality opinion declared "that the Constitution does not prevent a State subject to the Voting Rights Act from deliberately creating or preserving black majorities in particular districts in order to ensure that its reapportionment plan complies with [§]5" and that "The permissible use of racial criteria is not confined to eliminating the effects of past discriminatory districting or apportionment" (p. 161). Furthermore, the majority contended, the plan did not stigmatize members of the burden group (in this case whites) or brand them as second-class citizens. Chief Justice Burger, the lone dissenter, protested against any use of quotas or racial gerrymandering and denied that state action not otherwise constitutional is legalized by an attempt to comply with the VRA.

In 1982, in renewing the VRA for an additional 25 years, Congress voted to overturn the Court's decision in City of Mobile v. Bolden, 446 U.S. 55 (1980), that the Equal Protection Clause required proof of discriminatory purpose in voting rights cases. VRA §2 was amnded to allow challenges to methods of voting on the basis of "results" rather than intent. The amendment provided that a violation is established if, "*based on the totality of circumstances*," members of minority groups "have less opportunity than other members of the electorate to participate in the political process *and to elect representatives of their choice*." (Italics added.) The amendment further provided that "The extent to which members of a protected group have been elected ... is one circumstance which may be considered...."

Thus the drawing of legislative districts to reserve seats for black candidates became not only a judicially created policy by but now a congressional mandate.

The Supreme Court's first interpretation of the amended §2 was its fractured decision in Thornburg v. Gingles, 478 U.S. 30 (1986), involving a North Carolina redistricting plan for election to the state legislature. At issue were proposed multimember districts that the plaintiffs challenged as impairing the opportunity of black voters "to participate in the political process and to elect representatives of their choice." Applying the "totality of circumstances" test, the Court held that the redistricting plan violated §2 because it resulted in the dilution of black citizens' votes.

In his plurality opinion, Justice Brennan laid down three "preconditions" that plaintiffs must satisfy to prevail in a §2 suit: "First, the minority group must be able to demonstrate that it is sufficiently large and geographically compact to constitute a majority in a single-member district.... Second, the minority group must be able to show that it is politically cohesive.... Third, the minority must be able to demonstrate that the white majority votes sufficiently as a bloc to enable it ... usually to defeat the minority's preferred candidate." (Pp. 50-51.)

But, according to Brennan, the third precondition—racial bloc voting—did not require proof of white resistance to black candidacies. He said: "The reasons black and white voters vote differently have no relevance to the central inquiry of § 2. It is the difference between the choices made by blacks and whites—not the reasons for that difference—that results in blacks having less opportunity than whites to elect their preferred representatives." (P. 63.)

In her opinion concurring on other grounds, Justice O'Connor (joined by Burger, Powell, and Rehnquist) charged that "the Court is requiring a form of proportional representation," which "is inconsistent with the results test and with §2's disclaimer of a right to proportional representation." (P. 94.) If the reasons whites voted as they did were irrelevant, as Brennan said, then only election results—whether a sufficient number of black candidates had won—were of any significance. And, given Brennan's expansive definition of racial bloc voting, it could be found almost any time that a candidate supported by minority voters failed to get a sufficient number of white votes to win an election.[130]

---

[130] See Samuel Issacharoff, "Polarized Voting and the Political Process: The Transformation of Voting Rights Jurisprudence," 90 *Michigan Law Review* 1833 (1992).

Justice O'Connor rejected Brennan's primary focus on polarized voting practices in a particular jurisdiction and instead argued for a much broader inquiry into the political factors that promote or impede minority electoral ambitions:

> "The [reviewing] court should not focus solely on the minority group's ability to elect representatives of its choice. Whatever measure of undiluted minority voting strength the court employs in connection with evaluating the presence or absence of minority electoral success, it should also bear in mind that 'the power to influence the political process is not limited to winning elections.' ... Of course, the relative lack of minority electoral success under a challenged plan, when compared with the success that would be predicted under the measure of undiluted minority voting strength the court is employing, can constitute powerful evidence of vote dilution. Moreover, the minority group may, in fact, lack access to or influence upon representatives it did not support as candidates. ... Nonetheless, a reviewing court should be required to find more than simply that the minority group does not usually attain an undiluted measure of electoral success." (Pp. 99-100.)

In subsequent cases, starting with Shaw v. Reno, 509 U.S. 630 (1993), the O'Connor view became increasingly ascendant in the Court's decisions.[131]

SHAW V. RENO

Between the Court's decisions in *UJO* and *Shaw v. Reno*, much had changed, not only in the composition of the Supreme Court but also in its view of "benign" discrimination. Notably, in City of Richmond v. J.A. Croson Co., 488 U.S. 469, 493 (1989), the Court held that Richmond's set-aside program for minority contractors did not meet strict scrutiny and that the city's claimed "benign" purpose did not justify any lower standard.

In *Shaw v. Reno*, the Court in effect repudiated (ostensibly "distinguished" but did not overrule) *UJO* and reasserted the primacy of the Equal Protection Clause.

---

[131]Richard Pildes, "The Decline of Legally Mandated Minority Representation," 68 *Ohio State Law Journal* 1139, 1140-41 (2007).

Shaw arose from the 1990 redistricting of North Carolina by its General Assembly. As a result of the 1990 census, North Carolina became entitled to a twelfth seat in the U.S. House of Representatives. Although the eligible voting population of North Carolina is approximately 20% black, there had been no black congressional representation from North Carolina in the twentieth century. The black population is relatively dispersed and constitutes a majority of the general population in only five of the State's 100 counties. The redistricting plan initially enacted by the General Assembly provided for one majority-black congressional district (District 1).

To comply with the preclearance requirement of VRA §5, North Carolina submitted its plan to the Justice Department, which objected on the ground that the creation of only one majority-black district in the state was insufficient and that a second majority-black district was also required. In response, the General Assembly revised its proposal to create a second majority-black district, but rejected the Department's proposal to create the second district in the southeastern section of the state that contained a significant concentration of black voters. Instead, the Assembly insisted on creating he second district (District 12) in the north-central region of the state.

Both of the proposed majority-black districts had dramatically irregular boundaries. District 1 was compared to a "Rorschach ink-blot test," and a "bug splattered on a windshield." District 12 was approximately 160 miles long and, for much of its length, no wider than the I-85 corridor. It was described as winding in snake-like fashion through tobacco country, financial centers, and manufacturing areas "until it gobbles in enough enclaves of black neighborhoods." Northbound and southbound drivers on I-85 sometimes found themselves in separate districts in one county, only to change districts when they entered the next county. According to one state legislator, "[i]f you drove down the interstate with both car doors open, you'd kill most of the people in the district." Of the ten counties through which District 12 passed, five were cut into three different districts; even towns were divided. At one point, the area in the district remained contiguous only because it intersected at a single point with two other districts before crossing over them.

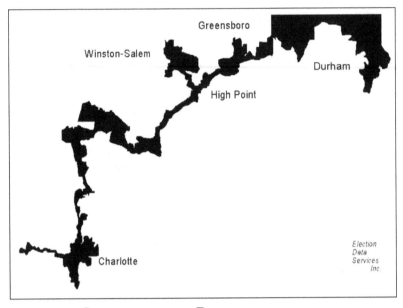

CONGRESSIONAL DISTRICT 12 - 1992

Although the Justice Department did not object to the General Assembly's revised plan, five white North Carolina residents filed suit claiming that the General Assembly had created an unconstitutional racial gerrymander. They claimed that their constitutional rights were violated by the deliberate segregation of voters into separate districts on the basis of race in order to guarantee the election of two black representatives. North Carolina defended the plan on the ground that it was attempting to comply with the VRA and, in the alternative, that it had a significant interest in eradicating the effects of past racial discrimination.

A three-judge District Court (2-1) dismissed the suit on the ground, among others, that under *UJO* favoring minority voters was not constitutionally discriminatory. The Supreme Court (5-4) reversed, holding that "...if [the plaintiffs'] allegations of a racial gerrymander are not contradicted on remand, the District Court must determine whether the General Assembly's reapportionment plan satisfies strict scrutiny" (p. 653).

In her opinion for the Court, citing Gomillion v. Lightfoot, 364 U.S. 339 (1960), Justice O'Connor pointed out that gerrymanders to *exclude* voters on a racial basis violate the Equal Protection Clause.

314

And, citing the *Croson* and *Wygant* opinions, she stated: "We have made clear...that equal protection analysis 'is not dependent on the race of those burdened or benefited by a particular classification'" (p. 650).

Justice O'Connor recognized, however, that "...redistricting differs from other kinds of state decisionmaking in that the legislature always is aware of race when it draws district lines, just as it is aware of age, economic status, religious and political persuasion, and a variety of other demographic factors." "That sort of race consciousness," she stated (p. 646), "does not lead inevitably to impermissible race discrimination" and "may reflect wholly legitimate purposes" since "The district lines may be drawn, for example, to provide for compact districts of contiguous territory, or to maintain the integrity of political subdivisions." Therefore race-conscious redistricting, unlike racial classifications in other contexts (in *Croson*, for example), does not automatically require application of the strict scrutiny standard.[132]

But in this case, Justice O'Connor pointed out, it was alleged that the reapportionment scheme was so irrational on its face that it could only be understood as an effort to segregate voters into separate voting districts because of their race (p. 647):

> "Put differently, we believe that reapportionment is one area in which appearances do matter. A reapportionment plan that includes in one district individuals who belong to the same race, but who are otherwise widely separated by geographical and political boundaries, and who may have little in common with one another but the color of their skin, bears an uncomfortable resemblance to political apartheid. It reinforces the perception that members of the same racial group—regardless of their age, education, economic status, or the community in which they live—think alike, share the same political interests, and will prefer the same candidates at the polls. The message that such districting sends to elected representatives is equally pernicious."

---

[132] See also, e.g., Justice Ginsberg dissenting in Miller v. Johnson, 515 U.S. 900, 944-45 (1995): "To accommodate the reality of ethnic bonds, legislatures have long drawn voting districts along ethnic lines. Our Nation's cities are full of districts identified by their ethnic character—Chinese, Irish, Italian, Jewish, Polish, Russian, for example."

Therefore, the Court held, "[A] plaintiff challenging a reapportionment statute under the Equal Protection Clause may state a claim
by alleging that the legislation, though race-neutral on its face, rationally cannot be understood as anything other than an effort to
separate voters into different districts on the basis of race, and that
the separation lacks sufficient justification" (p. 649).

Justices White, Blackmun, Stevens, and Souter each filed a dissenting opinion, contending that the majority's approach would unnecessarily hinder a state's voluntary effort to ensure minority representation
where the minority population is geographically dispersed. The dissenters further contended that North Carolina had a compelling interest to
comply with the Justice Department requirements under the VRA.

THE PROGENY OF SHAW V. RENO

The decision led to a remarkable series of rulings in which a sharply
divided Court sought to define the meaning and scope of the *Shaw*
decision.

On remand of the case, applying the strict scrutiny standard,
the District Court again upheld the plan, finding that creation of the
majority-black districts was justified as an effort to obtain the Justice
Department's approval.

But, on appeal, the Supreme Court (again by a 5-4 vote) rejected
that justification, concluding that the plan for District 12 violated the
Equal Protection Clause. The Court found that race was the "predominant" factor in creating the district and that the district was not
narrowly tailored to comply with the VRA. Shaw v. Hunt, 517 U.S.
899 (1996) (known as "*Shaw II*").

In response, the North Carolina legislature (1997) redrew the
boundaries, but the revised district lines were again challenged under the Equal Protection Clause. The District Court, without holding
a trial, found the plan to be unconstitutional.

On appeal, this decision was also reversed by the Supreme Court,
which held—this time unanimously—that a trial of the factual issues
was necessary. Hunt v. Cromartie, 526 U.S. 541 (1999). The Court
held that the plaintiffs had introduced only "circumstantial evidence"
in support of their claim that race had been the predominant factor
in creating District 12 and that therefore summary judgment was

inappropriate because of evidence that the General Assembly's principal goals were the protection of incumbents and preservation of a split between Republicans and Democrats.

The Court's opinion (written by Justice Thomas and joined by Rehnquist, O'Connor, Scalia, and Kennedy) noted that "[o]ur prior decisions have made clear that a jurisdiction may engage in constitutional political gerrymandering, even if it so happens that the most loyal Democrats happen to be black Democrats and even if the State were *conscious* of that fact.... Evidence that blacks constitute even a supermajority in one congressional district while amounting to less than a plurality in a neighboring district will not, by itself, suffice to prove that a jurisdiction was motivated by race in drawing its district lines when the evidence also shows a high correlation between race and party preference." (P. 542, italics in original.) Stevens (joined by Souter, Ginsburg, and Breyer) concurred in the judgment.

On remand, this time after trial, the District Court again held that the districting was race-motivated and unconstitutional.

But on appeal the Supreme Court (also 5-4) again reversed, invoking the Court's little-used authority to reject the District Court's findings of facts as "clearly erroneous." Easley v. Cromartie, 532 U.S. 234, 257 (2001). The majority opinion (written by Justice Breyer and joined by the other dissenters in the 1999 decision as well as Justice O'Connor) concluded that "The evidence taken together, however, does not show ... that racial considerations predominated in the drawing of District 12's boundaries."

According to the majority, since blacks in North Carolina vote Democratic about 95 percent of the time, the General Assembly's creation of a majority-black district could rationally be seen as using race for a constitutional political objective—the creation of a safe Democratic seat. The Court stated that, "... given the fact that the party attacking the legislature's decision bears the burden of proving that racial considerations are 'dominant and controlling,' ... given the 'demanding' nature of that burden of proof, ... and given the sensitivity, the 'extraordinary caution,' that district courts must show to avoid treading upon legislative prerogatives, ... the attacking party has not successfully shown that race, rather than politics, predominantly accounts for the result."

Thomas (who had written the 1999 *Hunt v. Cromartie* decision) dissented, joined by Rehnquist, Scalia, and Kennedy.

The practical effect of this series of decisions was to facilitate the creation of majority-black districts by substantially increasing opponents' burden of establishing that the purpose was "predominantly" racial. But a correlative effect was to accord greater legitimacy to traditional political tactics as an alternative explanation for gerrymandering a district.

MILLER V. JOHNSON

Two years after *Shaw v. Reno*, the decision was applied by the Supreme Court in Miller v. Johnson, 515 U.S. 900 (1995), to reject (5-4) a Georgia plan providing for three majority-black congressional districts.

The Georgia Legislature adopted the plan with the Justice Department's approval after the Department had refused to preclear two earlier plans that provided for only two majority-black districts. Voters in the third majority-black district (which joined metropolitan black neighborhoods together with the poor black population of coastal areas 260 miles away) challenged the plan on the ground that the district was a racial gerrymander in violation of the Equal Protection Clause.

In an opinion by Justice Kennedy, the Court restated the *Shaw* holding in a more comprehensive fashion, particularly concerning the appearance factor given such heavy emphasis in *Shaw*:

> "Our observation in *Shaw* of the consequences of racial stereotyping was not meant to suggest that a district must be bizarre on its face before there is a constitutional violation. Nor was our conclusion in *Shaw* that in certain instances a district's appearance (or, to be more precise, its appearance in combination with certain demographic evidence) can give rise to an equal protection claim.... Our circumspect approach and narrow holding in *Shaw* did not erect an artificial rule barring accepted equal protection analysis in other redistricting cases. Shape is relevant not because bizarreness is a necessary element of the constitutional wrong or a threshold requirement of proof, but because it may be persuasive circumstantial evidence that race for its own sake, and not other districting

principles, was the legislature's dominant and controlling rationale in drawing its district lines." (P. 912.)

Turning then to the record in the case, the Court found it unnecessary to base its decision on the shape of the challenged district, considered separately, since there was substantial additional evidence demonstrating that the Georgia legislature was motivated by a predominant purpose to create a third majority-black district. There was little doubt, the Court held, that Georgia's true interest was to satisfy the Department's preclearance demands and that the Department had exceeded its authority under VRA in utilizing §5 to require the maximization of majority-minority districts.

The Court declared that it did "not accept the contention that the State has a compelling interest in complying with whatever preclearance mandates the Justice Department issues.... Instead of grounding its objections on evidence of a discriminatory purpose, it would appear the Government was driven by its policy of maximizing majority-black districts." The Court added that it was

> "especially reluctant to conclude that [§]5 justifies that policy given the serious constitutional concerns it raises ... [T]he Justice Department's implicit command that States engage in presumptively unconstitutional race-based districting brings the Voting Rights Act ... into tension with the Fourteenth Amendment. ... We need not, however, resolve these troubling and difficult constitutional questions today. There is no indication Congress intended such a far-reaching application of [§]5, so we reject the Justice Department's interpretation of the statute and avoid the constitutional problems that interpretation raises." (Pp. 926-27.)

The Court's decision was bitterly condemned by civil rights leaders on the ground that it would reduce the number of black representatives in Congress. But that prediction proved to be incorrect. As related by sociologist Orlando Patterson, "when the same Afro-American candidates ran in non-gerrymandered districts with majority Euro-American electors in the 1996 elections, *every single one was re-elected*. Once again, ordinary Americans—both Euro-Americans and Afro-Americans—turned out to be far more progressive than the

Euro-American pundits and Afro-American leadership gave them credit for." (Italics in original). [133]

Recent elections, according to Professor Patterson, demonstrate that "even a small proportion of Afro-American voters can powerfully influence the elected leaders of both parties—whatever their ethnic ancestry—to vote in a manner that advances the interests of Afro-Americans and the less privileged," and that "the practice of specially concentrating electors into minority districts so as to ensure the election of a minority representative almost always makes all the other voting districts of such a gerrymandered state not only more conservative, but more self-consciously hostile to the interests of the Afro-American minorities in their midst."[134]

The following year, in evaluating three Texas districts in Bush v. Vera, 517 U.S. 952, 958-59 (1996), the plurality Justices explained that "Strict scrutiny does not apply merely because redistricting is performed with consciousness of race. Nor does it apply to all cases of intentional creation of majority-minority districts. ... For strict scrutiny to apply, the plaintiffs must prove that other legitimate districting principles were 'subordinated' to race." The Court concluded that strict scrutiny was appropriate in Bush v. Vera because the evidence demonstrated that racial motivation had a qualitatively greater influence on the drawing of district lines than political motivations.[135]

Georgia v. Ashcroft

In Georgia v. Ashcroft, 539 U.S. 461 (2003), the Court considered a Georgia Senate proposal that would reduce the number of majority-black districts but would, on the other hand, increase the number of districts certain to elect white Democrats.

The proposal was supported almost unanimously by all Georgia

---

[133] Orlando Patterson, *The Ordeal of Integration: Progress and Resentment in America's "Racial" Crisis* [Civitas 1997]: 67. In the 2008 presidential election, although Barack Obama did not receive an overall majority of votes cast by whites, his 43% share of this group was larger than that of John Kerry in 2004 (41%) or Al Gore in 2000 (42%). Abigail and Stephan Thernstrom, "Racial Gerrymandering Is Unnecessary," *Wall Street Journal*, November 11, 2008.

[134] Patterson, supra, at 67.

[135] In an opinion concurring in the judgment, Justice Thomas, joined by Justice Scalia, supported an even broader test, contending that strict scrutiny is appropriate in any case in which race is intentionally used in districting, even if it is not the predominant purpose. (Pp. 999-1003.)

black legislators—10 of 11 black state senators (including the black majority leader and the black chairman of the redistricting committee) and 33 of 34 black representatives in the Georgia House. They contended it would increase the influence of black voters, who were overwhelmingly Democrats. Other black leaders also supported the plan; Congressman John Lewis, for example, thought it was "in the best interest of African American voters ... to have a continued Democratic-controlled legislature in Georgia." [136]

Nevertheless, the Justice Department refused to preclear the change because it would reduce the number of black representatives. Despite the Department's opposition, the Court (5-4) sustained the proposal, holding that it would protect the interests of black voters even if the elected representatives in the affected districts were white rather than black.

The question to be decided, Justice O'Connor said in her opinion for the majority, was "whether the change 'would lead to a retrogression in the position of racial minorities with respect to their effective exercise of the electoral franchise.'"[137] Resolution of that question, she stated, requires consideration of whether "the gains in the plan as a whole offset the loss in a particular district." In the majority's view, securing a maximum number of safe black districts did not necessarily maximize black representation, and "...a court should not focus solely on the comparative ability of a minority group to elect a candidate of its choice." Instead, "the State may choose, consistent with §5, that it is better to risk having fewer minority representatives in order to achieve greater overall representation of a minority group by increasing the number of representatives sympathetic to the interests of minority voters." (Pp. 478, 483).[138] Under this view, the preclearance decision should turn on the totality of the political factors that might affect minority political advantage, instead of just the number of black representatives.[139]

---

[136] See Abigail Thernstrom, *Voting Rights—and Wrongs: The Elusive Quest for Racially Fair Elections* [AEI Press 2009]: 66-70.

[137] Quoting *Beer v. United States*, 425 U.S. 130, 141 (1976).

[138] In the following election, in two of the districts in which the black population had been reduced, the black incumbents still won overwhelmingly under the revised plan. See Thernstrom, supra, at 261 n.75.

[139] Samuel Issacharoff, "Is Section 5 of the Voting Rights Act a Victim of Its Own Success?," 104 *Columbia Law Review* 1710, 1717 (2004).

Despite the plan's broad support by black legislators in the state, the Court's decision in *Georgia v. Ashcroft* was harshly criticized in the civil rights community for allegedly substituting "coalition" districts for majority-black districts. In renewing the VRA in 2006, Congress responded to the criticism by amending §5 to require the denial of preclearance to any redistricting plan (or any other voting change) that "has the purpose of or will have the effect of diminishing the ability of any citizens of the United States on account of race or color ... to elect their preferred candidates of choice...." The amendment was enacted with the support of nearly a unanimous vote of both Democrats and Republicans.[140]

The preamble of the amendment stated that the Supreme Court in *Georgia v. Ashcroft* had "...misconstrued Congress' original intent in enacting the Voting Rights Act of 1965 and narrowed the protections afforded by section 5 of such Act." Although describing the amendment as only "partly" rejecting *Georgia v. Ashcroft,* the House Judiciary Committee report on the bill charged that the decision had created a "vague and open-ended 'totality of circumstances' test [that] opened the door to allow all manner of undefined considerations to trump the minority's choice of candidate." According to the report, the decision had encouraged "states to spread minority voters under the guise of 'influence' and would effectively shut minority voters out of the political process" and had allowed states to "turn black and other minority voters into second class voters who [could] influence elections of white candidates, but who [could not] elect their preferred candidates, including candidates of their own race."

[140] Although Republicans voted almost unanimously for the amendment, the Republican-controlled Senate Judiciary Committee issued a report *after the vote* that offered a sharply different interpretation. Disregarding the language of the bill that had already become law, the report claimed that the test in evaluating preclearance requests would be whether the change in voting practices was "purposefully taken ... to lock out racial and language minorities from political power." In applying that test, the report stated, "Courts and the Justice Department should ask whether the decision not to create a black-majority district departed from ordinary districting rules" and "If the State went out of its way to avoid creating such a majority-minority—one that would be created under ordinary rules—that is unconstitutional racial discrimination." Furthermore, "This legislation definitively is not intended to preserve or ensure the successful election of candidates of any political party, even if that party's candidates generally are supported by members of minority groups." See Thernstrom, *supra,* at 178-82.

THE LULAC CASE

In the same year as enactment of the 2006 amendment, the Court decided League of United Latin American Citizens v. Perry, 548 U. S. 399 (2006) [*LULAC*], holding that part of the 2003 Texas redistricting violated the VRA.[141]

In redrawing the lines of District 23, although Hispanics would retain a slim 50.9 percent majority in voting-age population (both citizens and non-citizens), the Texas legislature reduced the Hispanic citizen voting-age population in the district from 57.5 percent to 46 percent. In order to compensate for the reduction and avoid a "retrogression" problem under VRA §5, the legislature created a new District 25 that would be overwhelmingly Hispanic.

By a 5-4 vote the Court ruled that the exchange was insufficient. According to the majority, since it is the number of citizens that is controlling in assessing a group's opportunity to elect a candidate, the change had removed the Hispanics' opportunity in District 23 to elect their preferred candidates and therefore diluted the votes of the Hispanic population. In addition, in the majority's view, the newly created District 25 was not compact enough to be considered a qualifying replacement majority-minority Hispanic district.

But a differently constituted majority of the Court, also by a 5-to-4 vote, rejected the claim that the voting power of blacks in former District 24 had been illegally diluted by the legislature's dismembering the district into pieces assigned to other districts. The Court held that former District 24's black population, with only 25.7% of the citizen voting age population in the district, did not constitute a sufficiently large minority to elect their candidate of choice. Because establishing a §2 claim requires more than showing that a minority had substantial influence in a district, the Court concluded that dismembering District 24 did not dilute the blacks' voting power.

The majority opinion on the VRA issues was written by Justice Kennedy. Separate opinions were filed by Justices Stevens, Souter, Breyer, and Scalia.

---

[141] The Court also rejected the plaintiffs' argument that the Constitution does not permit a state to redistrict more than once per census. After the 2000 census, a federal court had earlier adopted a redistricting plan because of a political deadlock in the legislature.

In his opinion Justice Scalia (joined by Justice Thomas) focused on an issue that was not addressed by the other Justices—whether the Equal Protection Clause was violated by the state's action in moving Hispanics out of District 23 and the state's intentional creation of District 25 as a majority-minority district. Scalia withheld any judgment of unconstitutionality as to District 23 because of the lower court's finding that there had been no invidious racial intent in its reconfiguration. However, with respect to District 25, Scalia concluded that "when a legislature intentionally creates a majority-minority district, race is necessarily its predominant motivation and strict scrutiny is therefore triggered" and "the State's concession here sufficiently establishes that the legislature classified individuals on the basis of their race when it drew District 25." [142]

Prior to the *LULAC* decision, as Richard Pildes noted, "the Court had not upheld a single Section 2 VRA claim in any case the Court has given plenary consideration since the moment *Gingles* was decided." He nevertheless concluded that "The net effect of *LULAC* will be to limit substantially the legal imperative to design safe minority election districts." Pildes predicts, if the composition of the Court stays substantially the same, "a commanding Court antipathy toward legally-mandated safe minority districting."[143]

The 2010 census, furthermore, may have the effect of reducing the number and political advantage of black-majority districts. While the national black population increased 12 percent, eight of the top ten majority-black districts across the country actually experienced a substantial population loss, reflecting the movement of approximately 50% of the black population from major metropolitan areas—where most of these districts are located—into suburbs.[144] As

[142] As to the alleged VRA claims, Scalia stated: "I would dismiss appellants' vote-dilution claims premised on §2 of the Voting Rights Act of 1965 for failure to state a claim, for the reasons set forth in Justice Thomas's opinion, which I joined, in *Holder v. Hall* [512 U.S. 879, 891-896 (1994).]...." Thomas had argued in *Holder* that "The matters the Court has set out to resolve in vote dilution cases are questions of political philosophy, not questions of law" and therefore "are not readily subjected to any judicially manageable standards that can guide courts in attempting to select between competing theories." See Thernstrom, supra, at 104-106, 110.

[143] Richard Pildes, "The Decline of Legally Mandated Minority Representation," 68 *Ohio State Law Journal* 1139, 1141 (2007).

[144] Aaron Blake, "The decline of the majority-black district, and what it means," *Washington Post*, April 20, 2011; Jason Riley, "The Good News About Race in America," *Wall Street Journal*, May 18, 2012.

a recent study demonstrates, the nation's cities are now more racially integrated than at any time since 1910, all-white enclaves now "are effectively extinct," and black urban ghettos are shriveling.[145]

---

[145] Edward Glaeser and Jacob Vigdor, *The End of the Segregated Century: Racial Separation in America's Neighborhoods, 1890-2010* [Manhattan Institute 2012]. See Sam Roberts, "Segregation Curtailed in U.S. Cities, Study Finds," *New York Times*, January 30, 2012; "The dream is getting closer," *The Economist*, February 11, 2012.

AFTERWORD

Since the *Brown* decision and the ensuing federal legislation, we are now a very different nation. America is no longer governed as a racial caste system. Government discrimination against racial minorities has been effectively outlawed; and if instances of such discrimination arise, remedies are readily available for their correction. Legal equality has been achieved. Indeed, the principal demand of racial minorities is now no longer legal equality but instead racial preferences.

We also are now a very different nation in black-white relations. For example: Blacks are among the country's most popular (and best-paid) celebrities—Oprah Winfrey, Colin Powell, Michael Jordan, Will Smith, Derek Jeter, Denzell Washington, Bill Cosby, to name just a few. Blacks have a prominent position in the nation's universities and professions, including law and medicine. Blacks have served as CEOs of major corporations, president of the American Bar Association, president of the Conference of Catholic Bishops, chairmen of countless other prestigious public and private organizations, Secretary of State, chairman of the Joint Chiefs of Staff, Ambassador to the United Nations, Supreme Court Justices, governors of Virginia and Massachusetts, mayors of Atlanta, Birmingham, New Orleans, and other southern cities (as well as New York, Chicago, Washington, Los Angeles, Philadelphia, Detroit, Seattle, St. Louis, and Kansas City).

In 2008, in "a blow to the near hammerlock that white Protestant males have had on the presidency since George Washington,"

Barack Obama was elected President.[146] His election—with, more-over, a victory margin of nearly ten million votes and the largest majority for his party's candidate, and substantially more white votes, since Lyndon Johnson in 1964—constituted a historic event by any measure. His election led to the appointment of the first black United States Attorney General. And in 2012 the Southern Baptist Convention—a denomination of 16 million members (approximately 94% non-black) that was a spiritual home to white supremacists for much of the 20th century—elected its first black president.

The nation's indisputable racial progress is fundamentally inconsistent with assertions that America still remains a racist society. Clearly not all vestiges of racism (whether white or black) have been eliminated. In a country of 300 million, there inevitably will be some pockets of the incorrigible and the pathological. They plainly do not, however, typify the great mass of Americans.

Troubling racial disparities still remain—in poverty, learning achievement, employment, crime, and other areas. Yet, even as long ago as 1991, Orlando Patterson could conclude that "The sociological truths are that America, while still flawed in its race relations .. . , is now the least racist white-majority society in the world; has a better record of legal protection of minorities than any other society, white or black; offers more opportunities to a greater number of black persons than any other society...."[147] And in the following two decades, as Obama's election strikingly illustrates, there have been further significant advances.

A half century ago only a reckless optimist could have predicted the extraordinary changes that have taken place. That history provides a strong basis for expecting this progress to continue.

---

[146] Walter Russell Mead, "Honolulu, Harvard, and Hyde Park," *Foreign Affairs*, July-August 2010, p. 148. See also George Will, "Will Utah Send Its Love to Washington?," *Washington Post*, September 21, 2012.

[147] Orlando Patterson, "Race, Gender and Liberal Fallacies," *New York Times*, October 20, 1991.